SO-ACZ-727

ACTOR

By Jerome Lawrence

PLAYS AND MUSICALS
(In collaboration with Robert E. Lee)

LOOK, MA, I'M DANCIN'!
INHERIT THE WIND
SHANGRI-LA
AUNTIE MAME
THE GANG'S ALL HERE
ONLY IN AMERICA
A CALL ON KUPRIN
SPARKS FLY UPWARD
MAME
DEAR WORLD
THE CROCODILE SMILE
THE NIGHT THOREAU SPENT IN JAIL
THE INCOMPARABLE MAX
JABBERWOCK
INSIDE A KID'S HEAD
* * *

Also by Jerome Lawrence

OSCAR THE OSTRICH
OFF MIKE
LIVE SPELLED BACKWARDS

(Photo by Schuyler Crail. Collection of Henry Blanke)
Muni as Émile Zola.

ACTOR

The Life and Times
of
PAUL MUNI

by Jerome Lawrence

W. H. ALLEN · London
A division of Howard & Wyndham Ltd
1975

First British edition, 1975

*This book or parts thereof may not be
reproduced in any form whatsoever
without permission in writing.*

Printed and bound in Great Britain by
Butler & Tanner Ltd, Frome and London
for the publishers W. H. Allen & Co. Ltd,
44 Hill Street, London W1X 8LB

ISBN 0 491 01643 3

To
young, learning
ACTORS:
the Munis of tomorrow

Portrait of Paul Muni, actor, born Muni Weisenfreund.

Prologue

Down on Second Avenue on New York's Lower East Side, the theater addicts used to say, "There are actors and there are actors. But that Munya—that is an ac-TOR!" It was always said with a swell of personal pride: he was their own, everybody's son, brother, father, grandfather.

They were talking about Paul Muni, born Muni Weisenfreund, who went on to star in fourteen plays (twelve of them on Broadway), twenty-three films, and even radio and television. But in the fabled days of the Yiddish theater, Muni had acted more than three hundred different roles. And he prided himself on rarely repeating a characterization; once the run of a play was completed or the last take of a film was finished, he "shed his skin like a snake" and went on to become another man.

No wonder he was labeled "an actor's actor," and often his peers would pronounce it in rolling tones, using the Russian-Yiddish pronunciation: "AHK-*TYOR!*"

Muni shunned compliments, distrusted applause. But he liked the simple designation of "actor." There was only one other label he was willing to accept. Once he heard a woman at a stage door clucking her tongue in admiration and saying about him, "That is a *mensch!*" Muni smiled, knowing, like most Yiddish, it was untranslatable. (He always felt the average American parent's command to a child, "Be good!" had a puritanical, moralistic ring to it. The French had a more apt phrase: "*Sois sage!*"—be wise! But Yiddish parents said, "Be a *mensch!*" *Mensch* didn't mean simply "man." It didn't mean being masculine, muscular, with hair on your chest. The phrase meant: "Be a person, a human being with individuality and guts; have a distinctive place in the universe."

Was Muni, as many claim, the greatest American performer of our century? Muni himself would have shrugged and dismissed the whole idea with a wave of his arm. "I'm a difficult customer," he'd say. "But don't turn me into a headline, a public institution, a statue. Just say the words, the way it happened."

The words? He was an actor. He was a *mensch*.

**Muni weighing the Bible and Darwin in the final moments of *Inherit the Wind.*
The inscription reads: "To my son Jerry," then in Yiddish: "A leben auf dir
[A blessed life to you]—Paul Muni."** *(Photo by Fred Fehl)*

1

Each night on the stage of the National Theatre in New York, Muni would take a hurried bow, then turn his back to face the cast of *Inherit the Wind* and applaud it along with the audience.

On the night of August 29, 1955, Muni's wife, Bella, and I stood at the rear of the theater, listening to the applause, watching people leap to their feet, hearing the shouts of "Bravo!" We were both crying. Herman Shumlin, the producer-director, was pacing back and forth behind us, staring down at the red carpet, his fingers digging into his head, as if mourning for something forever lost.

It had been a magnificent performance that night: Muni as the Darrow-like Henry Drummond, crusader for the underdog, alternately impassioned and funny. As I watched the play, I kept saying to myself: "This is the last time I'll ever see Muni on a stage." He must have been thinking that, too, for there was an extra dimension that night: Muni certainly believed it was his farewell performance, not only of this play but of his entire acting career.

But the audience didn't know. Only Muni and Bella and Herman and I knew. And Muni's doctors.

My playwriting partner, Robert E. Lee, knew as well. I had phoned him in California just before the performance to tell him the heartbreaking news. Muni's left eye had been paining him; his sight had begun to blur. The medical experts detected a tumor, probably cancerous. To save the man, the eye would have to be removed. Muni, with courage, quietly said, "Let's do it right away. Tomorrow. No wait." The operating room was scheduled at Mount Sinai Hospital for the following day.

Our play, *Inherit the Wind*, had opened perilously late in the season, April 21, 1955. But the reviews were glowing, the lines grew longer at the box office, the "Standing Room Only" sign was out almost every performance. And there were ovations for Muni. That April opening night had been, for us, like "Dreams of Glory" in the Steig cartoons. When the audience, on its feet, began shouting "Author! Author!" we thought they were joking. But Bella Muni shoved us onstage. Muni hugged us, kissed us both on the foreheads, and put up his hand to silence the audience.

9

It was rare for him to make a curtain speech. Simply, quietly, he said one short sentence: "I did the play because I love the words."

Now, a mere four months later, on that night in August, the curtain was coming down for what we thought was the last time.

But Bella Muni grabbed my hand, squeezing it very hard, and in a voice quivering with conviction, she said, "We'll be back by Christmas! Wait and see: we'll be back by Christmas!"

I was at the hospital the next day, sitting with Bella during the long wait, then helplessly, silently, pacing the corridors. Finally the word from the doctors: the operation was successful. The tumor had been totally removed. But there would be a long, long recovery period.

Herman Shumlin closed the play, then daringly announced its reopening within two weeks with a new star, Melvyn Douglas. Broadway scoffed. How could a suave matinee idol follow Muni? With only two weeks of rehearsal, Douglas proved he was a fitting heir to Muni's dynamism. The reopening night critics cheered a new Douglas and saluted the genius of Shumlin's direction.

Muni was fitted for a prosthetic eye and went home to California to rest, presumably to retire.

But the play had a third Broadway opening night on December 1, 1955, without advertising, with no announcement in the press. The display signs and the marquee of the National Theatre still read: "Melvyn Douglas in *Inherit the Wind*." At eight thirty-five, the houselights dimmed to half. The audience settled back. Douglas walked out in front of the curtain. The audience moaned, sighing with disappointment—he wasn't in makeup or costume. Some unknown understudy was probably going to play the part.

Then Douglas spoke with eloquent understatement:

"According to the rules of Actors' Equity, a public announcement must be made from the stage whenever there is a cast substitution. Tonight the role of Henry Drummond will be played by Paul Muni."

Again I was standing in the back of the theater with Bella Muni. The audience was cheering. Bella grabbed my hand again. I have never seen such happy tears in a woman's eyes.

"Merry Christmas!" she said.

2

IN 1968, at the Plaza Hotel in New York, Bella Muni, now all alone except for her dedicated nurses, started a book about her celebrated husband. Bob Lee and I had urged her to write it. It would be good therapy, we thought, and besides, everybody wanted to know that amazing story.

"Will you help me?" Bella asked. "Will you tell me when I sound like Edgar Guest? Or like a goddamn fool? Muni was a somebody. I don't want a book sounding as if it were written by a nobody."

"No," I said, "I won't help a damn bit. Not until you write it."

She laughed and promised to "start scribbling." Weeks after we discussed it, she phoned me.

"Come on over, Jerrele," she said. "I've got some material to read to you."

She was seated in the corner of the parlor of her Plaza suite, her hands folded over a legal-sized yellow pad.

"Look," she said proudly. "I've got it. The title. The whole title page!"

She handed me the pad. It read:

> THE MEN I HAVE LIVED WITH!!
> *by Bella Muni*
>
> Dedicated to Muni—who else?

I flipped the pages. The rest of them were still blank.

"It's a good title," I said. "It even sounds a little racy, a little pornographic."

"You know how many people I've been married to?" she explained. "When Muni was playing a part, onstage or in Hollywood, maybe he could take off the makeup, he couldn't take off the part. When he was playing *Scarface*, who do you think I went home with every night? Al Capone. Oh, what a relief it was to be married to George Simon, that nice attorney in *Counsellor-at-Law*. It's a lot easier living with a good kosher lawyer than living with Al Capone."

We laughed about it. I told her she was the world's best polygamist.

Weeks passed. Every time I called I asked how she was doing with the book.

"I'm thinking about it," Bella said.

"Start getting it down," I advised. "Let me get you a tape recorder maybe. You can dictate."

"I can't. It reminds me too much of Muni."

"That's the idea."

"No, no. I'll write it in longhand. We used to have every kind of tape recorder known to man. I gave them all away or threw them out."

1968 turned into 1969.

It was winter, and Bella hardly went out, even to the theater. For her, playgoing was an experience, sometimes inspiring and exciting; sometimes it made her sick to her stomach. "But!" she said. "But! Breathing actors and a breathing audience both in the same place at the same time: that's what I call an *event!*" Bella had a way of indicating her loves with a brightness that came into her eyes. But those huge eyes would go dead when she wanted to turn off pain or erase something she preferred *not* to remember.

We could hear the shouts and laughter of kids on the Central Park skating rink that cold afternoon she handed me a few scrawled yellow pages.

"Chapter One!" Bella said as if she were presenting the crown jewels.

"The first time I met Muni he was one hundred and one years old!" I read.

Bella was leaning forward, hoping I'd like it.

"It's a great beginning," I said. I read a few more pages of what we had urged her to write, a warm and breezy account of how Bella Finkel and Muni Weisenfreund had met and married. Later Bella wrote a total of twenty-three pages. (I inherited those yellow pads, and they form the basis of some of what follows.)

Bella asked me what I thought. I told her I felt she should go back and tell what she knew about Muni's life before they met and her own life as a member of the Thomashefsky family, the "Barrymores of the Lower East Side."

"I want to know what Muni was like as a kid," I suggested, "and what you were like."

She glanced out of the window at her New York, now almost dead.

"Don't you remember?" I asked.

I hardly heard her answer; she was speaking half to herself. "Nothing to remember."

Suddenly the sounds of children's voices from the skating rink seemed to stop. Even the hum of traffic on the icy streets of Central Park West below us was gone. But the real silence seemed to be in Bella's eyes.

"Muni was never a kid. He was born old, maybe even with a long beard. And *I* was never a kid either."

She shrugged a little.

"Remember? Why?"

She tried to smile.

"Let me put it a different way," she said. "It's better everybody forgot about it."

It was a mystery to unravel. I have tried to put together the pieces of a jigsaw puzzle like the reporter in *Citizen Kane*.

During the run of *Inherit the Wind* in New York, I enriched my mind and my stomach with innumerable after-theater corn beef (occasionally pastrami) sandwiches with Muni, usually at the Sixth Avenue Delicatessen. He brandished a dill pickle quadrant as a pointer and re-created a theater and film past for me, half joyous, half painful, but always kosher-dill pungent.

A few times we took a cab from the National Theatre on West Forty-first downtown to Ratner's Dairy Restaurant on lower Second Avenue. Muni would spoon in vegetables and sour cream, his favorite dish.

"Most actors unwind with booze. Sour cream takes the tension out of my *kishkes*," he said.

The sour cream reminded him of the century's teens and twenties as he stared out onto a deserted Second Avenue, once the Yiddish Broadway, and recalled the days of the Thomashefskys and the Adlers and his in-again, out-again years with Maurice Schwartz.

I didn't run home and write it all down. I don't have a tape-recorder memory. But much of what he told me is letter-clear in my mind, and it keeps rerunning in my head like a cherished film.

One quarter to midnight after a performance, Muni said, "Let's go have a *schnapps*."

So we went to the bar next door to the National. They had Muni's photograph framed in the window, but he had never come in before in person. They were so flabbergasted they almost bowed. They gave us a table in the far corner and left us alone.

"I've played a lot of drunk scenes," Muni said, "but I don't think I've ever really been drunk. You've got to be pretty damn sober to play a drunk effectively, let me tell you."

Two shots of rye, with ginger ale chasers, seemed to mellow Muni. I'd never had a drink with him before, and it opened something in his memory, a kind of reluctant affection about the films he'd made. even the bad ones. His voice was very deep, like the organ tones of some of his early radio appearances. And the words came out slowly and with some difficulty.

"It's easy to kid Hollywood or to hate it. I guess anything or anybody that inflates itself so much, pats itself on the back with blown-up publicity, glorifies and magnifies itself, is a natural target for jokes. I suppose with Hollywood it was necessary to their existence to puff themselves up. But it doesn't take a mastermind to say, 'Christ, what a preposterous place!'

"But! Dreams are preposterous.

"Magic is preposterous.

"Lies are preposterous. And what else is acting or writing or painting or composing but elaborate, creative lying?

"Truth is preposterous. You can't really duplicate it, unless you're a photographer, and even that depends on the angle and the selection, and you can always crop out the garbage can. You can just pretend that you're approximating a moment of truth occasionally, by luck, by chance. Even then all you catch is the shadow of a shadow of it in the mirror of a mirror. The lens of a camera is a man-made eye, and it only looks at what it *wants* to look at."

Muni squinted at me. He wasn't really high, just enhanced.

"The idea of God in heaven, some animated old bellhop with a long beard, who answers every time you ring with a prayer—that's crazy-preposterous. But you know what's more preposterous? *No* God."

He stared at his empty shot glass.

"Booze is preposterous. Let's have another one."

He drank up and waved his arm in the air.

"What the hell could be more preposterous than a volcano or an earthquake or a tidal wave or lightning and thunder? Nature is constantly doing ridiculous, outrageous things. Look at a giraffe or an octopus or an aardvark or a typhoid-fever germ."

Suddenly his voice seemed very strange, like a man talking to himself.

"I suppose you could say that birth and death and everything in between are preposterous. And anybody who tries to photograph it, even catch a tiny glimpse of it to preserve on cel-

14

luloid—that's a fella who tries to rival God in creativity—and he's
HEADMAN PREPOSTEROUS!"

Since Bella's death, knowing her book about Muni would never
be completed, I have tried to fill in the missing pieces of a self-
labeled preposterous but often remarkable life. I have talked and
taped with everybody I could find who knew the Munis, who
had touched their lives: actors and actresses, directors, producers,
writers, agents, friends, brothers, cousins, and other relatives ("in-
laws and out-laws" Bella called them). Often there are a dozen
different versions of a single incident. It is amazing how people
we thought we knew well are really total strangers, puzzles even
to themselves. And we didn't know them at all.

Muni's parents, Salche and Nachum Favel Weisenfreund, were
"tingle-tangle" players, going from village to village of the old
Austria-Hungary. They were a two-person troupe, doing sketches,
songs, and dances, in a Yiddish vaudeville called *shantan*, which
meant variety, a tavern turn, a poor man's nightclub; rarely, if
ever, did this include anything as formal as a stage, a theater,
a playwright, or even a sober and attentive audience. The Weisenfreunds usually wore long black coats and wide-rimmed round
hats, and they would have looked like priests, except for the glued-
on curls along their cheeks. Both played men; women on the
stage were still considered prostitutes or worse.

Muni remembered his mother as being very beautiful, his father
as tall and stern and businesslike. Three sons had been born previously, all in the 1890's. One died in childbirth. Joseph was born
in June, 1891, Elias fourteen months later in August, 1892, both
in Budapest. The trouping parents had made a wide sweep
between the two births, with one-night stands in cafes and barns
and town squares. But Salche had wanted to come back to
Budapest, where there was a midwife she knew who was reliable.
Their performances were by kerosene lamplight. They sang *a
cappella*. Neither could play a musical instrument, but they swore
they would raise sons who could fiddle.

Salche kept letting out the *capota*, the long black cloak, and
continued playing to the very night of Muni's birth. They were
a long way from Budapest and from the midwife Salche trusted
on the night of September 22, 1895, when Muni was delivered
by candlelight in a rooming house for itinerant players directly
across the street from the city jail in Lemberg, Austria. (The city
is now Lvov, later part of Poland, now in the Russian Ukraine.)

15

(Courtesy of Joseph Weisenfreund)

(Courtesy of Rea Lindenberg)

The earliest picture of Muni with the entire Weisenfreund family: his brother Elias (with the hoop); his father, Favel; his mother, Salche; his brother Joseph.

The commemorative photograph in Budapest: Elias, Muni, Joseph with their first violins.

Philip Weisenfreund, Muni's father, attempts to break into New York's Yiddish theater.

Sallie Weisenfreund, Chicago, 1913.

(Courtesy of Joseph Weisenfreund)

(Courtesy of Rea Lindenberg)

Salche and Favel (she always called him by his second name) played until an hour before labor began. Their act was performed on boards across two wine barrels, set up in the corner of a farmer's field. Nobody in the audience realized the potbellied businessman on the makeshift stage was really a woman large with child.

Favel, thirteen years older than his wife, stood around helplessly while the baby was being delivered. He was glad to hear it was a boy. Three violinists, a string trio: that was something to give the world!

The midwife breast-fed the new *boychick*. Salche took three nights off, the act went badly without her, and the fourth night she returned to work. At the end of the week they were back in their carriage, the old horse, half-asleep, pulling the enlarged Weisenfreund family toward another oasis of light in the dark countryside. Joseph, four, and Elias, two, slept on potato sacks on the floor of the carriage. Salche held the new baby. Favel held the reins.

By morning light they searched for a farm with a goat. Milk for the new baby. A farm with a cow was a miracle. And they would literally sing for their breakfast.

A song from Favel sometimes brought half a loaf of bread and the loan of a pot of boiling water so they could cook their potatoes. A generous farmer would let them put their potatoes on sticks and dip them in the herring barrel. This delicacy was called *lok und bulbus*—and Joseph and Elias ate them like lollipops, the thick herring juice coating and salting and flavoring the hot potatoes.

A lullaby from Salche was always worth at least a boiled egg. So if there were an infant on the farm, she would rock it and sing, not to her own newborn, but to the farmer's baby. The farmer's wife would always weep, hearing the borrowed song from Goldfaden's operetta *Shulamith*, the folk melody that swept the world.

In dem Bes-Hamikdosh in a vinkel Cheder,
Sitzt die almona Bas-Zion allein,
Ihr ben-yokhidel, Yidele, vegt zi k'seder,
Und singt ihm zu shloffen a ledele shoen:

"Unter Yidele's vegele
Shteht a klor-weisse tzegele,
Das tzegele ist geforren handlen,
Dos veyt sein dein beruf,
Roshenkes mit Mandelen!
Shloff sie, Yidele, shloff!"

In a synagogue, in a corner of learning,
A widow of Zion sits all alone;
Her pride and joy she rocks with a yearning
To help him dream a dream of her own:

   "In a cradle rests a little child,
   Underneath's a goat, pure white and mild,
   The goat trots off to bargain and barter,
   That's the job you will reap,
   Selling Raisins and Almonds,
   Sleep, my Israel, sleep!"*

The swell of music always came with "Raisins and Almonds," and the tears would fall, as everyone dreamed of the beautiful utopia of being a merchant, selling only delicacies, of a life beyond black bread, rock-strewn fields, bad weather, and hungry stomachs.

It took three weeks to find a village where there was a *mohel* to perform the rites of circumcision. The Weisenfreunds were neither religious nor irreligious, but they occasionally went through ceremonies, when they had the time. Years later his father told Muni: "You were a *goy* for three weeks!"

A rare glass of wine followed the ceremony, along with a drop on Papa's fingertip, to moisten the lips of the baby, and a drop on Mama's fingertip for Joe, a drop for Elias.

They gave the new baby a name. In Hebrew it was Mehilem Meyer. Translated into English, it would be Michael. But they used the Austrian nickname of Muni, which was not unlike "Mickey" in English. They pronounced it *"Moo*-nee," but in later years it was always *"Mew*-nee." The family altered it, with affection, even further to "Munya." But to Mama it was *Munya-le*.

And occasionally she would perform in private, too, rocking her new son, and the name *Munya-le* fit the lullaby:

Shloff-sie, Munya-le, shloff!

The melody always stuck in Muni's mind. For years when he had to ad-lib a melody, the first sounds that came to his lips, as if waiting deep in his subconscious, were the notes that fit that phrase of *"Roshenkes mit Mandelen."*

The other early memories were a blur to Muni: being left for long weeks with strange-smelling relatives, being awakened in the middle of the night for a quick good-bye from his parents and then staring into the dark, asking, "Where did they go?"

*Translated, especially for this book, by Ted Thomas.

18

Muni was joyful when he was taken along and given the privilege of holding the kerosene lamps, their openings pointed toward the crude platforms, then swinging the lanterns around to face the audience while his parents made quick costume changes. He remembered vaguely, as if part of some dream, the rough outlines of the sketches his parents performed, always improvised, embroidered, tailored to fit the local audience. A favorite concerned two bumbling, stumbling Army recruits; what was more unlikely than a Yiddish soldier? Two were even worse, a *shlemihl* bumping into a *nudnick*, each vying with the other to lose the war single-handedly. In another sketch Mama played a drunken student, with Papa as her harsh taskmaster. Muni was always frightened that Mama was sick, but the people kept laughing, so Muni laughed, too. But he worried when she pretended to fall down drunk, and Muni didn't really feel like laughing.

"It's not enough just to make them laugh," Favel always said. "You must make them sad, too, so they *feel*. Then they laugh harder!"

When Muni was three, he was given the job of passing the plate, which was usually a tambourine. They told him that's where the expression "tingle-tangle" came from: the sound of coins rattling into the tambourine. But Muni didn't like doing it, didn't even like the sound. He had seen a beggar on a village street, holding out a hand like a claw, and he sensed that he never wanted to beg like that.

"It's not begging," Papa insisted. "It's like buying tickets. But *afterward*, not before. That's more of a compliment and less of a gyp. And when the tambourine bearer is young, with wide eyes—the customers tingle and tangle even more!"

Favel never spoke about his own parents. To the three boys, grandparents on either side were nonexistent. They knew that their father had begun performing as a choirboy in a synagogue in Galicia. He belonged to a Hassidic family and had run away from home at the age of twelve. Other than that, they knew nothing, and Favel would always shut them up when they asked.

Salche was more vocal. She had been born in Stanislavov, in the Polish area of Austria-Hungary. Her mother, her father's second wife, had died when she was very young.

"My father was a tradesman," she would say proudly. "A merchant. And very rich!"

"Where did all the money go, Mama?" Joseph once asked.

She laughed a little.

"When I met your father and he got me to go on the stage with him, your grandfather disowned me. And when he died, he left everything to the servants. To me, not a single kopeck —because I became an actress."

She said it flatly, factually, without emotion.

"So be musicians," Favel warned the boys. "It is more respectable, and if you're any good at all, you'll never go hungry. Or be disinherited. Nobody ever disinherits a fiddle player!"

Favel would get swells of conscience and enroll all three boys in a local *cheder*. Joseph was already a tall seven-year-old: it was all right to be tall, stupid no. Elias (they began calling him El or Al) was a gangling five-year-old. Muni was a silent, watching three.

"Sure, Munya's too young to learn," Favel said, "but he can go along and absorb. Everything doesn't come in through the brain; some of it sinks into the skin. So sit. And listen!"

The Hebrew teacher was a monster with pockmarked skin and thin wisps of a red beard. His teeth were stained yellow-brown with tobacco juice, and his breath was foul from garlic. He never talked. He either whispered or screamed.

He always patted Muni on the head, with a touch of fatherly affection, and he was patient with the older boys as they struggled through the Hebrew alphabet and learned all the strange symbols, the diacritical marks placed below the consonants, to indicate different vowel sounds. But one day he stormed into the cramped classroom and his patches of red beard seemed to be standing on end, bristling.

"You are the children of Gypsies!" he shouted.

"No!" Joseph shouted back, protectively. "Not Gypsies. My mama and papa are *actors!*"

"Worse! More sinful. Idolatry!"

The two older boys backed away. Muni sat, not moving. He was told to listen, so he listened.

The monster grabbed a thick black prayer book and shook it at Muni.

"The Talmudic scholars have decreed it, and I say this prayer at the synagogue three times a day each day of my life. With joy I say this prayer!"

He flipped the black book open, brandishing it at Muni as if it were a weapon. And he intoned the Hebrew, translating it immediately into half German, half Yiddish, pounding the words at Muni as if they were lightning bolts. Joe and El cowered in a far corner.

"I give thanks to you, O Lord my God and God of my fathers, that you have placed my portion among those who sit in the House of Prayer, and that you did not cast my lot among those who frequent theaters and circuses. For I labor, and they labor; I wait and they wait: I to inherit the World-to-come; they, the pit of destruction."

His voice rose to a crescendo, shouting into Muni's ear as if the child were deaf.

Joe grabbed Muni's hand, and the three boys ran out of the *cheder*. They could still hear the ringing tones of "the pit of destruction" half a block away.

"If he's going to the World-to-come," Joe said, "I'd just as soon go to—"

He pointed down, and El nodded agreement. Muni laughed. Something was certainly wrong with a person who didn't like Mama and Papa in the warm kerosene light singing and dancing and even falling down drunk.

Three days later Favel told them it was all right to stop going to *cheder* because they were moving on to another town. Joe and El had to admit to him that they'd stopped going anyway. Favel slapped them both across the face. Muni, he said, was too young to slap, but he hit him on the bottom.

Then Favel looked a little ashamed of himself.

"Maybe you did the right thing," he said. "I don't want you to be rabbis anyhow. I want you all to be violinists. When we get to Budapest, I'll buy three fiddles."

At the next town, still many muddy miles to Budapest, El and Muni were sent out, coins wrapped carefully in a handkerchief, to buy a jug of kerosene. Salche and Favel set up their stage at the edge of a field. It would be dark by the time the show would start. No kerosene, no performance.

At the shop, El stared at the colorless liquid, then motioned to Muni. They left the shop without making the purchase.

"It looks just like water," El told Muni. "We'll just fill our jug at the well, and nobody will ever know it's not kerosene. And we can use the coins to buy honey candy."

Muni nodded obediently. El was older. He knew a lot more. And what was wrong with candy?

They bought four mouth-watering honey balls wrapped in brown paper: one for each of them now, two to save for later to enjoy in the dark just before bedtime.

Cockily, El filled the kerosene jug at the town well. He held it up to the light. "See? The same. Who will ever know the difference?"

They skipped back to the field, their mouths full of sweetness.

The audience was gathering for the performance. Hastily, Favel took the jug from the boys and poured liquid into each lamp.

Behind a blanket strung between two trees, Salche, by candlelight, was getting into her long black costume. Favel motioned to Joe to ignite the lamps.

Joe lit a taper from the candle behind the blanket and went to the first lamp. The taper sputtered and died. He raced back to the candle, lit the other end of the taper, and tried the second lamp. Another hissing sputter, then darkness.

Favel, watching impatiently, shoved Joe aside. "You are stupid," he yelled. "A baby like Munya could light these lamps! Are you soft in the head?"

He grabbed the taper, felt that it was wet, tossed it on the ground, and took the candle instead. He went to the first lamp, bent the candle to it, and the candle flame hissed out. Muni and El huddled together under a tree, holding their breaths. Favel was panicky. He found some long crude matches and tried lamp after lamp. All went out. He lifted one of the lamps, almost viciously, as if it were an enemy, and swung back his arm, as if to fling its uselessness into the growing dark. Some of the liquid from it poured out onto his fingers. He stopped, smelled his fingers, suspiciously tasted a few drops.

He closed his eyes, turned to the audience, hoarsely controlling his fury as he apologized. There would be no performance tonight. The muttering, unhappy villagers emptied the field.

Then Favel screamed. "God! What kinds of sons did you give me? Donkeys! Brains made of pig vomit! I send them for kerosene, they bring back water!"

Favel walked over to the tree, where El and Muni were cowering.

"What did you do with the money?" he shouted.

Numbly, El opened his hand. It contained the brown paper wrapped around the precious remaining honey balls.

"Candy!" Favel thundered. "May it rot your *kishkes!* May it turn into snakes inside your stomachs!"

He grabbed the candy and flung it far into the field. The boys watched their treasure disappear into the night, while their father continued to rant.

"And did you expect water to flame into light? The day that water burns, the world comes to an end—all the oceans on fire! You must be intelligent to stay alive, but you will both die of stupidity!"

And he hit El and Muni across the faces with the full impact of the back of his hand. El staggered against the tree. Muni fell on the ground, whimpering. His father's voice lowered, but it was deep like the sound of doom.

"Cry! Cry, baby. Cry away your ignorance! Candy you can wait for. Candy comes later. But light for the stage means potatoes in our mouths—and that comes first!"

Muni, on the ground, sobbing, guilty, hurt, watched his father stalk around the field, a huge figure against the night sky. Years later he remembered it dimly, but always thinking: What a performance! No mere tingle-tangle player falling down drunk. A giant. A great actor, who thundered like some ancient god.

His father rose above him, lifted him to his feet, holding tightly to his shoulders, shaking him.

"So it's over. It's finished. You've learned a lesson?"

Muni nodded, but the tears were still in his eyes, running down his face.

"So stop crying. Munya, be a *mensch!*"

The Weisenfreunds found no work in Budapest. The dimly lit café where Favel and Salche had hoped to play had closed. The owners had moved to America. *"Am-yehr-itch-kee"* people would call it, always speaking of the streets paved with gold, a country where they liked Jewish people so well that one of their Presidents even had the first name of Abraham!

Europe was different. There was anti-Semitism, especially in Russia, where the Cossacks had burned villages. The Yiddish theater had been banned in Russia. Where would they strike next? One must save and have the courage to plan to go to England perhaps or even across the great ocean to *Am-yehr-itch-kee*. The papa of every family went first, then sent for the others.

"Soon," Favel told his family, "we will do the same. But first promises must be kept."

So he bought three quarter-size fiddles for his three sons. Of course, the shortage of money meant only the eldest could begin lessons; besides, Muni was still too young. But it was a beginning.

"You start with a string trio. That's on the road to being a whole orchestra!" Favel was emphatic about his plans. "Someday—a real theater. With a whole play by a real playwright. *Singen. Tanzen.* And a conductor in the pit, one of my own sons waving the baton!"

To celebrate their new acquisitions, there must be a commemorative photograph: the three Weisenfreund Brothers, violin trio deluxe! Striped knee pants for all three. Cummerbunds around their waists, like stars in a rich café in Vienna. And for Muni, a red and blue scarf, tied jauntily around his neck, and a podium to stand on.

First, haircuts. In the latest style. Flowing and artistic, to make them look like musicians, like the seventeen-year-old Kubelik who was already a virtuoso. See? It is easy. You just study, you work, you wait, and in a few years you are another Kubelik!

At the barbershop, where Favel left them, the boys insisted on short hair. Joe asked that his be shaved off completely, and the barber followed orders. When Favel returned, he was aghast.

"Flowing, like musicians, I said. Not bare and bald! You look like Cossacks, especially Joe."

"I have heard," Joe explained, "that if you have a shaved head, your hair never falls out."

"What's to fall out?" Favel roared. "Idiot. You have ruined the photograph! You don't look like a musician; you look like a convict!"

The picture was taken for posterity.

In the months that followed, Joe studied, scales and finger exercises, and hated it. Favel performed alone, in villages close by. Salche was sick and stayed in Budapest. She was pregnant again. *Am-yehr-itch-kee* was still very far away.

Less money bought fewer potatoes. So they ate less. To supplement his income, Favel would go listen to other entertainers, then later copy down their jokes, their routines, even the lyrics to their songs he could remember. For a few Austrian marks, he would sell the routines to other traveling players. Everything was lifted anyway, improvised, makeshift, borrowed, put together with love and a prayer.

He took Muni along. "Sit, Munya. Listen. Not just with your ears. With your brain. Even with your pores."

Salche gave birth to a baby daughter but almost died during the delivery. The three worried boys were shooed out of the room while the Budapest midwife sweated and prayed and moaned along with the laboring mother.

Two weeks later their new baby sister, born so small, died.

Favel, who usually prayed and fasted only one day a year, on Yom Kippur, prayed on this spring day in 1899.

"Give me courage, dear God. It is time to move. I am thirty-nine years old. If I am not to waste the rest of my life in grubbing potatoes, if I am ever to become rich, famous, to give my family 'Raisins and Almonds,' I will have to change countries."

It took persuasion and tears and pain, and even more courage than Favel knew. But they sold their horse and carriage and Salche's wedding ring and made the long trip to a new country called England and a new city called London.

Favel never became rich and famous. But one of his sons did: the silent one, who listened even with his pores.

3

IN London the family lived on Philpot Street in the Whitechapel area, the Jewish neighborhood not unlike the Lower East Side of New York. They had two rooms, four flights up, and the stairwells were dark, damp, noisy, and filled with rancid odors. (Years later, the Nazis leveled most of this area with their brutal blitz.)

The Weisenfreunds had traveled across half the width of Europe on third-class swaying trains, then on a Channel boat, huddled below decks, not daring to be sick, but pale with fear. They were met at the Port of London and taken to the Jews' Temporary Shelter in Leman Street, run by the Jewish Board of Guardians. They carried with them only the basic clothes on their backs, but each boy had been instructed to hold, as if it were an infant whose bones and skin were tender and breakable, his own carefully wrapped quarter-size violin.

Favel carried something else, inside his head: his memory of all the turns and sketches he had seen, a marketable commodity.

Even before their first meal in their walk-up flat, Favel went in search of a violin teacher. He found a music student in his early twenties.

"Teach all three," Favel ordered. "Every day if necessary. Keep track of the charges. We will pay you when we are able to pay."

He unwrapped Muni's violin and held it up to the light.

"Someday, Munya," Favel predicted, "when you are a great concert violinist, I will buy you a Stradivarius!"

"Righto!" Muni said in English, and the family and the new music teacher laughed, amazed that their four-year-old had picked up the first English word.

Favel managed to get a few roles, walk-ons, in the Yiddish theater on Mile End Road in Whitechapel, but he considered it degrading. No lines. No songs. Just an old Jew in a beard, crossing the stage, carrying a staff. But it paid enough for potatoes, even a piece of real herring, not just the juice, and large bags of day-old cakes and broken biscuits. Favel shut his eyes, pasted on his beard, and kept making the anonymous crosses.

"We must become Anglicized," Favel told his family.

So Favel became Philip and Salche became Sallie. The two older boys, dressed carefully by their mother in Eton collars, were sent

25

to the Jews' Free School, beside Petticoat Lane. Muni stayed home and practiced the violin. But he listened, and he learned. He was the first to master English, but his words had a Cockney flavor. He was the only one in the family not called a *greener* by the kids in the neighborhood.

"What an ear you have!" his father would tell him. "So imitate music, too. And you will be the great virtuoso of your time. A new century is coming. You will be the greatest violinist of the twentieth century!"

Muni nodded and went back to practicing. His fingers were very tired. So he never joined his brothers in after-school games: Tin Can Copper, Gobs and Bonsters, and gutter cricket with a ball made from a squeezed-together newspaper, a piece of wood for a bat, and a gas streetlamp for a wicket.

Rumors swept across the ocean from America. Not only were the streets paved with gold, but the Yiddish theater was at its peak, a true golden age. Thomashefsky. Adler. Kessler. In America they were like gods, rich and adored.

Philip Weisenfreund found a patron in Whitechapel, a shopkeeper who laughed and cried whenever he heard stories of the *shlemihls* and *shmendricks* in Rumania and the Ukraine, the tender songs and the tales of the *shtetls*, the tiny Jewish villages of Eastern Europe. And the shopkeeper had saved up enough pounds sterling to help Philip open his own theater.

A theater? It was a cramped meeting hall, up a creaking stairway. But the new Sallie Weisenfreund could perform, and the new Philip Weisenfreund could be the manager and the sketch artist. Whitechapel now had Yiddish variety: songs and dances, two Hassidic Yids falling down drunk.

The shillings and pence started to flow in. The music teacher could be paid. Sallie bought a new dress, a bright one, her first, not black as her dresses had always been on the Continent. And the audiences laughed and applauded; to Sallie it was more of a feast than potatoes and herring juice.

But she was a young woman, merely twenty-six, and there were stirrings inside of her. Three sons, one almost as tall as she was, and she had hardly lived at all.

"I want to go out," she told her husband.

"Out?" he echoed. "We are already out. It is the people of London who go out to see *us*."

"I have a new dress, and I have never even worn it. What's the use of a bright dress if nobody sees me in it?"

"I'll work out a new sketch, Sallie alias Salche, my love, and you will be seen. The dress will be seen. By everybody!"

26

So the sketches were brought up to date. Philip also played a woman, an old crone of a *bubba*, a hunched-over grandmother, and Sallie was the modern, young, protesting granddaughter. The sketch was a huge success, borrowed from Goldfaden to be sure, but improvised to include local references, including mentions of the fog outside, the creaky theater stairway, and the Jew named Disraeli who had been Queen Victoria's Prime Minister. The customers flocked. Business was good. Philip paid back the shopkeeper; the theater was all his own. Now he was the total "boss." And he started saving.

The street gangs of Whitechapel defeated him. Two gangs, teen-age young toughs, tried to rule the territory. One gang called itself Kid Twists, but the boys were more mature and muscular than anything in Dickens. The Kid Twist gang, spotting Philip's theater as a profitable business, decided to "protect" it and made their headquarters on the stoop outside. The rival gang used the theater as a target and pelted the entranceway with rocks and bottles. One night a paying customer, a poor peddler on his way into the theater, was caught in the crossfire of rocks. He fell, hit his head on the curbstone, and died of the injuries.

Philip was called to constabulary court. Terrified, through an interpreter, he declared that he knew nothing about it; all he did was run the theater.

"I only wish," he said, "to make people laugh and cry. I do not wish to make people dead!"

Philip was cleared, but nobody came to the theater again. Sallie and Philip waited, in costume, ready to perform; not one customer bought a ticket.

So Philip decided it was time to move again to another country. A country without gangsters.

"See?" He showed his family his savings. "I'm a rich man. Eighty-five pounds! All from playing a crazy old grandma with a beautiful granddaughter!"

To Philip, it was a fortune. In those days, his hoard was worth more than $400. (And $400 then was more than $400 now.)

"We are going to America, to New York, to the New Jerusalem!"

The family decided that Philip would go first. As soon as he found a place and a position as one of the stars of the American Yiddish theater, he would send for the others. And nobody would travel steerage, like cattle. Second class—like ladies and gentlemen! And while they waited: "Fiddle! Daily! Practice!"

Passage was booked on an ocean liner leaving from Liverpool. Everybody wept hopeful good-byes. They would meet again soon on the golden streets of New York.

But the train to Liverpool was a luxury. Philip managed a ride on the cart of a friendly neighbor from Whitechapel who was driving south to fish in the great ocean. After all, Philip had driven all over Eastern Europe with a horse and carriage. England was tiny: a few hours only to the sea. And the money saved could be spent in America.

The money saved also saved his life. The cart was slow, the horse asthmatic. It took days, not hours, getting to Liverpool. Philip fretted, cursed the cart, the horse, himself for his stupidity. When he reached Liverpool, the ship had sailed.

While he waited at the seacoast, he learned that a hundred miles out, the ship he had been booked on sank; all the passengers were lost at sea.

Panicked that his family would hear of it, he scrawled a note and gave it to his friend in the cart, who was heading back for London.

> Deliver please to my family the following message:
> I WANT YOU TO KNOW I AM NOT SWIMMING AROUND LIKE A DROWNED POTATO DOWN THERE WITH THE HERRING. GOD IS GOOD—I MISSED THE BOAT!

Philip booked passage on the next ship. The family received another message: "IT ARRIVED SAFELY."

In the months that followed, the reports from New York's Lower East Side to London's Whitechapel were sparse. Sallie was worried; to her no news meant bad news. The boys tried to cheer her up. Papa was probably so busy becoming the king of New York's Yiddish theater that he had no time to give them a full report.

But all three boys returned to scratching away at their fiddles, doing what Papa had ordered, covering up their own worries in endless practicing. Their one luxury: Joe graduated from a quarter-size to a full-size violin and hated it four times as much.

The few letters from Philip raved about New York City: "There are more Irish here than in Dublin and more Jews than in all of Palestine." But nothing about any jobs, no word about when the family was to join him.

Philip wrote vaguely about some relatives he had discovered in New York, and finally the envelope came with money for tickets and directions from Papa about when to come.

It took a month to straighten out their papers. The name Weisenfreund had multiple spellings: Joe's papers from Budapest read Waiszenfreundt. The stiff British officials and the friendlier clerks at the American consulate were puzzled and had to be convinced they were all part of the same family.

"What does Weisenfreund mean?" one clerk asked them. "Wise friend? White friend?"

Joseph tried to explain. It was originally "Waiss," which meant waif or orphan, so their whole name actually meant "The Orphan's Friend."

Right then, Elias remembered, he didn't feel at all like a friend of an orphan, he felt like the orphan itself. The clerk tried to transliterate it into English: Orphfriend? Friendorph? Then he decided to leave it the way it was. Their visas read:

Sallie Weisenfreund, 27; Joseph Weisenfreund, 9; Elias Weisenfreund, 7; Muni Weisenfreund, 5.

The day after Queen Victoria's funeral in 1901 the Weisenfreunds sailed from Liverpool, headed for the New Jerusalem.

Sallie had no doubt that the ship would sink. Another vessel had gone down. Was theirs different? How did it stay up anyway? She clung to railings and the side of her bunk, as if physically trying to hold the ship up. The boys tried to laugh, to cheer her up, but their laughter was thin; they were really cheering themselves up.

Sallie and Joe were sick most of the trip across, prisoners of their bunks, hardly eating anything. But Muni and El raced around the decks, feeling free as sea gulls, enjoying the adventure of open air and open sea.

It was dark, half an hour before dawn, when their ship nosed into New York Harbor. Through the mists of early morning, Muni saw the lifted torch of the Statue of Liberty, and he dragged his mother and Joe up on deck. The fog sat on the surface of the water and covered their view of the tip of Manhattan Island, but the statue was there, a giant figure emerging from the morning gray.

Muni had mastered enough English to read a tourist pamphlet. Proudly, he introduced his family to it.

"It is called 'Liberty Enlightening the World,'" he said in English with a slight Cockney accent and then again in Yiddish for his mother.

Sallie forgot about being sick; she was so impressed, not only by the sight, but by the fact there was this statue of a woman to welcome them to New York Harbor.

And suddenly they saw the very top of the New York skyline. The feet of the buildings were still hidden in the mist. Their peaks caught the light, gray at first, then rose-colored, then a flaming red, then golden. The towers seemed to float in space, insubstantial, hanging in the sky, a mirage out of an old folktale.

"Unbelievable. Unbelievable," Sallie said in Yiddish. "Truly the most beautiful city in the world. And *we* are going to live here. *We* are actually going to live here!"

They never could understand how they escaped the rigors of Ellis Island. Perhaps it was because they were traveling second class instead of steerage. It might as well have been steerage; twelve of them had been crowded into one stateroom belowdecks, including an infant who cried the entire trip.

But there were medical inspectors, who came aboard from a tugboat, who ripped off the boys' caps and examined their hair for lice. Sallie was indignant at this. But the boys diverted her anger by pointing again to the skyline, the piling up of golden towers in a crescent along the Battery. It was certainly magical, something from a dream.

Philip met them at the dock with a borrowed horse and buggy. He drove them proudly, the boys gaping all the way, to Clinton Street, far downtown on the Lower East Side. It was a cold-water flat, only one room and six flights up.

"This is progress?" Sallie complained. "One less room. Two flights higher to climb than Whitechapel."

"We are getting up in the world," Philip told them. But he was silent about his own work. When they began to ask questions, he told them that first there was a celebration for their arrival. A banquet at a very special delicatessen. And then an evening in the Yiddish theater! How was that for a welcome to the great city of New York?

With scrubbed faces and their Eton collars in place, the boys were ready. Sallie wore the bright dress. Philip sported a derby hat. Their father had discovered a nephew, the son of a brother, long dead and never before mentioned. Their newfound cousin owned a delicatessen on the ground level, down a few steps, right on Second Avenue, the Yiddish Rialto.

Their first meal in America was a feast: seven courses for fifteen cents each, including chopped liver, noodle soup, flanken of beef, steaming bowls of vegetables, dessert, and the climax—"a glass tea" with strawberry jam floating in it.

Their first theater-going was also a feast: the great Boris Thomashefsky, starring in the elaborate production of the *Yeshiva Bocher*. Loosely translated as *The Rabbinical Student*, the plot was familiar to Joseph, who had gone far enough in school in England to recognize it.

30

They sat in the balcony, agape at the wonders on the stage: Thomashefsky, an imposing man with thighs which made the shopgirls sigh, playing a rabbinical student, brought home to a village in Russia because of the death of his father. His uncle has just married his mother. His father, also a rabbi, has died of a broken heart when the mother fell in love with the pompous uncle. Mourning, the rabbinical student goes to the synagogue to recite Kaddish, the prayer for the dead. The Holy Ark is opened, and there stands the ghost of his father, chanting like a cantor for revenge.

Muni and his brothers gasped at the effectiveness of this moment, a staggering effect, and weeping swept through the audience. Philip poked his wife, nodded to his sons, as if to say, "See? See? Here is great theater!"

They watched the rest of the plot unfold: the rabbinical student singing his great love for the fair Esther; the evil uncle plotting against the young student, spreading a rumor that the boy is a nihilist who denies the existence of God. Somehow, the plot is discovered, and the scheming uncle is exiled to Siberia. Esther drowns herself after a mad aria. The fifth act takes place in the Jewish cemetery in the midst of a blowing snowstorm. Esther, shrouded for burial, is brought in. The rabbinical student rants about his undying love, and a marriage ceremony is performed between the still-living student and his lost sweetheart. The climax is reached with resounding chords from the orchestra as the student falls dead, his heart broken. Curtain. Moaning and sobbing from the audience amid the applause as the cast sweeps across the stage for their bows.

"Beautiful! Thrilling!" Philip said, blowing his nose. "A story which truly catches the Jewish character."

"But, Papa," Joseph protested as they made their exit through the crowd and the hawkers of seltzer water and political pamphlets, "it's really Shakespeare."

"It's what?" Philip asked.

"Hershel, the *Yeshiva Bocher*, is Hamlet. Esther is Ophelia. I studied it in school in London. It was written by Shakespeare."

"Shakespeare? Shakespeare? A Jewish boy?"

"No, Papa."

"It doesn't matter. That's some writer, lemme tell you. Someday maybe we get him to write us a sketch."

(Courtesy of Joseph Weisenfreund)

(Albert Fenn Collection)

The Weisenfreunds pose for a family picture in Cleveland. Muni, center; Joseph and Elias, Philip and Sallie, front.

Emma Thomashefsky, the "Gibson Girl" of the Yiddish theater.

THE boys, exhausted, were bedded down in the corners of their one-room walk-up flat. Only Muni stayed awake, staring at the cracked ceiling, listening intently as his father confessed in halting whispers to his mother their terrible predicament: they had arrived in New York too late.

"Tonight you saw one of the kings, the great Thomashefsky. There are other kings. Queens also. But two years ago, in 1899, a union was formed. Now the doors are closed. We should not have gone to London, but directly to America. Perhaps, then, we could be royalty, too. Now we are serfs."

Sure, he had made a few dollars: singing at a wedding, relieving his cousin at the counter of the delicatessen, selling one sketch, even acting as a fill-in prompter.

Philip had performed a *proba*, what later actors called an audition, for the union committee. The judges were stern and unsmiling; everybody said they were chosen because they were hardhearted. A set number of actors had been determined for each theater; only a death created a vacancy. (If there were 400 actors and 10 theaters, each theater had 40 actors on the payroll, whether they appeared onstage or not.)

32

"Perhaps," Sallie said, "if you're too talented, the actors on the committee are afraid of you."

"Possible, possible," Philip brooded.

"They see in you another great star, and they're afraid of the competition. Go again and don't be so good!"

Proba had a cruel double meaning. It was also the Yiddish word for rehearsal, so when the auditioning committee granted a hopeful actor a *proba*, they were implying: "You're not on yet, you're not *in* yet!" A few years later, when Actors' Equity was formed uptown, labor-fearing theater managers used the Hebrew Actors Union as a horrible example of the closed shop.

Philip sadly told Sallie about other, lesser classifications in the union. They would try for them. Classification Two was the road: Cleveland, Chicago, Philadelphia, Boston.

"But we have waited so long to come to New York," Sallie complained. "Tomorrow morning we leave already?"

He explained the third and lowest classification: for variety artists. For some unknown reason, it was called local #5, but #3 and #4 were nonexistent. Philip and Sallie would simply repeat what they had done in Europe. And they would wait. And hope. People died every day.

"*We* could die before we had a chance." And Sallie wept. Philip held her and turned down the gaslight.

Muni stared into the darkness, full in the stomach, full in the mind from a kaleidoscopic first day and evening in New York, but hungry still: hungry to know what would happen to them in this strange, terrifying, huge, unknown, yet alluring new country.

The two older boys were sent to Suffolk Street School and were bullied by the other boys because of their Eton jackets, their neatness, and their English accents. They were bounced down several grades because of their unfamiliarity with basic arithmetic and reading. Muni stayed at home and practiced the violin. Sallie and Philip found a job, weekends only, singing in a storefront variety house. And finally they moved their lodgings to another street, one block closer to Second Avenue, one flight lower, one room larger.

Muni first enrolled at P.S. 20 on the corner of Rivington and Eldridge streets. It was an all-male school with cavernous hallways and tall windows that had to be opened with poles. Teachers' pets were allowed the glorious privilege of staying after school to beat the cloth erasers together, which sent up clouds of chalk dust. Muni never said much. He sat. He listened. He hated the teachers' pets and wouldn't be caught dead slapping the erasers together.

The girls of the neighborhood (Muni was always shy and low-ered his head when he passed them) went to Public School 91, three blocks away. Both schools had high turrets and were sur-rounded by steel picket fences. They could have been medieval dungeons or penitentiaries.

A new P.S. 20 opened many years later in 1965, after the original building was torn down. In it is a Wall of Fame, a twenty-foot-high mosaic called "The Wall of Our Forebears." Included among the famous alumni are likenesses of George Gershwin, Edward G. Robinson, Senator Jacob Javits, Harry Golden, Irving Caesar (who wrote the lyrics for "Swanee" and "Tea for Two"), and Paul Muni. But Muni never went beyond the second grade there; the road to graduation, all the way to 8-B, was long, and Muni never traveled it.

Sallie and Philip were booked, on an irregular basis, into a dozen variety theaters around New York and one below the bridge in Brooklyn. Some other promising newcomers, doing "single turns," were Sophie Tucker and Belle Baker.

"But I am an *actor*," Philip complained. "A *schauspieler!* I should be allowed to play with the best. Why do they keep me out? Am I to be a nickel player all my life?"

One day he stormed into the union office, also the home of the Hebrew Actors Club, where the greats lounged and *shmoosed*. He demanded a hearing before the judging committee.

They heard him out. "Elevate yourself! Join Local Number Two," they advised. "Go on the road. To fine, growing cities like Cleveland or Chicago. After three years, come back. With such experience, you will have a better chance."

So in 1904 Philip Weisenfreund grimly packed up his family and moved to Cleveland. The boys were yanked out of school and away from their new violin teachers. Joe was now so proficient that he could play in the pit. They felt as if they were leaving the New Jerusalem to travel more weary years in the wilderness.

Sallie stood at the rear of the train like Lot's wife and watched New York slipping away, gone from their lives, Paradise forever lost. But Philip argued it would be better than the drafty saloons, the storefront variety houses, the whole degrading category so aptly named, he felt, not third but *fifth* class. In a place like Cleveland they could raise their income and their artistic stand-ards.

But none of them knew, and Muni didn't know until many years later, that a few weeks after they left New York, a great scandal rocked the Yiddish Rialto. For the rest of her life, the niece of the great Thomashefsky, Bella Finkel, later Mrs. Paul Muni, wanted to forget it, erase it, obliterate it, never talk about it or write about it. Why not pretend it was just something she read about that happened to somebody else?

The Yiddish theater in New York was dazzling, skyrocketing to its apex, comparing itself to a golden age in Greece or the Elizabethan Renaissance in England. But it was a short-lived Roman candle, blazing across the sky only briefly: twenty-five or thirty pyrotechnic years.

The fire blazed in its stars: Boris Thomashefsky, Jacob P. Adler, David Kessler, Sigmund Mogelescu, Madame Keni Lipzin, and in later years such titans as Maurice Schwartz, Jacob Ben-Ami, Ludwig Satz, Rudolph Schildkraut.

Bella often heard the story from Uncle Boris how the Yiddish theater in New York had been born. Somebody had to give birth to it: more Yiddish was being spoken in New York than in any other single city in the world.

Boris Thomashefsky, aged fifteen, worked with his father at the Samaplana Cigarette Factory. (The cigarette had a sulfur tip; it could be lit without the benefit of a match on the abrasive bottom of the packet: "a matchless cigarette.") Boris also sang on the Sabbath and on High Holy Days at the Henry Street Synagogue as a boy soprano, graduating to a very high tenor. The president of the synagogue, Frank Wolf, ran a saloon at the corner of Essex and Hester streets. Boris felt Wolf was impressive, since he had a large sign over his bar reading THE WORKERS' FRIEND, and he wore a large diamond stickpin in a brightly colored shirt and two large diamond rings on his fingers. Wolf was equally impressed with Boris: a six-foot figure with a barrel chest, yet only fifteen. Wolf often invited the young Thomashefsky to *Shabbas* dinner. And one Friday night Boris convinced Wolf to import a troupe of Yiddish actors from London. Wolf could be the godfather and patron saint and founder of New York's Yiddish theater! It would be good business for his saloon, and it would make him a *macher*, a big shot in the community. Wolf agreed to import twelve actors of assorted sizes and sexes from London. Thomashefsky was ecstatic.

The play Boris chose was *Die Kishuf Macherine*, which meant *The Witch* or *The Sorceress*. This old-fashioned Abraham Goldfaden play had plenty of songs and plenty of action. The theater was rented, Turn Hall on East Fourth Street near Second Avenue.

Next he hired a chorus from neighborhood synagogue choirs, a conductor, and twenty-four musicians. The posters were impressive:

Frank Wolf presents
THE FIRST YIDDISH PRODUCTION
IN NEW YORK
THE HEBREW OPERA AND DRAMATIC COMPANY
Goldfaden's
DIE KISHUF MACHERINE
For the benefit of ten poor Russian families
Tickets: $1.50, $1.00, 50¢, 35¢
TURN HALL
August 18, 1882

In very small letters, B. Thomashefsky was listed as "Manager and Chorus Master."

The troupe arrived, with a sense of history in their faces. No written text was available, but all the actors were able to re-create the work from memory from all the productions they had done in Europe. Thomashefsky threw in a few extra songs for good measure. How could they miss?

But the Yiddish theater in New York almost died before it opened because of protests from German-Jewish citizens, already uptown and appalled by this insurgent group threatening their very existence with this "vulgar public display." Yiddish theater would call attention to their Jewishness; they wished only to be assimilated, to become more American than Americans.

Despite threats of deportation on boats worse than steerage ("Pig boats. You will be sent back to Europe with the swine that you are!"), the actors carried on. Thomashefsky was everywhere, bubbling with enthusiasm and optimism, assuring everybody they were making history.

Huge crowds gathered outside the theater the night of August 18. Police were called. They tried to get the customers to form orderly lines at the box office but found it impossible. The audience waved dollar bills in the air and shoved, trying to get in. Giant vans moved in, one on each corner of the block, causing pandemonium: drums beating, trumpets blaring different melodies simultaneously from four different wagons. Speakers leaped up onto the backs of the vans and shouted to the crowd, "Don't go to this evil production. It is a shame and a scandal for every good Jew in America." They argued that the play made fun of their people. Bubba Yachneh, the witch of the play, sets fire to a Jewish home. The actors were accused of trying to spread anti-Semitism. "Jews must not be permitted to allow such a thing to happen!" The speakers even suggested that the actors be lynched.

Thomashefsky later wrote that by seven o'clock Turn Hall was so crowded "a splinter couldn't be inserted anywhere!" At eight o'clock the curtain was ready to rise and the orchestra was playing the overture. Then they discovered that the prima donna, Madame Sarah Krantzfeld, had failed to show up at the theater. She had the key role of Mirele (a popular name for heroines in the Yiddish theater). Bubba Yachneh was played by a man named Leon Golubok. (Thomashefsky himself played it in later years; so did Muni.) But the curtain couldn't go up without Madame Krantzfeld. Boris signaled for the orchestra to keep playing. When the waiting audience heard it for the third time, they started hooting, whistling, pounding their feet. Thomashefsky grabbed Wolf, and they ran to the prima donna's apartment. They found her in bed, a wet towel on her head. She swore she was dying. The young Boris knelt beside the bed, crying, pleading.

"We will all be without bread. We will starve. Besides you are murdering a beautiful baby about to be born. A theater! It is sinful what you are doing! God will punish you!"

Madame Krantzfeld continued her death scene, moaning about her pains. But suddenly her frightened husband, fearing the wrath of God, confessed to Thomashefsky and Wolf that the opposition forces had offered him $300 and promised him a soda stand right on the corner of Fourth Street and Second Avenue if his wife did not perform.

"If you will give me a better offer, I will permit her to perform," he bargained.

Trapped, Wolf gave in, promising $350 and the best seltzer stand on the Lower East Side. Exactly on cue, Madame Krantzfeld threw off the cold towel, and they all headed back for Turn Hall.

By the time they got to the theater, a large part of the audience had left. Those still in the auditorium were screaming, cursing, breaking chairs. The orchestra and the chorus had also checked out. Only a pianist remained. Madame Krantzfeld refused to perform without an orchestra. Thomashefsky shoved her on the stage, but she was still arguing and ranting when the curtain went up. Stubbornly, she didn't sing but *recited* the songs. The audience, many familiar with the work, began to hoot and whistle. Wolf came on to announce that all the ticket money would be refunded.

That's the version pieced together from reports in the *Jewish Messenger,* the *Jewish Gazette*, and the *Staats Zeitung*, newspapers of the time. Many years later Abe Cahan, the fiery editor of the *Jewish Forward*, and Boris Thomashefsky himself (in an autobiography never translated into English) told a slightly amended account in a hazy glow of recollected glory. It all took place in 1879, they claim—three years earlier—and Boris was only twelve at the time. Boris, still a boy soprano and known affectionately as the Berditchiver Nightingale (named after a town in the Ukraine), did indeed persuade Wolf to bring over the troupe. But, in addition, he rehearsed the choir, staged the play, built and painted the sets, and was slated to appear briefly as a bean vendor, and sing a song in Act Three. In this version, though La Krantzfeld went through all her death throes, she did *not* return to Turn Hall. Boris then climbed into her costume, padded himself out so that he had a prima donna's bosom, and the "Nightingale" sang and performed brilliantly. The reaction: "The Krantzfeld has never sung better."

Both versions agree on the disastrous finale. People who had bought tickets couldn't get in—and money had to be refunded. Wolf, disgusted, called it quits. With no money left and to keep his company together, Boris got all his actors jobs at the Samaplana Cigarette Factory. He was not so generous to Madame Krantzfeld, who never worked in a cigarette factory or on any stage ever again. Her husband, however, was able to support her from his thriving soda stand. In the Thomashefsky-Cahan version (1879 model), the enterprising twelve-year-old impresario then turned thirteen and went back to the Henry Street Synagogue, where some say he undoubtedly doubled as the rabbi at his own Bar Mitzvah.

Years later, every time Muni and Bella wanted to quit a play or a film and run away, Bella would recall the story about Madame Krantzfeld. "I'll put a cold towel on my head and say I'm dying," she'd tell Muni, "and then we can negotiate for you to run the soda stand on the corner of Fourth Street and Second Avenue."

"I think I'd like that," Muni would say. "I know that Krantzfeld character as if he were my own flesh and blood. Not too bright. He does you a favor selling you a 'For Two Cents Plain.' Most of the time, he just stands there, trying to pick his teeth with a kitchen match, but the match is too big for the gaps. So he keeps staring at the end of the match, accusing it as if it were an enemy."

Muni would play the part for thirty seconds, holding up a match, widening his eyes so they looked like a simpleton's. And he would dream of escaping to an area of innocence and irresponsibility. "Ah, yes! Except for his battle with that stubborn match, Mr. Krantzfeld is a totally happy human being!"

The Yiddish theater, which the Weisenfreunds were trying to join, even though they were being shoved to the far fringes of it, did not die a-borning. The need was too great for a meeting place, a watering hole in the ghetto jungle.

It struggled; then it thrived. Kessler and Adler joined in Thomashefsky's dedication, and the Yiddish theater became a cherished institution.

The immigrant who bought a seat seemed to be invited into the rich parlors of their stars. It was as if Otto Kahn or Vanderbilt or some other millionaire had said, "Sit down. Enjoy. Listen to my beautiful conversation." Who wouldn't pay thirty-five cents for such a privilege? "Look. Hear how they sing. See how they dance. How wonderful it is: their feet don't hurt from standing up all day pressing pants!"

And every ticket bought was an act of ownership. Buying a seat was like buying a plot of land, and if anybody else was in your reserved seat, you demanded he remove his *tochus*, even if every other seat in the theater was empty. After a respite in this palace of light and music and joy and tales of the old country, you had to go back to the sweatshop, to the night piecework, to the struggle to make a nickel. At the theater you sat in a private throne. Thirty-five cents helped you remember and helped you forget.

Even the playwrights were attaining respectability. Some of the early writers for the Yiddish theater had been hacks, and their works were labeled *shund* plays, crass plagiarism from every source known to man, and all the actors improvised and stuck in their favorite bits. Jacob Gordin was the first writer for the Yiddish theater who had the nerve and the literary muscle to demand the actors stick to his texts. It was a revolution.

Still the stars were the monarchs; the more outrageous they were, the more their fans adored them. *La Vie Bohème* was puritanical compared with the magic life of their fleshy gods. Was there a rumor that a young actress had refused to sleep with Thomashefsky? She was ugly, no doubt about it. Did the great Boris have to have a woman to bed down in his dressing room between every matinee and evening performance? Naturally, why not? What a favor to the girl!

After the curtain came down at one matinee, the skirts went

up for one young lady, nameless but now immortalized in the Yiddish theater's most famous pornographic legend. Thomashefsky whisked her into his dressing room, where she blissfully became his offstage leading lady in a performance reputed to be one of Boris' best. When they were finished, the great matinee idol put on his flowing red robe with the yellow silk lining and generously (he thought) handed the girl two tickets for the evening performance. She stared at them, aghast.

"I can't use these," she said. "I'm a poor girl. I need bread!"

Thomashefsky shrugged.

"You need bread—fuck a baker!"

The *Patriotten,* the fan clubs of the Lower East Side, jealously insist that happened not to Thomashefsky, but to one of their own idols, to Adler, to Kessler. Perhaps it happened to all three of them. It might even have been the same girl, ticket-wealthy, bread-poor.

Ted Thomas, a very perceptive writer (born to Boris and Bessie and named Theodore Herzel Thomashefsky), the father of the brilliant young symphony conductor Michael Tilson Thomas, describes the period around 1900: "The Yiddish theater made the Left Bank of Paris look like a convent. There was every form of degeneration you can imagine: murder, suicide, drugs, sex deviations of all kinds. These were the emergent Jews, after years of living a Torah-cloistered existence, suddenly free—and drunk with it."

Yet in other areas the aristocracy of the Yiddish theater was perversely puritanical; sisters and daughters were treated like Jewish nuns.

The most treasured of the lot was Emma Thomashefsky, Boris' younger sister: exquisite, talented, already a full-fledged attraction in the Yiddish theater at the age of fifteen.

Boris and his troupe had been performing at the old Garden Theatre at 113–113½ Bowery, but they could never quite erase from the public mind the fact that it had previously been a beer garden, a hangout for drunken sailors and Bowery bums. Artistic standards were going higher, and this was no place for Emma, their saintly youngest.

They teamed up with a European impresario, Morris Finkel, one of the few good directors around, who had come to America with a load of theatrical effects: costumes, scenic devices, mostly know-how in a period when the "big scenic display" was essential to theater, uptown as well as downtown. Finkel was much sought after by the half dozen other fiercely competitive managers who were elbowing into the Yiddish theater community. The

Thomashefsky family considered it a coup to be able to bring Finkel into the fold and leased a former German language theater right on Second Avenue: the Thalia.

And Emma was their brightest new star.

When the family found out that Finkel was falling in love with Emma, they insisted Boris "do something!" Finkel had been married before, divorced of course, with a child somewhere in Europe. But worst of all, the man was twenty-five years older than Emma! It was intolerable.

Finkel was distinguished-looking, with a flowing mustache, and he always wore a wing collar. He took Emma to plays on their days off, not the Second Avenue competition, but even worse, the *goyish* plays uptown, all the way up on Fourteenth Street. They had been seen at cafés, drinking; Finkel was reputed to be a great connoisseur of wines. He was a cradle snatcher, a roué, a drunk, a polluter of their fairest flower, a robber come to steal their purest, most talented child!

When they confronted Emma, she just smiled distantly like the Mona Lisa and said nothing. That sealed it. They had to take action.

That evening the entire family met Finkel at the stage door of the Thalia and told him he was not permitted inside. They didn't approve of his relationship with Emma, and he was ordered to stay away not merely from Emma, but from the theater and all the Thomashefskys for all time.

Finkel immediately got a crew of workingmen and moved all his costumes and scenic effects across the street to the Windsor Theatre, where yesterday's enemy was delighted to have them and him.

"It's all right," Boris called out in a petulant roar. "Let his cheap tricks and ugly costumes go. We have our beautiful Emma."

But to make doubly sure, they went to work on Emma. She was not only their sister-daughter, but a very valuable theater property. So that night a very unusual theatrical event took place. All 2,700 seats of the Thalia Theatre were sold. At the intermission following the second act, Boris gravely came onstage and begged the audience to remain in their seats at the end of the performance to witness a *shvier*.

According to ancient Jewish custom, a solemn oath is binding in the sight of God Almighty if performed publicly, a "swearing" before a minyan, ten adult males.

"In the theater tonight," Boris proclaimed, "we have two hundred times a minyan!"

The audience hardly watched the final three acts of the five-act play, so curious were they about the swearing ceremony. Who was to swear to what? Why did Boris Thomashefsky seem so tragic, so gloomy?

After the final curtain calls, the beautiful Emma was led onstage. Nobody in the audience seemed to breathe. Boris was at his most dramatic. He thundered the words at his sister and she repeated them in an obedient whisper filled with emotion.

"Before this audience, before God, do you swear. . . ."

"I swear. . . ."

"That you will never go out with. . . ."

"That I will never go out with. . . ."

"The man named Moishe Finkel. . . ."

"The man named Moishe Finkel. . . ."

"Or ever see him or have any dealings with him again as long as you live?"

A second's pause, then she spoke in a hardly audible monotone:

"Or ever see him or have any dealings with him again . . . as long as I live."

The applause broke like a tidal wave. Women wept. Emma's eyes were dry, but everybody shook her hand. "It's for the best, Emma child. An old man and a young girl—it never works. You have been saved for some great love which will come to you when you are truly a woman!"

Later that night Emma thought it all over, suddenly became indignant at her stage "performance," stalked across the street to the Windsor, found Morris Finkel, and they ran off together to Philadelphia. A few days later they were married. Finkel had all his stage effects shipped to Philadelphia, and they began working together at the historic Arch Street Theatre. Boris Thomashefsky had his own personal *shvier:* he swore he would never forgive either one of them.

Emma grew even more beautiful. She was immensely popular in Philadelphia; since she already belonged to Union #1, she had no difficulty making guest appearances back in New York. Finally, commercially and emotionally, the Thomashefsky family became reconciled to the marriage. Finkel was a devoted husband, a highly successful theater manager, now even a brother-in-law. An arm's-length truce was declared and they began exchanging theatrical treasures. Why should a Thomashefsky come to New York and play across the street at the Windsor, the competition, for God's sake? So Emma returned often to the Thalia. Boris even made a roaring guest appearance for the once-despised Finkel in Philadelphia.

Besides, three Finkel children had been born: Lucy, Bella, and

Abem—a whole new theatrical dynasty! See? What beauty, what happiness can come out of the most unlikely of marriages! Perhaps they had all been wrong. Nothing but *naches*, pride and joy, lay ahead.

But as Morris Finkel grew older, he grew more rigid, more inflexible. He was correct, honest, efficient, but somehow lacking in warmth. He would post cold, abrupt warnings backstage to the actors: "Fifty cents' fine for every minute you are late." "Thirty-five cents' fine for not returning costumes to wardrobe mistress."

He was somewhat of a mystery man as well. Before he married Emma, he had disappeared from New York for a while; years later it was revealed that he had made a long ocean voyage back to Europe. He traveled to Rumania, found his son by his first marriage in a boarding school, kidnapped him, literally stole him away, and brought him to the United States.

Shortly after he married Emma, that son, Erwin, came to live with them. But the boy was only two years younger than Emma, and he was no different from the public, who adored her offstage as well as on. After all, she was the idealized Gibson Girl of the Yiddish theater. Morris Finkel was more jealous and suspicious than anyone realized. He kicked his son out of the house. It was unnecessary. Nothing had taken place but adolescent adoration by a boy for a goddess in his own household.

In 1904, Lucy was seven, Bella was six, and Abem was four. Morris Finkel was fifty-four, but hard work made him look and act like a man of seventy. Emma, though twenty-nine, still seemed a radiant seventeen. When she paraded down Essex Street, her handsome children skipping beside her, the shopgirls and the pushcart peddlers would cluck their tongues in admiration. "A *shvester!*" they would say. "A sister, absolutely, no doubt about it; such a young creature could not possibly be the mother of three growing children."

Somebody else thought so, too: David Levinson, a young leading man who had joined the company at the Thalia. He was thin, tall, handsome, a celluloid-collar ad, and exactly Emma's age.

Levinson rehearsed with Emma, romantic roles mostly, but the romance didn't seem to stop when the scenes were over. What appealed to Emma most about her new leading man was his total lack of conceit. Good-looking actors were usually strutting roosters, arrogant and cocksure. David Levinson was as gentle as he was handsome. He looked at Emma with great puppylike eyes. Whenever Emma wanted anything, even a glass of water, he would race for it, coming back to her breathlessly, as if he were a lowly servant waiting on a queen.

They fell in love. The kids found him a happy companion, too. Their father was always busy, planning productions, counting box-office receipts. David romped with them, joked with them. Emma didn't sleep with David. She didn't want to be like other women of the theater in those days and just "have an affair." So she went to Morris Finkel and told him she was in love and wanted a divorce. He refused and ordered her never to see Levinson again.

She said she wanted time to think. Instead of touring that summer, she would take the children and go away from both Morris and David for a few months' vacation. Most actors went to the seashore or to the mountains. Emma found a farmhouse in Old Bridge, New Jersey, with cows and chickens and a farm family who didn't know Second Avenue existed. It would be a chance to breathe.

David Levinson promised to stay away for the entire summer. They needed a juvenile in Boston; he would try for that. Morris planned to work in hot New York City. By Labor Day Emma would come to her senses.

But the love-sick David couldn't stay away. He came to Old Bridge one warm Saturday afternoon. It was a happy surprise for everyone. The kids all hugged him. The equally joyous and love-struck Emma restrained herself and proposed a walk in the woods. Tall elm trees and ferns lined a quiet glade, and the kids could go wading in the stream.

The children skipped on ahead. David and Emma strolled silently into the peaceful, sun-dappled woods. Emma forced herself not to look at David. But he reached out and took her hand as they walked. She closed her eyes for a moment of total joy.

Twenty feet behind her a voice cried out.

"Emma!"

She turned, saw Morris, inflamed with suspicion, a pistol in his hand.

A shot was fired, whizzing by David's ear. It didn't touch him. Emma wheeled around to see if the children were safe and out of range. Another shot rang out. It hit her at the base of the spine. She fell to the wooded path as the children ran toward her, numb and disbelieving.

Morris saw her fall, evidently thought he had killed her, turned the gun on himself and fired. He died instantly. The children were petrified with fear, convinced that their beautiful mother was dead. Vaguely they remembered an ambulance that finally came, carrying away a dead father. Their mother was alive, they were told, but later they learned that she would never walk again, that she would be a cripple for the rest of her life.*

News of the tragedy of the Thomashefsky and Finkel families reached Cleveland. Muni Weisenfreund heard about it in hushed whispers. He had just finished the fourth grade at Case-Woodland Elementary School, and he was beginning to play second violin for his father and mother at the Perry Theatre, at the corner of Twenty-sixth Street and Woodland Avenue.

But Muni, age nine, had no way of knowing that a numb and horrified watcher, age six, on that once-quiet path in Old Bridge, New Jersey, would one day be his wife.

Bella's childhood? No wonder she wanted to forget.

5

MUNI's first appearance on stage was an accident. The Perry Theatre in Cleveland was a nickelodeon, with continuous performances all day long, from eleven in the morning until eleven at night. Customers would drop in when they had a free hour or two. Philip and Sallie and the character man could grab a quick glass of tea while they showed one-reel silent films (with English titles) which punctuated their Yiddish sketches and short plays. Otherwise the Weisenfreunds never took time off for meals, except breakfast, at which they stuffed themselves to last the entire day.

Admission was a nickel, ten cents at night, for their hour-long play. Muni played violin in the unsunken "pit," mostly by ear—printed music was an extravagance. Joe had graduated to the slightly tinny upright piano. Al was the major fiddle player, occasionally doubling over to the crude percussion when they needed the rhythm of a drumbeat or a comedy effect. The trio also played for slide shows; the projectionist flashed scenic wonders of the old and new worlds on the screen and the words of Yiddish folk songs for community *singen.*

*There are as many versions of the Finkel-Thomashefsky story as there are members of the Hebrew Actors Union. The most vivid variations come from people who weren't there, whose imaginations were not curbed by being eyewitnesses. They will swear on a stack of unproduced playscripts that the tragedy took place in a theater. Where else? After all, it was the Yiddish theater's equivalent of the shooting of Abe Lincoln. Even Bessie Thomashefsky insisted that it was a "tragedy of errors," compounded by Emma's desire to help a handsome young actor and by Finkel's wine-inflamed jealousy.

Muni was not allowed in the theater except at night. On nonschool days, Philip locked him in their walk-up flat a few blocks from the theater on Woodland Avenue and forced him to practice. From their twelve-hour-a-day, seven-days-a-week theatrical marathon the Weisenfreunds never cleared more than $40 a week. Eighteen dollars of that went every week for music lessons, six of it for Muni's violin instruction.

"Do you realize how many nickels that takes?" Philip would remind him. "How much sweat on the stage? So practice!"

As a reward for his persistence on the fiddle, Muni was given a pair of roller skates. Sallie complained it was a foolish luxury, but Philip pointed out that it was cheaper than hiring a strange and expensive musician.

During their brief time at home, the Weisenfreunds talked only of the theater: soon Philip would try again for New York; soon they would hire a better character actor—their present one was a *klutz* who couldn't remember his lines and who had to be paid an outrageous $10 a week, a fortune!

At the theater, while Muni wasn't sawing away at the violin, he would sneak a few pages of reading. He was indifferent to what was going on behind the gas lights up on the stage and had no particular desire to perform as an actor. But he knew all the sketches by rote, every line, every piece of business.

Late in the summer of 1908, when Muni was still twelve years old, a hot argument broke out backstage during the one-reel film. The customers complained that they couldn't concentrate on the exciting action on the screen: a baby lifted in the air by an eagle. "Put it on the stage!" somebody in the audience shouted.

Joe, who doubled at the box office, came back to the stage door to announce that they had sold out for that night's performance. The expensive ten-cent tickets were all gone. He would clear the theater of the nickel customers whenever they gave him the signal.

At that moment, the *klutz* of a character actor walked out into the stage alley. He was through with the theater, he declared loudly. People like Philip made it too difficult. He would rather starve than continue with such a slave driver.

"Go! And good riddance!" Philip shouted. "Go, you ham amateur!"

The character man stalked away, not looking back. Then Philip realized their predicament. They had announced a "thrilling presentation of a great play by Jacob Gordin, *Two Corpses at Breakfast.*" The old man, the lodge president, was a vital part.

"Shall I give back the money at the box office?" Joe asked.

Philip closed his eyes and tried to figure what to do. It wasn't possible to double; besides, he didn't know the part.

"Munya knows it, word for word," Joe said. "Better than the *klutz.*"

Philip turned and looked at Muni, short for his age, in knee pants, circling around the alleyway on his roller skates, still even too young to shave.

"Impossible," Philip said flatly.

Joe turned to go. "I'll give back the money."

Philip, desperate, turned to Muni. "You really know it?"

"Sure." Muni shrugged. What was so great about learning those lines?

"Try. The *klutz*'s costume is in the basement." He ran his hand across Muni's smooth face. "There are beards down there, and wigs. For God's sake, at least use a beard."

Muni took off his roller skates and went to work.

"It'll be a disaster," Philip predicted.

Muni climbed into the costume, padding it with pillows. He decided against a ready-made hang-on beard; with spirit gum and false hair he quickly fashioned one of his own.

Two Corpses at Breakfast was an early-day black comedy, a ghoulish Yiddish sketch about a starving husband and wife, whose only remaining resource was the death benefit from a lodge. Not unlike O. Henry's "Gift of the Magi," but on a comic level, each conspires to pretend to play dead, so that the other can collect the funeral expenses and death pension. Philip and Sallie had the roles of the husband and wife. The character man was the old lodge president, who was to arrive just at breakfast time to commiserate and investigate this startling seriocomic double death in the family.

Both Sallie and Philip were playing bodies supposedly ready for the grave, but the comic business included a sneezing corpse and one who swatted away flies. But this night the corpses were jumpier than ever. They kept glancing nervously toward the prop door for the arrival of the investigating lodge president.

Muni made his entrance onstage with complete aplomb. He wore a frock coat, long striped pants, a high silk hat, and a flowing beard. As he entered, he swung a cane nonchalantly.

Papa Corpse sat up. Philip, serious about the theater, saw no humor in a twelve-year-old playing an old man, but he was surprised and startled by Muni. That couldn't be the kid he'd seen half an hour ago roller-skating in the stage alley. My God, he looked more convincing than the *klutz!*

Out of Muni's mouth came a falsetto voice, which didn't sound like a playacting kid, but like an authentic old man.

After the final curtain, Philip just nodded to his son and patted him awkwardly on the shoulder. Sallie said nothing about his performance. She just stared at him for a minute.

"All right," she said, "the emergency is over. Take off those long pants."

"No," said Muni, quietly, still in character.

"What do you mean 'no'?"

Muni seemed to grow three inches taller.

"The president of a lodge, an actor, doesn't wear knickers!"

Then Muni, still in his beard, leapfrogged over the stage furniture.

After that night, Muni was hooked. When he was supposed to be practicing the violin, he would sit in front of a mirror, experimenting with makeup, pasting mattress stuffing on his face. His mother played the few male juvenile roles in their repertoire. Besides, Muni was too young to be believable as most young men. But most Yiddish sketches included a grandfather, an old rabbi, or a hardhearted landlord. And a beard made you automatically a holy man, a doctor, or a villain.

Philip reluctantly agreed that Muni should assume the roles of their former *klutzy* character man. After all, they were saving $10 a week in salary. But the arrangement was temporary—Muni was to continue to practice the violin.

One day Philip came home and found Muni in front of a makeup mirror. He lifted Muni by the ears and led him to the violin stand. Muni sighed and continued his fiddle exercises, a beard covering half his face.

"When you can be Mischa Elman or Fritz Kreisler, why would you want to be an actor?" his father yelled at him. "You want examples? Look at me."

Muni played a wild cadenza on the fiddle.

"Beautiful! Tender! Emotional!" Philip raved.

Muni deliberately played some discordant notes. Philip sighed, as if it were the music of the gods.

"When you can make music like that, Munya, why should you hide your face behind a mattress?"

Then Philip put his arm on the boy's shoulder and told him a story he had heard about the great Thomashefsky.

"What would you do," somebody asked the mighty Boris, "if a son of yours wanted to be an actor?"

"What would I do?" Thomashefsky replied. "I would take him to the theater, sit him in a box, and let him watch a beautiful performance. Then, when everybody had gone, I'd lead him onto the empty stage and let him look out into the audience and sense the majesty of the theater. Then slowly, slowly, I would bring up the footlights until the glow of the gaslight filled his face. THEN! Then I'd rip down his pants and get his *tochus* bare—and shove his naked ass smack against a hot footlight!"

Muni listened, but the story didn't change his mind. He had decided. But how could he ever tell his father? He didn't want to be Kubelik or Mischa Elman or Fritz Kreisler. He wanted to be Jacob P. Adler or David Kessler or Boris Thomashefsky.

His brother Joseph, busy at the box office or at the piano or doubling as a backstage violinist, didn't have much time to watch the stage. But he remembers most vividly the time Muni played a monologue as Bar-Kochba. In the scene, the ancient Palestinian warrior was being abused; the cries of pain from the actor made Joe turn and watch the stage. He was amazed. Muni wore wisps of a red beard and red side curls. And a chill ran up Joe's spine when Bar-Kochba, confident of victory before battle, raised his head to heaven and recited the classic line: "O, Lord of my fathers, we pray that you do not help our enemy. As for us, we need no help!" Onstage Joseph saw their Hebrew teacher from the *cheder* in Galicia. Muni alternately shouted and whispered like that terrifying man, as if the foul-breathed teacher had been transported from Europe and was standing on the stage of the Perry Theatre, taking the whiplashes of Bar-Kochba's tormentors.

In the longer evening playlets, Muni usually had to address his mother onstage as *tochter* (daughter) and his father as *mein kind* (my child). But Muni, the old man-little boy, still enjoyed roller-skating along the Woodland Avenue sidewalks.

The Weisenfreunds performed *The Wandering Jew*, a famous sketch filled with tears. ("A four handkerchief *pyessa*," Philip called it, "and the more the customers cry, the more they come!") They scheduled it as the climax of the afternoon performance, as well as the main event for the more prestigious ten-cent evening showing. Muni played an eighty-five-year-old patriarch, with a long-flowing snow-white beard.

Between performances Muni didn't have time to remove and put back all that makeup, so he took his recess roller-skating around the stage alley, while his parents had a glass of tea backstage. Occasionally, his long black coat touching the sidewalk, Muni would glide out onto Woodland Avenue, startling passersby. This same bearded patriarch was sometimes seen shooting marbles at the corner of Twenty-sixth Street. Some Clevelanders have never recovered from the shock.

One night the evening performance began to a packed house. Sallie and Philip as the children of the patriarch were bemoaning the fact that their half-mad father had been wandering lost and Lear-like in the forest. Would he ever come home? Would they ever see this pious old man again in their lifetime?

The door was supposed to be flung open for the ancient man's arrival and a tearful reunion. A pause. No patriarch. Philip repeated the cue. Joe, backstage, stuck his head out of the alley door and yelled to the Wandering Jew, who was blithely circling around outside on his roller skates, his white beard flowing behind him.

"Munya! You're on!"

Realizing his cue was upon him, Muni had to make a choice. Should he delay the performance or take off his skates? He was an actor. He made an instant and instinctive choice.

While Joe grabbed his fiddle to play the Yiddish equivalent of "Hearts and Flowers," Muni roller-skated through the stage door and glided onstage, his skates making him seem to float across the set. Stage historians have called it the goddamnedest entrance in theater history.

Legend spinners in the Yiddish theater will tell you that the roller-skate incident culminated in Muni's saying aloud, in character, to his mother: *"Tochter, hast du a skate key?"*

Almost a lifetime later I asked Muni if it was true. The first part, yes, he told me; the second part, the ad lib to his mother, was apocryphal, embroidery after the fact.

Muni, the constant perfectionist, shrugged and smiled, as if wishing he could have improved his performance forty-eight years before.

"But it's not a bad line. I should have said it!"

Muni, at sixteen, attempting to look suave and sophisticated.

(Albert Fenn Collection)

Muni Weisenfreund, Yiddish vaudevillian, in Chicago.

(Albert Fenn Collection)

PHILIP went back to New York to try again to get into Union #1. He was excited when he reached Second Avenue. New theaters were being built, and great Yiddish stars walked along the avenues like Olympian gods. The Café Royale had opened—a Parnassus where each star could hold court.

He saw as much theater as he could, trying to memorize the plots, the staging, the grand gestures, watching the audience as much as the stage—to see what made them laugh and what made them cry.

The Yiddish theater had a shorthand: stock characters as instantly identifiable as those of the *commedia dell'arte*. A *shammas* (a sexton) always used a snuffbox, a *shatchen* (a marriage broker) carried an umbrella, a student naturally made his entrance with an open book in his hand. Messengers from Yahweh and assorted angels invariably wore white, except for the angel of death, who wore black. A doctor without a beard and fine spectacles couldn't be trusted to ask you to say "ah." Capitalists and landlords wore top hats and smoked thick cigars.

Shund plays reigned. Ted Thomas defines *shund* as very loose excrement. Jacob Lateiner had written 90 plays or more, "Professor" Moshe Hurwitz boasted that his catalogue of plays exceeded 150. Often the plays were skeletons of plots, and the actors were encouraged to insert a song or digress into dance.

"Oh, say can you see?" sang a celebrated soubrette, kicking high.

51

"We see! We see!" the audience shouted back.

The Hurwitz-Lateiner era of Yiddish theater was dubbed "A Matzoh Factory—the dough is in and the dough is out and every week they bake a new historical operetta. They advertise, they rehearse, they make a huge fuss." And every star flamboyantly displayed his own brand of matzoh making.

That all stopped when Jacob Gordin came along. He demanded that actors stick to their lines. If they didn't, he would stand up in the middle of a performance and scream at them from the audience, threatening physical violence. This prompted the use of a prompter, the *souffleur* of the French stage and of the opera. Plays in the Yiddish palaces of Second Avenue changed so rapidly during a week that no actor, no matter how good his total recall, could commit all the lines.

So the actors memorized some of their long speeches, and when they went blank in conversation, they would invent business: cleaning their glasses, stalking up and down, slowly opening their watches, seeming to think or ponder or stare into the distance—but all the time waiting for the next line to be thrown to them by the prompter from his hooded booth downstage center. Sarah Adler used to call this vamping-until-ready technique "pecking corn," but it developed a whole new style in acting, the nodding, thoughtful performer. "Ah, how deep," the audience murmured, "how intellectual!"

When Jacob P. Adler and Jacob Gordin joined forces, Second Avenue trembled. The Yiddish *Koenig Lear* was their greatest success, and the audiences flocked. "Such a Jewish play—ungrateful children, the long-suffering father!" And Gordin adapted the plot into a female version, which he called *Mirele Efros*, who was indeed a *Queen* Lear. Madame Lipzin played it with all stops out.

All these Philip saw, as well as Thomashefsky in a wild adaptation of *Uncle Tom's Cabin*, advertised as "Where One Persecuted Race Portrays the Hardships of Another." Boris was Uncle Tom; his wife, Bessie, was Topsy. The Simon Legree was a villain recognized instantly by all the recent immigrants: a Cossack in a red blouse and high shiny black boots. They hissed and booed him. At the Café Royale the wits (speaking loud enough so everybody could hear) labeled this production "Uncle Thomashefsky's Cabin."

Philip prepared carefully for his *proba* at the union, trying to synthesize all he had learned in his years of trouping, adding what he could from the current style along the Yiddish Rialto.

Although he was nervous, he felt he gave one of the best performances of his life. He wanted so much to come to New York, to be part of the royalty of the theater, that all the juices inside him flowed. Before the stern-faced union committee he performed the comic *Shmendrick*, and they laughed, they actually laughed. "For other actors to respond like that," he reported later to his family in Cleveland, "is like God shining his light down from heaven. It was as much of a miracle as if a dramatic critic had laughed!"

And then Philip moved on to Goldfaden's tragic sketch *The Frightful Dream*. One woman on the committee wept and "even blew her nose in her handkerchief," Philip recalled. When he finished, he bowed—it was the wrong thing to do to bow before an auditioning committee; but he felt like it, and the committee applauded. He was certain he was destined to be the next major star of Second Avenue.

Then the chairman of the committee rose. "You are a very fine actor, Weisenfreund. But the union has new rules. To gain admittance, we no longer require three years on the road. It is now seven years. Apply again later on. Meanwhile, Cleveland is a lucky city to have you performing there."

Philip didn't answer. He walked out of the Hebrew Actors Union, stunned with disbelief. He didn't speak a word the rest of that day in New York or sitting up all night on the interminable train ride across New York State, the edges of Pennsylvania, and into Ohio.

Back in Cleveland, he walked numbly through the deserted early-morning streets into the Perry Theatre. The playhouse was empty, musty, and he hated it. All the brightness of New York seemed to be obliterated by the darkness of this provincial outhouse. He heard a sound in the basement and slowly descended the stairs.

Muni was seated at an improvised dressing table practicing makeup. His unused violin lay in a corner on a pile of rumpled costumes. Muni looked up and saw his father and leaped from his chair excitedly.

"How did it go, Papa? Are we moving to New York? Right away?"

The boy's face, half made up, looked like some elfin creature out of a folktale. Silently, Philip shook his head.

Philip turned away, hiding his emotion, so that Muni wouldn't see it. Then he slowly walked over and picked up the discarded violin.

"Why aren't you practicing?"

Muni took a deep breath.

"I no longer care for the violin, Papa. I don't have time for it. I want to be an actor—I can't do both!"

53

Without any expression on his face, Philip grasped both ends of the violin and broke it in two.

Twenty-six years later, talking to Jim Tully, Muni, then a major star, stared into his Broadway dressing room mirror and said, "The years may have given me much or little, but never the power to obliterate that scene. Boylike, I didn't realize I had stricken my father to the heart. After that, we never discussed the violin again."

His father didn't speak to him for almost two months, except when they were onstage together. Offstage, there was silence.

Then one day his father made an announcement: "We are moving to Chicago. There is better opportunity there." And that was all: the flat statement to the entire family. They didn't have to worry about transferring schools; the boys had already dropped out. Muni, age thirteen, was a full-time actor.

In Chicago, Philip leased a theater on Twelfth Street, later Roosevelt Road. It had to be "a step up in the world," so he hired a signpainter to emblazon the family name across the front of the theater:

WEISENFREUND'S PAVILION THEATRE

The Finest in Yiddish Drama and Entertainment!

"If certain parties wish to perform, to act, as artists, not Gypsies or bums," his father said, referring to Muni in the third person, "then they must have a proper platform. And their names must be placed in large letters on a large sign so the entire world can see!"

Sallie just shrugged. "It is *our* name, too. And *our* reputations. If people come to the theater, it will be to see the leading players, not the character man. Besides, you know the boy can't act!"

Muni's mother disapproved of his making a career of the theater and rarely spoke to him. "When we can afford it, we will find another actor, a better actor!"

Muni resented this hasty dismissal of his fledgling attempts. But he would catch Philip glancing at him with a hint of admiration, even approval. And occasionally his father would smile slightly at one of Muni's bizarre makeups.

Muni developed a series of convincing old men, with tremors in their voices and their hands. One day in rehearsal, Muni was so authentic Philip hardly recognized him.

"My son, the *alter cocker*," he said.

They graduated to full-length plays in the evenings, sometimes even with actual written texts, a great rarity, for they were only occasionally committed to paper. They hired another actor, not to replace Muni, but to supplement him. They called Adolph Gertner their *Yankel*-of-all-trades; he was alternately a prompter, a stage carpenter, an actor, a doorman. All the Weisenfreunds also performed multiple duties. They used to laugh when they heard about the "big-time *goyish* vaudeville," called "two-a-day."

"My God," Philip would say after a weary Sunday, "we then should be called 'ten-a-day'!"

Around the corner, on Halstead and O'Brien streets, was a rival Yiddish theater, the Casino, run by an entire tribe of Grossmans. Irving Grossman and the younger Joseph Grossman were Muni's contemporaries and friends. A block in the opposite direction on Jefferson Street, the Jacobson family ran the Metropolitan Theatre. Bessie and Joseph Jacobson spawned an entire theater dynasty. Their eldest, Hymie Jacobson, sang, danced, wrote songs, and occasionally (in knee pants) doubled as a drummer and curtain puller at Weisenfreund's Pavilion. Irving Jacobson (many years later the warm and jolly Sancho Panza of *Man of La Mancha*) was so tiny that even on a raised stage they had to put him on a pedestal. Irving was billed as "The Little Caruso"; Muni affectionately called him Peezik. Irving's remembered joy was tightening Muni's roller skates and watching with awe as Muni made the hazardous journey across the cobblestones of Chicago's back alleys. Henrietta Jacobson (later the mother in Neil Simon's first play, *Come Blow Your Horn*) was still an infant. Wandering among all three theaters was Jack Berlin, Elaine May's father, who translated English songs into Yiddish, fifteen cents a lyric.

The three theaters were friendly competitors. Business was good enough to fill all the 300-seat houses, especially on weekends. For living quarters, most of the actors gravitated to one apartment building on Center Avenue (later named Racine), which they called the "artistic ghetto." The Weisenfreunds finally had four rooms; the huge Grossman family had the luxury of five rooms on the floor below. The Jacobsons lived down the street, jealous of the fact that the Weisenfreunds and the Grossmans actually had steam heat. (It didn't always work.)

Rehearsals at the Pavilion were in the morning, without music because Joe and Al were sent to study at the Chicago Institute of Music. It was a lot of money, all those music lessons with "fancy long-haired professionals," but Philip was determined that somebody in his family would be respectable, at least two of his sons would rise above the rat race of the theater.

A rehearsal would begin on the stage of the Pavilion with Philip explaining, with tears, with gestures, with throaty eloquence, the plots of plays he had seen in New York. Muni and Sallie and Gertner would listen; then Philip would leap into the leading role, cuing them and goading them through their improvisations until the play took the semblance of shape.

When they expanded Goldfaden's *Bar-Kochba* from a monologue to a full evening in the theater (their Friday night special), Philip played the title role and humbly went to his fourteen-year-old son and asked him to apply the wild red beard. Silently, carefully, as an act of love, Muni transformed his father's face.

"Satisfactory!" Philip said as he glanced into the mirror, and Muni knew it was his father's highest compliment.

Muni played the part of Papus, the legendary avenging son of the martyred Bar-Kochba, but it was neither a juvenile nor a leading man. Papus had been played traditionally as a cruel, twisted, Caliban-like monster, distorted by his thirst for vengeance.

Muni's father, half a director, half a fellow player, gave Muni advice about the part, and Muni never forgot it.

"Do it a different way, Munya. No villain ever thinks of himself as a villain, just as no hero can be all-hero. Who would believe him? He couldn't even believe himself! Papus is bitter? Of course! But mix with the bitter some of the taste of humanity. The man is not all evil. He would like to be good. But he can't, because he has been hurt by other people. Or look at it this way: Papus may not be such a bad person. Unhappy people are usually bitter. Why not? If somebody steps on your soul, it leaves a scar. But let a small light show through. Remember, he is a human being, and even a monster has a soul!"

Muni listened carefully to his father's words. He rehearsed, spent hours making up his face and his fingers. During the performances he heard the silence of attention and awe from the audience and knew that he had brought a dimension of humanity to the role of Papus. Philip gave him another one-word compliment.

"Yes," his father said.

For a sketch one afternoon, Muni impersonated Woodrow Wilson: a slicked-back gray wig, pince-nez eyeglasses, a black top hat held rigidly in his hand. The audience cheered and applauded.

Everybody around the theater started to call Muni "Old Man Makeup." Joe Grossman remembers coming into the dressing room of the Pavilion Theatre at all hours to find Muni putting on and taking off makeup, trying wigs of all sorts.

"What part are you playing tonight?" Grossman would ask him.

"Oh, this isn't for a part," Muni would say. "Just an experiment. Just a hobby."

56

Several times Muni's experiments backfired. Muni himself described what happened:

"I developed one theory that I thought was going to revolutionize the whole art of makeup. I thought if we could only use putty and completely cover my face and so mold it that no part of the real face or expression could be seen by the audience, a great step forward would be taken in character impersonation."

So Muni bought several pounds of soft putty and plastered his entire face with it. That night he was playing, as usual, a very old man. He hadn't told anybody else about his revolutionary discovery. When he got onstage, the other actors and the audience saw a withered face, the age lines dug deep into it. It was an astonishing sight. He had even wiped out the telltale wig line with a careful blending of the putty into it. He looked a hundred and twenty years old.

"But my theory only went so far," Muni recalled, "I hadn't taken into account that putty, to remain plastic, must be constantly kneaded. My face became hard, frozen, petrified, and when I tried to move my lips to speak my lines, I struggled simply to get my mouth open. When I finally did, my false face cracked, broke into a dozen pieces and fell off! The audience howled, and the curtain had to be brought down."

Muni never read a book on the art of makeup or went to any school or took a lesson in the fascinating art of changing his face. Everything he mastered he taught himself, by trial and error. Over the years he became a consummate artist, whose canvas was his own face.

For a while he collected wigs; later he threw them all into a trash can. When there was money enough, he would buy crepe hair and occasionally even whole switches of human hair and fashion his own wigs. He often went to barbershops and collected specimens of human hair to study. Landladies in boardinghouses on the road used to complain that after Muni had passed through town, they found pockets of emptiness in mattresses and couches.

"Tonight"—Muni would shrug—"I play old mattress face!"

He had the role of the devil in Jacob Gordin's inventive reworking of Faust, *Gott, Mann und Teufel (God, Man and Devil)*.

"I tried another near-fatal experiment, trying to be one hell of a devil. I covered my eyelids with gold paper, pasting it on with spirit gum. I thought it would turn me into a wildly fantastic creature from the nether regions with the glittering sparks of hell streaming out of my eyes. As a matter of fact, the spirit gum hardening and the stiffness of the paper almost made me blind. What a payoff for a devil—falling over the furniture!"

The audiences at the Pavilion, the Casino, and the Metropolitan made a ritual of attending plays. Friday nights and Saturday afternoons were always sold out. Tickets were purchased in advance: religious Jews never carried money on the Sabbath. Nor did they ride in any public or private conveyances—so walking distance to their neighborhood playhouse was mandatory. All three theaters qualified; they were even closer to the major Jewish areas than the synagogues. On *Shabbas*, it was a sin to light a match, cook a meal, write a letter—but the theater was different. To laugh was no work. To cry was a pleasure. So orthodox Jews blinked, and the playhouses blazed, first with gaslight and then with the miracle of electricity.

The themes of the plays were usually repetitious: infidelity in marriage, the gap between generations, the loss of virtue of a virginal daughter or sister, the pain of prejudice, the nobility of self-sacrifice, the temptation of the pure by Satan in the flesh. All had unfettered displays of emotion. The titles of some of the plays suggest how much: *The Orphans, The Runaway, The Insane Woman, The Penitent, The Wronged Bride, The Fanatic, The Rich Land Owner, The Pogrom, The Last Hour of Life*.

The audiences loved death scenes, and they wept as if personally bereaved. Muni, inevitably the old man, died again and again and again.

"How often this week did your brother Irving kick the bucket?" he once asked Joe Grossman. "Me—I attended my own funeral twelve times!"

Tongue clucking swept through the audience when a maiden's virtue was being tested, and when it was lost, you heard a fateful word whispered ominously all over the house: *"Fakeert! Fakeert!"* It didn't mean seduced or raped; it meant "falling over the brink" or "losing life's most precious jewel." In short, it was untranslatable, but everybody felt the emotion.

Muni, the old father, would grasp the chin of the lost maiden, usually played by his mother, and turn it—and she would try to look away. His eyes would burn into hers; then indignation would flame in his face when he read the truth in her guilty eyes. Immediately a murmured flood of *"Fakeert!"* would sweep through the audience.

During the summer months, the New York theaters closed down and occasionally a major Yiddish star made guest appearances in the provinces. Adler or Kessler or even the flamboyant Thomashefsky would stoop to performing for a week in the far reaches of Philadelphia or Boston or Chicago. But the crowds were so huge they could not afford to use the tiny local theaters. So a Shriners auditorium or a symphony hall was rented.

David Kessler came to Chicago for one triumphant week in Leon Kobrin's *Yankel Boila*. The great stars insisted on playing sympathetic roles, never villains, never heavies. And each role included what was called a "tablecloth speech—it covered everything!" *Yankel Boila* had a tablecloth speech which Kessler tore to tatters, a declamation about homesickness for the old country, yet hope for the new.

Kessler needed an extra actor to play an old peasant, just a walk-on. "But," said the advance man, "it is with a beard." That was always the convincer. They borrowed Muni for the bit.

His walk, the tilt of his head, the animal-like alertness of his listening made a gem of the walk-on. Kessler was magnanimous enough to notice. At the curtain call on the final Saturday night performance, he took Muni's hand and led him out of the bowing line to the downstage apron. "I wish to make a prediction," he said to the audience. "This young actor—what's your name?"

"Weisenfreund," Muni muttered.

". . . will one day be famous. Remember that name—Weisenfreund!"

Muni was embarrassed at the applause and rushed out of the theater. His family, busy at the Pavilion, had not seen his momentary triumph. And he never told them about the curtain call and Kessler's compliment.

Nor did Philip ever understand the enlarged line of customers at his box office. Business had always been good on weekends; now people cued up for early-in-the-week performances. Perhaps his reputation or Sallie's was getting around Chicago, he thought, for ticket buyers would say, "I wish to see the Weisenfreund perform!"

Philip woke up one night hours past midnight to find a sleepless Muni pacing aimlessly around the dark apartment.

"What's wrong, Munya? Why aren't you sleeping?"

Muni stopped, stood very still. Out of the darkness his voice was deep and strange.

"Papa, I'm hungry."

"So go to the icebox and eat something. Thank God, we no longer have to grub for food, begging for coins in a tingle-tangle tambourine. No more boiled potatoes on sticks, Munya. There is plenty now—meat and chicken and cheese and white bread. Go eat, eat! Enjoy."

"No, no, Papa. I'm not hungry in the stomach. Just—empty. I can't explain it."

"Something happened with Kessler? He didn't like you?"

"Nothing happened, Papa."

"Then for what are you hungry? You want to be a millionaire?"
Muni just snorted.

"You want to be famous, everybody shouting your name?"

"No. I don't want that. I don't think that would matter."

"What then, Munya? Why are you hungry? What do you want, *boychick?*"

"I want to be better, Papa."

7

ON Argyle Avenue on Chicago's North Side a makeshift silent film company, the Argyle Studios, supplied most of the one-reelers which were shown between the sketches at the Pavilion, Metropolitan, and Casino theaters. Ben Turpin, Ford Sterling, and Mary Miles Minter were featured in silent comedies and quickie dramas. Shortly after that, for weather purposes, they all moved to California to join the newly formed Biograph and Mack Sennett studios.

The director at Argyle was the actor-producer King Baggott, who later did a dozen longer silent films in Hollywood. But Argyle studios never even considered the Weisenfreunds, the Jacobsons or the Grossmans for acting roles. To the performers at the Yiddish theaters, the flickering movies were a nickelodeon novelty, totally unrelated to the art of acting, having nothing whatsoever to do with theater.

Muni often walked the two miles to the lakefront on hot nights after the performance, saving the few cents of carfare, wanting the exercise and the cooler air off the lake. As the months passed, he found, with the exception of his brothers, he was the first one home. His mother would come in very late at night, and his father not at all. Then he discovered his father had been sleeping on a mattress made from old stage draperies in a dressing room at the Pavilion Theatre.

Muni waited one night after the performance, watched his mother leave by herself in suddenly elegant "civilian" clothes. Muni turned and looked at his father, whom he had always considered a man with few emotions, a Prussian martinet, unaffected by affection, unmoved except onstage. He walked closer and saw tears in his father's eyes.

Philip seemed pale and drained, gasping slightly for air as if

60

somebody had kicked him in the stomach. He glanced around quickly to make sure they were alone in the theater, and then spoke in a voice Muni had never heard before. How could his father be weak and helpless?

Muni was sure it was a scene from a very bad play which never should have been written.

"Your mother—" Philip said in Yiddish. "Your mother—" He gestured in the empty air, unable to continue.

"Papa, are you all right?"

"No, Munya. I am not all right. I am lost and sick, and I have nobody in the world to tell but you. I can't talk to your brothers. Only to you—and you are still a child. How can I tell you?"

And then Philip began to sob. It was the first time Muni had ever seen his father cry.

"Your mother is a *curva*, a *nafka*, a whore. She is sleeping with other men. Munya, what am I going to do?"

Muni glanced toward the empty auditorium, as if expecting an audience to murmur, *"Fakeert! Fakeert!"*

Helpless, not knowing what to say, Muni ran out of the theater. He walked all night, alone, along the lakefront, through the empty streets of Chicago. The next day he moved out of their apartment and stayed with the Grossmans. He continued to play at the theater, but he never looked directly at Sallie. And he didn't speak to her again for twenty years.

The life seemed to go out of Philip. He spent all his time at the theater, pounding on pieces of scenery, taking set pieces apart and nailing them together again, relieving his anger and frustration with hammerblows.

When Philip started getting back pains, Muni and his brothers urged him to go to a doctor. He protested it was nothing, just a man over fifty using muscles that hadn't been exercised for years.

"Onstage," he said, "an actor, unless he's a dancer or an acrobat, uses his brain muscles and his ass muscles. If you happen to shake up the ones in between, they're so surprised they yell with pain."

He promised to stop hammering so hard. But the aches persisted, and one night he struggled through a performance, then collapsed onstage when the curtain came down. They rushed him, by ambulance, to the nearest hospital, St. Anthony's. It seemed to Muni that it took ten years for a doctor to get there. He diagnosed the illness as pleurisy which had developed into pneumonia and said that Philip should have been brought in for treatment weeks before. Now, perhaps, it was too late.

Philip, bewildered by the nuns and priests, reverted totally to

Yiddish, forgetting the rudimentary English he had learned. Sallie came and sat silently by his bedside in the ward. The boys stood at the foot of the white hospital bed, stared at their father's pale face, and wished they had learned how to pray.

Weakly, he begged them to continue at the theater. Everything would be all right soon. The doctors would get rid of his crazy pains, and by the High Holidays maybe they would all be back in New York, walking like kings among the royalty of Second Avenue. Besides, they needed the money to pay the doctor bills. To humor him, they went back to the Pavilion. The audience laughed and applauded—but, without Philip, the theater seemed like a captainless ship.

On the night of June 2, 1913, Adolph Gertner was alone with Philip at the hospital while the rest of the family was performing at the theater. Philip thrashed around on the bed, then turned weakly to Adolph.

"Gertner, what will happen? I know my two older boys will do fine. They are musicians, and they can always make a dollar. But what will happen with my baby—what will become of Munya?"

An hour later he was dead. He was fifty-three.

Muni was lost, indignant at the indecency of a man dying so young, angry that his father, like Moses, had been forbidden to enter the Promised Land of New York theater. And he realized, totaling up in his mind the years of comic turns and tragic sketches, how much he respected his father as a performer and how much he had learned from him.

After the funeral, they closed the theater and pulled down the Weisenfreund sign. Sallie announced she was leaving Chicago, to take an offer from a small Yiddish theater in Toronto. Her companion on the trip was Morris Nassiter, who had been a prompter at the Casino. A year later Muni heard that his mother had married Nassiter in Canada.

Joe and Al took part-time jobs, fiddling with pickup orchestras and string trios, playing for weddings and Bar Mitzvahs and anniversaries. But Muni felt he never wanted to perform in public again. The whole business was a curse, a disease, a slave market where you sold your body and your soul to anybody who bought a ticket for ten cents.

Muni got a job with the gas company, peddling mesh wicks and trimmers for gas lamps. He went from door to door, avoiding neighborhoods where anybody was remotely related to the theater, trying to turn off his mind, playing the role of an automaton.

Adolph Gertner took over the building and changed the name

of it to Gertner's Pavilion Theatre. He offered Muni a job, but Muni refused.

The Grossmans told him of plans to tour their company through the Midwest and the South. They invited Muni to come along. At first he said no, but they persuaded him to join their traveling troupe; for him to keep working for the gas company was a waste of time. Anybody could peddle wick trimmers, but how many actors had the versatility of the youngest Weisenfreund? Muni proposed a novel arrangement: "I'll come along on one condition—that each time we start a new play, a new sketch, I can play a character I've never played. I want to lose myself in a hundred different men I never met before."

Muni didn't realize when he agreed to go that he would occasionally play female parts as well, usually old women with mustaches instead of old men with beards.

They traveled with a trunkful of costumes but without scenery, picking up props, stage draperies, and basic set pieces at each stop. Muni carried only a few clothes but most important his makeup kit; with it he made masks to hide Muni Weisenfreund.

Samuel B. Grossman was the star-manager, and the entire Grossman family filled out most of the cast. Among their three musicians was a drummer named Abe Lyman, later a popular orchestra leader. But after a month in such foreign territory as Galveston, San Antonio, and New Orleans, the Grossman troupe was ready and willing to join forces with another touring company, headed by Fanny Reinhart (famous for playing, as a man, the title role in a Yiddish *Hamlet*). The combined company did far better in St. Louis and other cities of the Midwest.

Newspaper ads were a luxury, but posters preceded the company into each town; they were strategically placed in kosher meat markets (in exchange for two free tickets) and in a synagogue lobby, when a *shammas* was liberal enough to blink at advertising in a holy place.

The Reinhart-Grossman poster included Muni's photograph as a handsome young man of eighteen or nineteen. His picture was the major attraction of the houseboards. A face like that helped sell tickets to marriageable girls and even old married ladies. Some local maidens announced beforehand that they were madly in love with the actor Weisenfreund and even brought marriage brokers to the performance. But they were disappointed, for Muni never played Muni. Once an angry girl and her apoplectic mother demanded their money back at the box office because "the Weisenfreund wasn't in the play." The manager of the theater showed them a program. "That old man!" the mother screamed. "I'd die before I'd let him marry my daughter." Muni, for his part, wasn't feeling very marriageable.

To make sure the fans waiting at the stage door didn't spot him, he would change makeup, put on a strange wig or grotesque eyeglasses when he stepped into the street. While other members of the company enjoyed recognition, Muni relished his anonymity.

"Are you in the play?" one girl asked.

"Sure," Muni said. "You remember that floor lamp in Act Three? With the fringe? That was me. I'm not even plugged in —and yet I light up. Did you ever see Thomashefsky as a floor lamp? Or the great Jacob P. Adler? Never. Any man can play a man. Let me tell you, it takes an *artist* to play a floor lamp!"

The older ladies of the troupe were insulted if asked to play old women; they considered themselves ingenues, prima donnas, leading ladies, soubrettes. (The same thing was going on in the Yiddish musicals along Second Avenue in New York; most of the "young chorus girls" were already grandmothers in personal life.) So Muni was drafted to play whatever old crones or grandmothers were required. Coincidentally, the first female role he played was a character called Bayle, the Yiddish for Bella.

In Omaha, Nebraska, the Grossmans announced a full evening's presentation of Jacob Gordin's *Kreutzer Sonata*. Presumably it was based on Count Leo Tolstoy's novel, but Gordin's "adaptation," plus the improvisations of numerous troupes Gordin couldn't supervise first hand, had taken the plot far afield. By the time it reached Omaha little was left of Tolstoy; Gordin himself probably wouldn't have recognized it.

The standard immigrant couple, Ephriam and Bayle, have the standard ungrateful and selfish son. The father is a musician, newly arrived in America and unable to get into the union. (A personal dig at the unfeeling unions by the weary actors who were wandering, like the children of Israel, for what seemed like forty years in the wilderness of Nebraska.) In the play, the arrogant son is already a famous concert violinist, a member of the union, and his excited father is supposed to say, "*I* can play better than you can."

But the actor playing Ephriam didn't even know how to hold a violin. So, in the spirit of "making do" in the Yiddish theater, Ephriam pointed to the old Bayle, bent over, with strands of gray hair spilling out of her *babushka*. "Why, your old mother can play better than you can!" At which point, Muni, his hands trembling like an old hag's, took the fiddle and played the emotional allegro of Beethoven's *Kreutzer Sonata*. He was a sensation.

Muni directed a sketch occasionally, the "director" being the actor or prompter (or even the stagehand) who best remembered the plot, the sequence, and the stirring climax of any given work.

In 1916 Muni came back to New York briefly. The season was over with the Grossmans, and he thought he would try for Union #1. But he decided against a *proba*, telling himself he would be terrible, that if his father had never made it, how could he? Besides, he was a character actor. How could they believe him barefaced on an empty platform? And he convinced himself that New York didn't want a minor Yiddish vaudevillian from the sticks.

Topical works were the rage along Second Avenue. Boris Thomashefsky had written a play about the celebrated Mendel Beilis ritual murder case, which was shaking the world in the manner of the Dreyfus affair. ("Where does Thomashefsky get time to write plays?" everybody asked. "Between all his acting and all his romances, he must have three heads and thirteen penises!")

A New York agent decided to book a Union #2 tour of *Mendel Beilis* to play a series of cities in the state of Virginia. Seven men were hired, including Muni. And—who could believe it?—they had a script, typed on a Yiddish-language typewriter: it was pure luxury. They planned to take turns as prompter when they were offstage. And the state of Virginia seemed romantic. Unfortunately, the actors and the agent had little preknowledge of the conditions and audiences in the South.

The play is significant since it was Muni's first "social document" drama and on alternate nights his first role as attorney for the defense. He had played many rabbis and scholars concerned with social issues, but this was the first dramatized public document, a pattern he was to follow in many stage and screen roles in later years.

The historical background of the play is terrible and fascinating.

On March 25, 1911, Andrei Yushinsky, a twelve-year-old Christian boy, was found murdered, with forty-seven knife wounds in his body, in a cave near Kiev, in Russia. The Czarist government used the case as a diversionary tactic during the time of growing revolutionary fervor and did nothing to stop the rumor that it was a ritual murder. This was an ancient canard: that Jews used the blood of Christian children to make matzohs during the Passover holidays.

The crime was attributed to the bearded Mendel Beilis, a superintendent in a brick kiln on the outskirts of Kiev. Two town drunks testified they had seen a "man with a black beard" kidnap the boy and promptly, though drunkenly, identified Beilis. But Mitshuk, an incorruptible police chief in Kiev, came forward, declaring the ritual murder was the fantasy of the mob, that the Yushinsky boy had been tortured and put to death by the very accusers of Beilis, because Yushinsky had gone to the police and informed on them. Mitshuk was thrown in prison for "fabricating false evidence."

The case attracted worldwide attention, involving people who had fought for Dreyfus, including Anatole France, the German playwright Gerhart Hauptmann, and, in America, Catholic John Cardinal Farley and Episcopal Bishop David H. Greer. All sent protests to Czar Nicholas II.

But the Beilis trial, which lasted thirty-four days, was a farce, rigged, with the defendant's life constantly threatened. Mobs outside the court shouted for his scalp. A bomb was thrown into the courtroom. Then the case took a startling turn. The attorney for the defense trapped the accusers on the stand; they broke down and confessed their lies. Beilis was acquitted, but the charge still read that "ritual murder had been committed by Jews unknown."

The play, melodramatic and flamboyant, was one of more than a hundred sired by Boris Thomashefsky, dramatist. Thomashefsky often produced topical works, "fill-in quickies," to exploit the excitement generated by the newspapers. (He even did a play about the Johnstown flood while the streets were still wet.) Later Thomashefsky imported Beilis himself to America—but he simply couldn't make an actor out of him. The group of seven actors, including Muni, brought the play *Mendel Beilis* to the sovereign and totally disinterested state of Virginia. They played to empty houses in Richmond and Norfolk. When they reached Lynchburg, they hunted for a Jewish section of town so they could get lodgings, put up posters, and spread the word about their play. They found nothing.

On the main street of Lynchburg they saw a distinguished old man; Muni later described him as "a double for Moses." Muni went up to him and started questioning him in Yiddish. He smiled but looked totally confused, so Muni repeated his questions more distinctly, thinking the old man might be deaf. Finally the Lynchburg patriarch said warmly, "Why, ah declayah, ah doan know what you-all're talkin' abow-aht!" Muni switched to English, asking him if he wasn't Jewish. The man said that of course he was, he had been born and educated right there in Lynchburg, but there were so few Hebrews around there wasn't even a synagogue or a kosher meat market. "As for me, ah doan know one single little ole woh-ad of Yiddish!"

They hurried to the town auditorium, where they were scheduled to play, set up their few movable props, and tried translating the play into English. When they began rehearsing, they discovered that Muni was the only one of the seven actors who knew enough English, so they raced out and wired their New York agent-booker to cancel the date. They waited in the Western Union office and finally received a return message: "Play!"

That night they performed *Mendel Beilis* in stumbling English for twenty-five people, with Muni prompting and translating while trying to play the title role, but he was so confused that he wasn't very good himself. Eventually even the stagehands couldn't endure it and refused to raise the curtain for the fifth and final act. The actors received no money, had only their train tickets, so carried their trunks on their backs to the depot.

Muni told me this on a warm summer night in 1955 at the Sixth Avenue Delicatessen after a performance of *Inherit the Wind*. "Lawrence and Lee should write a play about Beilis," he said. "But don't expect a movie sale. No studio will do it—they're scared of Jewish subject matter. Tell you what I'll do—in the play, I'll do Beilis one night, Mitshuk the next night, and the defense attorney the night the critics come. Okay?"

The waiter came over at that moment with Muni's order: a combination corn-beef–pastrami sandwich on rye, three and a half inches thick.

"Look at that!" Muni said, holding it up. "I could have used it in Virginia, let me tell you. In one town, there was a diner that served a Truck Driver's Breakfast for fifteen cents, but only until nine in the morning. After nine it was thirty-five cents. Did you ever know an actor to get up that early? In our case, by the time we stumbled into bed it was three or four in the morning and we stumbled right out again to make that nine A.M. deadline. We'd pretend to be a bunch of tough truck drivers. Well, you haven't lived until you've seen and heard a bunch of anemic Yiddish actors trying to be burly truck drivers! We got juice, cereal, eggs—hold the Virginia ham, please—and all the rolls we could eat. We filled our pockets with rolls and lived on them the rest of the day. That was our total food for twenty-four hours. Fifteen cents apiece. It was the first time a Yiddish theater company on tour ever gained weight."

In 1917 Muni headed back for Chicago again. The United States had entered the war, and patriotic fervor even swept the Yiddish theaters, which began doing appropriate plays: *Jewish War Brides,*

67

The World in Flames, Yiddish Martyr in America. Immigration had stopped, which should have slowed up attendance, but the Yiddish theaters were filled with *shund* plays. Audiences flocked to help forget that the old country was literally in flames. But some of the younger generation, who had arrived as infants at the turn of the century, were searching and hoping for better theater.

In Chicago Muni learned that both his brothers had married and were living in Canada. Gertner's company, still at the Pavilion, had its full quota of actors. Muni was promised the first available vacancy, but he didn't want to return to the theater which was once called Weisenfreund's. He made his headquarters at Printer's Restaurant, where itinerant Yiddish actors were cast, and when he registered for the draft, he gave the restaurant as his home address.

For three weeks, to keep food in his mouth, Muni went back to work for the Chicago Gas Company. The market was gone for the meshlike gas wicks or the trimmers, so he read meters. But an actor can't turn off his trade like a gas jet. So he decided to practice, to try a different accent each day. His first was as close an approximation as possible to the Southern drawl of the Lynchburg Moses. On trolley-car rides to the edge of town where he read meters, Muni struck up conversations with working people and then later tried to mimic their speaking style. He listened so intently to Polish and German and Swedish accents that often he missed what the people were saying in his concentration on how they were saying it. Then one night in Printer's Restaurant, he ran into an old friend from Gertner's Theatre, the Yiddish comic Berel Bernardi.

Bernardi, who had also been born in Lemberg, suffered the same problem Philip Weisenfreund had experienced for so many years, the inability to break into the closed Union #1 in New York. He had been traveling from town to town with his entire family: his actress wife, Laina, and his theatrically gifted children, Boris, Jack, and Faige. (Another son, Herschel, was to become Tevya in *Fiddler on the Roof*, Lieutenant Jacoby on the *Peter Gunn* television series, and Harry Golden in the West Coast company of *Only in America*; but he wasn't born until five years later, in 1922.)

When a season ended for the Bernardis in Detroit in 1917, they decided to try working as a resident company in Milwaukee. It had often been a way-stop for traveling troupes, but Milwaukee had never had a permanent Yiddish theater. Bernardi leased the Rose Theatre on Walnut Street, then came to Chicago to assemble a company. He hired Muni as his character man, and Max Hoenig and Moishe Dorf to fill out the company. Muni-Hoenig-Dorf came to be known as the "Three Musketeers of the Bernardi Troupe." But the Milwaukee adventure was as doomed as the hegira to Virginia.

Just before they left Chicago, Muni was called up for his draft physical. They dismissed him as unfit for military duty for "health reasons" but refused to tell him why. Muni worried for a while, but dismissed it in his mind as a mistake. "They're *mishuga*," he told Bernardi. "I'm as healthy as a horse. Of course, you haven't seen the horse!" Muni wasn't at all unhappy to escape the Army. He thought of his parents' falling-down soldier sketches and was convinced that he was well trained to be the worst rookie in the AEF.

Jack Bernardi recalls the total disaster of the Rose Theatre in Milwaukee. Muni continued his specialty of old rabbis and patriarchs and even once played King Solomon. He was known among his peers as "the Makeup *Expertnik*." Since the actor-manager's specialty was comedy, they played knockdown Yiddish farces, including *The Greenhorn Teacher* and *Mishka and Moshke*. Muni began to think of himself as primarily a comic performer. And he adored the Bernardi family, particularly Berel's malapropisms. When they could afford it, Papa Bernardi would take the family and Muni to a German restaurant and order: "One steak, please—well-to-do." Muni also considered Laina Bernardi "the only woman in the civilized world who can say four-letter words and still sound like a nice girl."

But the German-Jewish population of Milwaukee didn't want to be Germans because of the war and didn't want to be Jews. The Rose Theatre was losing so much money that Bernardi scheduled performances only on weekends, booking in burlesque shows and early Pearl White and Chaplin films for the other days. Muni spent one week, waiting for the weekend, learning how to juggle, instructed by a fleabitten burlesque juggler.

But finally Bernardi and the theater went broke, without even enough money to pay the actors their full final salaries. When Muni opened his envelope, he found it was $3 short. (The traditional time to collect salaries in the Yiddish theater was the final performance of the week, just before Act Two: Saturday night, a fortune of $15 in hand and only three acts to go!)

Holding his total worldly wealth of $12, Muni asked, "Berel, when do I get the other three dollars?"

"Soon, Munya. When I can," Bernardi promised. "You'll get it back some day! Take my word!"

Fifteen years later, in 1932, Muni was in New York, a famous picture star after *Scarface*. He was attending a performance at the downtown National Theatre to see his old friend Samuel Goldenberg play a Yiddish adaptation of the Wallace Beery movie *The Champ*. The child actor in the Jackie Cooper part was ten-year-old Herschel Bernardi. Papa Bernardi spotted Muni in the audience. After they had embraced like long-lost father and son, Berel handed the now-wealthy Muni $3.

"What's this for, Berel?" Muni asked.

"Milwaukee!"

After the theater in Milwaukee closed, they were all jobless. But rent on the theater had been paid for a month ahead. So the Bernardi kids, who had been playacting in their boardinghouse attic, took over the theater. Muni, their twenty-two-year-old onstage grandfather, gave them makeup lessons.

"He showed us exactly how to put a beard on properly," Jack Bernardi recalls. "How else could an eleven-year-old look like the Czar of Russia? The trick, Muni told us, was to start below the chin and build the beard up. He was warm with us; he was patient with us; he was affectionate with us."

Berel Bernardi managed to raise enough money from local Milwaukee *Patriotten* to tour their troupe for one-night stand's to St. Paul, St. Louis, and Omaha. When they arrived in Nebraska, Muni made an announcement.

"Omaha! The city where I was born. As an actress!"

When they finished a two-night stand in Minneapolis, they didn't have enough money to get back to home base in Milwaukee. The Jewish community took up a collection and paid their train fares. Muni returned to Chicago. He thought he could always go back to reading gas meters.

At Printer's Restaurant he found a letter from Jacob Kalich, who managed a Yiddish theater at the Grand Opera House in Boston. Kalich wrote that he had learned of the Weisenfreund reputation and offered him a job as character man in his Boston company. Muni hastily telegraphed his acceptance.

When he arrived in Boston, Muni discovered the most effervescent member of the company was a young lady named Molly Pyekoon, who usually was cast as twelve- and thirteen-year-old boys, parts Muni himself had never played. Molly had also been a convincing eleven as one of the children Madame Keni Lipzin slaughtered in *The Yiddishe Medea*. Later producer Kalich, madly in love with his starlet, announced his engagement to her from the stage of the Grand Opera House and simplified her name to Molly Picon. Muni's onstage relationship to Molly was only that of grandfather to grandson.

Kalich once asked Muni if he had ever gone through a Bar

Mitzvah, the Jewish rites of confirmation, which declares a boy a man at the age of thirteen. "Bar Mitzvah? Who needs a Bar Mitzvah?" Muni snorted. "At the age of thirteen, I was already a seventy-three-year-old rabbi. Molly Pyekoon should come to *me* to be Bar Mitzvahed!"

Five weeks after Muni arrived in Boston, the most virulent influenza epidemic in history hit New England. All theaters, Yiddish included, were ordered closed by the board of health. Muni was again out of a job.

He found his way to Philadelphia and managed to get part-time walk-ons with a second-rate company playing the Girard Avenue Theatre. The playhouse had seen better days; it had opened in 1891 with James O'Neill, the father of Eugene O'Neill, starring in Watts Phillips' *The Dead Heart*, alternating with the play which was the elder O'Neill's triumph and downfall, *The Count of Monte Cristo*. But now the theater sat in the center of Philadelphia's "Lower East Side" and performed only the *shund*, the offal squeezed out by Second Avenue. Muni made as much impression as a prop or a footlight.

"I was always an old Jew—with a beard, with a staff, with a pack, with a pain. They used me for crossovers in one while they were changing the scenery. If they needed more time, I would pad my part—with a grunt, with a cough, with a sneeze, with an elaborate blowing of the nose."

Muni lived at Mrs. Rolling's Theatrical Boarding House, 1215 North Marshall Street, just opposite the Girard Avenue Theatre's stage door. But he never had enough money for food or enough satisfaction for the soul, so he took a job at a tab burlesque theater near Franklin Square. He didn't speak in his "act," but he danced a little jig, played the violin, and even tried juggling.

Following one afternoon performance, a bulbous-nosed man came backstage. Playing in Philadelphia with the *Ziegfeld Follies*, he was visiting old haunts where he had juggled in earlier, less prosperous years, "before I performed for all the crowned heads of Europe." His name was W. C. Fields.

"You'll never make it as a juggler, m'boy," Fields told Muni. "Your eyes are too sad."

Muni's eyes must have looked extra-sad, because Fields added: "But don't listen to me, kid. My entire success is based on one rule: never take advice from anybody!"

Muni stopped juggling, and his turn consisted entirely of gags on the violin. When he purchased a fiddle at a pawnshop, he stared at it for a long time. How ironic that Papa had been right: he was eating because he knew how to coax a funny melody out of a violin.

The neighborhood where Muni lived was a tough one, full of Italians and Irish ready to fight if you looked at one of them twice. So he decided to take a few boxing lessons. At a one-flight-up gymnasium, he started working out, punching a bag, skipping rope, occasionally sparring with some Philadelphia fighters: Battling Levinsky and the young Lew Tendler, later—like so many boxers—a restaurateur.

Levinsky thought Muni could develop into a pretty good light heavyweight and urged him to continue to fight. "Hell, what other chance does a Jewish kid have these days?" Levinsky told him. "You can either be a boxer or some kind of show-business performer. And you sure as hell don't look like an actor!"

Muni quit boxing at the gym for fear he might break his fingers and wouldn't even be able to grub a living with a violin.

A few years later, he told Clifford Odets about this unlikely combination of prizefighter and fiddler, and Odets got his premise for *Golden Boy*, which Luther Adler played on the stage and William Holden in the film. Odets cryptically nodded his thanks to Muni by naming the fight manager of his play "Moody" and the fighter's girlfriend "Lorna Moon."

During the summer of 1918 Muni tried New York again. Along the Yiddish Rialto theaters were passing back and forth among managers in a game of musical chairs. Producers were feuding, snatching theater leases away from each other, using their major stars as pawns. As for material, it was the popular belief that "every Jew in New York has written a play."

One manager, Joseph Edelstein, with a fine nose for a dollar, established David Kessler and company (including the actor Maurice Schwartz) in the upstairs area of the Second Avenue Theatre called the Roof Garden; the airy name took the sting off serious plays being presented in the summer heat, long before the days of air conditioning. Downstairs, in the main Second Avenue Theatre, Edelstein presented Yiddish vaudeville and lightweight musicals, always with the persistent melodies of Joseph Rumshinsky. Since Union #1 didn't cover it, Muni managed to get a place in that company as a comic bearded old Jew who danced as he fiddled and sang comic songs. His capers were beneath the notice of the critics, who covered the "deeper art" upstairs. But one person did notice: Maurice Schwartz, who was planning a theater of his own that fall on Irving Place. He would come downstairs and watch this eccentric, talented young man, hiding behind a beard and a pawnshop violin. A few months later he remembered the name Weisenfreund.

At the end of the summer, the Second Avenue Theatre changed hands again, and Muni went back to Philadelphia, to the second-rate company on Girard Avenue. (The theater is still there at 627 West Girard, but it is now Klein's Self-Service Market. The seats have been ripped out, and the stage is used to display fresh produce.) Muni, feeling like a vegetable, heard reports of the new Yiddish Art Theatre in New York but never dreamed he could ever be part of it. He played bigger roles now in Philadelphia, but he was convinced it was a dead end.

What was happening inside Muni during these dismal days? Mendel Osherowitch, once a city editor of the *Forward* in New York, gives some insight in his book *David Kessler and Muni Weisenfreund: Two Generations of the Yiddish Theatre.* No published translation exists in English, but the late Joseph Tickman verbally translated pertinent passages to the theater scholar Michael C. Gerlach. The Osherowitch-Tickman-Gerlach account describes Muni's Philadelphia period vividly:

> Muni was very unhappy: long days, cheap performances, lousy acting, terrible dialogue—nothing for the soul. Faces that expressed no emotions. Heavy feelings weighed upon him. Is this how it's going to be forever? And once when he was sitting in the hot, stuffy dressing room trying to put on makeup, the actor Louis Gelrod came in as a special messenger from New York sent by Maurice Schwartz.

A later article in the *Forward*, by Milton Danley, quotes Muni's own words about that day:

> When the messenger from Schwartz descended upon me in Philadelphia with news of the projected engagement, I didn't believe him. To play in New York in Schwartz's Irving Place Theatre, about which I had heard so much, sounded too unreal, too good to be true. That day I didn't walk down the streets of Quakerstown, I floated in the air. My head was full of visions; my eyes looked and beheld dreams. That day was worth all that a human heart could wish.

He still had to pass the hurdle of the *proba* to get clearance by the union, but Gelrod said it was only a routine matter. Schwartz had already engaged his required number of union actors, and "the Weisenfreund" was to be a bonus hiring. Gelrod assured Muni that the union committee wouldn't dare turn down a special request from the new messiah of the Yiddish theater, Maurice Schwartz.

Back in New York, Muni had misgivings. He dreaded the *proba*, remembering his father's traumatic failures. And he had doubts about suddenly vaulting into the highly professional Yiddish theater. He asked the union to let him perform his *proba* in

73

makeup. They refused. Shrugging, he used only posture and voice as an old man in a short comic sketch and as the devil in *Gott, Mann und Teufel.* He performed indifferently, resenting the whole procedure. One committee member said about Muni's *proba*: "He's terrible. Let him in—he'll never put anybody out of work except himself. And if Schwartz wants him, that's Schwartz's funeral." But wiser watchers that day sensed a presence the moment Muni walked onto the platform. (Once, determining scholarships for Barter Theatre, Ethel Barrymore remarked about auditioning actors: "You'll know they *have it* the minute they walk out onstage, or you'll think your watch has stopped!") That afternoon at the Hebrew Actors Union nobody's watch stopped. But old-timers will tell you that if Muni had auditioned as a young leading man, he would have been turned down; the sixty-year-olds along Second Avenue were still playing all available juvenile parts.

In 1919 Muni had just passed his twenty-third birthday; he had been a working but wandering actor for eleven years. But now he was in New York to stay, and he had a Union #1 card in his hand.

"Papa," he murmured, staring at the card, "this is for you."

Left: One of Muni's multiple experiments with makeup. The nose has been changed, and the fingers have been elongated. Center: Muni as a clown in *Motke Goniff (Motke the Thief).* Right: Muni as Ossip in *Revizor (The Inspector General).* This pose became the unofficial logo of the Yiddish theater.

MUNI sensed from the start that Maurice Schwartz was both his benefactor and his enemy. He was honored and flattered to be a part of the distinguished company of actors at the Irving Place Theatre. And he was to be paid $40 a week.

"Why, if he had offered twenty dollars, I would have gladly accepted it," Muni said. "But there it was, the printed contract, and I signed it. Why should I argue?"

Then Muni began to read how Schwartz was bragging about him in the Yiddish press.

"I have acquired a young actor named Muni Weisenfreund," Schwartz is quoted as saying, "and I predict he will be a sensation in New York in my company."

When newspapermen dismissed it as the usual publicity puff, Schwartz went on to insist, "I'm telling you—Weisenfreund is a genius!"

The word for genius in Yiddish leaped out of the newsprint at Muni, and it frightened him. He rushed to confront Schwartz in person.

"Mr. Schwartz," Muni blurted, "you're killing me. What do you mean telling the newspapers that I'll be a sensation in New York? What happens if I'm not? They'll toss me back to Milwaukee or the dung heap in Philadelphia. Please. I want only very small parts."

Schwartz looked at him astonished. It was the first time in the history of the Yiddish theater that anybody had deliberately *asked* for minor roles.

Muni got his wish. His first part was little more than a walk-on, Zazulye, a government functionary, a bearded postal clerk who comes on briefly in Sholom Aleichem's *Tevya, the Dairyman,* scheduled to open the season on August 29, 1919.

The Promised Land Muni had entered was having its difficulties. The previous season Schwartz had battled with one of the leading members of his company, Jacob Ben-Ami. Schwartz had promised Ben-Ami he would present Peretz Hirshbein's *Farvorfen Vinkel (Forsaken Nook)* but then reneged, considering it "too literary." The play became a *cause célèbre*, was finally shoehorned into an off Wednesday night, and turned out to be the triumph of the season. As a result of the battle, Ben-Ami broke away and formed his own company, the Jewish Art Theatre. Beyond this new competition, there were further difficulties. Schwartz had promised his actors the end of the star system; his theater was to be truly an ensemble effort. But the audiences still insisted on their matinee idols. Partly from egotism, partly for commercial reasons, Schwartz starred himself.

The other major Yiddish actors were still holding court along Second Avenue. Swept along by the literary trend, they circumcised the plays of Dumas, Hauptmann, Ibsen, Strindberg, Chekhov, Tolstoy, and Shakespeare. The *Patriotten*, the fan clubs of the day, continued to mob Adler and Thomashefsky. Their fierce rivalry sometimes turned into near rioting in the streets. When Thomashefsky announced he was playing *Alexander the Great* astride a genuine live white horse, the Adler *Patriotten* managed to sneak a powerful physic into the horse's feed bag. Thomashefsky, in shining armor, rode triumphantly onstage. The disturbed horse reared back toward the footlights, blithely lifted its tail, and dumped a load of manure all over the prompter.

Theater in the Yiddish community was so vital and important that the editor of the leading newspaper, Abraham Cahan of the *Jewish Daily Forward*, was also the dramatic critic. Resembling Leon Trotsky, he was respected and feared by the performers. Cahan, enthroned in a box, would glower at the stage, or when he brought along his wife, who was hard of hearing, he would sit front row center and loudly repeat the lines to her. The reviews were not churned out overnight as in the uptown theater world but appeared every Friday. Actors would line up at the newsstands to get copies of the opinions of the mighty.

Though Muni had merely a sentence or two, fellow actors claim he stole half, if not all, of *Tevya.* He was comic, sad, and totally believable as the old government clerk; nobody in the audience conceived that he was a stripling of twenty-three. The critics, however, were indifferent. One even said, "Weisenfreund is no actor at all." Muni, discouraged, convinced it was because Schwartz had given him too much of a buildup, was ready to "spit on New York and run." Where? Perhaps back to the gas company in Chicago.

Muni had thought of the New York theater as a temple, a shrine where the actors were dedicated artists. He despaired when he discovered backstage at Irving Place the same jealousies and tricks he had found in the hinterlands.

During one performance of *Tevya,* another actor (not Schwartz) suddenly began speaking to Muni in Russian. The actor looked at Muni smugly, knowing most of the audience of Russian immigrants understood what he was saying but that Muni knew not a word of it. Muni was startled momentarily, shocked that an actor in this theater devoted to art would resort to a sleazy vaudeville trick. At first Muni thought he would do a somersault or dance; instead he picked up one Russian word and kept repeating it over and over again, as if he were drunk or confused, climaxing it with a violent sneeze.

The audience applauded, but Muni rushed offstage, furious at the trick. "What a horrible thing to do to another actor. If it's vaudeville horseplay he wants, I can do it better than him. I'll punch his teeth in." He was convinced there would be a scene and a scandal, and he'd be kicked out of the theater. But when the other actor came offstage, he saw how incensed Muni was and quickly apologized.

Muni's second role with Schwartz was in another Hirshbein play, *The Blacksmith's Daughter*, which had been performed the previous season after the unanticipated success of *Farvorfen Vinkel*. Muni was a replacement as the old grandfather for Jehiel Goldschmidt, who had left Schwartz to join Ben-Ami's new company. As the doddering, comic old grandfather, Muni opened the play, saluting the dewy freshness of the morning in this village idyll with a song, not unlike "Oh, What a Beautiful Morning," the joyful opening of *Oklahoma!* many years later. Muni was convinced that his place in the theater was in musicals and always as an old character comedian.

Luther Adler (then Lutha J. Adler), the son of the famous Jacob B., remembers that "the Weisenfreund became a cult among the *fineschmeckers*, the 'fine smellers,' the young blades of Second Avenue, who considered ourselves connoisseurs of fine acting." Muni had spent eighteen hours putting on his makeup for the walk-on in *Tevya* to read one pronouncement from the czar; in *The Blacksmith's Daughter* his old man on the stage was the genuine article, and the old men sitting alongside them in the audience seemed to be the made-up fakes.

"We were the smart asses of our time," Luther says, "and nobody could fool us. We'd say, 'Weisenfreund's opening in a new play tonight,' and though we knew it was just a bit part, we'd rush to see all the things he did. The young people in Schwartz's audiences were there because we wanted to see this glaring talent. At that time and for some time later, Muni was by far the greatest hope on the whole American acting scene. He was the prizewinner, among people who knew, the most gifted performer, male or female, in New York, in the country!"

Schwartz was trapped. He gave Muni what he had asked for: smaller and smaller roles. But the audiences kept shouting for Muni to take solo curtain calls no matter how insignificant the part. As actor-manager, originator, promoter of his theater, Schwartz wanted good performers, but at the same time he resented being upstaged by an upstart on his payroll.

An operetta was scheduled, Wolf LeRoy's *The White Lily,* and Muni was shoved into the chorus. Cahan of the *Forward* was outraged that "an art theater would slip back into *shund*!" and refused to review it, assigning a second stringer to cover the opening in May, 1920. Muni played an old man, with a combination of lechery and innocence in his eyes. Every time a girl danced near him he would hesitate for an instant, as if to say, "You're sure you want me to put my arm around your waist? You're sure I won't break anything?" And then when the girl smiled and danced with him, Muni would turn to the audience with a surprised look which said, "See? See? It's not so bad being an *alter cocker*. Maybe it's what the girls really like. Watch! Watch! Before the evening's over, I may even manage a tiny erection!"

The audience howled, cheered, wouldn't let the musical continue. But nobody above Fourteenth Street ever heard of Muni. Uptown they named the downtown gods on the fingers of one hand: Adler the elder, Thomashefsky, now Schwartz, Schildkraut, and Ben-Ami. Weisenfreund? Never heard of him. Weisen who?

The fall season opened on September 3, 1920, with *The Gold Chain* by Isaac Leib Peretz. Muni was assigned the role of an old flax merchant-farmer, a simpleton of a peasant, the kind of a part normally given to a super. Muni turned the bit into a classic, still spoken about, stamped into the memories of Yiddish theatergoers after more than fifty years.

The *Chain* of the title refers to the chain of *Rapunum*, the sun, the dynasty of rabbis, sons of sons of sons of rabbis, gifted with special wisdom and even the power of healing. The holy chief rabbi of the play was a judge, doctor, high priest, dispenser of wisdom. Muni, in contrast, was a half-witted flax merchant, arriving for a shred of advice.

With a mingling of faith and naïveté, the flax merchant bumbled apologetically into the presence of the great man.

"Rabbi," he said, "I have a problem. I want to know if I should plant flax or corn. I'll do whatever you say!"

The rabbi looked totally disinterested in this minor matter.

"Plant corn," he replied curtly, dismissing the man with a wave.

"Yes. Corn will be very good, but suppose there's a war? Flax would be a good thing."

"Well, then, plant flax."

"But what if there is no war, what should I do?"

The rabbi sighed. Muni bent forward. There wasn't a muscle, a vein, a fingernail in his whole body that wasn't alerted, poised to hear the words of wisdom from the learned rabbi. An unnamed theatergoer said later, "He even seemed to be listening with his *tochus*!"

Finally the rabbi said, "Well, I'll tell you what to do."

"Yes? Yes?"

"Plant a little corn and plant a little flax."

Pure joy bubbled out of the flax merchant.

"Marvelous! Listen to that brilliance. A little corn. A little flax."

And he began a grateful old man's dance of exuberance and adulation. "How wonderful to get such great advice from the son of a son of a son! 'A little of this, a little of that!' I will win no matter what!"

I. Friedman wrote in the Yiddish daily newspaper *Tageblatt*, under the pen name of Israel the Yankee: "Muni Weisenfreund truthfully portrays a Jewish simpleton. Fortunately, he's not a comedian or he would have overexaggerated it."

When Muni read it, he showed it to a fellow actor. "If I'm not a comedian, what am I?"

"You're working," the other actor said.

Muni's next part was in Fishel Bimko's play, *The Thieves*, in which he played Lepack. Again Muni had a bit, behind heavy makeup, a Yiddish thief—in a way his first gangster. Instinctively, without direction, he made a discovery. During rehearsal, Schwartz was shouting directions through a third person, to any other actor but Muni. "Tell that Weisenfreund to do so-and-so." Muni decided to demand attention with calm, with quiet, with whispers, sometimes with total silence, a technique he was to employ often throughout his professional career.

Another actor in *The Thieves*, with a part fifty times as important as Muni's, complained bitterly to Schwartz: "The *mumzer* is under-playing me to death!"

Schwartz decided to get Muni out from behind his beard. Their unspoken rivalry climaxed in October, 1920, with the play which inadvertently made Muni a major force in the Yiddish theater: Sholom Aleichem's *Shver zu Sein a Yid (Hard to Be a Jew)*.

Sholom Aleichem had originally written it as a short novel, *The Bloody Joke*, but "the Yiddish Mark Twain" died before it was performed onstage. It concerns an aristocratic Russian student, Ivanov, who offers to trade places and identities for a year with a Jewish student, Schneyerson, to prove it's not difficult at all to be a Jew and that discrimination doesn't really exist. The switch is made. In a distant city, Ivanov takes lodgings at the home of a bearded, rich Jewish merchant, David Shapiro, and falls in love with Shapiro's daughter.

This plot was to see many lives, including two English-language plays, *If I Were You* and *The Grass Is Greener*, and may have suggested a similar premise to Laura Z. Hobson when she wrote the novel *Gentlemen's Agreement*. In the Yiddish theater *Shver zu Sein a Yid* was a resounding favorite. (During the 1973–74 season, it reappeared on Second Avenue as a Yiddish musical, starring Joseph Buloff.)

Schwartz assigned the role of Ivanov to Muni, who was terrified. He begged Schwartz for the part of the old Shapiro—"with a beard." Schwartz insisted on the casting; he had decided to play old Shapiro himself.

"But I've never been to Russia," Muni protested. "I've never met a Russian student. I'll be a terrible flop. It will ruin the play and ruin me. I've never played a part with my bare face hanging out. My God, I'll catch cold!"

Schwartz was adamant, and rehearsals began. Muni worried and sweated and was certain they had given him such an important part to "show him up," to prove he was capable of playing only small roles. It was a pattern of self-doubt which was to remain with Muni all his life. Muni hardly slept at night. "A Jew playing a Christian playing a Jew—I won't know who I am!"

Berta Gersten, who played Shapiro's daughter, talked about those rehearsals for the rest of her life: how Muni, using his own uncertainty and nervousness, climbed inside the soul of Ivanov.

"It was remarkable," she once told some young acting hopefuls, "how he made up his face almost *without* makeup. The severe look of an aristocrat seemed to rise up into his cheekbones. His posture, the stiffening of his spine, his attempt to unbend but never quite making it—all added to the believability. I was so amazed watching him I would sometimes forget my lines, thinking I really was a Jewish girl in Russia, falling in love with this fascinating *goy*."

Luther Adler went to see the play again and again. "It was Muni's *'cognac*, his big fist,' which is what we called somebody's first important role in the theater. He was wonderful. It's not easy for a Jew to go on the Yiddish stage, speak Yiddish and give the impression of being a complete Gentile. But he did it."

Every day of rehearsal Muni quit. Schwartz took him to the union, where an executive told Muni, "If you don't play the part, you're out of the theater. All theaters!" Then Muni grasped at any lame excuse he could find. He didn't have a dinner jacket. Schwartz condescended to let Muni borrow his; the fact that it was ill-fitting added to the awkwardness of Ivanov's first tentative evening at the Shapiro house.

On opening night, Muni sat and stared at his dressing table, refusing to talk to anyone, appalled at the beardless face he saw in his mirror. He went onstage reluctantly, totally uncertain. When the lights hit him, magic began.

Nine days after his twenty-fifth birthday, Muni, with his own face for all the world to see, was a major star of the Yiddish theater. Even the difficult Abe Cahan, editor-critic of the *Forward*, joined the rooting section:

Muni Weisenfreund put his name in the Golden Book of the

80

Yiddish theater, his Ivanov makes him one of the most talented actors our theater has ever had. It is really too bad that Sholom Aleichem didn't live to see this great play of his with the wonderful Weisenfreund in the part of Ivanov.

Muni received multiple offers within the Yiddish theater community, but none from Broadway and none from motion pictures, then primarily interested in Rudolph Valentino-Milton Sills matinee idols. But down on Second Avenue, they offered to start a theater starring Weisenfreund as actor-manager. Muni politely refused. Yiddish playwrights rhapsodized about his performance and said they would write starring roles for him. Muni quietly answered that "I am a member of an ensemble company. I still have a lot to learn." Others urged him to try Shylock in *Merchant of Venice* or the leading role in *God of Vengeance*. In one weekend, they said, he could outdistance Kessler and Rudolph Schildkraut and become Thomashefsky-Adler-Schwartz rolled into one.

"Thank you, no," Muni said. "I am a member of the Yiddish Art Theatre. I am doing my work. This is where I belong."

The most surprising offer of all came from Maurice Schwartz. Muni had never heard Schwartz speak so quietly; usually his booming voice projected even in a dressing room.

"Weisenfreund," Schwartz said, not looking directly at Muni, "you were quite right. You are far better suited to the part of old Shapiro. You can have your wish, beard and everything. And *I* shall play the part of young Ivanov."

Muni shrugged his acceptance and went into rehearsal. His makeup as Shapiro obliterated the Russian *goy*. Besides, he found it a challenge to switch roles, and he was eager to see what Schwartz would do with the difficult part of Ivanov. He didn't complain; after all, wasn't this true ensemble playing?

Schwartz was quite good as Ivanov, Muni thought. Perhaps a little too old for the part, but austere and with a chilling stage presence. As for himself, he was delighted to retreat behind "a muff," as he called it, and relax into the role of an ancient patriarch. Rehearsals were so brief that during performances Muni had to "peck corn" occasionally and stroll close to the prompter for some of his lines. Consequently, he thought his own portrayal as Shapiro was terrible.

The critics raved about Weisenfreund's Shapiro. And they gave the star of the company one brief sentence: "The role of Ivanov was played by Maurice Schwartz."

Muni was not rehired by the Yiddish Art Theatre for the season of 1921–22.

9

LATE in 1920, Lucy Finkel, Bella's sister, saw young Muni Weisenfreund as Ivanov at the Irving Place Theatre. She joined the standing ovation, then rushed home to tell Bella all about it.

The sixteen years since the shooting at Old Bridge, New Jersey, had not been easy for the Finkel family with three small children to raise. Emma was as cheerful as she could be as she hobbled around on crutches or sank into the wooden arms of a wheelchair.

David Levinson did all he could: he fetched and carried, did laundry and washed dishes, drowning his feelings of guilt in attentiveness. There is a rumor that he married Emma, that the children called themselves Levinson for a while, but nobody has ever seen a wedding certificate or remembers an official ceremony. History has a cruel way of going in circles: eventually Levinson left Emma and married a still younger woman.

In the tradition of the Yiddish theater, Emma was given a benefit. The playwright Isaac Zolotorewsky wrote a play especially for the occasion, *The Second Wife*, about a cripple in a wheelchair, with Emma in the leading role. All her friends along Second Avenue knew Emma and her children needed money; but most of all, Emma needed the medicine of applause and laughter—no doctor could give her that, only her public, only the audiences she had enchanted and dazzled.

But nobody applauded at the benefit. The audience wept; it wasn't the Emma they had known, that they remembered, that they were never to have again. There was only silence and sorrow.

The great Boris Thomashefsky kept his distance, still not totally forgiving his younger sister for breaking her vow, made before God in heaven and the gods of the gallery. But Harry Thomashefsky, Boris' oldest son, insists that actor Leon Blank was Boris' emissary, keeping an eye on the family, slipping them a few dollars when it was needed. The children always called Leon Papa Blank.

Emma had a "glass tea" with a dollop of strawberry jam floating in it for any visitor who came to call, though she scraped pennies for the jam and tea was a luxury. They were holed up in a cheap flat deep in the Bronx and were down to their last twenty-five cents. On a cold day the family took a vote: should they drop the quarter in the gas meter to get a few more hours of heat and cooking power, or should they spend it for something to eat? If the quarter went to buy food, there would be no gas to cook with. At that precise moment, their Aunt Annie Thomashefsky arrived with a strawberry shortcake. Emma laughed and cried, dropped the quarter in the meter, and fixed everybody glasses of tea.

Uncle Boris eventually gave Lucy and Bella jobs singing and dancing in the chorus at his theater. Young chorus girls? It was a revolution. And thin ones? Unheard of in that array of blubber usually called the Kosher Beef Trust. "Lucy and Bella stood out," Ted Thomas wrote, "like two minnows in a tank of whales." Bella was primarily a comic. Lucy had a beautiful singing voice; she loved Puccini and hoped one day to play *Madama Butterfly*. The girls dutifully brought home their $18 a week: it would go to educate their brother, Abem.

Bella in her early twenties was slim, short, dark-eyed, with chestnut hair, slightly frizzy, pulled back in a bun. Lucy was far prettier, but Bella's large eyes were full of wit and energy. A powerful engine seemed to be racing constantly behind her outward calm. She loved to understate, yet she tended to be sarcastic, somewhat bitter, but always with a laugh. Somebody once said, "Bella invented worry." After Bella married Muni, she often referred to him as the Worrier's Husband.

The book Bella started to write in 1968 begins with a winter day late in the year 1920:

> The first time I heard about Muni Weisenfreund was when my sister, Lucy, came home after seeing a performance at the Yiddish Art Theatre and started raving to my mother and me about this new actor.
>
> She said, "He is simply wonderful and has the most beautiful expressive hands I have ever seen, and, Mama, I think he would be wonderful for Bella!"
>
> I hit the ceiling and said, "You are the older sister. If you like his hands so much, why don't *you* marry him?"
>
> A short while later I saw Muni in one of his greatest hits in the Art Theatre. I was very impressed with his performance, but that was it.
>
> Several months later the Art Theatre was going to do a production of the operetta *Maytime*. (Note: they called it *One Day in May* and listed the author as "Anonymous.") Muni was playing the role of the roué who chases girls all through the play. In the last act, at the age of one hundred and one, he is chasing a young chorus girl.

In Muni's own handwriting on the back of this photograph: "Saturday, March 5, 1921. I proposed to Bella, Atlantic City. 2 Squares from Breakers Hotel." With them is matchmaker Hymie Jacobson.

(Courtesy of Henrietta Jacobson)

The Art Theatre didn't have anyone in the company to play the chorus girl. So Maurice Schwartz asked my uncle, Boris Thomashefsky, at whose theater I was working, whether he could have me for the part. My uncle consented. I went to rehearsal and met Muni for the first time. He was so engrossed in what he was doing that he barely noticed me. I was very nervous and ill at ease with him. However, at lunchtime, he invited me to have lunch with him. So we had our first date, at the Automat.

As I recall, we spent the hour discussing our respective roles and how they should be played. He was twenty-five years old at the time, but in his mind he was already thinking of the old roué. I was not very flattered and decided this was a very self-centered young man.

A few days before the show was to open, my uncle changed his mind and wanted me back in his theater. So I never got to do *Maytime* with Muni and thought to myself: "Well, that's the end of Weisenfreund."

But I did not reckon with my sister and a friend of Muni's. They had plans about Muni and Bella, and they worked on them. Muni's friend finally persuaded him to call me for a date. I was quite pleased and accepted.

Muni had a "thing" about punctuality. He used to say, "If someone steals my money, that is one thing, but if they steal my time, they are stealing part of my life."

By sheer accident, I arrived at our meeting place right on the dot. He liked that and told me in no uncertain terms. I was off on the right foot; but I also had an infected toe on that foot, and when we got to the theater, I had to keep going to the ladies' room to put medication on it. But it gave me a good excuse when we came out of the theater to say, "Mr. Weisenfreund, do you mind if I take your arm and lean on you?" We hit it off well and he asked me for another date.

84

This time he was to pick me up at my house because I wanted him to meet my wonderful mother. The only catch was that he came a little early, so he had to wait until I finished ironing my brother's shirt.

Between Muni and my mother it was a case of love at first sight. As a matter of fact, after I had married Muni, she once said, "I don't remember; didn't I give birth to him, too?"

The following is a little hazy in my mind. The results are not. Somehow I was going to Atlantic City to visit some friends. By coincidence, Muni was going to Atlantic City with his friend, the matchmaker [Hymie Jacobson]. Well, there the serious courting began. One day, while we were walking on the Boardwalk, Muni suddenly turned to me and said, "You know, I don't like to spend money on a strange woman, and if I have the courage, by the time we reach the next corner, I am going to ask you to marry me." (He hadn't even tried to kiss me yet.)

My answer? "If you ask me, I will say yes."

So he said, "We're engaged. And when we get back to New York, we will tell your mother." Then he said, "I haven't got enough money to buy you an engagement ring, we'll get around to that later, but let's go in and buy a ring for your mother."

Also he said, "I want to warn you that I am a very difficult man to get along with. I am very moody and have a terrible temper." Who cared? All I wanted to do is say yes and settle the deal.

For my mother and sister and our friend, the matchmaker, there was only sheer joy—they had pulled it off!

Now came the business of getting married. Nobody in either family had any money, so any kind of reception or "affair" was out of the question. It was just going to be the closest family, the rabbi, and us.

But we had a problem. We were both working. Also I had signed with Muni's company to go on tour and my mother was not going to let me go on tour with him until we were married. So the date was set for May 8, 1921, a day that we both had matinees to do. The ceremony took place at noon; I came five minutes late, and Muni was angry.

At any rate, we went through the ceremony. Muni kissed me hastily (he couldn't be late for the matinee); I went to the subway and went to Newark, where I had a matinee.

At midnight, Muni met me at the subway entrance and said, "I know you, you're my wife!" Then he took me home. I spent my wedding night sleeping with my sister! A week later came the honeymoon in Atlantic City.

Then we went on tour together. I was new in the company and had very little rehearsal. In the first play we did together, Muni played my grandfather. At a certain cue, I had to walk downstage with a plate of soup in my hands and that was the end of the act. As I said, I had very few rehearsals and was not too sure of the timing. So I turned to Muni, who was standing near me, and said, "Darling, tell me when to start downstage." All I got was a grunt and a glare. Well, I did get downstage on time.

After the curtain came down, Muni came to me, saying, "How dare you speak to me in English and call me darling? We are doing a Yiddish play and I am supposed to be your grandfather. Don't you have any imagination and concentration when you are on there? Don't you ever do that to me again!"

I was stunned, went into the dressing room, cried and asked myself, "What kind of monster did I marry?" He came in later and apologized and explained that the only way he could function onstage was by deep concentration. I had interfered with that concentration, and that was what had made him so angry. I had had my first lesson. But that was the serious side of Muni.

No one could be a bigger clown on stage than Muni when he didn't believe in a part or didn't like it. For instance, his company had imported a French actress [Jenny Vallier] who brought her own play with her. It was a cheap melodrama and a terrible flop. Muni played one of those characters, the friend of the family who is always giving advice. At the last performance, when Mademoiselle Vallier said poignantly, "What will we do with the child?" Muni, with a straight face, answered, "We will eat it!"

Although Maurice Schwartz made Bella part of the touring company for the summer of 1921, at the start of the fall season he did not rehire either of them. Schwartz took over the Garden Theatre when Jacob Ben-Ami left for Broadway. It was a partial move uptown for Schwartz, into the Madison Square area. Presumably he was happy to be rid of his young competition. But Muni and Bella moved farther *down*town to the operetta *shund* at Joseph Edelstein's Second Avenue Theatre.

Muni clowned and cavorted as a musical-comedy performer playing flamboyant barons in long black opera capes with red satin linings or hoofing in white tie and tails (that was Bella's favorite view of him and she never forgot it). "It was remarkable," Osherowitch wrote, "that even in an operetta, if you possess the talent, an artist can create something that others can't."

Bella and Muni both loved playing with the warm, often raucous, wise, and wide-hearted Bessie Thomashefsky. In one operetta, Aunt Bessie played the title role in *Susie Brenn*. Muni had an incredible one-scene show-stealing bit as a rubber in a turkish bath, reeking with alcohol and eucalyptus oil. As a red-faced slob, Muni invented clacks with his tongue which sounded like slaps on a bare ass.

Midseason, Schwartz found he missed "the Weisenfreund" very much; business was not booming, despite his addition of the great German-Yiddish actor Rudolph Schildkraut to his company. Schwartz tried to get Edelstein to release Muni, but Edelstein refused. Muni, even in bits, was bringing the audience into the Second Avenue Theatre.

"Down here," Edelstein is quoted as saying, "we have two purposes: to make the audience happy and to make money. We don't fart around with 'art'!"

Aunt Bessie, in later years, used to hold court, spinning yarns about the Adlers and about her favorite nephew-in-law, the incredible young Muni Weisenfreund.

"When Munya was a fugitive from the Art Theatre, we were doing an operetta together—not the turkish bath one, another, I don't even remember the name—and he had his tablecloth speech someplace in the second act. During such a long spiel, I had nothing to do. So I sat behind, as far upstage as I could get, at the kitchen table, and I poured myself a glass tea, squeezed in a little lemon, dropped in a lump sugar, another lump, a third lump—why not? he was only halfway through the speech—and folded a napkin.

"All of a sudden, Munya stopped, right in the middle of a sentence. He didn't even turn around but said right to the audience, 'And now if Mrs. Thomashefsky will kindly stop moving around behind my back, I'll go on with the play.' So I stopped."

Muni, a master of stage concentration, often commented on how fragile it was, how easy to shatter.

During the summer of 1922, Muni and Bella rented a bungalow at Brighton Beach, then decided to live there all year round. Emma Finkel had been moved to Brighton a few months before, and Bella wanted to be close to her mother. Muni agreed to return to Schwartz's Yiddish Art Theatre early that fall, and he spent most of the summer rehearsing new and unfamiliar roles by himself in the attic of the Brighton bungalow.

Bella fixed up the attic as a study. Muni had begun to collect books, dictionaries mostly. He loved to "dance with language." He tried his hand at painting, but, impatient with imperfection, gave it up and destroyed everything he had painted. But he kept experimenting with makeup.

"I can't paint like Michelangelo," he told Bella, "but I can begin to *look* like him."

Bella recalled what went on up in that attic:

One night I was sick in bed with the flu and had a high temperature. All of a sudden I heard this sad dirge. I thought: "Oh, my God, I'm dying and they're saying prayers for me." What it really was: Muni was studying a part!

Despite his previous battles, spoken and unspoken, with Maurice Schwartz, Muni was not unhappy to be returning to the Yiddish Art company. At the Second Avenue Theatre, the melodies of Rumshinsky had been enchanting, and he had proved to himself that he could "make a dollar in the commercial theater." But he had the feeling that everything he did as an actor had to say something, total up, add dimension to the audiences' lives and to his own.

"Create characters and you are like God," Muni said. "Six performances a week and rest on the seventh day. One difference: God doesn't have a contract in the Yiddish theater. There—eight or nine performances a week and no *Shabbas!*"

Attempting to explain and perhaps rationalize Schwartz's love-hate relationship with Muni, Luther Adler says:

"Muni was too visible, too highly visible. Muni would walk onstage, and Schwartz would disappear, as if you'd turned off the light on him. Years later, when I was asked to perform in something, I always said, 'Look, I don't go on with monkeys, I don't go on with babies, and I don't go on with Zero Mostel.' Well, to Schwartz, Muni was the same way."

The roles Muni was assigned to play for the season were exciting. And he was pleased- to be part of a company which included, in addition to Schwartz, some of the best actors in the Yiddish theater: Ludwig Satz, Celia Adler, Berta Gersten, Morris Strassberg, Bina Abramovitch (whom Muni described as the Yiddish Dusé) among others.

Celia Adler had departed to join Ben-Ami but was back again. She battled with Schwartz, and she was accident-prone. Her mother, the celebrated Sarah Adler, once commented, "You know *Electra*? Well, *Electra* is like *one day* in my daughter's life!"

Muni himself felt like part of a Greek tragedy that summer. Believing his responsibility as a husband included adequate life insurance, he went into Manhattan and casually applied. It would be a surprise for Bella. He had the scene all rehearsed. "Here," he would say, handing her the policy. "When I die, you'll be the richest widow on Second Avenue. Never again will you have to worry about quarters for the gas meter!"

The physical examination seemed routine. But when it was completed, they told him that life insurance was not available to him, he was a "poor risk." Baffled, Muni asked what was wrong. They told him he had a rheumatic heart, that he might drop dead at any moment.

He refused to believe it. They must have made a mistake. He was alternately angry and frightened, perplexed and indignant. He found a lawyer. Muni told him he wanted a legal document, binding for the rest of his life, stating that for every dollar Muni earned, Bella would get fifty cents of it; for every dime he made, Bella would get a nickel. The lawyer advised him that such a document was unnecessary, inadvisable, and completely unorthodox. But Muni insisted, so the lawyer drew it up.

Several days later, Muni, who had been mysteriously silent and uncommunicative at home, brought Bella into Manhattan, took her to the lawyer's office, and asked her to sign the document. Suspiciously, she started to leaf through it.

"Don't read it," Muni said. "Just sign, and then it will be notarized and completely settled."

But Bella continued to read it and refused to have anything to do with it. It was heartless and cold-blooded, and who needed it? Muni pleaded with her not to ask questions, but to be a good wife and do what her husband said. She tossed the document down and said, "No."

Then quietly, Muni told her the whole story. He had confirmed the insurance company's diagnosis by going to another doctor. Evidently Muni had suffered rheumatic heart damage as a child. Now insurance was impossible. He wanted this arrangement: it would give him more peace of mind.

"Please, Bella, do as I say."

With tears running down her cheeks, Bella signed.

THE 1922–23 theater year was a season of maturity, uptown and downtown. Art and commerce were being married on Broadway, experimentation and classics were announced on Forty-second Street, and Maurice Schwartz at the Yiddish Art Theatre proclaimed a program of "the highest literary standards."

Broadway promised John Barrymore in *Hamlet*, two Juliets, Ethel Barrymore and Jane Cowl, Jeanne Eagels in *Rain*, John Galsworthy's *Loyalties* (a British view of anti-Semitism), Karel

Muni as David Leizer in _Anathema_.

Capek's experimental _R.U.R_, and Pirandello's _Six Characters in Search of an Author_. The Theatre Guild scheduled Elmer Rice's expressionistic _The Adding Machine_ and a production in English of Sholem Asch's _The God of Vengeance_, transplanted from the Yiddish theater to Broadway. To top the excitement, the world-famous Moscow Art Theatre, with Constantin Stanislavsky himself as a member of the company, was coming to New York for the first time.

The journey uptown, from Fourth to Forty-second, a mere thirty-eight city blocks, often seemed a rougher crossing than the Atlantic. There was no Castle Garden or Ellis Island where officials stamped your papers to let you in or examined your head to see if you had lice. Many performers in the Yiddish theater tried swimming it alone. Others sailed along in the hopeful arks of their companies. And quite a few drowned.

Schwartz scheduled Halper Leivick's _Different_ for the opening of his season at the Garden Theatre, but Muni was not cast in it. Leivick was considered the outstanding literary figure writing in Yiddish at the time. A lot of the audience didn't understand Leivick's symbolistic poetry, but they attended dutifully. They seemed to be waiting for the second play of the season and for "the Weisenfreund."

Revizor, Gogol's savagely comic attack on petty bureaucrats and thievery in government, has often been called "the greatest play ever written in Russia." As *The Inspector General*, it is performed constantly throughout the world, timelier than ever in this era of corruption. Aware of the importance of the play and that critical eyes would be comparing his company to the Moscow Art, Schwartz was astute enough to engage a Russian director, Vladimir Viskowsky.

Muni had studied the role of Ossip, the salty old servant, for the entire summer, but as usual he was terrified. He went to Viskowsky and pleaded to be cast in a smaller, more insignificant part. The director gently urged him to stay on as Ossip. Later, after one of the first public performances, Viskowsky told Muni to learn the Russian language, then he would recommend that the Moscow Art Theatre hire Muni to play Ossip: he had never seen a better performance of it.

When the Moscow Art Theatre came to Broadway, many of its players visited Schwartz's company. Vassily Kachalov, second only to Stanislavsky as director and performer in that famous troupe, told Osherowitch that "Muni could have been one of the finest players in the Moscow Art company."

Muni's opening scene, stretched out on his master's bed, his sagging boots still on, impertinently mimicking his superior's voice and attitudes, totally enchanted the critics and the audience. They even bravoed his boots; they were certain he had been wearing them for sixty years.

His opening line, in Yiddish—"Oh, hell, I'm so hungry, my stomach is making more noise than a whole regimental band" —drew applause. His beady-eyed knavishness delighted them. The photograph of Muni as Ossip, the old servant carrying a trunk on his back, became an unofficial logo, a symbol of the Yiddish theater. "People would say 'wonderful actor,'" Luther Adler remembers. "And they were difficult to impress. There were a lot of good actors around, audiences were used to superb performances, so in order for them to say 'wonderful,' you had to be *super*wonderful!"

Muni didn't take time off to revel in success. He shrugged off compliments and went to work on his next role in *Motke Goniff (Motke the Thief)* by Sholem Asch. Playing the title role frightened him; he was certain he would be the target of virulent attacks this time.

Motke is a congenital thief, unable to stop stealing, who hides out as a clown in a circus, finally reforms and comes home, convinced he is cured. But in order to save his village, he is forced to become a thief once more. The reviews were mildly approving, but the audiences demanded more performances of *Revizor*; consequently *Motke* was not scheduled too often. David Kessler had performed it before, and Muni was unhappy with the role. "I know what they're saying," he complained. "That Weisenfreund isn't as good as Kessler." He felt his Ossip was a more original creation.

Broadway was beginning to hear about this "wonderful actor." When somebody told the management of the forthcoming *Humoresque* by Fannie Hurst that Muni not only was authentically Jewish but also could play the violin, they invited him uptown to meet the star, Laurette Taylor, and her director husband, J. Hartley Manners. The appointment was set for two o'clock one afternoon, and Schwartz was generous enough to excuse Muni from a rehearsal. Muni arrived in the producer's office exactly on the instant. At two ten Miss Taylor and Mr. Manners had not shown up. Muni rose from his seat, told the secretary, "I have great respect for Miss Taylor, but I'm afraid the Manners have no manners." And he walked out.

Humoresque opened the following February at the Vanderbilt Theatre with Lutha J. Adler (he changed it to Luther during the run) as the grown-up boy prodigy. Though he had played many roles in the Yiddish theater, it was the first appearance on the Broadway stage for this brilliant and somehow underapplauded actor. Burns Mantle reported: "The Jews did not think Laurette Taylor was Jewish and the Irish did not admire her for trying to be." *Humoresque* lasted thirty-two performances.

Muni was so absorbed in his next role that he probably didn't even notice. He was scheduled to play David Leizer in Andreyev's *Anathema*. It involved an elaborate makeup, which Muni spent months perfecting. He had an entire greasepaint factory in the attic of the Brighton Beach bungalow. Piety was the keynote of the character, and Muni attempted hair by hair to shape himself into a white-bearded old man who would be the ultimate patriarch—not merely an Old Testament prophet, a Lear, or a crazed John Brown. He was reaching for the childhood concept of the Almighty Himself.

Bella was startled when "God" emerged from the attic.

"Hallelujah!" she shouted.

They decided to test the effectiveness of the transformation on Emma. So they walked over to her cottage, Bella holding the old man's arm as he hobbled along the beach path. Emma, although wise in the ways of the theater, was totally convinced that her visitor was a holy Galician rabbi, newly arrived in America.

Suddenly, Muni did a little jig, whirled Emma's wheelchair around, kissed her on the cheek, and laughed at the success of his characterization.

"Mama Emma," he said joyfully, "I'd rather fool you than the critics!"

The humanity, the humility, the bewilderment of the pious old David Leizer were the convincing elements which captivated the critics, far more than the painstaking makeup. It was Muni's triumph in the Yiddish Theater. Maurice Schwartz was equally brilliant as Anathema, a thinly disguised devil. Bina Abramowitz was Leizer's wife. The play, a highly theatrical variation of the *Faust* legend, begins with an argument in heaven between God and Anathema, a wager in which Anathema boasts he can tempt the most righteous of men. He carries to earth a legacy for the simplehearted old man in a Russian village. This sudden enormous wealth has no meaning for Leizer, except as charity, and he begins to distribute all of it to the poor and the sick. They regard him as a miracle worker, begin to erect monuments to him in the marketplace. Appalled at this sacrilege, Leizer flees to the desert. The money gone, the angry crowd follows him and stones him to death. The triumphant Anathema returns to heaven, boasting he has captured the soul of the pious old man. But he finds David Leizer seated at the right hand of God's throne.

The role was difficult, exhausting, but highly effective. Even the still photographs bear no discernible resemblance to Muni the man. Not yet thirty, Muni played one of the most convincing elders in the history of the theater.

Revolutions were occurring on the Yiddish stage. ("Do you suppose," somebody once asked, "that we can reduce the acts of a play from five to four and possibly let the audience go home before midnight?" "Sure," an expert answered, "but you'll go broke!") One of Schwartz's innovations was the elimination of flamboyant curtain calls after each scene, which had been the custom in the manner of grand opera. A note in the program of *Anathema* cautions theatergoers about this startling change:

> The audience is respectfully requested not to destroy the illusion
> of the play by curtain calls until the end of the performance.
> If called upon after the epilogue, the company will deem it an
> honor to respond.

But the program still contained elaborate descriptions of each character:

DAVID LEIZER . . . a poor sick Jew, who wanders eternally by the seashore, seeking from the waves an answer to the question of human destiny. Tenderness toward little children and compassion for the world's unfortunate rule his heart.

(Muni's lifetime could be described in the same words: he was constantly heading for the sea, he had a great affinity for children, and he never wanted to perform a work which did not contain some compassion for humanity.)

Muni was next cast as Koppel, the meek, almost silent little tailor in Sholom Aleichem's *Das Grosse Gevin (The Big Lottery)*. Koppel was a total transformation from David Leizer, and Muni often played the two parts at alternate performances, sometimes one at a matinee and the other at night. As Koppel, he was praised for "the profundity of his silence." Schwartz played the owner of the tailor shop who wins 200,000 rubles in a lottery. The almost serflike tailors in his employ are given the tailor shop as a gift while the new "rich man" eats rich goose, buys himself golden chairs and expensive clothes. In the final scene, they discover a mistake has been made: the winnings were 20 rubles, not 200,000—and the old boss has to come begging to his former near slaves for a tiny piece of herring. Muni accomplished his role almost entirely with his eyes and the shrugging of his shoulders. And he made the knotting of a handkerchief into a small masterpiece of stage business.

More and more Yiddish actors were moving uptown to the greener pastures of Broadway. Rudolph Schildkraut starred in and staged *God of Vengeance*. Sam Jaffe, also in the cast, recalls they were closed by the police, not because of the play's brothel theme, but because of one line: "Cut his bowels out!" which the censor-driven police thought was "Cut his balls out!"

Muni attended as many productions as possible of the visiting Moscow Art Theatre, which played a repertoire of Gorky, Chekhov, and Turgenev at the Fifty-ninth Street Theatre in January and February, 1923. But Muni never met Stanislavsky; he was literally too shy to go backstage. (Later Maria Ouspenskaya and Akim Tamiroff of that company left Russia and migrated to Hollywood.)

Was Muni a "Method" actor? "What method?" he always used to ask. But he admitted being tremendously influenced by Schildkraut, by the convincingly naturalistic theater of Stanislavsky and the Moscow Art troupe, and later by Max Reinhardt. Lee Strasberg, the guru of the Actors Studio, says that Muni probably "prepared beforehand" more thoroughly than any actor in American stage history.

"Whatever he did," Strasberg says, "he needed a mask; he

needed the sense of being somebody else, in order to be himself. He was a real character actor. And to characterize, he used what every good actor uses: some kind of imaginative stimulus that often is fed by things that are highly personal. Sometimes he's not even aware of it, as writers are not necessarily aware of it, but it feeds them, gives flesh and substance to what they do on-stage. Muni had a sound, respectable sense of responsibility to his craft and to his art—he never just swept it off the cuff. He was careful, detailed, painstaking in his *preparation*."

For his own part, Muni disdained any set or pet theory of acting. "The only way to learn to ride a bicycle," he said, "is to get on and ride it. You'll never learn by reading a book or having some-body tell you about it. You know how to roller-skate, don't you? Well, if somebody asks you, 'How do you do it?'—what's your answer? Who knows? Practice, I guess. But if you try to think about what you're doing *while* you're actually rolling along the sidewalk, if you look down at the wheels and try to figure out how you're managing it, you'll fall right on your ass!"

In later years, young Method-mad acting students who managed to get a word with him, always purred: "Mr. Muni, tell us! What is *your* method?"

"Well, I'll tell you," he'd drawl. "My wife's grandmother used to bake the best apple pie in the world. And people were always asking her, 'Grandma Thomashefsky, how do you do it? What's your recipe?' Grandma would think, nod her head and say, 'Well, I get up in the morning, I wash my hands, put on my apron, and I bake apple pie.' Well, it's the same way with me. I go to the theater, I put on my makeup, I go out on stage, and I act!"

In April, 1923, Maurice Schwartz (spelling his name *Swartz*) made the journey uptown, presenting at the Forty-eighth Street Theatre two plays in English: *Anathema* and *The Inspector General*. Ossip in the latter and David Leizer in the former had been Muni's most resounding successes, but Schwartz left Muni downtown at the Yiddish Art Theatre. In the uptown *Anathema*, Schwartz switched roles again and played the part of David Leizer himself, realizing that despite the title, it was the choice role, at least the way Muni portrayed it. For the record, *Anathema* ran fifteen per-formances uptown and *Inspector General* eight.

Schwartz did not rehire Muni for the 1923–24 season.

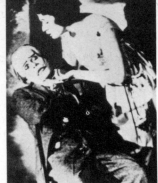

Muni as Kyril Pyatak, the philosophic drunk of *Moshke Chasser (Morris the Pig)*.

Muni as an old roué in *One Day in May* **(alias** *Maytime***) with the beautiful Berta Gersten.**

Bella Finkel as a chorus girl.

Muni as Shnell, the fast-talking publicity man of *Ven Starpt Er? (When Will He Die?)*.

11

IN the summer of 1923 Muni became an American citizen. Bella, born in Philadelphia, didn't have to go through the rigmarole of first papers, second papers, and finally naturalization. Oral tests had to be passed, but Muni wasn't worried. He had been reading omnivorously, especially American history. He was fascinated by Abraham Lincoln and collected every book he could find on the Great Emancipator.

"Don't ask Munya how to add two and three," Bella often said. "He couldn't pass third-grade arithmetic. But he knows American history like a college professor."

Muni played his final naturalization ceremony as if it were a scene from a play. He started out slightly bent over and spoke in a halting and heavy *mittel-Europa* accent, squinting his eyes as if he didn't quite understand each question. Bella was seated in the front row at the federal courthouse, watching and listening fascinated, knowing how Muni loved to play games. During the quizzing, Muni began to straighten up and gradually lost his accent. The startled judge heard his final answer in impeccable English.

Muni smiled. "Your Honor, it's remarkable. Now that you've made me a citizen, I can speak perfectly!"

Bella applauded. Muni raised his right hand, took the oath, and became a citizen of the United States.

Muni didn't sign with any particular Yiddish theater company that fall, though he had many offers. He agreed to appear at Samuel Goldenberg's Cooperative Irving Place Theatre. Goldenberg, an excellent actor-singer, varied his schedule between *shund* and theater literature; one night he would present an appalling melodrama and the next night a work of sensitivity and power. "Half art, half crap," one actor noted. Goldenberg, who also played the piano, liked to interpolate pyrotechnic keyboard solos in the midst of highly dramatic scenes: one even took place during a scene in a graveyard, where the piano was hidden behind the tombstones; the actor-manager seemed to be picking macabre melodies out of the graves. Muni considered his stint there merely "a way to make a buck."

Schwartz had returned to the Garden Theatre from his fiasco on Broadway, complaining so all could hear, "The whole trouble was that a British, not a Yiddish, actor played the title role of Anathema. If Weisenfreund and I had played our original roles, it would have been a triumph." But Schwartz never told anybody why he hadn't invited Muni to make the trip uptown with him.

During that time Muni was busy playing all of Schwartz's roles downtown. So he wasn't even aware that on March 12, 1923, a play by Sacha Guitry had opened uptown at the famous Empire Theatre, adapted for the English stage by Arthur Hornblow, Jr., produced by Charles Frohman. It was called *Pasteur*, it starred Henry Miller in the title role, and it lasted sixteen performances.

With Goldenberg's company, Muni played a grizzled old hermit in *The Holy Tyrant*, a man who retreated from the world to help the poor and the suffering. Simultaneously, Goldenberg produced *Die Hopt Sach* (*The Chief Thing*) by Nickolai Evreinov, in which Muni played a broken-down comedian who was pretending to be a doctor. In this minor role, Muni stole the show. Bella was also in the cast.

The play, most of which takes place in a boardinghouse, is thematically not unlike *The Passing of the Third Floor Back* and is a heady mixture of comedy and drama, with mystic and philosophic overtones. Muni's big moment comes when he must reveal himself: "I am not a doctor, I am a comedian!" which brought both laughter and tears from the audience. The critics singled out Muni for his outstanding performance. Three years later the Theatre Guild presented the play in English uptown, with a cast which included Edward G. Robinson, Estelle Winwood, Edith Meiser, Henry Travers, Harold Clurman (as an actor), Lee Strasberg, Romney Brent, Kate Lawson, McKay Morris, and Helen Westley. But Ernest Cossart, the actor who played the comedian-doctor, went unnoticed and was not even mentioned in a single review.

Muni, without knowing how he did it, *commanded* an audience's attention: with his face, his manner, his presence.

Two other plays with Goldenberg were not as soul-satisfying. In both, Muni played doctors, which he was to do often in his later film career. Zolotorewsky's *The Spider and the Fly* was, Muni said, "a play, if you'd call it a play, which I'd rather forget." *Shver Ungelt (Bad to Be Without Money)* is described by Jacob Ben-Ami as "a play Muni did so that *he* wouldn't be without money."

Actress Henrietta Jacobson (who recalls her mother chasing her brother Hymie and Muni around a Chicago playground with a baseball bat years before—for letting Henrietta, age three, mess in her pants, while Muni was hitting a home run) tells of Muni's constant backstage kidding. Muni told an uppity actress, Stella Gold, "You know what Shakespeare said, Stella? 'Screw 'em all!' " "I'll try my best," Stella answered with great dignity. Miss Gold bragged that she had read "absolutely every book I can get my hands on." "Oh?" Muni commented. "How about that great classic, *Chayam Putz* [Muni's made-up title, meaning "huge penis"]? Have you read that one, Stella?" "Sure," she boasted. "A hundred times!"

Midseason, Maurice Schwartz planned a triumphant tour of Europe and invited Muni and Bella to rejoin his company. Despite previous arm's-length coolness between the two actors, Muni was happy to climb out of his intermittent *shund* experience.

The entire Yiddish Art Theatre troupe sailed for Europe on the SS *George Washington* in April, 1924, prepared to storm the theatrical ramparts of London, Paris, and Vienna. It was Muni's first trip back to the "old country."

Actor Morris Strassberg, a member of the troupe, kept a scrapbook filled with antic snapshots of the company on the high seas in what was apparently a smooth and joyful crossing. Muni, with a cap tilted rakishly on his head, keeps poking his face into photographs and was the clown prince of the trip, ordering food with a different accent at each meal and generally keeping the troupe in constant laughter.

Schwartz seems to have been equally genial, promising reforms and goodness and light, swearing that Europe would see a company celebrated for its ensemble playing, with everybody getting equal billing. They rehearsed every afternoon in the Grand Salon. Muni went up to Schwartz one sunny afternoon on deck and shook his hand. "I want to apologize. I have been thinking of you as the son of a bitch. But *I'm* the bastard. I'm the pain in the ass." Grandiloquently, they bowed to each other.

They arrived in London, scheduled to play not in the remote ghetto of Whitechapel, but in the elegant West End, at the Scala Theatre. Schwartz's inflated promises of equality were punctured when the company saw the theater marquee and the billboards: MAURICE SCHWARTZ AND COMPANY. The tiny houseboards listed the names of the cast in very small letters, alphabetically, with Weisenfreund at the very bottom. "Down there where the dogs pee on it," Muni remarked. In New York, the Hebrew letter *vov* is sixth in the alphabet. "But here," Schwartz explained limply, "Weisenfreund begins with an English *W*, not a Yiddish *V*. In England, we must do things in the English manner."

"Listen," Muni retorted, "I spoke English before I spoke American! And I take back what I said on the ship. It was the *George Washington*, I'm a citizen now, and I cannot tell a lie!"

Despite the conflicts, the company opened at the Scala in London on April 18, 1924, with *Sabbethai Zvi*, author unlisted, a play based on an apocryphal messiah of the seventeenth century. Schwartz played the title role, and Muni was Nehamia Kohn, a believing peasant who becomes disillusioned. Muni also played a bit in *The Dybbuk*; though a classic of the Yiddish theater, Muni was never fond of this play: he found the mysticism murky and the Yiddish Art Theatre production lacking either humanity or the alleviating grace of humor.

In Andreyev's *Seven Who Were Hanged* Muni played a general whose son is about to be executed. At the start of the third act in a dimly lit scene in a dungeon, only a long low bench was visible in the murky shadows. Seated were characters portrayed by Muni, Bella, and Lazar Fried. The "artistic" lighting was arranged so that when Schwartz entered and sat at the end of the bench, a key spotlight faded in subtly, suffusing his face, while the others still remained in shadows. This annoyed Muni, so at each performance, just before the third act curtain went up, he moved the bench ever so slightly; when the pinspot bloomed, it hit Bella's face or Fried's or an empty spot on the stage floor. When the scene was over, the infuriated Schwartz raised hell with the stage manager.

"Believe me, Mr. Schwartz," the stage manager said. "I measured it. The bench is precisely on the marks on the floor. I'm absolutely positive."

Schwartz fumed. His art was being sabotaged! He finally realized the practical joke being played on him. Muni, disillusioned by "art" in the theater, asked for his release and got it; naturally Bella went with him. After London, Schwartz and company moved on to Paris and Vienna. Bella and Muni, with their return tickets dated six weeks off, decided to take a European vacation. In Vienna the Schwartz company, without Muni, made a silent film with Yiddish titles: *Thou Shall Remember*. Nothing much ever happened to it. In fact, Muni never made a silent film, but if he had been in this one, it would have been a collector's item.

Bella and Muni had a joyful holiday. In Basle, Switzerland, they sat at an outdoor café, drinking beer. "Munya was so happy to be free (always an obsession with him)," Bella remembered, "that he cried."

Their next stop was Paris. They drank champagne, stuffed themselves with French food, and danced in the streets. It felt as if it were their first honeymoon.

The trip home on the SS *Champlain* wasn't as much fun. There were no jokes, no clowning. Muni and Bella kept to themselves. Schwartz never spoke to him once during the entire crossing.

Muni felt bitter and disgusted. He seriously talked to Bella about taking up a "respectable trade," starting a candy store or going into the cloak-and-suit business. Bella listened and nodded and let him get it out of his system.

Back in New York, Muni was startled and disbelieving when a messenger brought him an offer from Schwartz to sign a contract for the 1924–25 season. Other actors in the company, whom Muni respected, urged him to accept.

He looked quizzically to Bella. Should he sign? Bella's shrug never meant "yes" or "no"; it was a more eloquent "why not?" Slowly she was becoming the decision maker in the family; perhaps Muni wanted somebody to blame for his mistakes. The three new scripts which arrived with the contract offer had parts which tantalized Muni; all had dimensions he had never played before. Bella also read them, and her "why not?" turned into an "absolutely."

"I'm an actor," Muni said. "I don't know how to do anything else but act. I accept."

The season opened with Schwartz's moneymaking production of *The Dybbuk*. Muni played merely a walk-on as a messenger. He was delighted to have this breathing time for more careful preparation of the three plum parts ahead.

I. D. Berkowitz's *Moshke Chasser* (loosely translated as *Morris the Pig* or *Morris the Swine*, though *Chasser* has fringe meanings of "slob," "messiness," far beyond any literal translation) opened in New York on September 29, 1924. In it Muni had the opportunity to create a role which pleased his creative soul: the drunken philosophic bum Kyril Pyatak, who drinks to blind himself to the meanness in the world. Muni played no ordinary drunk. Critics remarked that it was the first stage drunk they had ever seen who made you understand why the man obliterated himself with liquor. Constantly fantasizing, alternately sarcastic and warm, he was a stage ancestor to Elwood P. Dowd of *Harvey*.

Less than a month later, on October 21, Chone Gottesfeld's *Ven Starpt Er?* (*When Will He Die?*) was added to the repertoire. It was a joy and a lark for Muni to play Shnell, a fast-talking, wisecracking theatrical publicity man. The often hilarious backstage plot concerned a play which was dying at the box office. Shnell has the brilliant idea that if the author (played by Schwartz) were to die, the play would prosper, since audiences have greater respect for a deceased playwright than for a live dramatist-next-door. So they convince the author to feign death, funeral and all. Muni couldn't help remembering his first exposure in theater. *When Will He Die?* had overtones of *Two Corpses at Breakfast*. Schwartz as the body in the coffin, swatting away flies, sneezing, and rising to make pointed comments on his own eulogy, reminded Muni of his parents in similar antics at the Perry Theatre in Cleveland.

Satirizing the plethora of plays by every housewife and pants presser on the Lower East Side, Gottesfeld included a telling cameo

Maurice Schwartz and Muni Weisenfreund in Romain Rolland's *Wolves*.

of a butcher, played by Morris Strassberg, who comes to the management to announce portentously that he has "WRITTEN A PLAY!" "Is it a good play?" the butcher is asked. "Of course it's a good play," the butcher answers indignantly. "Everybody dies in the second act!"

Abe Cahan and other critics praised the work beyond its worth primarily because the playwright, Gottesfeld, was a fellow Yiddish newspaperman. But for Muni it was a romp.

Six days after the opening, the Yiddish Art Theatre itself died temporarily. The Hebrew Actors Union called a strike, demanding payment for some undelivered wages for the European trip. Muni joined the walkout in sympathy, though he was not personally involved in the controversy. Schwartz tried to protest that the actors making the claims were no longer with his company; but he finally paid up, and the season continued. The Yiddish community felt that actors striking were behaving as immorally as if firemen or schoolteachers or doctors would go on strike. The bread of life was being taken out of their mouths.

The literary highlight of the season, planned for a December 4, 1924, opening, was Romain Rolland's *Wolves*, a high-minded social drama, fervent in its plea for justice and the rights of man. As a production it was the most elegant and unusual of the Yiddish Art Theatre's history. Muni, accustomed to playing simple and earthy peasants, found a challenge in the role of the powdered, coiffed, and snuffbox-proud Du Arun. Muni had never played drawing-room comedy, and he was a stranger to aristocratic elegance. He had to construct an entire epoch in his mind in order to crawl inside the skin of this French dandy. He tried to find by posture and gesture a way to express the rigidity of militarism and the proud disdain "as if considering everything in the world except himself smelled slightly rancid."

During rehearsals, Schwartz was all over the place, directing, shouting, playing every part, Muni remembered, "including the stagehands." There were no women's roles, but Schwartz had in his company most of the best male actors then alive in the Yiddish theater.

Halfway through rehearsal, Schwartz had what he considered a brilliant notion: Du Arun would be played entirely facing *up*stage. Symbolically, he explained, this would show the audience the progressive forward face of tomorrow with the French revolutionists, while the decadent aristocracy, on its way out, would be backward, retreating. At first Muni was appalled at the idea. How could he play a role when the audience never saw his eyes? He boiled inside, certain he was being tossed to the wolves by a jealous and vindictive actor-manager seeking revenge for the sliding bench in London.

Ted Thomas remembers Muni's grappling with the problem in the brief respites between rehearsals, as he paced along the boardwalk at Brighton Beach. The opening scene of the play was set in a sidewalk café, and the curtain was to rise, according to Schwartz's direction, with Muni's back to the audience. Muni leaped around the boardwalk, the problem tossing in his mind like the flying clubs of a juggler. Muni suddenly sat down on a bench and turned his back on Thomas.

"Watch! I'll sit this way, and then I'll sit that way, and I'll arch my back, stiffening it when one of the scum passes in front of me."

And he slapped the seat of the bench.

"By God, I'll do it, Teddy! I'll keep my back to the audience during the whole goddamn play, and I'll take it away from him anyhow!"

The production was done with bravado and panoply. The climactic scene involved Schwartz as the revolutionary leader ripping the epaulets off Muni as the military aristocrat, taking away his sword, and ordering him to the guillotine. "Swine!" he spat, in a moment nobody who saw it has ever forgotten. "You swine!"

Muni's back stiffened, quivered, his head shot up in arrogant defiance, refusing to plead for mercy. And he never faced front, even in the curtain call.

The critics raved.

After Muni left the company (according to an undocumented rumor), Schwartz tried the part of Du Arun himself, playing it with his back to the audience. The comment along Second Avenue was: "What's-a-matter? Schwartz has a pimple on his face, he doesn't want us to see it?"

Muni did quit this time, rather than waiting to be fired and then rehired the next season. "Acting is difficult enough without living your entire life on a seesaw," Muni said. In March, 1925, Schwartz ended the season with Goldfaden's *The Witch* and assigned Muni the role of Bubba Yachneh, the old crone traditionally played by a man.

"I've done it," Muni said, refusing the part. "I was an old lady years and years ago, when I was still a kid. Why should I do it again? My God, the whole Yiddish theater is right back where it began. Where can we find Madame Krantzfeld?"

Schwartz had grandiose plans for the 1925–26 season. He announced a move uptown to the Nora Bayes Theatre within the precincts of Times Square and the glamor of Broadway itself.

The season was to open with an exciting new Yiddish play by a most talented new playwright: *Shakespeare & Company* by M. Charnoff. When Muni found out that M. Charnoff was really Maurice Schwartz, he decided it was definitely curtaintime for him at the Yiddish Art Theatre.

In retrospect, through the years, Muni always praised Schwartz, expressing his gratitude for the variety of parts he was able to play. "Schwartz was daring on many occasions, there was always something new and different, an adventure, a challenge. Most of all, he trouped; he helped to promote theater. Sometimes working with him was a struggle. But he was an artist. Schwartz had only one incurable disease: he was an actor!"

Muni needed a job for the next season, so he went to work for Max Gabel at the People's Theatre. Gabel, who had married the popular Second Avenue actress Jennie Goldstein when she was sixteen, had written 114 plays, mostly for his wife and himself. The 1925–26 season opened with *Vas Vill Menchen Zugen? (What Will People Say?)*. "The answer to that question," the wags noted at the Café Royale, "is that Weisenfreund is playing *shund* again."

Gabel was a theater hack, a hammy actor, and, though past fifty, was still playing juveniles. Muni, facing thirty, played the old father. "I'm thirty years old," Muni noted, "going on a hundred."

Muni felt as disillusioned as he had been in Philadelphia. What was the use of being in New York when you felt as unartistic and unfulfilled as when you fiddled in a cheap burlesque house?

He switched theaters and signed a contract with Nathan Goldberg to play a series of operettas at the National Theatre. Bella was in the company: at least they'd be working together. Muni was a comic grandfather in his first assignment there: William Siegel's *The Garden of Love*. When I asked Jacob Ben-Ami what it was like, Ben-Ami replied, "William Siegel was the world's worst playwright. Don't even ask about him. As a writer, you shouldn't even know about him—it might be contagious!"

The role was wafer-thin. Despite a newly shaped beard (Muni tried a different one for every role), he was desperately unhappy.

"A difficult part is much easier than an easy part," Muni said. "You can climb inside the fortress of a great character; it's almost impossible to cloak yourself with toilet paper!"

At home, Muni had nobody to play but Muni, and he was not fond of the character. With nothing else but himself to think about, Muni began to be overly concerned for the first time with his heart, with the fear of sudden and unannounced death. Bella babied him and slowly, almost unconsciously, began to turn into a mother hen. Muni did not resist.

For five years their married life had been totally theatrical: comic, tragic, hits, flops, high romance with violins playing in a moon-blue spotlight, or bungled cues and missing props. Years later Bella told Ellen Siegel Perkiss about their delayed wedding night: the first time they'd had a chance to sleep in the same room and the same bed together had been a week after the ceremony. Bella was frightened, but Muni was more frightened. He spent half the night standing by an open window singing "The Skater's Waltz," clowning to cover his embarrassment.

"Sex is for whores," Muni said. "Does a fine lady do anything like that?"

"Somebody," Bella said quietly, "should ask the lady."

12

Muni was playing an inspired bit of a doddering old waiter in Sigmund Romberg's *The Student Prince* (Yiddish edition) at the downtown National when he was finally "discovered" by uptown Broadway. Even then it was a fluke.

Acting buffs flocked to see what a "genius could do with a walk-on." He had two pieces of business, invented but appropriate, which were Chaplin-esque, Muni-esque. Carrying a tray, he would suddenly look down at the polished parquet floor as if to say, "What am I doing here? I'll soil it, break it," and he would begin to tiptoe, watching the floor with awe and respect, as if trying to walk on it without touching it with his feet.

Later, sitting in a chair was an exquisite exercise. Slowly, slowly he would settle into it, and his face lit up when his rear end hit the bottom of the seat. When a *zoftig* waitress came and sat

Left: Mr. and Mrs. Muni Weisenfreund the day Muni became an American citizen, 1923. Right: Muni's final role in the Yiddish theater: the doddering old waiter, surrounded by military cadets, in *The Student Prince*.

(Inscribed to Bella's mother.)   *(Photo by Rappaport)*

on his lap, he looked delirious with joy. But only for a moment. Suddenly his lap would go, collapse, disappear from the weight of the pretty lady. Muni would look around as if he had dropped his lap and couldn't find it. "Where did it go?" And he would stare accusingly at the audience: somebody out there had stolen his lap from him! That one piece of business drew Yiddish cheers.

In his offices above the Music Box Theatre on West Forty-fifth Street, Producer Sam H. Harris was having a problem. *We Americans*, a play by William Herbert Gropper and Max Siegel, scheduled for Broadway, was doing well on the fringes of New York at the Bronx Opera House and down in Atlantic City. But a still unfamous Edward G. Robinson, playing the key role of the old father, had a previous commitment to the Theatre Guild (how irrationally coincidental the theater is!) to play in Franz Werfel's *Juarez and Maximilian*, scheduled to open in New York on October 11, 1926. *We Americans* was announced for the following night.

Morris Strassberg, who had moved uptown to be part of the *We Americans* company, had never forgotten Muni's convincing old men from their days together in the Yiddish Art Theatre. He urged Harris to have a look at Weisenfreund, the sensation of the Yiddish Rialto.* Albert Lewis of the Harris office and playwright Siegel and his bride, Pauline, made the fortuitous trip to the tip of Second Avenue and joined in the cheering. They kept poking each other during the performance: the old man was perfect for their play.

Afterward, they went backstage and knocked on Muni's dressing room door. They were startled when a very young man, his makeup already off, answered the door.

"Oh, excuse us," Siegel said. "We've made a mistake. We're looking for Mr. Weisenfreund."

Muni asssured him he was the genuine article, and they were astonished. They invited him to come to the Music Box offices the following day to meet producer Harris and the play's director, Sam Forrest. Muni told them he was under contract to Nathan Goldberg for the entire season, but they urged him to come nevertheless.

Fortunately they didn't keep him waiting. Sam Harris looked up at the youthful Muni when he walked in and immediately dismissed him with a peremptory wave.

*In Edward G. Robinson's autobiography, *All My Yesterdays* (with Leonard Spigelgass), he gives Clara Langsner credit for the suggestion of Muni. A single-spaced list of people who claim to have "discovered Muni" would take up the rest of this book.

"Too young. Are you out of your minds? He's just a kid!"

Muni turned to leave the room. Siegel put up his hand to stop him. Muni looked back at Sam Harris; then he bent over and tottered toward the producer's desk. He wore no makeup, but his voice seemed as wise and ancient as time.

"Oh, sir, you're right. We old bastards shouldn't let any of those young punks into the theater. What do they know—still wet in the diapers, still shitting their pants?"

Harris looked up, laughed, then glanced over at the equally startled director. Forrest, who hadn't said a word, now said just two: "Sign him."

Harris glanced at the co-author.

"You want him, Max?"

"Very much. I think he'll be a sensation."

They called in their publicity man, a kid named Sidney Skolsky. Then Harris and Lewis contacted Nathan Goldberg, who was generous enough to release Muni from his contract at the downtown National.

Muni said, "Wait a minute. Maybe I won't like the play."

Then he looked at the suddenly crestfallen Siegel.

"I take that back. If you wrote it, I think I'll like it."

It was the beginning of a friendship which lasted the rest of their lives. Rehearsals were scheduled for the following Monday at the roof theater of the New Amsterdam on Forty-second Street. Muni was handed a script. He touched it gingerly. Then he rocked it like a baby, and everybody laughed. He was thirty-one years old, he had worked in the Yiddish theater for eighteen years in more than 300 different parts, and finally he was about to make his debut on the English-speaking stage.

Young actors of today, impatient that they are not stars by the time they can vote, can take a lesson in patience and perseverance from Muni, who never appeared on Broadway until he was around the bend of thirty.

The Yiddish theater community congratulated him but sensed a loss they would never regain. Milton Danley wrote in the *Forward*:

> Weisenfreund did not leave the Yiddish stage because of any
> monetary considerations. Nor has the fame which Broadway can
> offer tempted him. It was the wide opportunities, the chance
> to play that lured him. Weisenfreund is an actor, first and last.
> On the Yiddish stage, his scope is naturally limited. Here, if
> you are not a star-manager, you have to limit yourself to roles
> offered by the director who is susceptible to whims and caprices.

But the death knell had already tolled for the golden age of the Yiddish theater, and Muni knew it. With the passage of the Johnson Immigration Act in 1921, which cut off Yiddish-speaking audiences streaming in from Eastern Europe, the "fountain" stopped flowing. Appropriately enough, *We Americans* dramatized the growing up and the breaking away of the new generation from the near ghetto of New York's Lower East Side.

It was graduation day for Muni, but he never denied or regretted his schooling, his background, the rich opportunity to "practice and prepare" which he found in the Yiddish theater. There were many things about his childhood Muni wanted to forget, but never his debt to the Yiddish stage. Many performers, who went through the sea change of name and nose and nationality, ultimately abandoned any connection or association with their Jewishness. But never Muni.

Sam Harris was concerned about Muni's last name. "The audiences like to pronounce actors' names. They say 'Barrymore,' it can't be anything else but Barrymore. They say 'Fred Stone,' it doesn't sound like Izzy Lipshitz. But with your name, they won't know if it's 'Wize' or 'Weeze,' 'Froynd' or 'Froond.' Why not just simplify it to Wisenfrend? Then everybody will know it's just like a wise friend. Very good for the part."

"More wizened friend," Muni suggested.

"It's better for publicity, for the ads, for the billboards," Harris said.

"Sure, why not?" Muni shrugged. "What's in a name? A ham by any other name would still be as unkosher."

"Oh, we're not trying to say you're not Jewish," Harris said quickly. "The part is definitely a Jew."

Muni smiled. "Don't worry, Mr. Harris. The last time I looked I was still circumcised."

The first day of rehearsal, going up to the roof of the New Amsterdam Theatre in the tiny elevator, Muni was more frightened than he had ever been in his life. Bella was with him, and she took his hand: it was clammy cold.

"Shah, shah!" Bella said, trying to calm him down.

Muni gestured with his head toward the girl operating the elevator.

"Tell her to stop, reverse, take it down. I don't belong here. We'll go back downtown. We'll buy out Krantzfeld and operate the soda stand!"

"Nerves," Bella said, "are the sign of a professional. If you didn't care, you'd be a goddamn amateur."

Muni kissed her on the cheek and then pretended to try to bite the ear of the unaware elevator operator, facing front. Bella and Muni laughed, and the elevator reached the top floor.

Muni was sure all the other actors would hate him: he was an outsider, a beginner, an interloper; they had all been together, they knew their parts, he was the "greenhorn." But the director, Sam Forrest, was a teddy bear of a man, and the cast greeted Muni warmly. A few were old friends: Luther Adler, Clara Langsner, Morris Strassberg, all alumni of the Yiddish stage.

Playwright Sylvia Regan, who later wrote *The Fifth Season* and many other Broadway plays, was an actress then; her name was Sylvia Hoffman, she was seventeen, and she played the Rumanian girl in the night-school sequence. She recalls that first day of rehearsal vividly:

"We had Eddie Robinson in the show originally, and when we were called into rehearsal in the fall this gorgeous young man arrived. We didn't know him from the Yiddish theater. Ethel Henin, another young girl in the company, and I looked at this man and we thought he was going to be the new schoolteacher. Then we found out he was going to be the father, and we were terribly disturbed, and we kept whispering to each other. When Eddie was doing it, even though he was still young, he had that craggy look of a character actor, so that even without the beard he seemed right for the part. But within a day or two we realized that this handsome young man was suddenly hunching over and didn't need the beard. He *was* the guy. We both had a terrible crush on him."

Forrest, lumbering and white-haired, was easy and fatherly in his approach, and Muni tried to relax.

We Americans had its genesis in a vaudeville sketch by Max Siegel, chronicling the mishaps, malapropisms, and language hurdles of a polyglot bunch of night-school students. It was the precursor of *The Education of H*y*m*a*n K*a*p*l*a*n* by Leonard Q. Ross (Leo Rosten). As a full evening's play, Sam Harris felt it needed an experienced playwright, so Milton Herbert Gropper, the author of *Ladies of the Evening,* was called in as a collaborator. The Act Two night-school scene remained the play's highlight.

Hair by hair in his makeup, moment by moment and word by word in his interpretation, Muni transformed himself totally into the skin and soul of Morris Levine. Fashions in writing have changed, and no writer today would set down the seeming-burlesque dialect bits, not only for the Jewish players, but for the black, Irish, Italian, and even the Rumanian characters. Muni, for example, had to say:

LEVINE: Ei, ei, America! Children! In de old country de parents vas alvays right. Over here even ven dey're right, dey're wrong.

On the printed page of a playscript this might seem like part of a vaudeville routine. But the warmth of Muni's playing, the truth of his comedy, saved it from the standard stereotype. He wasn't playing every immigrant father: he was Morris Levine, an original, one of a kind.

Muni's personal sense of humor (and his onstage equivalent) was the put-down, the self-deprecating quality he found in the great men he admired: Lincoln, Einstein, and, many years later, John Kennedy. Perhaps it comes from a kind of awe at one's own powers—and a disbelief in them. Muni never played sophisticated drawing-room comedy, never indulged onstage or off in the cruelty of insulting others. In effect, it was always a mild self-insult: "I ain't so much. Spit on me. I'm ugly." It wasn't masochistic as much as "Let's not tempt the gods with too much self-praise."

Consciously or subconsciously, he had absorbed the commonman, folk quality of the Tevyas, the Koppels, the Leizers of the Yiddish stage. The *nebich*, the *shlemihl*, the *shmendrick*, the *nudnick* of Yiddish comedy tradition found inheritors in Chaplin, Keaton, Harold Lloyd, Stan Laurel, and later in Bert Lahr, Jack Benny, Red Skelton. Muni's impact as a serious actor has obscured the memory of his comedy genius.

Coupled with this (and Muni never analyzed it) was his uncanny skill at exposing a character's vulnerability. Perhaps he learned this from his father when he had tried to humanize the usually inhuman Papus in *Bar-Kochba*. There were always hints of humanity in Muni's characters, not only in villains, but in heroes: uncover some fallibility and you do not diminish your man; you turn him from a marble statue into a breathing human being.

Muni's quality of restrained indignation has often been noted through the years: great power of anger, near violence—reined-in, under control. He used sudden flare-ups of temperament not lethally, but to puncture pomposity, not to stop a human heart but to let the hot air out of overinflated balloons.

If somebody had told Muni that he was skillfully combining his dual capacity to play comedy and near tragedy in *We Americans,* he would have said, "What are you talking about? Shut up already. Tell me what I'm doing and I won't be able to do it anymore. I'll fall off the roller skates!"

The other members of the cast were amazed at his hard work. He was in his dressing room long before the others arrived, and after rehearsals were over, cleaning women and stage doormen, wanting to get home to the Bronx or New Jersey, had to kick

110

him out of the theater when only Muni and the spiders remained.

Ailsa Lawson, who played Muni's rebellious daughter in the play, was the young wife of the fabulously successful operetta composer Rudolph Friml. He had three shows running simultaneously on Broadway, including a revival of *Rose Marie*. Mrs. Friml would turn up at rehearsals in elegant basic black, wearing diamond rings that seemed the size of ostrich eggs. Muni would joke with her.

"How many operettas did your husband write this week: five, ten, a baker's dozen?"

The night-school teacher in the play was Charles Ellis, who in private life was married to Edna St. Vincent Millay's sister. Herbert Polesie, who played the bit part of a greenhorn, was later a stage and film director. Muni was concerned about Clara Langsner as his wife. She seems to have brought from the Yiddish theater too much overt sentimentality. She was a "crier," and Muni couldn't stand "that dripping emotion business." Muni and Luther Adler, who played his son, used to kid about it.

"You'd say hello to Clara and the tears would fly," Adler remembers. "She literally *drowned* the stage in tears!"

"Did you ever see anyone cry like that?" Muni said to Adler, "My God, she cries at the drop of a good morning!"

The director tried to restrain her tendency to weep buckets. Once Forrest called out to her from the dark of the rehearsal theater, "Mrs. Langsner, you sound as if you're feeling sorry for yourself. Please keep in mind that if you do that, the audience won't!"

The company went out of town to Philadelphia and had a mild reception at the Garrick Theatre. Muni visited none of his old haunts, sticking to his hotel room with Bella, having his meals sent up, never fraternizing with the other actors, concentrating totally, onstage and off, on his first Broadway part. But Muni was discouraged; they were playing to half-empty houses.

We Americans opened at the Sam H. Harris Theatre, 226 West Forty-second Street, on October 12, 1926. At the end of Act Two Clara Langsner as Mrs. Levine read Lincoln's Gettysburg Address. During the final moments of Act Three Sam Mann as Mr. Goldberg recited Patrick Henry's "Give me liberty or give me death." But nobody who saw it remembers the actors speaking the lines. All attention was focused on a watching, listening, feeling Morris Levine, *re*acting. It was Muni living the title of the play, discarding the Old World and the old ways, without speaking a word. It was the birth of a new American.

The audience and critics cheered Muni's performance. One critic was indignant: "What an outrage that this old man should have spent a lifetime waiting for a chance to appear on Broadway."

The New York *Times* sent a third-stringer, whose approving review was unsigned. Two other shows opened that same night, and the top *Times* critic, J. Brooks Atkinson, was not on hand to welcome Muni to Broadway: he was covering an instantly forgettable Kern-Harbach musical, *Criss Cross*, starring Fred Stone as Christopher Cross, along with the whole Stone family and the Tiller Sunshine Dancing Girls.

Skolsky placed two large photographs in the lobby of the Harris Theatre, side by side: Muni as himself, Muni as old Morris Levine. Playgoers were amazed, and it helped sell tickets. *We Americans* played 118 performances in New York (in those days 100 performances constituted a long run) and traveled to Chicago and Detroit in February and March, 1927.

Muni refused to bask in the publicity. He came to the theater hours before the performance, locked himself in his dressing room, and meticulously prepared his makeup. He reshaped the entire contour of his face, used three different carefully prepared wigs, and changed his beard, hair by hair, three times during the performance as the character of Levine became more Americanized. He never spoke to anybody before the curtain went up, losing himself totally in the character he was playing.

Juarez and Maximilian had opened the night before at the Guild Theatre, but Juarez was an offstage character. Alfred Lunt played Maximilian, Clare Eames was Carlotta, Edward G. Robinson was Porfirio Diaz, and the bit players were all warming up, grouping for the Group: Sanford Meisner, Morris Carnovsky, Harold Clurman, Cheryl Crawford (all as actors!). It ran forty-eight performances, the standard Guild subscription run. Clurman played two parts, not even turning himself into George Spelvin for the double. Muni never saw a performance. In fact, he hardly even saw a newspaper or seemed to realize he had an offstage wife.

Bella stayed in Brighton Beach, feeling neglected and unused —as a mind and as a body. She visited with her mother. She spent time with her sister, Lucy, who had begun a small business as an actor's agent. She wept on the telephone to her brother, Abem, who was trying to write.

In an outburst one night, she told Muni, "I can't lie on the beach like a seashell or a piece of driftwood. I belong in the theater. I'll go back downtown—there's still some Yiddish theater left. I can't just do nothing."

"One career in the family is enough," Muni said, but Bella

looked at him strangely. It was Morris Levine talking. And Morris Levine tottered off to his own room, exhausted and alone. Muni was sorry he said it. He tried to indicate he didn't mean it. But words are touchy things—once you say them, even apologies don't erase them.

Two weeks later Bella moved out and into a suite at the Martha Washington Hotel in Manhattan. Muni, dazed and silent, closed up the beach cottage and took a bachelor apartment on West Seventieth Street.

He went to Max Siegel. "You're my friend, Max. I can talk to you. What am I going to do? I don't have a twelve- or thirteen-year-old son to talk to. I've got to talk to somebody. I wake up in the morning. There's nobody there. Nobody to nod yes. Nobody to say, 'Good morning, Munya.' And, Max, it's terrible. That apartment—by myself—it's like living on an iceberg or on the moon or nowhere. I shave. I look at myself in the mirror and have long dialogues, like in a play. 'Hello,' I say, 'who the hell are you? Where did you get such a lousy face? Send it back to the factory and demand a replacement!' Then the face laughs at me—and it begins to look a little better. 'She's crazy,' I say out loud, 'a lady idiot. Why would she want to go out with anybody else when she's married to that handsome devil? I don't want to go out with another girl!' And while I'm shaving, I notice: I'm not even putting on a beard—I'm taking one off, for God's sake. No Bella and no beard!"

"Knowing how much you like beards," Siegel said quietly, "I suppose Bella would consider that a compliment. But she's a woman, Muni, not a beard!"

Muni forgot day-by-day living by coming twice alive on the stage eight times a week. Edward G. Robinson had played Levine with deep seriousness, emphasizing the tragic side, leaving the laughs to the two seasoned comedians in the cast, Sam Mann and Morris Strassberg. Muni's comic dimensions caused the only backstage tension of the run. Strassberg was more generous since they were old friends from the Schwartz troupe and their trip to London together, but Mann fought for every laugh.

In one comedy scene, Muni, impatient in the background, unconsciously began to tap his fingers. For a few performances, Mann smiled wanly, then finally came offstage and confronted Muni.

"Listen, kid," he said to the made-up old man, "this is my bread and butter. Any laugh I get helps me get a job in the next show, because I'm a professional comedian. So stop wiggling your fingers during my big scene!"

"I'm sorry," Muni said. "I didn't realize. I won't do it again."

But at the next performance, during the touching end of Act Two, there was an unexpected laugh from the audience. Muni turned and saw Mann wiggling his fingers playfully, while he was supposed to be sitting silently at one of the schoolroom desks. At the end of the act, the smoldering Muni stormed offstage and hit Mann in the face with his fist. They never spoke to each other again. But all finger wiggling stopped.

Mrs. Friml didn't go along for the short road tour. Muni kidded her about it. "I understand. If you leave New York for six weeks, you'll miss three of your husband's openings."

Mildred Leaf played Beth Levine for the Chicago and Detroit engagements. Sylvia Regan was the understudy.

"I had never played the part," Sylvia recalls, "and it never entered my mind that I might. The morning of the final Saturday matinee in Detroit, the very last day of the run, I received a phone call from the stage manager, Milton Herman: 'Brush up your lines, honey, you're playing this afternoon!' Well, I got myself together and ran to the theater and had about a fifteen-minute line run-through, and that was it. In my big scene where I'm having a row with my father, I had to jump up and really let him have it. Muni turned his back to the audience and let me take stage. I was ranting on and on, and suddenly I heard him mutter, 'Put down that damn napkin, you're ruining your scene.' I'm still convinced that since it was the last day of the run, Muni and Mildred Leaf had connived to let me play the part at least once."

A short time later, *We Americans* was purchased by Universal Pictures for a silent film. Muni was thought unsuitable. (Not Jewish enough?) George Sidney, the standard stereotype film Jew, played the role. Thus Muni missed doing a silent film altogether. Strangely enough, Muni was never to re-create as a film, silent or talking, any role he had originated on the stage.

The director of the film, Edward Sloman, explains it this way: "Wisenfrend was very anxious to do the picture, but all we saw was a young man in the stage makeup of a middle-aged man, and we were afraid he wouldn't be convincing on the big screen. Only a few years later, Muni became the biggest star on the Warner lot, celebrated for his makeups."

Broadway's 1926–27 season had been tumultuous. Producers turned to what was then judged to be pornography to combat the competition of the film palaces and radio's magnetic ability to keep people at home. A wave of censorship broke over Manhattan: Gilbert Miller was forced to close *The Captive,* which was about (dirty word) lesbians. Mae West, as author and co-producer of a play called simply *Sex*, was fined $500 and spent ten days in the workhouse.

That season director-playwright-actor George Abbott collaborated on and staged *Broadway* and directed Maurine Watkins' theatrical *Chicago*. For the theater year coming up, Abbott was scheduled to stage *Coquette*, which he had also co-written, to star Helen Hayes. And veteran producer John Golden had assigned him to collaborate on *The Prisoner* by Dana Burnet, which had been gathering dust on various managers' desks for several years. They changed the title to *Four Walls* and began what seemed like a hopeless search for the perfect young man to play the part.

"We needed that impossible thing," George Abbott says, "an actor of power and maturity who was young in years."

Albert Lewis took John Golden to see a matinee of *We Americans*. They ran into Sam Harris in the lobby at intermission, who told Golden, "John, you won't want Wisenfrend. He only plays old man parts!"

Golden sent George Abbott to see a performance just before the company was scheduled to leave for Chicago. "I saw this old, old man with whiskers," Abbott recalls. "I was told he was a young fellow and couldn't believe it. Later, in an interview, I discovered him to be not only young but personable. How exciting theater business becomes when you suddenly strike gold in this fashion."

John Golden was celebrated for "Goody Two-Shoes" type plays, clean, comic, and warmly sentimental; the tough *Four Walls* was a departure for him. Recalling Golden, George Abbott told me, "John would claim that he was like a father to me. He considered

Muni (here called Wisenfrend) in his first Broadway role: Morris Levine in *We Americans*.

(Photo by White Studio)

Muni as Benny Horowitz in *Four Walls*.

himself my mentor. I worked for Golden for a long, long time. I was in his office for fifteen dollars a week, so 'Father' wasn't overgenerous, but I didn't care. I absorbed a lot. I learned, I think, the foundations of good management in the theater, which I hope I've passed on to Hal Prince: how to plan a production. I was, in effect, John Golden's Hal Prince."

Muni read the play, and although he was terrified at the prospect of appearing on the Broadway stage without a mask of a heavy beard, he had determined not to do another old man on Broadway. He wanted very much for Bella to read the play, but he heard a rumor that she was going out with another man. He was hurt and felt it would be degrading to go begging to her for help.

No decision was made before the road tour of *We Americans* left New York, but when he arrived at the Olympic Theatre stagedoor in Chicago, Muni found a telegram from John Golden offering him the role of Benny Horowitz in *Four Walls*. Muni wished he could consult with Bella, personally, professionally. They had a joke between them: "Two heads are better than none." But now he had nobody to laugh with, to worry with. He had to make the decision alone, and he hated the burden of it.

He scrawled an answer on the back of the telegram, quickly accepting before he changed his mind, gave the stage doorman a dollar and asked him to get the return wire over to Western Union. Early in April when he returned to New York, Muni was offered a written contract. Muni told Golden it wasn't necessary as long as they really wanted him and believed in him. They shook hands; no other contract was ever drawn.

Muni thought he would have the entire summer to study the part, but rehearsals were scheduled in May for an out-of-town tryout in Hartford, New London, and Atlantic City in June. There would then be a hiatus before a September opening in New York. These were perhaps more sensible times in the American theater, when playwrights and directors were permitted to see their plays onstage first, then have the summer off to ponder, to revise, to edit, without the hotel-room madness of frantic 2 A.M. rewrites, hundreds of thousands of dollars at stake, and the inevitable rollercoaster ride into Broadway.

When he arrived for the first rehearsal at the old John Golden Theatre on Fifty-eighth Street (more recently, it was the studio for Dick Cavett's television program), Muni found the conventional semicircle of chairs, the director's table near the footlights beneath a bare work light, and the terrible but exciting moment when you first step into the virgin territory of a brand-new play.

Whenever he was introduced to strangers, Muni always seemed

to hunch a little, as if he were trying to hide his entire body inside his vest, to crawl away and quickly be somebody else and somewhere else. He realized how much he had retreated in time to the young man he really was when he saw who had been cast as his old Yiddish mother in this play: Clara Langsner, who had played his wife in *We Americans*, the actress who wept at the drop of a *yarmulke*.

And then he saw a familiar back, a neat, compact young lady chatting with some other actors. The figure turned, smiled respectfully at him, and walked toward the circle of chairs. Abbott cleared his throat.

"As Bertha, the girl who's secretly in love with you, Mr. Wisenfrend," Abbott said, "we've cast to type. Company, may I introduce you all to Mrs. Wisenfrend, whose professional name is Bella Finkel."

Muni managed to stumble through the first reading. Afterward Bella went home to the Martha Washington Hotel and Muni retreated to his apartment. Without being asked, Bella helped during the rehearsal period. Muni had several long, complicated, philosophic speeches, and he had not yet committed them to memory.

"Because Muni was used to prompters in the Yiddish theater," Abbott recalls, "Bella stood behind the scenery near a window and, in her little monotonous prompter's voice, said the speeches just ahead of Muni, who gave them with authority and feeling out on the stage. But he had the play all memorized by the time we reached Hartford."

Hartford was throat-cutting time. "The opening was not quite a disaster—but almost," Abbott remembers. "It was a serious play, and the audience didn't want a serious play. Dana Burnet, the co-author, was a very sweet man—he wrote novels in addition to his famous short stories—but he drank too much, and he had some wife troubles. When we met for rehearsals the morning after the opening, Dana said, 'I woke up this morning wondering—*who's dead?*'"

The reviews were passable but unenthusiastic.

Muni never forgot the craftsmanlike way Abbott, as both director and playwright, brought the play and the performances into focus. "When you make changes, remember—it's just as easy to make changes for the worse as to make changes for the better," Abbott would say. "It's suicidal to throw out an entire act. Make one change at a time, and be sure it's a step forward, not a step backwards."

Bella played a wide-eyed innocent, Bertha, who adores Benny

Horowitz, just home after five years in Sing Sing Prison and determined to cut himself off from his previous gang connections. Muni played the key speech with great conviction:

> BENNY: Listen, Ma. When I first went up there it was tough, see. I was mad—I was sore. I'd hear them other guys cursing and kickin' the doors half the night—and I'd do it too. I wanted to smash down the walls. And then I got to thinkin'. It ain't only the walls that make you a prisoner—it's the things inside you. Well, I made up my mind that when I got out I'd never do anything that would keep me from bein' free. That's all I want. If there ain't another free guy on earth—there's goin' to be ONE, anyway—and that's me.

During the summer months, knowing they had an actor who could play comedy, Abbott and Burnet fed some humorous relief into the tense melodrama, lines like: "I ain't drinkin', Tom. I got out of the habit. In the boardin' house where I been, they don't serve no wine with your meals." Or a scene where Benny clowns as a waiter in a fancy restaurant, elegantly serving his mother and Bertha. "He could be an actor, yet, Bertha," his mother says. Or when he encounters his former gang associates, who now euphemistically call themselves the East Side Political and Social Club, Benny says, "Well, ain't this nice? My three favorites— What you doin'—electin' the next President?" Or his comment when asked what book he's reading: "It's about a big gang leader named Napoleon." Or "Naw, I wouldn't kill a cop. It's against the law." All these Muni gave the lemon-twist edge of wryness, kidding himself, alleviating the tension with shafts of humor and pointed self-denigration.

Benny Horowitz lived vigorously onstage, and Muni Weisenfreund—no, Wisenfrend (what the hell's my name this week?)—was a listless stranger who walked around in his body, ate his meals to "stoke the furnace," and slept in his bed, alone, at night. Fiction has an uncanny way of parroting fact. Onstage as Bertha and Benny, Bella and Muni had this scene:

> BENNY: Bertha—would you marry me if I was to ask you?
> BERTHA: I—I like you, Benny. I love you, Benny. (She sobs)
> BENNY: Whadda y' cryin for?
> BERTHA: You don't want me. You don't love me.
> BENNY: Bertha, I—it's best I don't lie to you. No, I don't love you. I gotta be on the level about that. But we could get along. I'd treat you square. You're good, Bertha. You're strong!

BERTHA: Yes, all my life I been strong—and inside, my dreams
              burning me up. You don't love me and if I can't have
              love, I'll stay alone.

Offstage, Muni and Bella tried several reconciliations, but none
lasted more than a few days. They always ended up with her returning to her hotel suite and Muni staying alone again at his West
Seventieth Street flat. During that summer Muni bought his first
car, a Dodge touring model, and he treated it like some happy
toy. He drove to Tamiment, the adult "borscht circuit" camp,
along with Max and Pauline Siegel. Herb Polesie, who had been
in the cast of *We Americans*, was the social director, and Sylvia
Regan was on the staff. Hearing from Max that Muni was en
route, Polesie scheduled the night-school scene from *We Americans,*
hopeful that Muni would make a guest appearance.

Bella had refused to go along on this vacation trip. The Siegels
remembered how much Muni tried to be humorous and light-
hearted during their road journey. Clowning at the wheel, Muni
would swoop around a curve in the road and shout out, *"Curva!
Curva!"*—the Yiddish word for whore. And he kept referring
to the Adirondacks, where they were heading, as the "Adira-
done-dacks."

At Tamiment, Muni told Polesie that he wouldn't act in the
scene, but he'd direct it, and he did. Half the cast were doubling
as waiters, and Muni lost himself working for his week of vacation
as a director. "Acting isn't really a job for a grown man," he
told Pauline Siegel. "I'd much rather have been a shoe salesman.
Why the hell couldn't I have been able to write or direct?" He
was directing and brilliantly, but it was the only time in his life
he ever did officially.

Back in Manhattan, Muni concentrated on the revised *Four
Walls* script. Rehearsals were scheduled for August, but it seemed
like an endless summer. He would often meet his friend Hy Kraft
(who later wrote the joyful play *Café Crown* about the Yiddish
Sardi's, the Café Royale). Kraft lived close by in the West Eighties,
and they would dangle their feet over the end of the pier at
West Seventy-ninth, and talk about the futility of life, an old Lower
East Side syndrome.

"The conversations would always end on some desperate note,"
Kraft says, "as if Muni were ready to kill himself. It's too bad
that he didn't go to an analyst. I think it would have done him
a lot of good. I'm not sure, it might have done the analyst a
lot of good. The problem with Muni was that he never thought
he was attractive. I used to introduce him to a lot of girls, he
was separated from Bella then, and the girls would say, 'Oh, Jesus,

that man! *Oi, oi, oi*—what a handsome guy.' But he never believed it, he thought they were lying. He had such a low opinion of himself that he thought that if any girl seemed to like him, she must have bad eyes or bad taste."

Muni, faced with playing the first young man he'd ever played, with the exception of *Hard to Be a Jew*, was agonizingly trying to find the young man in his own life.

In his book, *On My Way to the Theater*, Hy Kraft recounts several incidents of that traumatic summer:

> One Saturday afternoon Muni asked me to go out to Long Beach, Long Island. So we drove out, rented a locker. I don't swim, so I dunked. But he swam, and after a couple of hours the beast in man asserted himself. We looked around for a couple of gals. He hadn't been in any movies, so he wasn't recognized. The chances of identification were nil. (In any case it was during one of his bachelor periods; it was later that he and Bella settled down to undivided affection) As night was falling over Long Beach we fell over a couple of very agreeable girls who seemed to have definite possibilities. We offered them dinner and dancing at one of the nearby Long Island roadhouses as down payment. They were summer residents, so they went home to change. Muni and I lingered awhile, then dressed and picked up the two girls. With the moon and stars as confederates we drove off, Muni at the wheel, a girl at his side. (Since it was his car he had the better-looking gal.) The conversation was pleasant and flirty. We knew nothing about them and they knew as much about us, but there was a promise of togetherness and a rewarding evening. I don't remember how or why, but one of the girls mentioned the word "actor"; there was something unmistakably pejorative in the way she said it. "Me," said the girl who was sitting beside Muni, "I certainly would not have anything to do with that type person." "What have you got against actors?" demanded Muni. And when Muni demanded he demanded! "I just don't trust them," said the girl. "I mean here today, gone tomorrow." Whereupon Muni pulled over to the side of the road with a jerk (me). He leaned over, opened the door and ordered the girls to get the hell out of the car. The girls were frightened. I should have said something or made some chivalrous gesture, but Muni was really in a rage. The girls got out. Did they ever realize that it was Pasteur, Zola, Juarez and Scarface who kicked them out and left them standing on a lonely Long Island road? It would be some consolation.
>
> He wanted me to write a play for him. The scene, a theatrical boarding house: the principals, three actors—an actor who played juvenile leads, good guys on the stage; a character actor who played bad guys; and a girl, the target of their love. The

120

play would prove that the character actor, the heavy, is, in real life, a good guy, whereas the juvenile is, in fact, a scoundrel. Muni, of course, intended to play the character actor; it would be the one chance that had so far been denied him—getting the girl. Obviously, this was a psychoanalysis session for Muni; at least it had the same effect. He said we'd talk further about it and I said I'd think about it. I never thought about, he never talked about it.*

Four Walls opened in New York on September 19, 1927. Muni received a standing ovation, rare in those days. The following afternoon, Muni's name went above the title in the newspaper ads and in lights on the theater marquee.

But Muni was panicked before his first entrance. "I reached up to see if my putty nose was all right and my whiskers on straight, and they weren't there. All at once I felt naked and helpless. Like a dream in which you think you are out on the street and have forgotten to put on your clothes. Then I looked out and saw hundreds of white splotches which were faces in the audience turned toward me, and they looked friendly. I was not an old man, but a young man who was having his big chance, and it was up to me to make the most of it."

The critics agreed that he did. Two other plays opened the same night, including *The Trial of Mary Dugan* at the National starring Ann Harding; J. Brooks Atkinson of the *Times* elected to cover that, but he did an approving Sunday follow-up of *Four Walls,* giving more praise to Muni than to the play. The unsigned second-stringer of the *Times* thought the play overly stagey, but called it good theater: "The psychology of the gangster, muddled as it is in his own mind, becomes equally muddled in the minds of his audience, and only the tremendous believability of Muni Wisenfrend's performance makes it appear credible."

Bella, whose name somehow got transposed in the program from Finkel to Finkle, also got a nod from the *Times* critic: "Bella Finkle, making her debut in an English-speaking role, plays the understanding sweetheart with sincerity and a commendable restraint."

It was Bella's debut and her farewell performance on the English-speaking stage; she was to be the "lady-behind-the-scenes" in all the years ahead.

Abbott's theatricality was tremendously effective: a block party, a speakeasy bar crowded with rival gangs, and a climactic rooftop

*From *On My Way to the Theater* by Hy Kraft. Copyright © 1971. Reprinted by permission of Macmillan Publishing Co., Inc.

scene (John Golden called it "Benny Horowitz's *Seventh Heaven*") in which Benny inadvertently shoves a rival off the parapet to his death. The girl who tries to blackmail Benny into marriage turns up later in a remarkably similar situation in the film of *I Am a Fugitive from a Chain Gang*. The role of Benny set a pattern, which Muni tried to vary and break away from, of convicts incarcerated by a quirk of fate, prisoners who shouldn't really be in prison. The love scene on the rooftop in *Four Walls* was brief and unfulfilled. Muni rarely ever even touched a woman in the multiple works that followed on stage or screen. His passion was usually cerebral, philosophic, spiritual, almost never physical.

George Abbott remembers an opening night miscue.

"Oh, gosh, there was one terrible thing. John Golden wanted to make certain that Muni's climactic speech in Act Two went well on opening night, so he had his telephone girl planted in the balcony to applaud at the end of it. But she got mixed up and applauded in the middle of the speech, at a place where there was no real climax, and bitched up the whole thing. That's what the commercial theater gets for monkeying with the artistic theater!"

On opening night, the New York *Herald Tribune* prophetically sent its film critic, Richard Watts, later the distinguished and astute drama critic of the New York *Post*. Watts wrote: "Wisenfrend's sincerity smashed through the artifice. He fairly lived his part."

Percy Hammond followed it up in the Sunday *Herald Tribune* with an equal tribute to the human being Muni had created onstage: "What is needed in the theatre is not histrionic wonderworkers, but actors such as Muni Wisenfrend who know the difference between acting and effigy."

George Abbott himself noted that Muni had a style that combined realism and old-fashioned acting power without becoming bombastic. "He had everything: the technical equipment, the emotion, the intelligence."

Frank Vreeland, in the New York *Telegram* made an amusing comment on Muni's name:

> He is a real personality, despite the evidence of his name, which would make him out to be a figment of the imagination. . . . You will hear more of this young man, but I hope with a name which sounds less like a typographical error. I suggest the name of Reginald Maltravers instead.

Nobody in the memory of man along Broadway remembers

any newspaper trumpeting an actor's talent in an editorial. The New York *Post* did:

IN PRAISE OF MUNI WISENFREND

Wisenfrend's acting in *Four Walls* is extremely imaginative. We are told that though he is still very young, he has already played over 300 Yiddish roles. We can easily believe this, for Mr. Wisenfrend's vigorous flexibility is the work of a mature actor. But experience alone is not enough. He has the kind of depth and intelligence which would bring him to the front, no matter how much training he had, or how little.

We hope to see him in a new role, for he is one of our most interesting and original performers.

It was a brilliant season on Broadway. "I felt as if I were surrounded by all the aristocrats," Muni said. Eleven plays opened up one night, December 26, 1927, and on the following night, the Kern-Hammerstein *Show Boat*, a great step forward in the musical theater. *Royal Family, Good News, Porgy, Funny Face* (with both the Astaires), and O'Neill's *Strange Interlude,* with Lynn Fontanne in the lead, were all playing. Censorship was still in the air, with threats to close two Theatre Guild productions, *Strange Interlude* and the classic *Volpone,* but no action was taken. There was a statute on the books, the Wales Padlock Law, and the Shuberts helped joke it out of existence with a revue called *Padlocks of 1927*, starring the raucous Texas Guinan.

Max Reinhardt's imported troupe was attracting lovers of more classical theater to the Century with *Jederman, Danton's Tod,* and *Midsummer Night's Dream* (in German, along with tons of scenery). Muni went to as many performances as he could, including Thursday matinees. Several times he rushed the seventeen blocks uptown to catch the last ten or fifteen minutes of a Reinhardt-directed work, standing in the back, in the shadows.

One night, shortly after his first entrance in *Four Walls*, Muni began to clown. Bella, onstage with him, whispered between clenched teeth, "Cut it out, Munya. Reinhardt's in the audience." Then, as if it were a line of dialogue, Muni said, "The lady is kidding!" He was convinced Reinhardt, the great artist, would never stoop to attend a commercial Broadway play.

After the performance Reinhardt came backstage, along with Kenneth Macgowan, overflowing with compliments for Muni's acting. But Muni wouldn't let him say a word. He began by apologizing for his "miserable performance" and then told Reinhardt how much he admired and appreciated the work at the Century Theatre, how important an influence it was on Ameri-

123

can actors. Reinhardt told Macgowan later, "I felt as if I didn't go backstage to see Muni, but that *he* came backstage to see *me!*"

Offers poured in for roles the following season. One was from Mae West; her manager, Jack Linder, offered Muni $1,000 a week (John Golden was paying him $250, which Muni considered a fortune) to play opposite La West, who found Muni "the sultry kind of dangerous leading man I like. And the son of a bitch can act!" That kind of money was astronomical in those days; major stars on Broadway made $500 or on rare occasions $750 a week. Muni read the play, found it a tawdry melodrama, and, without even consulting Bella, turned it down.

The flamboyant Broadway producer Jed Harris asked Muni to come into his office to discuss forming an entire on-Broadway repertory company, with Muni as the leading player. Harris kept Muni waiting in his outer office, and when he came out to greet Muni, Harris found him doing a handstand on the leather couch. "Who the hell is this acrobat?" Harris demanded. Nothing came of the interview.

Four Walls ran 144 performances on Broadway, then a month on the "Subway Circuit," legitimate theaters in New York's out-lying boroughs, including a sold-out run at Teller's Shubert Theatre in Brooklyn. Then in April, 1928, the company traveled to Chicago for a four-week run at the Adelphi Theatre. Some cast changes were made before the tour began. George Abbott was busy on his next project, so the stage manager, George Wright, Jr., directed the replacements, including a young actor-writer, Dore Schary, who took over Wright's role as one of the gangsters, Jake, and worked as assistant stage manager. Josephine Wehn, who played Mrs. Clampman, described in the text as "a large slovenly woman and an expectant mother," also decided not to go on the tour, and Muni asked John Golden to consider an actress named Sallie Nassiter.

"She's my mother," Muni said quietly. "Or used to be."

Muni had not been in touch with Sallie for years, but she had written letters from Canada, pleading hardship. Muni always felt that the greatest gift you could give an actor was work, not a handout. The actress playing Mrs. Clampman also understudied his onstage mother. Golden hired Sallie, and Muni felt how ironic it was that they were heading back to Chicago and that she might be playing not his daughter or granddaughter this time, but his mother. When she arrived for rehearsal, they were cool and reserved with each other, like two actors in a play meeting for the first time. For her billing in the program, she wanted to go back to Weisenfreund or Wisenfrend, but Golden felt it smacked

124

of nepotism, so she was listed (name-changing time again) as Sallie Nestor.

Wright warned Schary never to touch Muni. As Jake, Schary had to cross to Benny Horowitz on one line, "It's a lot better than taking your money in a pay envelope," and pretend to put his hand across Muni's shoulder. "When you do that," Wright said, "don't touch his back; he doesn't like to be touched."

It was rare for Muni to lose his stage concentration, but one night, apparently worried about his relationship to his mother, he went blank. Schary said the line again. Still no reply. Staying in character, Schary filled the pause with: "I said something to ya, can't ya hear?" There was still no response, so he slapped Muni on the back and said, "Wake up, Buddy!" Muni shook himself out of his near trance and blurted, "What did you say?" Schary repeated the line, and Muni was back on the track again.

Later Schary wrote some speeches Muni had to deliver at the B'nai B'rith and elsewhere. In return Muni gave Schary makeup lessons, on matinee days, between shows. Muni showed him how to transform his hands so they'd look thin and gaunt and spare, by lining the heavy veins with white. After the show closed, Schary supported himself by giving makeup demonstrations at YMHA's and Jewish community centers, for which he was paid $15 a lecture. He'd come in with a makeup kit, starting as a juvenile and ending up as an old man. "I learned it from the master," Schary said.

One warm spring matinee in Chicago Sallie was playing the mother's role in *Four Walls*. The ladies of the cast were sunning themselves and gossiping in the stage alley. Sallie didn't make her entrance on cue. Schary recalls Muni going to the door of the set and shouting off, in character, "Ma, where are you?" And she ran on, saying, "I'm sorry, I was busy."

"When the curtain came down at the end of the act," Schary remembers, "he turned on his mother furiously, shouting in Yiddish, bawling the piss out of her." And then suddenly Muni stiffened.

"What the hell were you doing out there—roller-skating?"

Muni (now officially Paul Muni) in seven different roles: Don Juan, a Cockney, Diablero, Franz Schubert, Joe Gans, Napoleon, and Papa Chibou in *Seven Faces*.

13

TALKIES were revolutionizing the motion-picture industry. The panicked studios enlisted any actor who could speak dialogue, anybody who didn't sound like a phonograph record playing backwards at the wrong speed.

Muni was gun-shy of Hollywood. Several actors he knew had returned from the Land of Milk and Money beaten and confused, "used like sides of beef," Muni was warned. But his old friend Albert Lewis was made an executive of Fox Films in New York, and Hy Kraft urged Lewis to give Muni a screen test. Winfield Sheehan, the vice-president of the studio, trained in from the West Coast in search of actors-who-could-talk and was impressed by Muni in *Four Walls*.

Kraft helped Muni prepare some material for his test. Muni had once performed a Chekhov one-act play, *The Stage Doorman*, at a Yiddish benefit, and Kraft wrote some English dialogue. Muni took a load of makeup to the Fox Manhattan Studios on Tenth Avenue. The eight-minute sketch was one of the longest and most expensive screen tests ever made. Muni played not only the old stage doorman, but six other roles, including an *Anathema*-inspired

Leizer-Lear and a drunken peasant, all actors in a backstage montage, each with a different makeup and a different voice. When William Fox and Sheehan saw the test, they were certain they had discovered "the new Lon Chaney," a title which was to plague Muni for many years.

Fox studios offered him a seven-year contract, beginning at $500 a week, going to $1,000 a week after the first year, and then to $1,500 a week. Muni had been living apart from Bella for almost two years. He went to her, a copy of the contract in his hand.

"What should I do, Bella?" he asked her.

"I think you should turn them down," Bella said. "You have a great career in the theater and I think you should stay here. You're only beginning on Broadway—why leave it so fast?"

"Is it possible to do both?" Muni pondered. "I'll be frank with you. Films fascinate me. Like a toy."

"So go," Bella said. "Try it."

"Not alone," he brooded. "I can't do it alone. I realize I can't check you in and out of my life like a library book. But will you come back, Bella? Will you go out to California with me?"

"To do what? I'm an actress. But my kind of actress they don't want. I don't look anything like Mary Pickford or Clara Bow."

"You could help me. I need you. Not to tell me what to do, but to tell me what *not* to do. I don't ever want to be a *ham-faddo*. I need your eyes and your ears to tell me when I go wrong. On the stage, the audience tells me. I need you for my audience."

Bella wanted time to think about it. Meanwhile, the pressures kept building, with daily telegrams and phone calls from the West Coast. Albert Lewis reported that William Fox carried around the can containing the reel of Muni's screen test, showing off his exciting new discovery.

No new Broadway plays tantalized Muni. Jed Harris suggested that Muni play Rasputin, but the dramatization wasn't finished. When Harris muttered that he thought Muni might be too young to play the part anyhow, Muni shouted to him over the phone, "Mr. Harris, you're a damn fool and you don't know a goddamn thing about the theater!" Harris never did a play about Rasputin.

Bella came to Muni. "If you still want me to go with you," she said quietly, "I've packed my suitcase." Muni was delighted. "Don't be so happy," she said. "*I'm* not. Here I am, thirty years old. A widow who's still got a husband; I might as well be living with him. It'll be the first time I've ever been so far away from my mother. It'll be the end of my career, which I love—" She sighed, looking into that complicated face. "What are we standing around for, Munya? Let's go."

Further note to impatient young actors: Muni signed the Fox contract when he was thirty-two years old. With the exception of the screen test, there was not a frame of film on him until he was thirty-three. But for the next thirty years he was destined to star in some of the most notable motion pictures in history.

On the five-day train trip across the country, Muni was sure he'd made a mistake. He studied his face in Bella's vanity mirror. "I'm lopsided! My ears don't match!" From Albany to Albuquerque, he fretted. He should have demanded script approval. Why had he turned his back on theater, which was home, to wander off into some crazy wilderness?

They arrived in California. There were photographers and a studio limousine waiting on the station platform in Pasadena.

"I feel ridiculous," he told Bella; then he shouted at the photographers. "What are you taking my picture for? Who the hell am I? I'm not a star. I'll bet you don't even know my name."

Sheepishly, one of the photographers dug into his coat pocket and consulted a slip of paper. "We know it, mister, but we don't know how to pronounce it."

"Oh, God," Muni moaned to Bella. "We've sold ourselves into slavery. We'll be sausages in a big sausage factory. And without labels even! When's the next train back?"

Bella patted his hand. "That's a good sign," she said. "When you don't want to do something, it usually turns out pretty good—like going up in that elevator at the New Amsterdam."

Muni looked out the limousine window. "What's that?" he asked, perplexed.

"A palm tree," Bella answered. "Don't worry—it'll learn to live with you."

Their first meeting at William Fox Films was with executive producer Sol Wurtzel and with Winfield Sheehan. They were greeted with what Muni later called "the usual baloney," promises of epic productions and seven years of unalloyed bliss. Then Sheehan cleared his throat.

"The first thing we have to do," he said, "is change your name."

"Why?" Muni protested. "You want to change my body, too, and my voice and my brain?"

"Just your name," Wurtzel said. "It's been decided."

"There's a lot of confusion," Sheehan went on, fingering some newspaper clippings. "Is it Weisenfreund or Wisenfrend? But frankly, neither of them would look good on a theater marquee."

"It's just *been* on a theater marquee!" Muni said, getting angry. "Why don't you call me Tom Mix?"

"What's your real name?" Wurtzel asked.

128

Muni read it out slowly, right in Wurtzel's teeth: *"Mehilem Meyer ben Nachum Favel*—how the hell would that look on a theater marquee?"

"How about using Muni as your last name?" Sheehan suggested.

Muni threw up his hands. "People'll pronounce it 'Mooney,' and everybody'll think I'm an Irishman. Or is that what you want?"

"I like Muni," Wurtzel said. "It's catchy, and it's short."

"So's Rin-Tin-Tin," Muni grumbled.

At the end of a lengthy argument Muni gave in. When it came to choosing a first name, Muni paused thoughtfully, then mentioned that it might be a way to pay tribute to his father.

"What was his name?" Wurtzel asked.

"Favel. He translated it as Philip. But it was like Paolo or Pablo."

"Philip Muni doesn't sound quite right," Sheehan declared. "What about Paul?"

"How about St. Paul?" Muni said. "Why not Minneapolis? Minneapolis Muni! I played there once."

"Paul Muni. It's a beautiful name," Wurtzel insisted, "and to me, it sounds like a star's name."

"Put it in writing!" Muni snorted, as he left the meeting.

The first publicity release Muni read astonished him: "William Fox has personally discovered and placed under a seven-year contract the celebrated Russian actor Paul Muni."

"Hell," Muni said, "I not only have a new name, I have a new nationality!"

"I think," Bella noted, "that in the picture business, 'Russian' is the polite word for 'Yiddish.'"

They had been rushed to Hollywood, but now they sat and waited. For six months nothing happened, no camera turned. Finally, Muni stormed into Wurtzel's office.

"I've got a complaint to make. You brought me out here to make pictures. But every week I come into the studio, go to the cashier, and collect my check and that's it. It's embarrassing, it's got to stop!"

"Oh," Wurtzel said, "that's easily solved. You don't have to go to the cashier. Stay home. Or go to Honolulu or somewhere. We'll mail you the check."

"No," Muni insisted, "I refuse to take any more money. Until you make me work for it!"

Muni's trouble was due to what was called "the reluctant revolution to sound." The studio was geared for silent pictures, not enough equipment was available, and nobody knew quite what to do with this new unknown actor. "All dressed up in a new name," Muni commented, "and no place to go."

The studio purchased a one-act play, *The Valiant,* by Robert Middlemass and Holworthy Hall, which had been a staple along the vaudeville circuit starring Bert Lytell. Sheehan thought it would fit Muni, since it was about a heroic prisoner. Two writers, Tom Barry and James Hunter Booth, were assigned to do "Adaptation and Dialog"; the picture was to be billboarded as *THE VALIANT* (ALL DIALOG!). Muni had never seen the play but read a published copy of it while awaiting the screenplay. He felt the best speech in the play was James Dyke's quiet explanation to the prison chaplain of his belief in immortality:

DYKE: If it will make you feel any better, Father, I do rather think there's going to be a hereafter. I read a book once that said a milligram of musk will give out perfume for seven thousand years, and a milligram of radium will give out light for seventy thousand. Why shouldn't a soul—mine, for instance—live more than twenty-seven?

When he was sent a copy of the screenplay, Muni found that speech omitted. He went to see Sheehan, who shrugged and tried to explain the commercial approach to filmmaking.

"Sure, movie audiences want to hear actors talk. But not too much. And if you start in with all that lofty crap about immortality, they'll walk out in droves."

"But they've left out something else," Muni said, flipping to the end of the screenplay. "When James Dyke goes to the electric chair, he recites something from *Julius Caesar,* which explains the title. Look, I've never played Shakespeare and, as a matter of fact, I'm no great Shakespearean buff—but how can you do the play and leave this speech out?"

He showed Sheehan the quote from the original play:

Cowards die many times before their deaths;
The valiant never taste of death but once.
Of all the wonders that I yet have heard,
It seems to me most strange that men should fear;
Seeing that death, a necessary end,
Will come when it will come.

"Nobody'll know what it means," Sheehan said.

"But nobody'll know what the title means," Muni complained.

"We can't use that Shakespeare stuff," Sheehan insisted. "It's too highbrow."

130

"In that case," Muni said, "why don't you call the film *Uncle Wiggly*?"

"Stop worrying!" Sheehan said. "Just remember—nobody gave birth in *Birth of a Nation*."

William K. Howard, who had previously directed only silent films, was assigned to the picture. Since it was his first talkie, Howard was frightened and unsure. Bella remembered it this way:

> Here was poor Muni in an entirely new medium with everybody around him overwhelmed by this new monster, talkies. The sound man was master on the set. Every time they finished a scene all eyes would automatically go to the sound man. Nine times out of ten he would say, "That's fine"—but poor Bill Howard was ready to cut his throat. Muni had to have microphones attached to the inside of his jacket. Imagine trying to play a dramatic scene under those circumstances!

Boom microphones which follow the actor around from aloft had not yet been developed. Technicians experimented with microphones on fishing poles, trying to catch actor's voices like fish. The sound man sat at his console, a newly appointed monarch on a throne. The sound expert on Muni's first film was famous for putting an international celebrity in his place. Fox had gone to great expense to bring the magnificent tenor John McCormack all the way from Ireland to do a musical short. After the first take, this sound wizard went up to McCormack and said, "Frankly, mister, tenors don't record very well. Can't you sing lower, like a baritone?"

Marguerite Churchill played the ingenue in *The Valiant,* making her film debut, most of it in a cloche hat. Johnny Mack Brown

Muni with Marguerite Churchill in *The Valiant.*

(Fox Films photo)

was her fiancé, a character invented for the film. For some unexplained reason, the real name of the character Muni played was changed from Joseph Anthony Paris to Joseph Anthony Douglas, but it's likely that today his assumed name of Dyke would be changed instead.

A few more lines of Shakespeare were in the original play: "Good night, good night! parting is such sweet sorrow,/ That I shall say good night till it be morrow," and the answer to it: "Sleep dwell upon thine eyes, peace in thy breast!/ Would I were sleep and peace, so sweet to rest!" This exchange had also been deleted from the screenplay and a nursery rhyme substituted. When they got to the set, Muni refused to read the new lines, which he considered asinine. So the original was restored. But there was no mention of that dirty word "Shakespeare"—they were called "verses" or "a regular little *Romeo and Juliet* farewell of our very own."

William Fox had been away from Hollywood; a reel and a half of *The Valiant* were completed when he returned to the studio. Fox ran the footage in a projection room and hit the ceiling. "Stop the shooting on this picture right away," he shouted. "This Muni guy is terrible. How did we ever sign this monkey? And his screen test was so damn good. Maybe we should junk the picture and release the test!"

They didn't tell Muni the real reason filming was suspended; they merely said it was lack of equipment. But Winnie Sheehan and Albert Lewis convinced Fox to let them finish the picture on the economic grounds that the sets had been built, a sizable portion of the film was completed, and it could always be shelved as a last resort. Fox gave his consent reluctantly; but the budget was trimmed, and the complete picture was only four and a half reels long.

"I didn't really blame them," Muni said later. "What was I? Rugged maybe. Not handsome. The movies were in the half zone between silent pictures and talking pictures and leading men had to be Adonises. I didn't qualify."

The studio released the picture as if it were letting it out on parole or as if it had bad breath. "It wasn't a sneak preview," Bella said, "it was a sneak release."

To everybody's surprise, particularly William Fox's, the critics liked the film. The young Robert Landry, writing in *Variety,* said:

> Paul Muni, the former Muni Wisenfreund of the Yiddish stage, brings to his role a wealth of humanity. He registers splendidly with utter naturalness and while he will be difficult to cast he

should find an important niche in the talkers. His voice is rich and pleasant, his personality strong and virile, and if he is not pretty, neither is Lon Chaney or Emil Jannings, and Muni has what those fellows have not, dialog utility. It's going to require much smart showmanship to exploit this young Yiddish-American actor, but directed and handled intelligently, he looks like one of the legits who will survive in the talkers.

Mordaunt Hall, the first New York film critic to get a by-line (he died at the age of ninety-four in 1973 as this book was being written), wrote in the New York *Times*:

At the Roxy this week is a talking picture called *The Valiant*, which is blessed with considerably more originality than most screen offerings. . . . The voices are well recorded most of the time, but occasionally there is that artificial touch that seems like a person is talking through a short megaphone. . . . Paul Muni is splendid as the determined Dyke.

It was S. L. Rothafel, whose nickname Roxy was also the name of his theater at Seventh Avenue and Fiftieth, who personally promoted Muni to movie stardom along the Great White Way. Rothafel, not Fox, paid for ads like these in all the New York newspapers:

Every once in a while a motion picture comes before the public quietly, unheralded, without the blaze and blare of advance publicity, and by the sheer strength of its merit, attracts the overwhelming attention and patronage of the masses. Such a picture is

THE VALIANT

Fox Movietone All Talking Production
with PAUL MUNI

So great is my faith in this picture, confirmed by the opinions of the critics and the thousands who have sat spell-bound and enthralled by its stark drama and human emotion, that I have persuaded Mr. William Fox to permit me to hold it over another week.

I want to give those who have not yet seen it an opportunity to be thrilled by the performance of this great young actor, Paul Muni, formerly known on the stage as Muni Wiesenfriend. With his first appearance in talking pictures, he has proved himself a master of this new and exciting medium, and one of the outstanding personalities of the talking screen.

The ad was signed with a flourishing and illegible S. L. Rothafel, but the "Roxy" under it was clearly readable. As for his own name, Muni was beginning to be glad he had changed it: neither *Variety* nor Roxy had hit Weisenfreund *or* Wisenfrend exactly on the nose.

"The picture was a Cinderella success, and nobody was more surprised than William Fox," Muni recalled later. "And we even managed to sneak in a couple of lines of Shakespeare. In those days the whole country accepted the verdict of the Roxy Theatre as final, so *The Valiant* managed to make it."

Despite the fact that Muni was a success without extensive character makeup, Fox Films rushed him into a project in which he could be billed as "the new Lon Chaney." The compliment-joke around Hollywood was that Chaney was making $5,000 a week and his disguises were so effective he could convince anybody that he was a porcupine, an egg beater, or Mount McKinley. William Fox kept running Muni's screen test and intended to capitalize on the "quick-change artist" he had under contract.

Muni resented the comparison. "I'm myself," he said. "I guess it's flattery when well-intentioned people call me a young Chaney. I don't mean to minimize his art—he's a master. But we choose our characters differently. Chaney likes to enact the grotesque. I take my characters from the street, real types everyone recognizes. I've been playing these characters on the stage for nearly twenty years."

The studio bought another one-act play, Richard Connell's *A Friend of Napoleon*. As a tour de force, Muni was to play seven different characters: Papa Chibou, a lovable, rheumy old caretaker of a wax museum (not unlike the famous Madame Tussaud's), as well as six of his charges, who eventually come to life. These included Franz Schubert; Willie Smith, a busker; Don Juan; Diablero, a hypnotist and blood cousin of Svengali's; Joe Gans, a black boxer; and Napoleon Bonaparte. The prospect fascinated and frightened Muni. He wondered if the end result would justify all the energy, time, research, and experimentation so necessary before filming could even begin. With the jumpiness of the film industry, Muni worried whether there would be any result at all.

Two factors partially quieted his fears. The studio hired Dana Burnet, co-author of *Four Walls,* to prepare the screenplay. Muni liked Burnet's pithy dialogue, found it "easy to fit in the mouth." As director, they engaged Berthold Viertel, whose work Muni admired. Viertel had directed numerous plays in Vienna, later worked with Reinhardt in Berlin, and was the first German to produce Eugene O'Neill plays. Viertel was the model for Christopher Isherwood's film director in the fascinating short novel *Prater Violet* (which we have long wanted to fashion into a play).

Unfortunately, Viertel's thick accent frightened the executives at Fox, so they assigned Lester Lonergan, who was also cast as the judge in the film, as co-director. The final absurd credit was: "Dual direction—Berthold Viertel, camera; Lester Lonergan, dialog." A second unit had been sent to Paris to get authentic background boulevard shots; these were peppered into the conglomerate broth. George Middleton, who had some direction ideas of his own, was hired as production executive. Tall, lumbering, fiftyish, amiable, he was the son-in-law of Senator Robert M. La Follette. Some of the ingredients he wanted to add to the stew were good; others turned it into mulligatawny.

Bella was another cook, director-without-portfolio in the shadows behind the camera, extra eyes and extra ears for Muni. They worked out secret signals between them after each take. Muni would glance quickly at Bella. She would never nod or shake her head, nor would Bella deign to do anything as obvious as touch her ear or wave a handkerchief or blow her nose. She had a Yiddish way of "shrugging with her face." Then, even if the directors were satisfied, Muni would ask for another take. This glance-at-Bella technique lasted through most of Muni's film career.

The title of the film was changed to *Seven Faces*. "That means," Muni fretted, "that I can be seven times as bad as usual."

"Or seven times as good," Bella added, trying to bolster his confidence, not playing her usual role of doom crier.

Marguerite Churchill, the ingenue of *The Valiant*, and Russell Gleason, James Gleason's ebullient son, were assigned the roles of the young lovers, whose trite romantic story helped sink the picture. Salka Viertel, Berthold's wife and one of the most gracious and brilliant ladies I have ever met, had the bit part of Catherine the Great, another of the wax statues, which comes to life. Later Salka became a screenwriter and mentor to Greta Garbo. She recalls her role in *Seven Faces* in her book *The Kindness of Strangers:* "The experience did not make me wish to become a movie actress. Acting in fragments is like drinking from an eyedropper when you are parched."

Muni was frantic with fragmentation. He would arrive in the makeup room at 4:30 in the morning and would not always be ready for the first shot scheduled for 9 A.M. The makeup for

Napoleon and for Franz Schubert were both the easiest and the most difficult: there were familiar portraits to copy, but that meant they had to be more literal; the other characters left more room for creative and imaginative concepts.

"The problem with Napoleon," Muni recalled, "was that there wasn't a single feature of my face that looked anything at all like his. He had a sharp narrow nose, I have a thick, rather small one. And, alas, he wore no beard or sideburns, which can often be used to shadow certain parts of the face. We had to start from the bottom and reconstruct my entire face."

For the Svengali-like character, Muni concentrated on the hands, fashioning long, eloquent fingers which seemed three-dimensional on the screen, reaching right to the audience. Don Juan was the easiest. "The good fellow left no portraits to be followed. So I could freely imagine a face of a man who had made love to so many women." It turned into a remarkable duplication of Du Arun of *Wolves*. Muni drew on many facets of his past: for the black boxer, Joe Gans, nobody had to teach him how to box; the difficulty was the total body makeup, since the character stripped down to fighting togs. And nobody had to coach Muni for the lyrical Cockney accent he used as the strutting, tapping busker; it sang right out of his subconscious.

The character of Papa Chibou, walrus-mustached, gentle, one of Muni's most affectionate old men, dignified the picture. Wryly humorous, it had the "look at me, I'm nothing" attitude which gave the comedy warmth and truth. He is introduced first drowsing in a chair, the figure of Napoleon behind him. A woman tourist says, "Look at that funny wax dummy!" Poked in the ribs with an umbrella, Chibou wakes suddenly, the effect like a wax statue coming to life. When the startled tourist shouts, "He's alive," Chibou bows, smiles, touches his cap, and says, "Madame, I always have been!"

After the young lovers of the story have quarreled, the old caretaker, dusting off Napoleon, sounds pertinently self-revealing as both Chibou and Muni: "Did you hear that, my friend? They love each other, yet they have trouble. Perhaps it's better to be alone as we are. . . ."

The whimsical plot of *Seven Faces* involves the sale of the museum and the threatened melting down of Chibou's beloved wax figures. The dream sequence in which the statues turn to flesh is too much like the stock toyshop where all the toys spring to life. The often-valid sentiment becomes sugar-candy sentimentality. This treacle aspect of the film, released just after the stock-

136

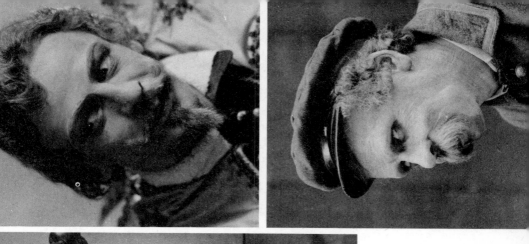

Joe Gans.

Don Juan.

Papa Chibou.

Cockney SEVEN FACES busker.

Napoleon.

Franz Schubert.

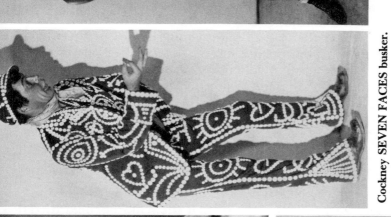

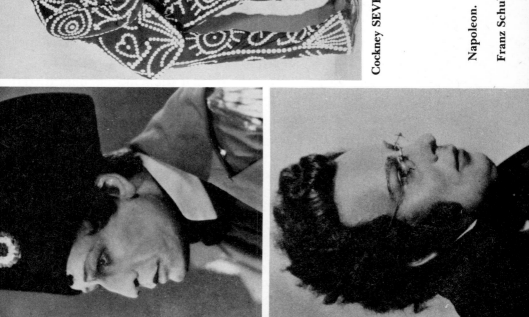

market crash in 1929, didn't go down with a food-hungry Depression audience.

But film buffs still count old Chibou walking through the streets of Paris carrying a stolen Napoleon under his arm as one of the classic moments of film history. Arrested for the theft, Chibou is thrown in jail with a trial scheduled, one of the many times Muni enacted roles at the bar and behind bars.

Muni was as painstaking creating seven distinct and different voices as he was with the physical transformation of face and hands and posture. At this point in his career he discovered the Dictaphone, which recorded on black wax cylinders and had to be scraped for reuse. After an exhausting day at the studio, Muni would come home and "practice voice makeup." Although each character had just a few lines of dialogue, Muni would play them over and over, rehearsing, experimenting, changing inflections and vowel sounds. In a burst of perfectionist fervor, he bought a second Dictaphone machine, placed the two on tables to match the positions of the characters on the set. He would record each voice, then flip the machines on alternately, making certain not a single inflection was similar in any of the seven voices.

"It was a seven-ring circus," Bella said. "The problem was—when you live with all those men, which one do you kiss good-night?"

The heads of the studio, seeing the daily rushes, seemed ecstatic. Muni watched the dailies one evening but was horrified "at that stranger up there on the screen." He rushed out of the projection room and never watched dailies again.

Muni respected one director and was patiently civil with the other. Berthold Viertel had a wonderful face and a short but powerful body; Muni always said that a film should be made about Viertel, starring Edward G. Robinson. Muni addressed him as Papa Viertel. The Viennese director, accustomed to being the ultimate authoritarian on a set, was hampered by the division of responsibility and lost in the maze of camera tricks.

Halfway through the shooting of the picture, word came from Lucy and Abem Finkel in New York that their mother had died quietly in her sleep. Bella had never been in an airplane before and was terrified. But Jewish law demands burial within two days; how else could she get back in time for the funeral? Muni requested permission from the studio to accompany her; they refused. Bella flew alone. The trimotor plane made eight stops and took thirty hours between Los Angeles and New York.

The headline story, blazoned across four columns in the New York *Telegram* of April 4, 1929, describes the funeral:

EMMA FINKEL, ONCE YIDDISH STAGE STAR, TRIUMPHANT IN DEATH 25 YEARS AFTER TRAGEDY ENDED HER CAREER

Throng of Weeping Men and Women Pay Tribute to Stage Favorite

by Earl Sparling
New York Telegram Staff Writer

It would be nice to tell Emma Finkel that her funeral was a success—even a greater success than her "Second Wife".

Emma Finkel was pathetically afraid that she would die unknown and that she would be buried unremembered.

Before she went to Atlantic City for a last vacation she hobbled first on her crutches to Sigmund Schwartz, the east side undertaker who has been burying Yiddish actors and actresses since the time his hair was black and not white.

"Sigmund," she said, "I have not long now. You have been my friend in life and you will be my friend in death. I want I should have a good funeral and my children will pay. They are able."

It would be nice to be able to tell her now that her funeral yesterday was so good that Sigmund Schwartz ordered the theatrical choir not to chant in the streets for fear the multitudes might get beyond control. The undertaker had made the mistake of asking for only ten policemen.

Men and women wept along Second Avenue as Emma Finkel's body passed, and when the forty liveried cars in the cortege reached Washington Cemetery, hundreds of mourners were already there, held back at the gates by the uniformed guard. More were arriving every moment.

When Emma Finkel, once darling of the Yiddish stage, was buried, it was hard to obtain a taxicab on the east side; the sidewalks of Second Ave. were solid with humanity and every theatre there was draped with black.

Irish cops toiled to keep order, producers and players came down from Broadway to bear witness and aging Jews came from Baltimore, St. Louis, Chicago and Detroit to mourn. Even Molly Picon, the comedienne of today, had trouble keeping her eyes clear.

It was twenty-five years ago that Emma Finkel's career ended, when her jealous husband, Morris Finkel, shot her, crippling her for life, and then committed suicide, which is when she really died, though she lived to be 52 years old.

When beauty has turned to deformity, youth to old age and

a woman has been "dead" a quarter of a century, there is usually little mourning along the sidewalks, even on Second Ave.

Emma Finkel, old men on the east side will tell you, was the most beautiful girl the Yiddish stage has known, which perhaps is only the "pathos of distance" again, but there was no illusion of time in the tears that rolled down the faces of Isaac Zolotorewsky and Leon Blank and Cantor Brie himself as they stood in Washington Cemetery, where so many are buried who have twinkled in the Yiddish lights along the old Bowery and the newer Second Ave.

All of the famous of the Yiddish theatre of today followed Emma Finkel to her grave. A choir of 100 men, picked from the ensembles of the Yiddish theatres, lifted voices in the Jewish Actor's Club, 31 E. Seventh Street, where the ceremony was held, and Yiddish chorus girls carried the flowers.

As the cortege passed down Second Ave., a music store phonograph was throwing Aaron Lebedeff's comical "Al Chet" into the street. But in front of the crepe-draped Second Avenue Theatre the cortege stopped and the red-bearded Cantor Brie stepped forth and a sadder chant was heard.

Emma Finkel was buried with her book of yellowed press clippings resting on her bosom, as she had desired. Her three children of the theatre stood at the edge of the grave, Bella having flown from Hollywood by airplane.

"We buried her in her plain white *tachrichem*, as she should be, with just one piece of lace," said Sigmund Schwartz, the undertaker. "But I fixed make-up on her face, with rouge and everything, as I used to know it when she was a girl on the stage twenty-five years ago."

Muni, alone in Hollywood, felt lost without Bella on the set. He phoned New York every night, urging her to return as soon as possible. Bella refused to fly again, so she made the long journey by train.

The shooting lumbered on. Technical difficulties pushed the filming into the hot-weather days. Air conditioning was still a thing of the future. Muni sweated through seven heavy makeups and lost twenty pounds.

The Academy of Motion Picture Arts and Sciences had been formed, and Muni was invited to join. He accepted gladly; it was an honor to be a member of the select group which considered film as an art form. But the Munis did not attend the first banquet at the Roosevelt Hotel in May, 1929; Bella was still in mourning. The awards were somewhat late, for the season of 1927–28, and went to *Wings,* the only silent picture ever to win, to Janet Gaynor

STAGE   BROADWAY   SCREEN

VARIETY

PRICE
25¢.

Published Weekly at 154 West 46th St., New York, N. Y., by Variety, Inc. Annual subscription, $10. Single copies, 25 cents.
Entered as second-class matter December 22, 1905, at the Post Office at New York, N. Y., under the act of March 3, 1879.

VOL. XCVII. No. 3   NEW YORK, WEDNESDAY, OCTOBER 30, 1929   88 PAGES

WALL ST. LAYS AN EGG

Going Dumb Is Deadly to Hostess In Her Serious Dance Hall Profesh

DROP IN STOCKS ROPES SHOWMEN

Kidding Kissers in Talkers Burns Up Fans of Screen's Best Lovers

for three films (*Seventh Heaven, Street Angel,* and *Sunrise*) and to Emil Jannings for two (*The Last Command* and *The Way of All Flesh*). Muni's *The Valiant* would be eligible for the following year, but he shrugged away the suggestion, certain that not only the film but he himself would be forgotten by then.

Plans were already being made for Muni's next picture. The studio agreed to try to get the rights to Molnar's *Liliom,* and Muni was intrigued with the possibility; it was a full-blooded role which had both guts and poetry. But Muni promised Bella a leisurely cruise to Hawaii first.

The stock-market crash stunned Hollywood. The famous *Variety* headline of October 30, 1929, WALL ST. LAYS AN EGG, was more than a joke. Show people on both coasts were wiped out. Bella, who had begun investing cautiously in the stock market, never dealt on margin, so their financial loss was minimal. Muni insisted on going through with the trip to Hawaii; they both desperately needed a vacation.

Two days before they were to sail, there was a frantic call from the studio. *Seven Faces* had been booked into the Roxy Theatre in New York, and the studio wanted Muni to make personal appearances with the picture. Sheehan was sure it would help bolster attendance and get the film off to a rousing start, despite the market crash.

He offered to fly Muni and Bella to New York, but Muni turned him down. Once a fortune-teller had told Muni he would die in a plane crash. "I'm not afraid for myself," Muni said, "but

141

why should I kill the pilot and all the other people on the plane?"
Bella described their train trip back to New York:

> We were sent off to New York in a blaze of glory, flowers and fruit baskets in our drawing room and a very sad man, Muni. He felt the picture was no good and he was headed for trouble, but no one (except me) believed him.
>
> So we arrived in New York, still in a blaze of glory, photographers, a beautiful suite of rooms at the Savoy Plaza, flowers and the phone going all day with requests for interviews, etc., etc.
>
> Muni kept saying, "Wait till they see the picture; they will be sorry they wasted all this money on us." He was right. The picture was a flop. The critics tore it to pieces as a stunt, and they were right. Poor Muni had to go through the anguish of personal appearances to empty houses. The flowers stopped, the telephone calls stopped, and we sat in that beautiful suite of rooms all by ourselves and thoroughly miserable.

The New York *Times'* Mordaunt Hall praised Muni's performance as Papa Chibou but dismissed the rest of the film with a shrug. *Variety*'s editor-publisher, Sid "Sime" Silverman, reviewed it personally and called it "Six characters in search of a screen story . . . nothing wrong with Muni. It's the stories."

Still Muni carried out his part of the bargain and made personal appearances at the Roxy in New York and in theaters in Washington, Detroit, and St. Louis during late November and early December through the worst blizzards in years. "Mr. Muni," the ads read, "will appear in person at all deluxe performances."

Muni dutifully came onstage, introducing himself without the help of the master of ceremonies, looking surprisingly young to an audience which had just seen seven of him on the silver screen, including the ancient Papa Chibou. He smiled winningly, modestly talked about the tricks of makeup.

"Sometimes," he said, "the makeup was so elaborate that when there were two days of shooting in a row for Franz Schubert, for example, I would go home as Schubert and come back the next day to finish the unfinished! But I never went to bed as Napoleon. You see, my wife didn't like being Josephine."

The rest of the live bill, enthusiastically billboarded by an unnamed master of ceremonies, included acrobatic dancers and other standard Fanchon and Marco acts. During their week at the Fox Theatre in Washington, the MC introduced Eddie Peabody, instrumentalist, playing "Painting the Clouds with Sunshine" with a line which has become part of show-business

142

history: "Eddie Playbody," he announced flamboyantly, "will now pee!" For Muni it was a brief patch of humor in stormy days.

No limousine greeted Muni and Bella on their return to Hollywood. Nobody from the studio met them at the station platform. They took a taxi home and began a long wait. The studio was silent. When Muni phoned to inquire about *Liliom*, they said, "We're working on it." Muni read a book on Rasputin, *The Holy Devil* by Philip Miller, and sent it to the studio story department as a possible property; it seems to have been deliberately misplaced there. "In Hollywood," Muni warned other actors, "never say 'Take me to your reader!'"

The studio did send over a huge stack of fan mail. One letter in particular amused Muni: "I liked you very much in all the roles you played in *Seven Faces* but I liked you best in the part of the judge!" Muni roared with laughter; Lester Lonergan had played the judge.

Finally, there was a call from Wurtzel's secretary: would Mr. Muni come in to confer with Messrs. Sheehan and Wurtzel the next day? At the meeting Sheehan hemmed and Wurtzel hawed. Yes, they were persuaded that *Liliom* should be made into a motion picture, but the fantasy elements would have to be minimized and the leads would have to be "big box-office stars." In view of what had happened with *Seven Faces*, Muni had not reached that exalted heaven. So they had decided to cast the famous Charles Farrell and Janet Gaynor in the leading parts, and Muni as Ficsur, the conniving, villainous supporting role. Perhaps later on Muni would be ready for "starring parts." Muni shrugged. He had played walk-ons in the Yiddish theater, bits, crossovers—why was this different? Nothing in his contract required him to be starred. He had wanted to play Liliom, not because it was the main part, but because he loved the double nature of the character. Reluctantly, Muni told the studio heads he would go along with them.

When he got home and told Bella what had happened, she began to shout, one of the few times in her life she ever got violently angry. "You were good enough to star in your first two pictures, weren't you? Are you going to let them demote you? Go back to the studio and tell them it's the leading role or nothing."

"What if they want to rip up the contract?" Muni asked.

"So they rip!"

Bella's anger was infectious. Muni pounded the table with his fist and shouted back. "That's exactly what I'm going to do! I'll either play Liliom or we'll get out of this dungeon!"

He drove back to the studio and told them his decision. Sheehan was fairly flippant about it.

"If you're sensitive about all this and it's any comfort to you," he said, "William Fox has just been fired, too."

When Albert Lewis, then stationed on the West Coast, heard about Muni's contract termination, he stormed into Sheehan's office, protesting that the studio was "letting go one of the great acting geniuses of our century."

Sheehan, the ex-New York fire commissioner, was unconcerned. "Good riddance!" he said.

A few days later, on April 3, 1930, the second annual Academy Awards banquet (for work in the 1928–29 season) was held at the Ambassador Hotel. The ceremony had been delayed because "the Academy wishes this year's bestowals to cover the new medium of talking pictures."

Muni was nominated as best actor for *The Valiant*, the first of five such nominations over the years, but lost to Warner Baxter as the Cisco Kid in *In Old Arizona,* described as an "outdoor talkie." *Broadway Melody* was named best picture; *The Valiant* was not nominated. Mary Pickford was named best actress for *Coquette*. Strangely enough, Tom Barry (but not his collaborator, James Hunter Booth) was nominated for "Writing Achievement" for the screenplay of *The Valiant*, but no mention was made of Robert Middlemass and Holworthy Hall, whose plot and dialogue constituted 90 percent of the picture. Barry received two nominations: he also wrote the "dialog" for *In Old Arizona,* but he lost to Hans Kraly, screenwriter of *The Patriot*.

A local Los Angeles radio station, KNX, broadcast one hour of the Academy Awards banquet that night from ten-thirty to eleven-thirty. The Munis did not attend.

Their first sojourn to the Land of Milk and Money was over.

BELLA and Muni decided to drive back to New York and forget about Hollywood completely. But no Broadway producer offered Muni a play, and the Yiddish theater had almost slowed to a stop. Muni was convinced he could never make a living as a motion-picture actor.

"Maybe I'll go into the cloak-and-suit business," he said again.

Pessimist Bella pointed out that people were buying as few cloaks and suits as they were theater tickets. The era was over when eleven plays opened in one night on Broadway.

Albert Lewis, feeling responsible for Muni's unhappy treatment in the film business, called a lot of New York casting directors. "Find a play for Muni," he told them. The young man he spoke to at the Crosby Gaige office was an ex-Californian, Arthur Lubin, an actor, stage manager, and in later years a celebrated film director. Coincidentally, Jake Wilk, a prominent literary agent (who became New York story editor for Warner Brothers several years later and consequently a close friend of the Munis'), asked Lubin to help his nephew, a young man just beginning as a writer.

Lubin was assigned as director-producer of an early-day indus-

Muni as Tony Camonte in *Scarface.*

Muni as the Capone-like gangster in *Scarface.*

trial stage presentation, *The Seven-Way Insurance Policy*; he agreed to give Wilk's nephew the job of writing it. That young man was Sidney Buchman, and he wrote the industrial with his left hand. With his right hand he was simultaneously working on three plays: *The Man Saul, Storm Song,* and *The Acute Triangle.*

Hearing of Muni's availability, Lubin and Buchman raced to get two thousand insurance salesmen fully briefed on how to sell insurance seven ways so they could concentrate on *The Man Saul,* which they felt was a perfect play for Muni. The ribbon copy, with directions in red, was shipped to California, hot off Buchman's typewriter.

Muni and Bella were packing to leave when the play arrived. They stopped to read the manuscript, unbinding it so that Muni could hand it page by page to Bella sitting alongside. When they finished, neither said a word. They just looked at each other and nodded yes.

The play has a guignol quality; it is a combination of symbolism and psychological probing with stageworthy melodramatics. Saul, the role for Muni, is a brutal, unfeeling, soulless thug; his brother, Marvin, is tender, sensitive, able to weep. One is flesh; the other is spirit. It deals with transmigration of a soul, not unlike *The Dybbuk.* Perhaps the playwright's intention that the two characters were really one was clarified when the title was changed for Broadway to *This One Man.* Muni saw in it overtones of *Liliom.*

When Muni agreed to do the play, Lubin teamed up with Richard Krakeur, general manager for Edgar Selwyn and scion of the Maison Le Blanc linen-store fortune, to become Broadway's newest and youngest producing organization. Lee Shubert offered to put up part of the money, but suggested a West Coast tryout since it was an expensive play with multiple sets. Lubin contacted Gilmore Brown at the Pasadena Playhouse, who agreed to a summer professional production; the playhouse was to get a small percentage of the profits if the play ever reached New York.

Muni was delighted with the idea of working in Pasadena. He didn't relish returning to the furnace heat of a Manhattan summer, and he found the palm tree quiet of this suburban oasis a change from the pressures of Broadway and the film world. He laughed when somebody described Pasadena as "the place people from Forest Lawn go to die."

The play did not die in Pasadena, where it played July 31 to August 9, 1930. But the producers were forced to advertise it as "NOT A BIBLICAL PLAY." Muni received a standing ovation on opening night, and the Los Angeles critics praised both the acting and the play. There were cries of "Author! Author!" and the joyful Sidney Buchman announced publicly that all three of his plays would be produced on Broadway during the 1930–31 season.

Arthur Lubin and Gilmore Brown were listed as co-directors of the Pasadena Playhouse production, but Lubin did most of the staging, with Brown adding his notes and comments along the way. "I ran into a problem as director," Lubin recalls. "Muni didn't listen to me or to any director; he listened to Bella. Once during rehearsals he got so temperamental that he bit a chair onstage. But he was brilliant in the play: a born performer, a great, great actor."

The rumor mills which grind alongside every stage production would have you believe *The Man Saul* was an exercise in self-analysis by Buchman, a trip through the playwright's own psyche. Buchman, it was whispered, once accidentally shot his own brother. The gossip was pure speculation; Sidney's only brother, Harold (later co-author of the stage play *Snafu*), is alive and bears no gun wounds. Muni, however, found the play an amazing exercise in psychoanalytical probing. His love scenes with his stage wife were brutal, almost sadistic. The role of Saul, a man denying tenderness, yet secretly longing for it, was achingly close to Muni's own double nature.

On a wave of theatrical euphoria, the young producers scheduled a Broadway opening for October at the Morosco Theatre, with way-stops in Hartford and New Haven. As scenic designer, Lubin hired his former professor at Carnegie Tech, Woodman Thompson. Muni requested a new director, somebody with art theater experience who could help probe the depths of the play. The producers, with Muni's approval, hired Leo Bulgakov, a pupil of Stanislavsky; Bulgakov abandoned a Greenwich Village season of classic repertory to accept the assignment.

Bella recalled the trip East:

> We decided to drive cross-country in our car. We were supposed to leave early one morning. But we were both so excited about the idea of going back to New York that neither of us could sleep. So at three o'clock in the morning Muni said to me, "How about getting up and leaving right now?" Which is just what we did.

Worrying that New York audiences might also think the play was a Biblical pageant, the Messrs. Lubin and Krakeur convinced Buchman to change the title to *The Man Holland,* which was used for the New Haven and Hartford performances. A second title, *Twice Born*, was announced for New York; it finally opened as

147

This One Man. The press agents, overselling, proclaimed Buchman the great hope of the American theater, and a fourth play of his, *Salvage*, to star Jeanne Eagels, was announced in the columns (where too often plays, like this one, have their total life and are then forgotten).

For his part, Muni kept saying, "Spit on it, it's ugly," and urged the press people to play down his Hollywood connections and the rave reviews from Pasadena.

"For God's sake," Muni advised, "let the critics come to the play in a state of virginity. And don't do the author the disfavor of writing his reviews in advance. As for me, I'm a bum. And then if the critics say I'm *not* a bum, it'll be a pleasure and a surprise!"

Muni was convinced that the opinion makers of New York had a built-in prejudice against anything even vaguely connected with Hollywood: any writer who had written for motion pictures or who voted in Los Angeles County was automatically a literary whore; any actor who had descended to films had sold his soul to Mammon.

For many years Muni told a story about Thomas Edison, which he felt bore a striking parallel to critics who come to the opening of a New York play with preconditioned opinions. Before he hired anybody, Edison would invite the job candidate to dinner and serve a rare and delicious soup. If the guest poured salt in the soup before he tasted it, Edison would not hire him.

"Some critics are the same way," Muni noted. "They arrive at a play and pour salt and pepper and a soupçon of shit into the soup before the curtain even goes up!"

A new cast was hired for Broadway, except for two other members of the Pasadena company, Robert Griffin and Mike Donlin, a one-time outfielder for the New York Giants. Additions to the New York cast included Paul Guilfoyle as the poetic brother, Constance McKay as the gun-moll wife, and Victor Kilian as one of the highly effective cross-examiners.

The three days at the Shubert Theatre in New Haven and the following three days at the Parsons Theatre in Hartford brought the play enthusiastic reviews but sparse audiences. Despite the low prices (tickets ranged from 50 cents to a $2 top), the Depression-wracked public stayed away. In New Haven the company met the scenery face-to-face for the first time. (Actors, enduring an uncivilized Broadway custom, rehearse on bare stages and only encounter scenery brief hours before the first out-of-town performance.) The sets for *The Man Holland* were heavy,

148

large, and mounted on a series of wagons. Whether all of it would work was as much a part of the theatrical suspense as the play itself.

Herschel Williams, Jr., the critic of the New Haven *News*, praised Muni's "devastating vitality" but reported: "Last night the panic-stricken moment was (much to our delight!) when the sliding door of the underground hideout of Scene II momentarily left its track. We didn't breathe freely until it got safely back on again."

It was no delight to members of the cast or to the director and producers, who screamed at the mild-mannered and professorial scenic designer. He assured them that all would be in good working order by the time they reached New York.

It wasn't. The scenery, which had squeezed into the theaters in New Haven and Hartford, was too mammoth to fit the smaller Morosco stage in New York. Carpenters were summoned to saw off pieces of the cumbersome wagons. Jack Daniels, the stage manager, recalls that they even had to cancel the dress rehearsal and "open cold" in New York. Arthur Lubin begged Lee Shubert to let them postpone the opening. Shubert protested that it would cost too much money and that postponements were always bad luck. "Besides," he added, "what does it matter? That Muni is only a Yiddish actor, and nobody will care too much about him."

On opening night at the Morosco on October 21, 1930, scenic changes caused tedious delays, but the audience received the play with rapt and hushed respect. John Mason Brown reported in the New York *Post*: "At the lowering of its final curtain it was greeted with more enthusiasm than any other opening of the new season."

As far as Muni's performance was concerned, none of the critics had presalted the soup.

J. Brooks Atkinson in the New York *Times* (he had not yet dropped the J.) proved himself an astute Nostradamus in his vivid description of Muni's performance:

> With only *Four Walls* and *This One Man* offered in evidence, it may be too early to salute Mr. Muni as one of the giants of his profession. But as this notice is being written fifteen or twenty minutes after his concluding scene, it is difficult to think of anything in the drama beyond Mr. Muni's capacities.
>
> As Saul, the unregenerate, Mr. Muni is overpowering and magnificent. He is an actor of virtuosity, with variety of vocal

149

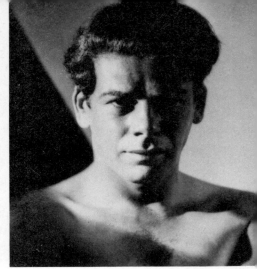

(Photo by White)

(Photo by Wm. Mortensen)

Constance McKay and Muni in a scene from *This One Man*.

Muni as Steven Moorhead in *Rock Me, Julie*.

inflections and great physical stamina. In his acting Saul becomes a character of many qualities—fright, rage, bravado, perplexity and remorse. Mr. Muni discriminates. He can play like a caged lion which he has to, but he can also retreat from destiny like a man stunned with fear. He has a considerable career behind him. That is all the more reason for believing that he has a great career ahead.

The acclaim for Muni convinced playwright and producers that they had a hit. The daily notices were followed up by even greater raves for Muni in the Sunday papers. But there were few ticket buyers at the Morosco box office. Burns Mantle roundly bawled out his readers in his *Sunday News* column:

> Personally I do not believe you are interested in acting. Or that any considerable number of your neighbors, associates or friends are interested in acting for itself alone. . . . For Mr. Muni gives one of the outstanding performances of this particular season. It is inspired by that inner conviction that is the fire of genius.

The producers fought to keep the play open. But it melted into slush with the pre-Christmas snow. Total performances in New York: thirty nine.

The playwright, understandably discouraged, abandoned his other projects and turned his back on Broadway. In the years that followed, Buchman wrote some of Hollywood's most notable screenplays, including *If I Had a Million*, a near classic, as well as *Theodora Goes Wild, Here Comes Mr. Jordan, Holiday,* and the unforgettable *Mr. Smith Goes to Washington.*

Muni was not ready to forsake Broadway. "I won't go up in a plane," he said, "but if a play crashes, I'll get into the next one that comes along and take it up for a spin."

Muni accepted the first play offered to him and went into rehearsal three weeks after *This One Man* closed. It was probably a mistake. The play, *Rock Me, Julie* by Kenneth Raisbeck, was undoubtedly inspired by O'Neill's *Beyond the Horizon.* Helen Menken, who had created a stir in New York in *The Captive,* and was married briefly to Humphrey Bogart, was its star; Muni was Miss Menken's personal choice as her leading man. The love affair seems to have ended with the casting.

Broadway necrophiliacs were blaming "the disastrous season" on the Depression, unemployment, cheaper prices at the talkies, and the fact that all good playwrights had been lured away to Hollywood. But *Once in a Lifetime* was flourishing at the Music Box, kidding the beginning of sound and Hollywood's treatment of writers; Muni could have given Kaufman and Hart stories about sound and writers to match that comedy scene by scene. *Girl Crazy* with a Gershwin score was flourishing at the Alvin, and in November Lunt and Fontanne opened in Maxwell Anderson's *Elizabeth the Queen.* Herman Shumlin produced *Grand Hotel* at the National. (The barometer of the times indicated that money was so scarce that Shumlin had to take as co-producer Harry Moses, an underwear magnate from Cleveland.)

The producers, Morris Green and Lewis E. Gensler, were astute enough to engage one of the theater's top professionals, Donald Oenslager, to design the spacious and sunlit Illinois living room for *Rock Me, Julie,* but they went through several directors. Helen Menken's tirades caused the quick disappearance of directors, but Muni's record for temperament led the gossips to blame him.

"We seem to be changing our directors," Muni noted philosophically, "about as often as we change socks."

But Muni could never find the producers when he had a complaint. They were simultaneously producing a musical, with a score by Gensler and a book by Russel Crouse, Oscar Hammerstein, and Morrie Riskind, called *The Gang's All Here.* (Years later when we asked Crouse for permission to use that title for a straight play, he said, "Help yourself. It didn't last long enough for the paint on the scenery to dry!")

During rehearsals for *Rock Me, Julie*, a comely but talentless starlet suddenly appeared, assigned to play a no-line walk-on. The members of the cast were convinced she must be sleeping with one of the producers. A few days later the young lady arrived at the rehearsal with several lines which had been added; there was no doubt in anybody's mind—she was now sleeping with the playwright. A week later the new director spent an entire day blocking the starlet into a more prominent downstage position. "Aha!" said somebody in the cast, as all eyebrows went up simultaneously. "Now she's sleeping with the director!"

Then the young lady dared to go up to Muni, who was hunched in a chair studying his part. "Oh, Mr. Muni," she gushed, "you are such a great actor. You have so much experience. Could you give me some hint, some basic rule of the theater?" Muni stared at her steadily.

"Yes, my dear young lady," he said slowly, "there is one fundamental rule of the theater you ought to know. You can't fuck an audience!"

For the record, the director was changed the next day, the part was written out, and that sexually athletic young lady shall be forever nameless in theater history.

Rehearsals plodded on. Christmas was forgotten with the opening scheduled at the Broad Street Theatre in Newark on December 29, with further stops at Brandt's Flatbush Theatre and the Bronx Opera House. If you are out of town with a disaster in Philadelphia, you can take a walk in Rittenhouse Square or go think alongside a Rodin; in Boston you can get some air in the Common. But where do you go in Newark for solace?

They were out of town but not far enough out.

When a play is spitting distance from Shubert Alley, all the Broadway wisenheimers begin to spit even before it arrives on Forty-fifth Street. Kenneth Raisbeck, the playwright, had won some renown as a lieutenant to Professor George Pierce Baker at Yale; he was bitten by Broadway when his one-act play *Torches* was part of a little theater tournament at the Nora Bayes Theatre in 1923. He seems to have attempted an American *Cherry Orchard* with *Rock Me, Julie*, in which he tells of a family reunion on a riverbank homestead in Illinois. Helen Menken played the daughter of the family who goes to New York for a career as a singer; she returns to Illinois, large with child (illegitimate) but totally unpregnant with success. Muni played Steven Moorhead, an adopted son, longing to leap beyond the horizon, but grounded by the discovery that he, too, is illegitimate. The unfortunate title of the piece comes from an old popular song about childhood innocence and purity.

The author had worked on the play for years. There is a special purgatory for playwrights; they are tortured by play doctors, cast changes, and producers who love a play passionately when they option it, then abandon it the moment one fat lady in Flatbush walks out during Act Two to go to the toilet. The dramatist suffers the ultimate damnation when the play opens on Broadway on a Tuesday night and closes the following Saturday.

Actors in a flop are equally sensitive, feeling every member of the audience is an assassin, ready to shoot down their lives, their careers, indeed blast apart their souls.

"Love is love when it is," Helen Menken's Charlotte says to Paul Muni's Steven in the play. Muni was directed to listen and nod and absorb this wisdom.

"I listened," Muni recalled many years later. "My God, I listened. And I pretended to understand what the hell it meant."

Hope brightened for the Broadway season during January. Tickets were at a premium at the Times Square Playhouse, where Noel Coward and Gertrude Lawrence were starring in *Private Lives*. (Nobody paid much notice to the comparative unknown Laurence Olivier, who played Victor Prynne, or to Olivier's wife then, Jill Esmond.) A pleasant folk item by Lynn Riggs, *Green Grow the Lilacs*, also opened in January and managed to eke out sixty-four performances; who would have dreamed that it would blossom into *Oklahoma!* a decade later?

Dr. Leo Michel, whose patients included many of the notables of the theater, remembers being backstage at the Royale Theatre the night of *Rock Me, Julie*'s dress rehearsal. He found Muni, depressed and disconsolate, in his dressing room. "Leo," Muni wailed, "I can't go through with this. Helen Menken is okay, but I'm terrible. But what can I do? It's her play—the lines, the words, the situations, they're all hers. I feel miserable." Michel sneaked out, tiptoeing along the corridor. Helen Menken called to him from her dressing room. She was in tears. "Leo, what am I going to do? I can't go on. What there is in the play, Muni has—the lines, the situations, everything—all Muni—nothing for me. I'm miserable!"

The play opened on a cold night, February 3, 1931. It closed seven performances later. *Rock Me, Julie* was Muni's shortest and most disastrous Broadway run. Atkinson in the *Times* confessed bewilderment at the play, but added: "Paul Muni's solid personality and the candor of his acting bring something of reality to the part of the adopted boy. But Helen Menken, as the delinquent sister, leaves Mr. Raisbeck's character still swimming in the air."

Plays which open on a Tuesday night usually omit the matinee the following day. *Rock Me, Julie* played on. But the audience was limp and sodden. Suburban dowagers clutched their fur coats, soaked from the sleet outside, and seemed fully briefed by the morning critics what a soggy play they were attending. The weather was equally gloomy backstage; the closing notice had been posted.

Muni was hurt and stung by a personal attack from Robert Garland in the New York *Evening Telegram*:

> Mr. Paul Muni is not as Paul Muni-ish as expected. In the first place, his Ben-Ami-like accent has as good as disappeared. In the second place, he projects his role without the hysterical histrionics which went far toward shortening the run of *This One Man* earlier in the season. As a matter of report, he uses no more than three and a half of his seven celebrated faces.

Muni was never to forget this; somehow it erased in his mind all the good reviews he had ever received. Bella tried to comfort Muni by pointing out that Helen Hayes also had two hasty arrival-departures on Broadway that season, but Muni's misery was not lessened by company.

He grabbed the first offer which came along. The Theatre Guild's Lawrence Langner and Theresa Helburn invited him to join their acting company. The prospect seemed a happy one; he would be a member of an ensemble group of distinguished players, and the Guild had high standards in its selection of plays. Muni felt it would be like being back in the Yiddish theater at its best.

The first script the Guild gave him was *He*, a play by Alfred Savoir which had been produced in Paris under the French title of *Lui* and which had been presented for a single performance at the Arts Theatre in London. Chester Erskine, a talented young man working with the Frohman company, adapted the play and was set to direct it. The Guild planned a spring tryout in Princeton, Philadelphia, and Boston, a summer layoff, then an early fall opening in New York.

Muni plunged into rehearsals. Though he had the title role, he felt playing a character called simply "He" was a disadvantage. He wanted to play flesh and blood, not a symbol, and tried throughout his career to avoid generalizations, characters called "The Soothsayer" or "The Stranger," nameless, faceless creatures. This part had slightly more substance; it was a sane madman pretending to be God (or was he *really* God?) to rankle a convention of freethinkers who had just voted to deny the existence of a

154

deity. The end of the play finds the Man-who-played-God returning to a mental sanitarium with his keeper. Muni enjoyed one telling line: "If God really did walk the earth, that's where you'd put Him—in an insane asylum." But it was not enough. The play seemed murky, and Muni was uncomfortable in the role, feeling he could not add flesh or feeling to "He"—or, as he began calling the part, "HIM."

"I just can't play a man I have to hold at arm's length and look at like some kind of stranger," Muni told Langner. He asked for his release from the company, promising he would come back to the Guild whenever it might need him or want him. Reluctantly, it let him withdraw from the cast. Two weeks into rehearsal, Tom Powers took over the role. Muni also felt that the Guild was producing this work with its left hand, using the cream of its acting regulars for O'Neill's *Mourning Becomes Electra* and Sherwood's *Reunion in Vienna*, both on the Guild production schedule. When the cast of *He* regrouped in the fall, it faltered, despite the addition of Claude Rains as a Napoleonic elevator man. After playing to forty half-filled houses, *He* expired before the Guild subscription period was even concluded.

Muni was desperate.

"A writer can write in an attic," he told Bella, pacing up and down in their New York apartment, "or on the top of a bus. Or with a sharp stick in some wet cement. To act, an actor has to have words. A stage. A camera turning. I can't go into the middle of Times Square, stop traffic, and start acting."

"Why not?" Bella said. "I've seen you do it."

Jonas Silverstone, later Muni's New York lawyer and close counselor, recalls how Muni bundled Bella into their Dodge touring car and drove out to Manhattan Beach. Silverstone's father, Harry Silverstone, a successful real estate man before the Depression, held court in his dining room, and Muni rushed to him for advice.

"I'm thoroughly disgusted with show business," Muni told the elder Silverstone, "and I want out. To hell with the theater. I'm through with it. I've had a bellyful!"

"Oh?" Silverstone said wisely, letting the younger man spill out his venom. "And what do you want to do?"

"Make a living. A regular living. A weekly paycheck. In the theater, that's impossible. Look, we've got a couple of thousand dollars saved up, enough to eat on, but in a few months that'll be gone. Help set me up in some kind of business. Real estate maybe. Ladies' garment business."

"What do you know about the ladies' garment business?"

"Nothing. Find me a partner. He'll know."

For an hour Harry Silverstone tried persuasion and allowed Muni to go through frustration letting. Finally, Silverstone stood up.

"I've seen you perform, Munya. Many times. Yiddish. English. In between. You're not good."

Muni blanched.

"You're great! One of a kind. Not a job lot. Not merchandise. What do you know? Acting, yes. *Shmattas,* no!"

Bella, sitting silent during the entire exchange, smiled and sighed.

"Do what you do best, Munya," Silverstone advised. "You might not like it too much for the time being. But real estate and the theater have got to get better. God knows, they can't get worse!"

Several days later, three thousand miles away, H.H. teamed up with an archrival, H.H.; otherwise Muni's career might have staggered to a stop. Howard Hughes had purchased a book called *Scarface* by Armitage Trail. Although his lawyers were pressing a lawsuit against Howard Hawks for alleged similarities between Hughes' film, *Hell's Angels,* and Hawk's film, *Dawn Patrol*, the young multimillionaire was savvy enough to realize Hawks was the only director to make *Scarface* explode onto the screen.

In August, 1973, Hawks, tall, seventy-seven but still as athletic as a young flier, proclaiming, "I never eat lunch," sat in walking shorts over his long legs in the cool of his adobe house in Palm Springs (it was 108° outside). He smiled, recalling Hughes rushing to make peace forty-two years before in 1931.

"I was just teeing off at Lakeside Country Club, when the golf pro came up to me and said, 'Howard Hughes is on the phone and wants to come out and play golf with you.' I said, 'Tell him I don't want to play golf with him.' 'Why?' 'The son of a bitch is suing me, that's why!' The pro went back to the phone, then rushed over to me on the fairway. 'He says he'll call the suit off.' Well, he came out, and we had a good game, and we decided to make a picture together. *Scarface.*

"I went to Ben Hecht and said, 'Ben, I've got a story.' 'What's it about?' 'It's a gangster picture.' 'Oh,' Ben said, 'you don't want to make one of those.' 'Well, I've got a little different idea,' I told him. 'The Borgia family lives today in Chicago. And Caesar Borgia is Al Capone.' 'Let's start tomorrow,' Hecht said.

"Ben wanted a thousand dollars a day, at the end of each day, in cash. Well, we wrote the whole damn thing in eleven days, story, scenario, everything. I'd originally offered him twenty thousand dollars to do the script, so I said, 'You made a bad deal, Ben. Let's take the train back to New York, and we'll work another week or ten days on it.'

"First I showed the script to Howard Hughes, who read it, grinned, and asked, 'Where's the brother?' 'There isn't any brother,' I told him. 'Well,' he said, 'you haven't used a damn thing from the book I bought except the title, but this is a great story—you'd better get at it right away.'

"It was terribly important to get solid, experienced actors. But all the best actors in Hollywood were under contract to the major studios, who weren't about to lend us anybody. We were independents, and they didn't like independents. To a major studio dealing with an independent was like sleeping with a leper. Oh, there was one exception. Irving Thalberg, an old friend of mine, heard about the story and said: 'We've got a fella over here at MGM and maybe you'd like him. His name is Clark Gable.' Well, I'd seen his first picture, and I turned him down. We needed a fantastic ACTOR, not just a personality. Nothing wrong with a personality; the camera likes certain people and turns them into something special and wonderful. But we needed *actor* actors, and I told Hughes I'd go to New York and look for some.

"Ben Hecht and I played quite a bit of backgammon on the Chief and the Twentieth-Century Limited, but we did a lot of work, too. When we got to New York, I saw Osgood Perkins (Tony Perkins' father) playing a kind of romantic lover on the stage, and I hired him as Johnny Lovo, the gang leader. I always had the theory that heavies had beady eyes, and Osgood certainly had them.

"A lot of people told me about Paul Muni and I remembered seeing him in the Yiddish theater in a fine scene with his back to the camera,* where he was such a purist he'd even made up his hands to fit the character. So I went to see him and told him about the movie. He was very pleasant and smiled but said he couldn't play that kind of man, he wasn't that kind of person, he wasn't physically strong enough. Besides he protested that Cagney had made *Public Enemy* and Robinson had made *Little Caesar*. What more could be done in *Scarface* that hadn't already been done?"

Bella remembered how charming and persuasive Howard Hawks was. He urged Muni to do a screen test in New York, not to convince Hughes or Hawks, but so Muni himself would be convinced he was right for the part.

*This is verbatim from the interview with Howard Hawks. It's interesting that a film director considers the watching eye a *camera* rather than a live audience.

Hawks rented a small studio, hired a cameraman and built a suit with padding to give Muni a heavier, huskier look. He deliberately cast supporting players for the test who were shorter than Muni; in addition, he had Muni walk around on planks to give him even more contrasting height. They shot one brief scene from the Hecht screenplay, with costumes and some rudimentary props, but without makeup or sound.

Though Muni had sworn off Hollywood, he was tempted to accept when Hawks ran the test for him. Muni admired Hawks' no-nonsense pragmatic approach to picturemaking; he stripped films of nonessentials and always said, "I'm a storyteller—that's the chief function of a director. And they're moving pictures, let's make 'em move!"

Muni also was a Hecht fan. He liked the screenplay's hard-bitten dialogue, laced with humor, and the epic quality of the rise and fall of Chicago gangster Tony Camonte. He was ready to sign when word came from the West Coast that Howard Hughes wanted Muni to fly out to make two additional tests, one for makeup and one for sound.

"It's insulting," Muni said, "and I won't do it. I've got a voice and I've got a face, and if Mr. Hughes doesn't know I can act by now, he'll never know. If I never do another picture, I won't make another test!"

Muni received a wire from Hughes in reply:

> OFFER TWENTY THOUSAND DOLLARS SUBJECT
> TO VOICE AND MAKEUP TESTS
>
> HUGHES

The giants squared off against each other. Muni dictated a wire:

> TWENTY-SEVEN FIVE AND NO MORE TESTS
>
> MUNI

Hawks kept phoning from New York; Hughes' office continued to wire and phone from the West Coast. Bella had a photographic memory of what happened next:

One evening we were sitting at home, and it was raining outside, and Muni was very restless. Then he suddenly said to me, "Bella, will you please pack a bag for me? I want to get in the car and just ride. I don't know where I'll land. I'll call you at midnight

158

and tell you where I am. I have to get away from these constant calls from the Coast and all the bickering. I don't want to go back to Hollywood, I am not a movie actor, my place is in the theater."

So I packed a bag for him (a thing I did many times throughout the years when the going got rough), and he left. He called me at midnight and told me he was in Greenwich, Connecticut. So. I was alone and I had to take the calls from the Coast. This went on for a few days, and Muni kept riding. Finally, I met with Mr. Hughes' New York representative, and it was agreed that Muni would not have to make another test. Also, they came around to the salary Muni had asked for. So—I made the deal. When Muni called me that night, I said, "Come on home, darling, we are going to Hollywood and you are going to do *Scarface!*" He pretended to be angry about the whole thing, but I suspect he was pleased. Here was another chance to prove whether he could make good in pictures. He always liked a challenge, and this was a big one.

Scarface was filmed in late spring and early summer of 1931 in an abandoned Hollywood studio rescued from the spiders by Hawks and his crew. Hawks cast Ann Dvorak as the sister, Karen Morley as the gun moll, Vince Barnett as Tony Camonte's "secretary," a pre-*Frankenstein* Boris Karloff, and a totally unknown hoofer named George Raft.

Hawks first spotted Raft in the audience at a prizefight, thought his Valentino-like smoothness ideal for Camonte's henchman Rinaldo, and asked him if he wanted to act. Raft was a dancer in cafés and had little or no experience onstage or in film. He asked for $500 to do the picture. Hawks paid him more, since the shooting schedule stretched over fifty or sixty days. The director, who later became the idol and inspiration of many of the French "New Wave" filmmakers, invented a piece of business for Raft, which has passed into history: Rinaldo's constant flipping of a nickel. Hawks devised the business so that the inexperienced performer would have something to do with his hands, but it became the standard symbol of the cool and poised hood. Later in the film Hawks had Raft cutting out paper dolls. To this day Raft is the prototype of the gangster, and though he has become a major star, Raft still says, "I don't know what the hell I did in *Scarface*, but it sure as hell wasn't acting!"

Hughes routinely submitted the script of *Scarface* to the Hays Office, a self-regulatory agency cooked up by the Motion Picture Producers Association to help combat the wave of Hollywood criticism from the bluenose press and pulpit—and presumably from the public. Will H. Hays, a God-fearing Presbyterian and

159

onetime national chairman of the Republican Party, stood with righteous sword unsheathed, ready to strike down onscreen or offscreen moral misbehavior in Hollywood.

The script of *Scarface* was returned to Hughes within a matter of hours, with a warning signed by one of Hays' chief censors, Colonel Jason Joy:

> Under no circumstances is this film to be made. The American public and all conscientious State Boards of Censorship find mobsters and hoodlums repugnant. Gangsterism must not be mentioned in the cinema. If you should be foolhardy enough to make *Scarface*, this office will make certain it is never released.

Hollywood studios had produced fifty-one gangster films in 1931, and Hughes felt the Hays Office was becoming moralistic after-the-fact. He sent a simple memo to Hawks:

> Screw the Hays Office. Start the picture and make it as realistic, as exciting, as grisly as possible.
>
> H.H.

Muni read as much as was available about Alphonse "Scarface" Capone for this story of a man who shoots his way to the top of a Chicago gang. He experimented with an arrogant, shambling walk. He tried a variety of accents. When they rehearsed the opening lines, Hawks said, "It's too Latin, too Italian. Cut it down. In half." "There won't be enough," Muni said, "but I'll try." He read a few more lines. "Cut it in half again," Hawks directed. "Howard, this isn't right," Muni protested. "Look," Hawks said, "we just want the *suggestion* that you're Italian. It's more in the inflection than in the accent. Besides, we want to understand you." Muni smiled. "That makes sense." Hawks reports that Muni found a rhythm and a subtle oily lilt which "worked beautifully through the whole picture."

As for the characterization of the contemporary Borgia, Hawks felt Muni began attacking Scarface as "too forbidding a man"—so together they evolved an approach to a character who attempted to be jovial, playful, despite his thick skin. As an illustration, Hawks told Muni of an actual incident in the career of the real Scarface: Capone once gave a banquet for an enemy, praised him, lifted toasts to him, joked, smiled, then killed him with a baseball bat.

"So many actors visualize characters as too dour, and they editorialize against them in their portrayals," Hawks says. "You

160

can't do that. I had a similar experience with another great actor, Edward G. Robinson. We were making *Tiger Shark*, and about four o'clock in the afternoon of the first shooting day, I said, 'Eddie, this is going to be one of the worst pictures ever made. I can't imagine anybody sitting for an hour and a half and looking at this. Let's make this a guy who tells bad jokes and laughs at everything.' And we did, and, by God, the picture is still playing!"

Hawks adds: "Incidentally, I think Muni, Robinson, and Walter Huston are the finest actors I ever worked with. I say actors because I'm usually fonder of personalities; I get more out of them —with the exception of that trio. All three were brilliant: they leaped out of the screen."

Hawks commented that most performers don't know stories and don't know what's good for them. He said he could sell a story to a famous Western star by telling him, "It's about a very handsome guy, he rides a horse, all the girls are crazy about him, and he's got a cock a foot long!" And the Western star would say immediately, "That's my kind of story. That's for me!"

Muni is entirely in silhouette in the opening shot of *Scarface*, spitting gunfire, setting the rhythm of violence which surges through the film. In the second sequence, the camera doesn't move in for a close-up; it remains stationary and a rising barber chair propels Muni into the close-up; the shadow becomes flesh—marred, scarred—the cross on the left cheek vivid in the key light. All the violence of the age is suddenly slapped at the audience.

Muni is surly, sultry, insolent, but even as a bloody gangster and wholesale murderer he has flashes of humor: winking, striking a match on a police officer's badge, clowning as he mimics Karen Morley plucking her eyebrows.

Although Hawks disdains tricks ("I've failed if the audience notices the camera shots more than the story"), he created some running effects which are collector's items in the opinion of film buffs. Thematically, through the picture, he uses X. Newspapers at the time always labeled their photographs of killings and accidents with a point of reference: "X MARKS THE SPOT WHERE THE BODY WAS FOUND." Hawks' opening credit is over an X, and the most remembered instance in the film is the killing of Boris Karloff during a bowling match; the camera moves in for the X on the bowling scoresheet: a strike.

"I got the crew together," Hawks recalls, "and I said, 'We're having a lot of killings and I want each to be labeled 'X MARKS THE SPOT' in a cinematic way. So anybody who comes up with a notion we can use will get fifty bucks. No, make that a hundred.'"

The grid above the garage in the St. Valentine's Day massacre is a series of X's; a body is sprawled on the ground, arms akimbo to shape an X; Raft's apartment number is the Roman numeral X; there are many others. Game players, seeing *Scarface* (mostly bootlegged through the film underground, it has never been released for television), try to spot the X's the way Sunday New York *Times* readers try to find the Ninas in Al Hirschfeld drawings.

They filmed a car wreck, a spectacular, splintering crash as a gunned-down driver loses control. Hughes saw it in the rushes and told Hawks, "Great shot! Let's have more of those. A lot more. All through the picture." So they made sixteen and used every one of them. When Hawks' friend and fellow director Lewis Milestone saw a rough cut of the picture, he said, "You're not going to use all of those, are you?" Hawks replied, "I think we are, Milly, because the total effect shows the whole reign of terror. And that's what the picture's about."

"Muni was an instinctive actor," Hawks says. "There aren't many of them around today. I wanted Muni to hit somebody in one scene. I hired a prizefighter, a friend of mine, and told him, 'During rehearsal, put your hand up to your jaw, but when the camera is rolling, take your hand away and really let Muni hit you.' Well, during the shot, Muni socked him, and the fighter toppled over; Muni just stared at him, not expecting to knock the guy out. I shouted, 'Act, you son of a bitch! Act!' And Muni went right on with the scene without even a glance at me.

"We had a shot where Muni had to poke his fist through a plate-glass window and the glass cut him and he began to bleed. He stopped for a second to glance down at his hand, and I yelled the same thing again: 'Act, you son of a bitch. Act!' He did, and he was tremendous."

Hawks also recalls how he and Muni got together to trick a trickster. Vince Barnett was a professional practical joker; he was often hired to impersonate waiters at private parties and spill tureens of soup into people's laps. Hawks got some snuffpowder and put it between the clapboards just before one of Barnett's major close-ups. When the cameras were rolling, Barnett began to wrinkle up his nose and sneeze. Muni pretended to be furious. "It's an insult to a fellow actor to do a thing like that!" Muni shouted, getting madder and madder at the apologetic and sneezing Barnett. Bella finally came over and tried to calm him down; Muni acted the gag outrage so convincingly he even fooled Bella. Later that day Barnett was gunned down in a scene and Hawks said to him, "Vince, you just lie there until I tell you to move." Then Muni, in on the prank, walked off with Hawks and the crew. Everybody went to lunch and left Barnett lying there for an entire hour.

"I never make a picture that's supposed to be a big one" Hawks says. "I like to take a little picture and make it big." *Scarface* followed that pattern: it made history, and it made Muni a picture star. The wealth of authentic, almost documentary detail gave the film a vivid reality. Gangsters would come visit Hawks, curious how he had found out things that had actually happened: a shoot-out from a moving hearse, for example. Once a hood named Charles White came to see Hawks, who kept his visitor waiting in the outer office until he was able to phone Chicago and find out everything possible about the man. When White walked in, Hawks looked up casually and said, "Oh, hello, Puggy, how are you?" White's jaw fell open. "How'd you know my name?" "Oh, I know quite a bit about you, Puggy. You started as a pimp on the South Side, you carried a gun for Al, and you were in on the killing of Jim Colisimo on Twenty-second Street." Puggy stared back. "No," he said, "you got it all wrong. I wasn't never no pimp!"

The major battle of *Scarface* was offscreen with the Hays Office. Officials were indignant when they saw the completed picture. They insisted on a title change and suggested the moralistic *Shame of the Nation*. "I'll change it," Hughes said, "if some other producers will change their titles to *Sweetness and Light* and *God, Ain't We Pure Though?*" The Hays Office also sent down an edict from on high that there would be no official Seal of Approval without dozens of cuts, the addition of a scene in which gangsterism is solemnly denounced, and an entirely new ending where the villain is tried and hung instead of being gunned down in the gutter.

"They objected to strange things in the picture," Hawks recalls. "They thought that the relationship between Muni and his sister [Ann Dvorak] was too beautiful to attribute to a gangster. They didn't recognize that it was supposed to be Borgian incest. All they worried about was that it was too tender an emotion. To them a gangster was not supposed to have any human dimension whatsoever."

Bella had her own problems at home. She described it this way:

> I sensed a change in Muni which worried me. He seemed to have become a different person. His whole manner toward me was different. At one time I thought: "Aha! Hollywood has got him. He is giving me the brushoff. He is not my Muni anymore." Suddenly it dawned on me. "Of course he isn't my Muni. He is bringing *Scarface* home with him."

On the final day of shooting, Muni received a letter from Elmer

Rice in New York. Rice, who had won the Pulitzer Prize for *Street Scene* and international admiration for *The Adding Machine*, had just completed a new play, *Counsellor-at-Law*, and thought Muni would be ideal for the leading role of George Simon. Muni wired back: SEND THE PLAY. The playscript arrived. Muni read it, loved it, and wanted to take the next train back to New York. There was a hitch: Howard Hughes had an option to do another picture with Muni. Bella conferred with David Tannenbaum, their West Coast lawyer. Nobody could reach Hughes. Finally, word arrived that Hughes was thoroughly disgusted with Hollywood, that he would never make another film, and that he was not going to pick up Muni's option. Muni and Bella, already packed, were on the Chief the following day, heading back to New York and the Broadway stage.

Hughes, faced with a film in the can, no available release, and $600,000 down the drain (far below what the production would cost today), decided to give in to the Hays Office demands. Over the objections of Hawks, multiple cuts were made, the title was euphemized, and several scenes were added, not directed by Hawks. One scene, which Hawks describes as "the most sickening piece of film I've ever seen," is a total break from the relentless rhythm and style of the picture. A bunch of do-gooders are seated around an office asking for a moral battle against the gangsters, sermonizing, advising that "We declare martial law. The Army will help. The American Legion will help." No wonder Hawks wanted to throw up.

The final scene was brilliant in the original cut: Scarface, trapped in police crossfire and driven outside by tear gas, breaks into the babble of a craven coward, then is shot down, ending like a rat in a sewer. The camera pans up to an electric advertising sign, carefully planted throughout the picture: THE WORLD IS YOURS. COOK TOURS. It said dramatically far more than any moralizing or righteous hanging-by-the-forces-of-law-and-order could ever convey. For the Hays Office-dictated ending, the court scene and hanging had to be shot with a double, since Muni was already in New York and in rehearsal for *Counsellor-at-Law*. Muni was amused when he heard that the sentencing was done with the double's back to the camera. "At least it could have been *my* back," he said. And when they showed the trip to the gallows with only feet plodding across the "last mile," Muni remarked, "I showed emotion once with my back—but never with feet—particularly *somebody else's* feet!" Ben Hecht, also tweaked by the irony, used a parallel incident at the ending of his short story about the filming of the final passion of Jesus, "The Missing Idol," a devastating attack on the film colony in his masterpiece, *The Book of Miracles*.

Hawks felt the film had been totally emasculated, but it now had the doubtful testicle of a Seal of Approval. Hughes booked a New York theater. Instantaneously, the New York State Board of Censors refused to allow it to play. Hughes was certain that Will Hays had secretly urged the New York Board to turn it down despite the seal. He issued a fighting statement, which a great many newspapers printed:

> It has become a serious threat to the freedom of honest expression in America when self-styled guardians of the public welfare, as personified by our film censor boards, lend their aid and their influence to the abortive efforts of selfish and vicious interests to suppress a motion picture simply because it depicts the truth about conditions in the United States which have been front page news since the advent of Prohibition.
>
> I am convinced that the determined opposition to *Scarface* is actuated by political motives. The picture, as originally filmed eight months ago, has been enthusiastically praised by foremost authorities on crime and law enforcement and by leading screen reviewers. It seems to be the unanimous opinion of these authorities that *Scarface* is an honest and powerful indictment of gang rule in America and, as such, will be a tremendous factor in compelling our State and Federal governments to take more drastic action to rid the country of gangsterism.

The banning of the film only made the public hungrier to see it. But Hughes, normally unconcerned about anything resembling public issues, was suddenly a champion of civil rights. The New York *Herald Tribune* even wrote an editorial: "Hughes is the only Hollywood producer who has had the courage to come out and fight this censorship menace in the open. We wish him a smashing success."

The film was banned by other state censorship boards and by many individual cities, so Hughes began a series of lawsuits. He won the case in New York State and issued the picture with its original title, the cuts restored, and only that one sickening office scene remaining. It opened at the Strand Theatre in New York almost a year after the filming had been completed.

The reviews were raves, particularly for Muni and Hawks. Mordaunt Hall in the New York *Times* said, "The picture is dominated by Mr. Muni's virile and vehement acting." But *Scarface* did not receive a single Academy Award nomination, nor did anybody connected with it. The major studios, despising the fantastic commercial success of this upstart independent, voted in blocks against it. So actors, director, writers, cinematographers (Lee Garmes and L. W. O'Connell created some of the most startling camera work in film history) went unsung, except at the box office.

The Producers Association did issue a public statement. This, they promised, would be the last of the gangster films. Ever. Never again, they swore, would the silver screen show such violence and brutality.

Muni saved and treasured another review, sent via Postal Telegraph on December 6, 1932:

DEAR PAUL MUNI MAY I CONGRATULATE YOU ON YOUR VERY GREAT PICTURE AT THE STRAND I HAVE NEVER SEEN A FINER PERFORMANCE

NOEL COWARD

Howard Hughes changed his mind about remaining in the picture business and rushed to New York. Muni was enjoying a double triumph, onstage at the Plymouth and onscreen at the Strand. Muni, who had never seen Hughes in person before, was surprised when a meeting was requested.

Hughes arrived at Muni's hotel in a rumpled sweater and dirty tennis shoes, slouched into a chair, and muttered that he was sorry he hadn't taken up Muni's option. He blamed the oversight on his attorneys. He said he wanted to put Muni under contract for several more pictures.

"I thank you for the offer, Mr. Hughes," Muni said. "But all during the time I was shooting *Scarface,* you didn't have the courtesy of coming on the set to shake my hand and say hello. You're just not the type of man I want to be associated with—so I'll never work for you again."

He didn't. *The Outlaw* was the climax of Howard Hughes' contribution to the motion-picture art. It starred Jane Russell.

15

MUNI was playing a lawyer on Broadway, but he was unable to participate actively in fighting what he considered "the obscenity of censorship." He felt that his portrayal of the gang lord in *Scarface* and Hawks' vivid direction would be tract enough, without

(Photos by Maurice Goldberg)

The various moods of a lawyer. Muni in *Counsellor-at-Law*.

the added sermon. And he was convinced that the cuts would soften the power-mad brutality of the work, merely lessen its impact on the public. Watering it down would divorce the film from reality, fictionalize it into a never-never land: Chicago would be a mythical kingdom invented by Hollywood.

During the year *Scarface* was imprisoned in the film vaults, Muni was outraged that a good piece of work—and seven months of his own life—was being wasted. He rehearsed speeches which were never delivered. "How, ladies and gentlemen of the jury, do you get rid of the rats if you don't even know what a rat looks like? How do you eradicate a deadly disease if you refuse to believe it is virulent in the land? Can you find the cure for a pernicious destroyer of our lives if you won't put the bug on a glass slide and examine it under a microscope?"

Muni channeled all his passion and anger into playing the volatile George Simon onstage at the Plymouth, convinced that his motion-picture career, which had never really begun, was now totally finished.

In the fall of 1965 my partner and I flanked Elmer Rice on a TWA flight from New York to Columbus, en route to the borning meeting of American Playwrights Theatre. Elmer often frightened people away, for he had no truck with *politesse*; he was fierce in his battle against sham, onstage and in anything which touched his own person. If you met Elmer and fled after his first lightning bolts, you would label him merely acerbic and irascible. If you waited out the thunderstorm, you would find whole areas of quiet sensitivity and a sometimes bitter but often warm sense of humor.

167

When I asked Elmer to autograph a copy of his autobiography, *Minority Report*, he flipped open the cover, uncapped a pen, and drawled, "You sure you want me to sign this? Y'know an *un*autographed book by Elmer Rice is pretty valuable these days."

Then he told us about his adventures with Muni and the birth-pains of *Counsellor-at-Law*.

"I never met Muni, and I only saw him perform once—in *Four Walls*. I didn't think that play was very good, and the character of the young gangster was nothing at all like George Simon in *Counsellor*. But there was a quality in Muni that I admired. Energy. High voltage.

"Everybody who read my play said one thing: it would only work if we found the right actor to play Simon. Otherwise, forget it. I had two plays scheduled for that season, first *The Left Bank*, then *Counsellor*. And I was wearing three hats on both of them: playwright, producer, director. I didn't have time to give anybody acting lessons.

"Well, we read or interviewed every actor in sight. The damned play was more difficult to cast than it was to write. I had knocked it off in about six weeks at St.-Jean-de-Luz, on the Basque coast of France near the Spanish border. It came easy because I'd studied law and I'd been a flunky in a law office. So it was sort of a *Street Scene* of the legal profession. Lots of characters. Lots of atmospheric touches. Simon's not autobiographical at all, nor is the play based on any actual incidents. But that aggressive young New York attorney who's risen from a poor family to great success in a fashionable law office was focal, the key to the success of the play. Who the hell could act it?

"Everybody I talked to, including my production associates, said that Muni was all wrong for the part, and there were the usual rumors that he was very hard to work with. For a while I listened to them. But when I couldn't find anybody else, I wrote Muni in Hollywood, where he was making a picture, then sent him the script. His enthusiasm for the play got me enthusiastic about him—isn't that a playwright's disease? We quickly reached an agreement on terms, and I sent him a run-of-the-play contract. Everybody said I was crazy. Well, you have to be a little crazy to write a play in the first place, and when you put your own money in it, you should be committed to an asylum. I began to get a little worried, making this binding commitment to an actor I'd never met in person, never auditioned for the part, and had seen perform onstage only once. Muni wasn't due to arrive in New York until the day before rehearsal began. I don't pray very often. I prayed.

"When I met him, I stopped worrying. He was absolutely right for the part. And he was never difficult, not in rehearsals or during the entire run of the play."

Jonas Silverstone, the attorney, remembers coming into his office one morning and finding Muni slouched in the waiting room.

"Do you want to see me, Munya?" Silverstone asked his cousin by marriage.

"No, Yoina, I just want to sit here and drink-in your office routine. Watch a little. Listen. Absorb. Smell."

During the weeks of rehearsal, Muni would show up often at Silverstone's office, browsing, probing, trying to become involved in the "feel" of a practicing attorney's day, so he could pick up stances, postures, atmosphere, words, phrases, intonations, rhythms.

"Someone said I worked like Muni and Muni worked like me," Silverstone says. "Whether he saw anything in me he'd want to imitate, I don't know, but watching him onstage in *Counsellor* and then later in *Inherit the Wind* made me proud to be an attorney. And Muni loved playing lawyers—far more than playing doctors!"

Rice's *The Left Bank* was set to open early in October and *Counsellor-at-Law* by mid-November. Rice had agreed to the latter date so that he could guarantee getting the Plymouth Theatre, then managed by Arthur Hopkins. But this meant only five weeks between the two plays and ruled out the possibility of an out-of-town tryout. Opening cold in New York with only one preview worried Muni, but he was fascinated by the part and the play, and he intensified his concentration.

The playwright-director didn't want casual passersby to drop into the Plymouth during rehearsals. Muni would walk offstage if he saw anybody in the theater other than Rice and Bella. So Rice had the lobby doors tied from the inside, and screens and a curtain were stretched across the back of the theater. This offended several reportorial snoopers from New York papers, accustomed to ferreting out gossip by dropping in unannounced at play rehearsals.

Muni's nervousness was compounded when he learned what happened that season to the monument of the Yiddish theater, the immortal Boris Thomashefsky, on his first excursion uptown to Broadway. Thomashefsky's oldest son, Harry, was shocked that his famous father was playing in nightclubs because of the startling decline and fall of the Yiddish theater downtown. So Harry translated a famous Yiddish operetta, *Chasanta (The Cantor's Wife)*, into English and called it *The Singing Rabbi*. He convinced his father that they could make a fortune presenting the work on Broadway, if they advertised:

The great Boris agreed. The king would no longer have to descend into a Rumanian cellar and perform a nightclub act in an "upholstered toilet." And if he earned enough money on Broadway, he might convince Bessie to divorce him and he could marry the love of his life, the *zoftig* red-haired Regina Zuckerberg.

The Selwyn Theatre on Forty-second Street was booked, a cast of English-speaking professionals was assembled, and the opening night was set: September 10, 1931. The theater was packed.

Thomashefsky made his entrance to cheers and applause. He looked out at the audience, bowed, then lapsed into Yiddish. The rest of the cast, confused and bewildered, stumbled between English and Yiddish, even lapsing into Russian. Disappointed members of the audience walked out indignantly. Thomashefsky persisted, not uttering a single word of the King's English for the rest of the performance.

When he came offstage at the end of that opening night, he found Harry waiting in the wings, weeping.

"Papa," Harry moaned, "how could you do this to me? We promised, we promised the whole world, you would perform in English. You've ruined me!"

Boris just stared at his son.

"For forty-nine years I have been performing in Yiddish," he said. "Successfully. So, my dear, loving, devoted son, go fuck yourself!"

For the record books: *The Singing Rabbi* closed that Saturday night. Total performances by B. Thomashefsky on Broadway—four.

The Munis wired BREAK A LEG and two days later their condolences. Only Western Union showed a profit.

During the third week of rehearsal of *Counsellor-at-Law* Elmer Rice confronted his cast with some disconcerting news. Three other plays were also scheduled to open on Monday night, November 9. Which one would the first-string critics attend? *The Social Register* had Anita Loos as co-author and stars of the magnitude of Lenore Ulric and Sidney Blackmer. Rice told them they didn't have to worry about *Peter Flies High*; the leading role was played by an unknown named Brian Donlevy. But S.N. Behrman's *Brief Moment* marked Katharine Cornell's debut as a producer, it starred Louis Calhern, and—woe to anybody else who opened that night—a fat part had been especially written by Behrman for Alexander Woollcott. Major reviewers wouldn't miss the onstage debut of a fellow critic. (Woollcott was a New York institution, a walking Mount Rushmore.)

Rice advised that they move their opening to the preceding Friday, November 6, with a preview the night before. "Otherwise," he told his cast, "we'll get reviewed by financial editors, police reporters, sportswriters, and snot-nosed office boys."

Muni was panicked, but he reluctantly agreed. Rice's *The Left Bank* was a hit a block away, and he respected the playwright's total knowledge of theater.

The preview, before a packed and enthusiastic audience, was almost too good. It worried Muni because everybody backstage seemed to be floating on a cloud of success. Muni was superstitious. He wanted no compliments. "Wait!" he said. "Wait. Tomorrow is the important night. The critics may hate us."

Muni had worked carefully on the infinite details of the character of George Simon, probing the man's vulnerabilities, slowly revealing to the audience Simon's weaknesses and strengths. He wanted a full-blooded character onstage. Not Paul Muni. Not something invented on paper by a playwright. But George Simon, breathing, laughing, terrified. If he could make the audience believe it was all happening *now*, for the first time, never before, then he thought he could consider himself an actor.

Elmer Rice recalled to us his opening night anguish:

"I sat in the light booth, way at the top of the Plymouth, with Arthur Hopkins. The first scene went fine. Then Muni made his entrance. Something was wrong. Suddenly I realized he had gone blank, dried up. And he had to be prompted. He was used to it from the Yiddish theater, but his frequent crosses to the stage manager's side disrupted the blocking and the timing. I was sweating and terrified. Hopkins, pacing behind me, kept saying, 'He's throwing your play, Elmer. He's throwing your play.' But Muni recovered and at the final curtain received an ovation."

Afterward, in his dressing room, certain he had destroyed the play, Muni confessed to Bella, "All I could think of was that Robert Garland was in the audience and he hates me."

Muni needn't have worried. Garland praised his performance lavishly in the *Evening Telegram*, stating, "Mr. Muni is Elmer Rice's best friend!"

Muni's ability to make his audience laugh, then cry, his quick near-pyrotechnic changes of emotion, swept the production on; it was the longest-running play of the 1931–32 season.

Playgoers indulged in a guessing game. Was this a *drama à clef*? Was Muni impersonating Untermyer? Darrow? Dudley Field

171

Malone? It was all of them and none of them. It was every lawyer who had clawed his way to the heights, and it was George Simon, born November 6, 1931.

Atkinson wrote in the New York *Times*:

> Mr. Muni gives one of those forceful and inventive performances that renew faith in the theatre. . . . In the playing of this part, he is at the top of his form, less showily dynamic than usual, more lucid and precise. Life comes spurting and bubbling out of this part in the gusto of Mr. Muni's playing.

Elmer Rice's fears of asylum commitment for financial madness were unfounded; the production was paid off in three weeks. Total cost of mounting the play: $11,000. Today *Counsellor-at-Law* would cost between $300,000 and $350,000. Good-bye, Broadway.

Universal Pictures bought the screen rights for an unprecedented $175,000. Muni was not even considered. Scared Hollywood took every Jewish element out of the work. John Barrymore was cast as George Simon.

Muni had only one comment: "They should also change the title to *Goy Meets Girl!*"

Muni's favorite performance of *Counsellor* was a Sunday night on a bare platform at Sing Sing Prison before an audience of two thousand convicts. The company had accepted the invitation from warden Lewis E. Lawes with fascinated trepidation. Muni watched the prisoners, appalled at how young most of them were. That evening was an emotional experience for Muni; the prisoners cheered and applauded throughout the play.

Muni never collected press clippings or reviews, but Bella did. (We arranged for all her scrapbooks to go to the Library and Museum of the Performing Arts in New York's Lincoln Center for a special "Muni Collection.") But he saved and treasured one review, a clipping from the Sing Sing newspaper, sent to him by Warden Lawes:

> Over two thousand men in gray, prisoners doing sentences from one year to natural life, vigorously applauded the cast of *Counsellor-at-Law*. Was it merely a polite gesture? Or did they witness something keenly alive and intensely human? To us prisoners George Simon is not an unfamiliar figure. He fights our battles. He is sympathetic with the underdog . . . it wasn't really George Simon we prisoners were watching. We were seeing life.

The review was signed "81–284."

In the spring of 1932 *Scarface* was playing around the clock at the Strand. Just a few blocks away, *Counsellor-at-Law*, despite the Depression, was doing sellout business. Muni had simultaneous hits on stage and screen.

Then Warner Brothers called.

Jake Wilk, their New York story editor and a great respecter of literary and performing talent, had purchased a property. The interoffice memo at the studio in Burbank described it this way:

> On Thursday, March 10, break the story that we have bought the motion picture rights to the much discussed and widely-read novel, "I AM A FUGITIVE FROM A PRISON CAMP" by (call Howard Smith's office and he will give you the author's name). Also be sure and not insert the word "Georgia" in the event Howard Smith's office gives you the complete title; the correct title of the story is "I AM A FUGITIVE FROM A GEORGIA PRISON CAMP" but for censorship purposes we have purposely eliminated the word: "Georgia."
> Oh. AUTHOR IS ROBERT E. BURNS

And at the bottom of the memo was the standard printed reminder:

VERBAL MESSAGES CAUSE MISUNDERSTANDING
AND DELAYS
(PLEASE PUT THEM IN WRITING)

Samuel Goldwyn said it another way: "An oral agreement isn't worth the paper it's written on."

The correct title of the book, ghostwritten by Burns' brother, an Episcopal priest in New Jersey, was *I Am a Fugitive from a Georgia Chain Gang*. Georgia was dropped immediately and never again mentioned by man or beast in beautiful downtown Burbank.

Darryl Zanuck was then in charge of production at Warner Brothers. Other shrewd heads at WB were the brothers Warner, Jack and Harry, and Hal Wallis, the unbilled executive producer; all realized they had a piece of cinematic dynamite. They assigned Mervyn LeRoy, who had brilliantly made *Little Caesar*, as director. LeRoy immediately took the train back to New York to see Muni in *Counsellor-at-Law* and wired back to the studio executives: THIS IS OUR MAN!

Wallis chose Sheridan Gibney (a double in looks for F. Scott Fitzgerald) to write the screenplay. Gibney, still in his twenties, was the author of a Broadway play Jed Harris had produced the year before, *The Wiser They Are*, starring Ruth Gordon and Osgood Perkins, coincidentally also at the Plymouth. The *Fugitive* story fascinated Gibney, who wrote the screenplay in five intensive weeks.

The book, not a novel but a harrowing documentary, rapidly became a best seller and was faithfully translated to the screen. A World War I veteran, unable to get a job, is innocently trapped into a holdup. Imprisoned, he is subjected to the inhumane cruelties of a Southern chain gang, manages to escape, becomes a living Jimmy Valentine by building a respectable life, is betrayed by his wife, returns to jail on the promise of an immediate pardon. The prison authorities, revenging themselves on him for revealing chain-gang conditions, deny his pardon. He escapes again, doomed for life as a desperate fugitive.

It was the true story of Burns, who was still free but hunted. Like Daniel Berrigan in later years, he moved through the underground, always in hiding. Warner Brothers spirited him to Burbank to work with Gibney, to give the screenwriter details of chain-gang life not covered in the book.

A Warner Brothers interoffice memo from Darryl Zanuck reads:

> The author of I AM A FUGITIVE FROM A CHAIN GANG leaves New York Saturday, arriving at the studio, Wednesday, April 13th. Top secrecy is required. We will not even mention his name. As in the film, he will be called JAMES ALLEN.

Gibney recalls how Burns jumped with fright at every sound. A crime film was being shot on a company street adjacent to the Writers' Building, where Gibney and Burns were conferring. When he heard police sirens and gunshots, Burns hid behind furniture and cowered against a wall. Gibney calmed him with the assurance it was all make-believe.

"They're shooting," he said, "but only a film."

Jake Wilk delivered the first-draft screenplay to Muni backstage at the Plymouth and offered him a seven-year contract if Muni liked the script and the role. Before he even read it, Muni said, "No! The mere idea of becoming an acting robot at the beck and call of a studio is too terrible even to think about! No more long-term contracts. I might do one picture if it's any good, or even a couple. But I always want to be free to come back to the theater."

Wilk studied him, aware that Muni was not just bargaining. He glanced at Bella, who was seated in the dressing room, watching and listening.

"All right," Wilk said flatly. "How about settling for a three-picture contract? We'll pay you fifty thousand dollars a picture."

174

"That's too much," Muni protested. "I only got twenty-seven thousand five hundred dollars for *Scarface*."

Bella smiled at Wilk's confusion; he had never before been bargained *down* by an actor.

"Shut up already, Munya," Bella said. "After the success of *Scarface*, I think you deserve a raise."

Muni and, of course, Bella read the screenplay of *Fugitive* that night before going to bed. The next morning a deal was made. There was a clause in Muni's contract with Elmer Rice that he had June, July, and August free. Part of his deal with Warner Brothers was the understanding that he return to *Counsellor-at-Law* in the fall for the entire next season. (Muni always hated summers in New York.) And the screenplay was daring and challenging. Otto Kruger was borrowed from the Chicago company of *Counsellor* to replace Muni at the Plymouth for the summer.

The *Fugitive* shooting schedule was set for fifty days in July and August, 1932. LeRoy, Wallis, Warner all remember the sense of expectancy in the air at the Burbank studios. There was something special about this film, particularly the fortunate wedding of actor and subject matter. The project had good vibrations and the "feel" of significance. Their sensory perceptions proved to be right. *Fugitive* was to be a landmark film, the beginning of an era of social consciousness in Hollywood, particularly at Warner's. Busby Berkeley musicals were sinking into the west; prison reform and the rights of man were part of the rising sun from the east.

With a month off before shooting was to begin, Muni and Bella decided to book passage on an ocean liner through the Panama Canal to California. Muni was weary, and he had a new script to memorize. His Dictaphone was his most important piece of luggage. Aboard the SS *Pennsylvania*, Muni spent most of the thirteen days of the voyage in his stateroom, with his Dictaphone as his leading lady. He rehearsed hour after hour, over and over again, until the words seemed entirely his own.

A lifelong friendship began on that voyage. The Munis met Ben Goetz and his wife, Goldie. Goetz was then executive vice-president of Consolidated Film Industries, the biggest film lab in the world; he had been a movie pioneer and had directed Pearl White one-reelers at the Crystal Film Studios, a converted laundry in the Bronx. Later Goetz spent twenty years as head of MGM's London office and produced many notable films. In the years that followed, Goldie became a second sister to Bella. Knowledgeable in the tricky waters of the film business, Ben helped navigate Muni throughout his screen career.

The advice from Goetz to Muni began as they hiked for their

daily constitutional around the upper deck. Muni wore a pedometer and wouldn't stop until he had clocked three miles.

"I'm not a picture actor, I'm a stage actor," Goetz remembers Muni telling him. "And I'm frankly doubtful about doing another film."

"You'll be great," Goetz told him.

"I'm thirty-six years old," Muni said. "What kind of job is *acting* for a grown man? For children, yes. Put on a beard and pretend to be somebody else. Do you suppose they'd let me direct a film? Then I could retire as an actor and become respectable."

"You'd be a good director," Goetz advised. "You should try it sometime. About fifty years from now."

Goetz told Muni a helpful trade secret about the technique of film executives like Samuel Goldwyn, the Warners, Harry Cohn, and particularly Louis B. Mayer.

"Mayer, for example, categorically disagrees with *everything*. That's so the other fellow will spill his guts. Mayer wants to find out how much the other guy knows and how much he believes in his position. Now, most people's convictions wither under that kind of barrage—and then they're dead."

Muni never forgot that. When he believed in something, he stood his ground, Jack L. Warner and all his archangels notwithstanding.

Goetz had worked with John Barrymore, and the Great Lover's escapades fascinated Muni. Goetz said that someday he wanted to write a book about Barrymore, but at the moment all he had was the title page:

Title: YOU CAN'T LAY EVERYBODY
Sub-Title: YOU DON'T KNOW EVERYBODY

Bella told me about another "celebrity" on that ship.

"Bugsy Siegel, the West Coast hood, was aboard. He'd walk around the decks with his bodyguards and entourage and glare at Muni as if the production of *Scarface* had soiled the virginity of the whole innocent gangster business. But they never talked. It was quite a show."

One of Bugsy's bodyguards did manage to corner Muni one night in the dining salon.

"Bugsy and us went to that Strand The-ay-ter to see that moom picture," he said. "Hey, that-there was no actor. He was the real goods. Tell me, mister, what mob was you with?"

Muni lowered his voice. "The Schwartz mob. Lower East Side."

176

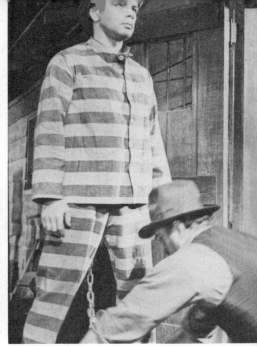

(Photos by John Ellis from the Mervyn LeRoy Collection)

Muni as James Allen in *I Am a Fugitive from a Chain Gang*.

Muni and other prisoners in *I Am a Fugitive from a Chain Gang*.

(Warner Brothers photo)

16

MUNI had several intensive meetings with Robert Burns in Burbank, studying the way the real fugitive walked and talked and breathed. Mostly he tried to catch "the smell of fear." "I don't want to imitate you," Muni told Burns. "I want to *be* you."

Muni asked the research department at Warner Brothers to give him every available book and magazine article about the penal system.

Did Muni actually read all the research material he asked for? Muni respected scholarship, longed to be a student. But he found a great deal of material beyond his depth. Half his reading time consisted of trips to the dictionary. But books were bulwarks for him; heavy volumes were sandbags against the flood of uncertainty.

Muni met with several California prison guards, one who had worked in a Southern chain gang. He asked if it was possible to meet with a guard or a warden still working in Georgia, but Warner studio executives discouraged the idea.

Bella remembered the rapport between Muni and Mervyn LeRoy. "They were on the same wavelength. They wanted to make the same picture, a gutsy film with no holds barred. Sometimes that doesn't happen. Often a director can be going north while an actor is going south."

Sheridan Gibney had returned to New York to work on a new play and was unavailable for rewrites. Two other writers contributed material: Brown Holmes and Howard J. Green.

"It's an old saying that the play's the thing, but by God, it's always been true," LeRoy told me. "If you don't have it on paper, you don't have it anyplace. You can talk about all these Hollywood geniuses, but I never saw a director walk on a set and say '*Act!*' They've got to have the *words*. They've got to have the jokes on paper."

A replica of a prison camp was built on the Warner ranch and the vivid rock-breaking scene was shot in an actual rock quarry in Chatsworth, about ten miles from the studio. Muni, a stickler for realism, refused to allow the use of a double, despite the brutal 5 A.M. shooting, made more difficult through the day when the July sun turned the rock pile into a searing furnace.

Drawing of Muni in the famous fade-out scene of *I Am a Fugitive from a Chain Gang* **by artist Winfield Meggs.**

(Warner Brothers Archives)

He and several hundred extras engaged as "convicts" broke stones with pickaxes and sledgehammers into sharp-edged "sprouls." As the stones split, their surfaces reflected the blistering sun, as if there were several million tiny, burning mirrors on that hillside. Nearly the entire company suffered from eyestrain, blisters, and sunburn. But the result was an epic scene, still a highlight in film history.

"Muni was one of the great actors of all time. There was no way for this man to be bad," LeRoy says. "He was a perfectionist, which is probably the reason he was never a really happy man. I don't know whether he liked being an actor or didn't like being an actor. He must have liked it because he worked so hard at it. What made him such a great performer? Heart. Guts. And one other important thing. He *listened*. He always listened. All the great actors listen. And the ones who don't, who are just thinking of their next line or who they're going to bed with tonight, might as well not be there. When young kids come to me for advice about acting, I tell them you can steal a scene when somebody else is talking. If you're really *listening*, you can take the scene right away from the guy or woman who's talking. Muni did that—not intentionally—instinctively."

Today only one line of the film seems dated, when the girl says, "I'm free, white, and twenty-one." No screenwriter would put that into a script these days. But the rest of the film remains fresh and suspenseful, with Muni giving a stirring and understated performance.

The ending of the picture, a scene which lasts less than a minute, is mentioned constantly in film histories, both here and abroad. It is not a pat pretty ending. No "they lived happily ever after" frosting was added to make the film more palatable or commercial. Muni as James Allen, weary, hunted, appears out of the night, for one last meeting in a garage alley with his girl. When she asks, "How do you live?" he answers, "I steal," as the black maw of night seems to swallow him up.

"It was an accident," LeRoy recalls. "I was shooting way downtown in Los Angeles. As we were doing a take, there was a sudden power failure. Muni was haggard and bleary with fatigue. As he backed away, the light drained out of his face as if the life were ebbing out of him. We shot it again with lights, but when we saw both takes in the projection room, we knew intuitively that we had stumbled onto a kind of God-given accident. It was a great ending."

Many have claimed credit for that stark final scene. Darryl F. Zanuck will tell you at the drop of a cigar ash that after the first sneak preview he personally sat down and wrote the ending dialogue and added it to the picture. He didn't. It can be found in Sheridan Gibney's first-draft screenplay. However, Zanuck did make a major contribution. He prevented more timid executives at the studio from cutting the scene. Perhaps putting a halt to that kind of "creative subtraction" turns you into the author.

I Am a Fugitive from a Chain Gang made the motion-picture industry realize Paul Muni had dimensions rarely seen on film: a man's soul in pain caught on celluloid.

"In Russia," LeRoy reports, "they thought we were all Communists. Because the film showed the brutality of the system. But we did a lot to help eradicate the chain gangs in the South. For years Jack Warner and I were barred from Georgia."

Abel Green in *Variety*, covering Muni on film for the first time, called it "a pip of a performance." The critical reaction was unanimously favorable, climaxed by the National Board of Review, which named the film the top picture of the year. Wilton A. Barrett of that organization wrote:

> The tragedy of a scrub-woman can be as great as the tragedy of Lady Macbeth, and a man caught in a prison, trying to escape from it and failing to do so, can be as awakening to our sense of the unfortunate, terrorful and pitiful as King Oedipus trying to escape the Furies. When a motion picture can make us feel and recognize this, it has not only said something, it *is* something. *I Am a Fugitive from a Chain Gang* has performed a service in

behalf of the dignity and meaning of the art of the American film.

Muni was nominated for the second time by the Academy as best actor of the year.

Robert Burns disappeared. There is one report that he was captured again and extradited to Georgia just after the film was released. But all records indicate he was never caught.

Muni and Bella made the transcontinental train trip, arriving back in New York just two days before Muni was scheduled to return to *Counsellor-at-Law* at the Plymouth Theatre on September 12, 1932. He read his entire part into his Dictaphone and kept it running in his compartment all the way across the prairies. Just before they reached Chicago, he turned to the machine and addressed it as if it were a person: "You can stop already. I know the part."

Getting back into the skin of the lively, alert George Simon was a joy for Muni and he loved the feedback of a live audience. His co-workers backstage at the Plymouth seemed like a family; though he almost never fraternized offstage with the cast, he felt it was like coming home.

Lester Salkow, who was to become one of Hollywood's leading agent-managers, was sixteen then, playing the office boy. (Typical of the times, the character in the play gets a salary of $10 a week, joyously raised from $9.) Salkow's understudy, who took over the part on the subsequent road tour, was Jules Garfield; later Warner Brothers dejeweled him into John Garfield. Salkow remembers Muni's return to the play.

Scarface had been running all summer at the Strand, and Muni was to replace Muni there. Warner Brothers announced a November opening at the same movie palace for *I Am a Fugitive from a Chain Gang*. The exuberant young Salkow rushed up to Muni when that news hit the Plymouth. How rare it was for an actor to have that kind of double exposure, twice, in New York.

"Gosh, Mr. Muni," Salkow said, "you're a big movie star. One of the biggest."

"I don't know what that means." Muni shrugged. "Here at the Plymouth, I walk through the stage door, I put on my makeup, and I do a performance. Back there, I'm a lot of little pieces of film glued together. In November, they'll ship me back here in a couple of cans—and I'll be frank with you, I don't understand how that happens. I get very confused. Where the hell am I? Here or there?"

When the juggernaut of a major studio's press department in the thirties moved into action, there was no stopping it. They concocted adjectives; they hypoed the nation's pituitary glands; they shouted in type; they screamed from billboards. Usually, they knew they were kidding themselves, but with *Fugitive*, it was not "puff." Everybody had total belief and conviction. The memos flew from coast to coast, from George Thomas in Burbank to S. Charles Einfeld in the Warners' New York office and back again:

> Charlie, here is the cinematic shot that will be heard round the world! The artistry of Paul Muni in this picture is beyond words. There is no use in attempting to describe it. You can piece together all the adjectives in your dictionary and when you are through you still have to see the picture to know what we are talking about.
>
> What a tremendous sensation this picture will make! And what a ten-strike it was to get Muni for the role!
>
> You can bet all the poppies in India that rival producers would give their right eye to have this at the top of their program for this or any other year. It is the hit of hits on a hit program, our biggest picture, not only from the standpoint of entertainment, but exploitation, advertising and publicity possibilities.

Every lady and gentleman interviewer from Maine to San Diego requested a "personal and exclusive interview with the new star." The press agent on *Counsellor-at-Law,* not wanting to be outdone, scheduled interviews with all the drama desk reporters. Muni was inundated with press.

The deluge was overwhelming. Muni's lifetime distrust of compliments and praise was compounded by the personal prying of the standard interview, which he found appalling.

"That fella Muni is extremely uninteresting," he told reporters. "And why the hell does anybody care what color pajamas the guy wears, or whether he sleeps in both ends or only the top or only the bottom or in the altogether? Besides, it's nobody's goddamn business."

Startled by this reverse of the usual star on the make, reporters began calling him "Muni the Hermit," "Muni the Silent," and "Garbo Man." Muni was even more infuriated. "Why can't they be satisfied with what they see onstage or on the screen?" he shouted to Bella. "Next thing you know they'll each want a urine sample."

Just before *Fugitive* opened at the Strand, Muni agreed to a group interview at their suite at the Delmonico Hotel. Muni promised Bella he would be calm and patient. He began with the reporters by discussing what the theater meant to him, the way an audience helped an actor, buoyed him up. Suddenly one female newshawk said, "Mr. Muni, we're not interested in what you think of the theater, we want to know about your personal life, particularly your love life."

Muni didn't say a word, walked over to the woman, lifted her out of her chair, piloted her to the door, and said, "Out!" It was the end of the news conference.

Counsellor-at-Law played 412 performances in New York, the first season a total of 292, then beginning in September, 1932, another 104 performances before setting out on a long and prosperous tour, which included Boston, Philadelphia, Pittsburgh, Detroit, and Chicago.

Bella's brother, Abem Finkel, was beginning to have some success as a writer and had married a pert and pretty secretary at Paramount, Ruth Rothman. Muni felt he needed a personal secretary to answer mail and keep reporters at arm's length during the *Counsellor* tour, so he hired Ruth. Bella's sister, Lucy, had been in a near-fatal automobile crackup, and Bella, who had conquered her fear of planes, was now terrified of automobiles. Muni loved to drive, to whiz down a highway, to explore unexplored roads. Bella was reluctant to be a fellow passenger, so Muni took Ruth Finkel along on his excursions.

Just before the tour left New York, Ruth and Muni drove up the highway winding alongside the Hudson River. They stopped and sat looking out at the river and the passing boats. Suddenly Muni saw a garbage scow, pulling up to shore.

"Y'know, Ruth," Muni said, "it would be damned interesting to find out how a man feels when he has to live on top of garbage all the time. I want to go talk to him. Wanta come along?"

She nodded yes, and they raced down the incline. The man on the scow was fascinated that anybody would be interested in him. Muni fired questions at him, studied him, and was amazed at the garbage man's joy in his job, despite the overwhelming aroma, about which the man seemed totally oblivious.

"I want you to know," the man said proudly, as if he were talking about the crown jewels, "that I have the cleanest garbage scow on the Hudson River!"

"Good for you," Muni said, pounding him on the back, delighted that the garbage man had no idea who Muni was.

On the way back into the city, Muni was contemplative. Then

suddenly he said, "Y'know, Ruth, if that man ever visited a perfume factory, he'd probably pass out. And they'd have to throw a pail of garbage in his face in order to bring him to!"

They laughed all the way back to the Plymouth Theatre.

Warner Brothers was preparing another property for him. The studio had purchased a story by Sheridan Gibney, *America Kneels*. Muni read it and liked it. Hal Wallis assigned Edward Chodorov to write the screenplay; shooting was scheduled for early July, 1933. "What do you want to do after that?" Jack Warner asked him. "One of two things," Muni replied. "Either a comedy, something light and frivolous, or the story of a Slovak coal miner." "We'll try to find a comedy," Warner said quickly.

But Muni was obsessed with the idea of what happens to a man who digs in the earth like a mole. So he began reading, in his spare time on the road, about mining laws, strikes, and the risks and calamities of the sometimes forgotten workers deep in the mines.

When *Counsellor* played the Nixon Theatre in Pittsburgh, Muni met Common Pleas Court Judge Michael A. Musmanno, who came backstage to tell his "fellow lawyer" how much he had admired his portrayal. Muni, as usual, switched the subject immediately and told the judge about wanting to do a coal-mining film.

"That's a coincidence," the judge said. "I'm writing a book at the moment about the mines." Musmanno told Muni about a case he'd worked on back in 1929. A miner named John Barkowski, totally innocent of any crime, was clubbed to death by company police at Imperial, Pennsylvania. Musmanno helped prosecute three sadistic policemen who were charged with the murder. In his book, the judge planned to fictionalize it a little, calling the miner Jan Volkanik—but otherwise it was fairly documentary.

"Send me a copy the minute it's finished," Muni urged. "Even before it's published."

During the time they were in the coal-mining area, Muni asked for a chance to visit the mines and see the lives of miners up close. Judge Musmanno arranged a trip.

Muni had two performances on Wednesday of his first week in Pittsburgh. But on Thursday he was up and ready to go at seven in the morning.

"Bella, you want to ride out to the mines?"

Bella, suffering from sinus trouble, hadn't slept at all. The dust was so bad the tears were running down her face.

"Munya, I can't," she moaned. "I'm sorry. Why don't you take Ruthie with you?"

184

So Muni rang Ruth Finkel's room, and within a half hour they were on a strange little train headed for Pottsville, Pennsylvania.

Ruth, today Mrs. Ruth Jacoves, was close to the Munis for the rest of their lives and recalls that trip to the mines on a soot-filled Pennsylvania morning forty years ago:

"The train ride took several hours. The foreman in Pottsville gave us each a hard hat with a light in it. I thought when we went down the shaft that Muni would ask about the miners' work, but he didn't. He wanted to know about their backgrounds. One miner had the most beautiful teeth you've ever seen. Muni said, 'You have such white teeth; how do you keep them so clean in this dirty mine?' And the man said, 'You should see my son. As a matter of fact, you'll meet him, 'cause he works here, too.' Muni was amazed, because the man looked about thirty. 'You're not old enough to have a son who works here,' Muni said. 'Yeah,' the miner said. 'He's eighteen. He's been digging in the mines for three years.'

"The mine manager took us into several homes in Pottsville, just shacks really. Muni studied family pictures on the walls and showed an intense interest in everything: what they ate, what time they got up in the morning, what they wanted for their children. Muni got so absorbed in drinking in the whole atmosphere of a coal town that we almost missed the train back, the last one if Muni was to make his performance that night in Pittsburgh.

"We ran for the train, just as it was about to pull out. There was no dining car or even a sandwich hawker on that little train, so Muni said to the conductor, 'How long can you stay here?' 'I gotta go right away,' the conductor said. 'Well, we missed lunch and we had a seven o'clock breakfast.' . . . The conductor pointed to a diner across the way and held the train for us. When Muni came running back with a paper sack full of sandwiches, the conductor said, 'I know. You're a honeymoon couple. But what you're doing in mine country, I don't know.' And he fixed seats facing each other and gave us a board to put the sandwiches on. We laughed. And Muni didn't correct him. 'A mine shaft,' Muni said. 'There's a perfect place for a honeymoon!' "

To climax the tour of *Counsellor*, a final two weeks was scheduled back in New York City in May, 1933. Then Muni was due in Burbank to film the remaining two projects of his three-picture contract with Warner Brothers. Jake Wilk phoned often during the tour, offering to scrap that contract for a longer-term deal.

"Wait," Muni said. "First see how the other two pictures turn out. One flop and I'll be rat poison."

(Collection of Helen Lovett)

Muni with director Mervyn LeRoy and Bella during the shooting of *The World Changes*.

Home at the Plymouth, Muni found a telegram awaiting him:

> FOLLOWING COMPLETION OF YOUR WARNER
> BROTHERS COMMITMENT I HAVE ROLE FOR
> YOU JUST LIKE SCARFACE. WOULD YOU BE
> INTERESTED?
>
> CECIL B. DE MILLE

Muni's answer:

> THANK YOU FOR YOUR OFFER
> BUT I HAVE ALREADY DONE
> SCARFACE.
>
> PAUL MUNI

Muni bought a new model Dictaphone; this one didn't require a change of cylinders every four or five minutes. The studio had sent him the shooting script of *The World Changes*, a switch on titles from *America Kneels*, which Harry Warner said sounded like "everybody in the country was either a Catholic or a goddamn queer." Muni was pleased that Mervyn LeRoy would be his director again and he was promised the hottest cameraman in Hollywood, Tony Gaudio.

Bella cued Muni on the train all the way across the country, playing every other part, and having a joyful time being what she called "the preshooting stand-ins for Aline MacMahon, Mary Astor, Margaret Lindsay, Anna Q. Nilsson, a nine-year-old Mickey Rooney, and even Guy Kibbee."

Shooting began at Burbank on July 12, 1933. *The World Changes* had a near-epic quality, a combination of *Cimarron* and the later *Citizen Kane*. Muni looks amazingly young and virile as Orin Nordholm in the opening prairie-farming days in Dakota. The action moves to Chicago, where he prospers as a meat-packer. He develops a fortune inventing refrigerated freight cars. The most quoted and remembered line from the film is Nordholm's Eureka shout: "Iceboxes on wheels! Iceboxes on wheels!"

Bella was on the set every day. Mervyn LeRoy bought her a director's chair of her own, with her name painted on the canvas back.

"I loved Bella," LeRoy says, "but she was so *sad* all the time. She always seemed to have a tear in her eye. No, I didn't resent her at all; she was there to be helpful. It gave Muni reassurance and a sense of confidence."

Others on the set weren't always as kind when referring to Bella. She was called the Witch of Stage 14, often switched to a capital *B*, and somebody once said, "Stage mothers are bad enough; stage wives are lethal." Perhaps this vituperation was caused by Bella's built-in phony detector. She had a nose for incompetence; consequently, people who were slightly wobbly in their duties sensed that Bella saw through them like an X ray. That's why many of them were afraid of her, gossiped about her, and hated her. Even for Muni the role Bella played was not an unmixed blessing. When he said a weary good-night to the grips, the carpenters, and the cameramen, he had to go home with his most perceptive critic. It is probably not surprising that they usually had separate bedrooms.

In the film, Mary Astor played his down-the-nose wife, who despises him because he's a butcher who "smells of blood." She writes about Muni in her book, *A Life on Film:*

> Personally I thought Muni was a very attractive man, and as an actor he was very scholarly and as dedicated and hardworking as the character he was playing. . . . I remember thinking during the making of the picture that this was a warm, strong, wonderful guy. I didn't approve of his method of working: his total attention to externals, makeup, hair, clothing, manner of walking, gesturing. Every word of the script memorized and actually recorded and rerecorded before he even went on the set. . . . O.K. So I didn't agree with him. But this wasn't *all* of Muni, and

187

(Warner Brothers photos)

Muni as Orin Nordholm with Mary Astor as his wife in *The World Changes*.

Muni as the old man in *The World Changes*.

I had a disturbing feeling that the snobbish idiot I was playing could have liked *something* about him, the character. Ah, no,no! that would have been confusing, you see. There would have been people in the audience who would have said to themselves, "I thought she hated him?" . . . I was as two-dimensional as the screen itself: cool, indifferent, looking lovely in close-ups. Period. Period. Period. When was I ever going to learn to act? You can't learn if you can't experiment and find what works, and doesn't work. But the hours are long, the schedule rigid, so I did what I was told and saved time and money for the front office. And got a lot of jobs that way.*

The transition of Nordholm, as played by Muni, from a young man with a flat prairie accent and a curl falling across his forehead, through three generations to a doddering patriarch, is the triumph of the picture. Muni is so convincing as an octogenarian that fellow workers treated him even off-camera with the respect usually paid to the aged, reaching to take his arm, helping him into chairs, shouting at him as if he was hard of hearing. Muni went far deeper than makeup; his old man was created not merely by a Rudyard Kipling-like mustache and withering hands. Age came from the depth of his eyes and the throaty hoarseness of his voice. When he sees his son dead on the floor, there is total grief in his eyes and Muni's entire face seems to turn into a skull.

*From *A Life on Film* by Mary Astor. Copyright © 1971 by Mary Astor. Reprinted by permission of Delacorte Press.

Muni had great respect for Rome-born cinematographer Tony Gaudio, who had a huge family and a voice with a musical Italian lilt. After the first rough cut was assembled, Muni asked Gaudio what he thought of the film. "It's great," Gaudio said, "one of the best pictures we've ever made here."

"Of course you'd tell me that," Muni answered with a wave of his arm, dismissing the flattery. "You say that to all actors."

"People tell lies," Gaudio said softly, looking straight at Muni. "My camera doesn't know how. I'll tell you something: Muni isn't in the last twenty minutes of the picture at all. He disappears completely. It's all that old man. Nordholm. He steals the whole picture. Nobody knows that's you playing him."

"Ah!" Muni said. "Now you're talking!"

The reviewers liked Muni, treated the film with grudging respect, but complained that there was too much similarity in theme and treatment to another Warner Brothers picture, *I Loved a Woman*, which starred Edward G. Robinson. Both films unfortunately disappeared into the hungry mouth of block booking and have been forgotten.

Muni's next film was to be a comedy, as promised. Jake Wilk bought a short story by Roy Chanslor, a newspaper yarn in *The Front Page* manner. A wisecracking managing editor is demoted to the Siberia job of Nellie Nelson, heart throbs editor. It was sheerest coincidence that two other similar works, a novel and a film, appeared that year: Nathaniel West's far more bitter near-classic, *Miss Lonelyhearts*, and a hastily made B picture, *Advice to the Lovelorn*, which starred Lee Tracy. Perhaps in 1933 everybody needed advice, economic and romantic.

Abem and Ruth Finkel had moved to the West Coast, and Muni recommended Abem as a screenwriter. Hal Wallis teamed him with a more experienced hand, Sidney Sutherland, and the newspaper story blossomed into a romp for Muni and the Warner Brothers stock company: Glenda Farrell, Ned Sparks, Edward Ellis, Donald Meek, a young Sidney Miller (Muni began referring to them as "My West Coast almost hundred percent *goyish* Yiddish Art Theatre").

Muni had been hesitant recommending a relative, even an in-law. The joke around town was that you couldn't get anywhere in the film business unless you were somebody's son-in-law. MGM, the wags said, stood for "Mayer's *Ganze Mishpuche*," the impudent Yiddish for "Mayer's Entire Family." But Muni was delighted with the breezy dialogue Finkel and Sutherland wrote. And he was happy to be working for the third time with his friend Mervyn LeRoy. Only the title of the film made Muni cringe: *Hi, Nellie!*

An interoffice memo indicates that the publicity department agreed:

> Just learned today that *Hi, Nellie!* is to be used throughout with the exclamation point. Have been trying to pin them down on this for some days, and the title went through yesterday. So see that it's on, will ya, Pal—and then later, perhaps, they'll change the whole title!
>
> GEORGE THOMAS

Perhaps the death knell of *Hi, Nellie!* was its title, including the exclamation point. Years later, after my playwriting partner and I came back from a New York stage disaster with our rear ends dragging, the usually pessimistic Bella was Chairman of the Cheerfulness Department.

"Everybody has flops," she reassured us, "but this business is charitable enough to forget them. You ever hear of a picture Muni did called *Hi, Nellie!*?" We had to admit we'd never even heard the title before. "See?" Bella said. "Go write the next one."

But watching the picture in a Warner Brothers projection room in 1973 convinced us that the plot had a lot of cockiness and bounce, and it afforded a welcome change of pace for Muni. More felt hats are tipped rakishly back on reporters' heads than in any newspaper city room since the dawn of linotypes. But even in the movie-compounded world of fake newsprint, Muni exudes integrity. And it proved that Muni, with sarcasm, with irony, could read a comic line with the best of them. Furthermore, the film is a rattling good detective yarn, much in the Sam Spade manner. Columnist Sidney Skolsky has a fleeting bit in the picture; he stares at deadpanned Ned Sparks and asks, "What are you laughing about?" Sparks, his face looking like a depressed basset hound, answers, "Because I'm happy!" The line was made up, Skolsky remembers, right on the set.

While praising Muni's acting skill in *Hi, Nellie!*, Richard Watts, Jr., in the New York *Herald Tribune* tells of the managing editor's demotion to the dog house of the heart throbs department, and adds: "There were, I cannot help telling you, cruel souls in the audience at the Strand last night who insisted that the publisher was showing mercy to his rebellious employee when he didn't insist that he become the paper's film critic."

Hi, Nellie! was shot in October and November, 1933, and played in New York and Hollywood in February, 1934. Bella and Muni were out of the country when the picture opened. They decided, on the spur of the moment, to take a trip to the Soviet Union.

"I swear to you," Bella told us, "it wasn't an escape. We didn't

190

run away. We really wanted to go visit the Moscow Art Theatre."

Muni's future at Warner Brothers was still indefinite. He was eager to do another play on Broadway but couldn't find a playscript which excited or challenged him. In any new contract with the studio, he would insist on more rigid story control, including the chance to do his cherished coal-mining project. But haggling and bargaining were not Muni's glass of tea. He decided for the first time in his career to get an agent.

Muni, an inveterate radio listener, loved Fred Allen's dry wit and through the years quoted Allen's biting line about the film capital: "You could take all the sincerity in Hollywood, and stuff it into a gnat's navel—and still have enough room left for an agent's heart."

He found one who was an exception. David Tannenbaum, the Munis' West Coast attorney and longtime friend (later mayor of Beverly Hills), recommended an agent who didn't fit the pattern of the run-of-the-mill flesh peddler. He was M. C. Levee, an honest, direct, down-to-earth businessman who handled less than twenty top actors and directors and devoted all his time and attention to them (including Bette Davis, Joan Crawford, Leslie Howard, Douglas Fairbanks, Jr., later Greer Garson and Vivien Leigh). Muni left all negotiating of a new Warner Brothers deal to Levee and Tannenbaum.

With Muni's desires in mind, they managed to get a contract rare in film-industry history. Muni was to do two pictures a year, which would be shot in the May to October periods, so that he was free to do a Broadway play in the fall and winter months. The producers and story department were to offer him three outlines and rough treatments (a bastard art form which often killed ideas a-borning). If Muni turned down all three, he then had the option to offer the studio three basic ideas or concepts of his choosing. The contract also stated that press interviews were to be at a minimum and at Muni's choice. The studio agreed that any script revisions would be submitted two weeks before shooting; this was designed to eliminate last-minute changes, often shoveled in the night before filming, a procedure which had given Muni sleepless nights. Muni was to get $100,000 a picture, twice a year, for seven years.

Muni and Bella received a letter outlining the deal the day they arrived at the National Hotel just off Red Square in Moscow.

"It sounds," Bella commented, "like a capitalist plot. But not bad!"

The Munis found Moscow grim but the Moscow Art Theatre, the Maly, the Vakchtangov, and the Puppet Theatre glowing with energy, pride, and incredible acting. Muni was riveted by the depth of the performances, especially productions of Tolstoy's *Resurrection* and Gogol's *Dead Souls*.

"I sat and watched them," he said, "like a student trying to learn how to act. In the Puppet Theatre, where half the cast were flesh-and-blood actors and half were dummies, even the puppets made acting in almost every other country seem shallow."

When Bob Lee and I were invited to visit the Soviet theaters many years later, Bella helped brief us for the trip and laughed as she recalled an experience she had at the Bolshoi Theater. At the intermission of *Prince Igor*, Bella left the elegant auditorium to go to the ladies' room, but found no toilet paper. In her limping Russian, Bella asked for some. The fat woman attendant rose to her full height. Bella knew enough Russian to make out the indignant reply: "Paper! In the Soviet Union? We are a literary nation! Paper we save for our poets!"

Muni and Bella saw nineteen plays in their seventeen days in Moscow and Leningrad. In many ways it was like being back in the audience at the Yiddish theater in New York; the repertory system meant a variety of dramas and comedies in one playhouse during the course of a week, with actors stretching themselves in a wide range of roles. The Soviet performers and directors they met had never seen an American stage play and rarely an American film; the only foreign picture star they knew was Charlie Chaplin. But a few of them had seen Muni in *Fugitive*, and they rushed for the brandy bottle when the Munis came backstage: a custom reserved for only the highest-ranking and most respected visiting artists.

They conversed backstage one-third in English, one-third in a gesture-punctuated Russian, and one-third in Yiddish (Muni and Bella were amazed to find how many of the Soviet actors were Jewish). Toasts were raised back and forth. "A variety of parts is wine to the actor!" Applause and the clinking of glasses. "What a horror to be typed—it is the death blow to any performer!" Cheers and bear hugs.

But Moscow in February was freezing cold, the food was bleak, and distant California suddenly seemed a paradise of warmth and comfort. Muni and Bella woke one morning in their twin-bedded room at the National Hotel. Even under the feather-thick quilts, they were each bundled up in heavy mufflers, sweaters, and double layers of long woolen underwear. Muni stared up at the ceiling, painted lentil-soup brown.

"Bella, are you thinking the same thing I'm thinking?"

192

"I'm thinking." Bella nodded. "But how do we do it? They expect us to stay a month. It's only been seventeen days."

"We have to go home. Somebody in the family is dying."

"They'll know it's a lie," Bella pointed out. "We never got a message like that. They keep track of all cables that come in."

"It's no lie."

"Oh? Who's dying?"

"Me. I'm a member of the family, and I'm sick of the food, and I'm dying of the cold."

Bella tried to urge Muni to fly home.

"That sick I'm not," Muni said.

The sea voyage was long and rough. They slept for most of the cross-country train trip.When the Chief pulled into Pasadena, a smiling Mike Levee was waiting for them on the station platform. The distinguished-looking Hal Wallis was there to shake their hands and welcome them home. Warner Brothers had respected Muni's wishes: no photographers were on hand to poke their cameras in his face. And the prepollution air of Pasadena smelled of orange blossoms and seemed like ambrosia to breathe to the travel-weary Munis.

Wallis was bubbling with news. The studio had platoons of writers at work on two properties for Muni. One screenplay was about a Mexican lawyer; the other was Muni's pet project, the coal-mining story. Jake Wilk had purchased Judge Musmanno's authentic account of the mine trouble, and Bella's brother, Abem, was already at work on the screenplay in collaboration with Carl Erickson. Archie Mayo and Michael Curtiz were being considered to direct the two pictures, Tony Gaudio would be behind the camera, and the pick of the studio's acting roster was awaiting Muni's return.

The Warner Brothers publicity department urged the Munis to attend the forthcoming Academy Awards banquet. *Fugitive* had been nominated as best film in a field of ten nominations, but there were only three nominations for best actor: Charles Laughton for *The Private Life of Henry VIII*, Leslie Howard for *Berkeley Square*, and Muni for *Fugitive*.

"Why go?" Muni said. "I won't win. Americans don't like American actors. Besides, I think it's the shame of the nation that Howard Hawks and Mervyn LeRoy weren't even nominated."

Muni signed the Warner Brothers contract the morning of the Award ceremonies, which the Munis attended at the Ambassador Hotel the night of March 16, 1934. Bella had a new fur coat, and Muni bought his first tuxedo. As Muni had predicted, Charles

Laughton won the gold statuette, but neither Laughton nor Katharine Hepburn was present to accept. Winfield Sheehan flamboyantly rushed up to receive from Will Rogers the award for best picture: *Cavalcade*.

Duke Ellington began playing for dancing, and Muni whirled Bella around the floor.

"So you didn't win," Bella sighed. "There'll be another time!"

"Still," Muni said, "we've come up in the world some. Look. My own tuxedo. Not borrowed from Maurice Schwartz!"

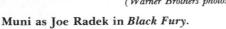
(Warner Brothers photos)

Muni as Joe Radek in *Black Fury*.   **Muni as Johnny Ramirez with the fabled Bette Davis in *Bordertown*.**

MUNI liked the two properties. *Bordertown*, the first, intrigued him; he had never played a Mexican before, and it was a challenge. The second property, then called *Black Hell*, had bones and guts and blood in it.

Muni thought Judge Musmanno's documentary book needed additional plot and urged the studio to buy an unproduced play, *Bohunk*, by Harry R. Irving. Bella's cousin, attorney Jonas Silverstone, negotiated for the rights, which Muni acquired, then transferred to the studio. The finished film script would be a blend of the two works.

An actor, Muni felt, should participate in the development of a screenplay, not as a writer but as a contributor to the sense of time and place. An actor could say early on in the drafting and polishing of a working script, "Here are dimensions to be explored. Here are questions I want to ask. Maybe we won't give any answers. But somebody, maybe just the actor's face, has to ask the questions."

Muni explained his one acid test for a script: "If I don't have the chance to play it, I'll die. And for me to get that feeling, a screenplay has to have more than a role; it has to have an *idea!*"

Feeling he had to soak up atmosphere for the first film, Muni haunted Olvera Street, Los Angeles' oldest Mexican neighborhood. It wasn't enough. "I have to go swimming in tequila," he said.

Wearing an old beat-up sweater and dark glasses, Muni traveled to Mexicali with Carroll Graham, the author of the novel on which the film was based, as his guide. Both men tried to act as non-touristy as possible, so they could explore the seamy side of the town, the saloons, the gambling casinos, the sagging shacks. When he got back to Los Angeles, Muni began taking private Spanish lessons.

Robert Lord, who had won an Academy Award a few weeks before as the writer of *One Way Passage*, was assigned to do a further story development, and then two seasoned screenwriters, Laird Doyle and Wallace Smith, wrote the final script. Muni phoned them every day to ask questions. Graham's best-selling novel had been called *Border Town*; Warner Brothers decided it was a more commercial title as one word.

Bette Davis had made fifteen pictures for Warner Brothers, but she recalls, "I might just as well have been any of the stock girls under contract. Until *Bordertown*, in which I was allowed some dramatic range."

Bordertown was made before Bette Davis was lent to RKO to film *Of Human Bondage*, but the Maugham story was released first. As Mildred, the sluttish waitress, Miss Davis was suddenly a major star. Warner Brothers cashed in on the fact, and all their publicity and promotion featured the two pyrotechnic players, Paul Muni and Bette Davis, together for the first time in *Bordertown*. Previously, Warner Brothers had largely ignored her as a star attraction.

The shooting schedule, originally set for summer of 1934, kept being pushed back, until it seemed as if the two Muni pictures for that year would be made almost in tandem. Muni continued to study, to probe, to perfect his accent and his attitude. "Perfection is impossible," he told Bella. "There's got to be something better."

Bella began to relax more when driving with Muni at the wheel of the Dodge. They were looking for land, a home, a place to settle. They explored deep into San Fernando Valley, then pure country, filled with walnut ranches, cow barns, and grazing sheep. One afternoon they stopped at a street corner to buy some flowers from a shy Mexican youth. Muni listened to the swarthy young man as he counted out the change.

"I'll buy all the flowers in your pails," Muni said, "if you'll just keep talking to me."

"That is one fine beez-ness deal, señor," the flower seller said, smiling with all his teeth and shoving carnations and gladioli into the back seat of the Dodge.

Intrigued by the easy, lazy flow of the Mexican boy's dialect, Muni offered him a job as soon as they found a ranch, first as a gardener, later as a chauffeur.

The next day the Munis bought a five-acre walnut ranch in Van Nuys. And Manuel came to work for them. For nine years he was their gardener, chauffeur, and friend. But he began by being the voice model for Johnny Ramirez, the young Mexican lawyer of *Bordertown*.

The Munis moved from their rented temporary bungalow in Burbank to the rambling ranch house. There was a guest cottage at the far end of the property. Muni was conscience-stricken at his treatment of his·mother. Nassiter, Sallie's second husband, had died in Canada. So with the reluctance of duty, Muni invited her to move out from Toronto and "come visit for a while."

Bella, allergic to most in-laws, wanted to object but didn't. She wished her own mother was still alive, so she understood Muni's feeling. "He had enough to worry about," she once mused, "without feeling guilty, too. In fact, if Muni had nothing to worry about, *that* worried him!"

"Besides, it's one of the Ten Commandments," Muni pointed out, ineffectually trying to convince himself as well as Bella. "All that honor thy mother and father business."

Sallie (once Salche) Weisberg Weisenfreund Nassiter came to live in the guest cottage on a walnut ranch filled with sunshine and hummingbirds, a long way from Lemberg, where thirty-nine years before she had borne a son she never really knew.

Muni kept his respectful distance, said a polite good morning every day, answered his mother's questions, but rarely began a

196

conversation. Sallie was constantly critical, complaining about the heat when a door was closed, the draft when a door was open, the seasoning of the soup. Muni never hugged her or kissed her. Or forgave her.

She had never seen *Fugitive*. Muni arranged a screening for her in a studio projection room. Bella took her to Burbank, with Manuel driving. Muni, on the verge of becoming Johnny Ramirez in *Bordertown*, refused to go along. "It'll just confuse me. That's James Allen up on that screen. No relation to Ramirez. Different skin. Different soul. Besides, when I do something, it's done. I don't want to eat the same meal twice."

Muni retreated to his study and his Dictaphone records. Near midnight Sallie walked into the house and stared at her son with dazed amazement.

"I always said you were the best actor in the family," she said.

"I guess the one thing I inherit from you, Mama," Muni said, "is a bad memory."

"Bad memory?"

"You forget. You told Papa, and me, too, that I couldn't act worth a plug nickel!"

"You're wrong, Munya. It must have been somebody else. No *mother* would ever say anything like that."

Shooting began on *Bordertown* on September 17, 1934, in a tight four-week schedule. *Black Hell* was to begin filming immediately afterward, with an October 18 starting date. This overlap, "with hardly room to catch my breath," worried Muni, who had hoped to film *Bordertown* during the summer months. Constant rewrites of the screenplay caused the delays. Muni's philosophy of work was summed up in one question: "Do you want it tomorrow or do you want it good?" The development and deepening of both screenplays pleased him, so the delay was a mixed blessing. And besides, he was only happy when he was working; if he were totally inside the skins of Johnny Ramirez and Joe Radek, the Polish miner, then that prickly Paul Muni would go away and stop bothering him.

Archie Mayo, basically a comedy director, was fat, jolly, and understanding. The opening sequences of *Bordertown* were shot on a roped-off Olvera Street in downtown Los Angeles. Often they worked all night. Mayo had a strolling Mexican band playing before every shot, not part of the action and not filmed or recorded, but "to get the company in the mood."

Margaret Lindsay had equal feature billing alongside Bette Davis. It was ideal casting: the tall, imperious, handsome aristocrat, a civilization apart from Bette Davis' gutter spitfire. Somebody

197

once asked director John Ford if it was true that he had once said, "A director's job is ninety percent done if he casts a picture correctly."

"No, goddamn it, I never said that," Ford shouted back. "What I said was ninety-*five* percent!"

When Miss Lindsay, as Dale Elwell, sketches Muni during an early courtroom sequence, she scribbles the word "SAVAGE" across the bottom of her drawing. It was a perfect description of the held-in coil, the inner fury which Muni made such an important part of the role. Her own cool, civilized detachment was striking dramatic contrast. Director Mayo and Warner Brothers had cast well. She had played the young English girl in the film of Noel Coward's *Cavalcade;* the legendary scene aboard ship shows her and her new husband walking away from a ship's railing as the camera moves in for a close-up of the life preserver: SS *TITANIC*. Miss Lindsay had gone to England to study, to perfect her English accent, and Fox was convinced on her return that this was her first time on American soil. "The perfect, authentic British ingenue" they called her. Hollywood irony: Margaret Lindsay was born and brought up in Dubuque, Iowa.

The story of *Bordertown* has dime-novel overtones, rescued mostly by the performances. Muni plays a night-school-manufactured lawyer from a squalid Mexican area of Los Angeles. Disbarred when his temper gets out of hand in court, he retreats below the border as a bouncer, then manager of a casino, in a near-gangster image. Muni had more experience playing lawyers than many full-time attorneys, and gangsters were getting to be an unhappy habit; as Ramirez he played both.

Muni portrayed the hard-driving, ambitious character with the tempering grace of humor. "It's a beautiful orchestra," a guest comments on his new casino. "You should hear the cash register," Johnny Ramirez smirks, but it has the added dimension of Muni laughing at himself. Muni, by his acting, demands that you like this often unpalatable Ramirez, that you understand him, that you are on his side.

Tony Gaudio had been the cameraman on all of Norma Talmadge's early film triumphs. "Muni," he said, "I'll make you look as pretty as Norma!"

"Don't do me any favors," Muni said, poking him in the ribs.

Muni and Bette Davis had unverbalized respect for each other's fire and acting flexibility. Muni watched admiringly as Miss Davis battled Mayo on her interpretation of her final mad scene on the witness stand. "If you want me to do it obviously, silent picture style, then why don't we bring back silent picture titles, too?" she protested with that clipped, icy precision which mimics have found so fascinating. Miss Davis won her point for a subtler approach, and the critics praised the scene.

Other portions of the picture could have used a stronger directorial thumb. "Less!" Bella commented sagely. "That one word may be the key to all movie acting. Less!"

The balloon-shaped Eugene Pallette with his bullfrog voice is the stock, overinflated capitalist, who could have stepped out of a Gropper cartoon. For story purposes, he is instantly identifiable as physically repulsive to Bette Davis. Arthur Treacher is Margaret Lindsay's butler: no explanations are needed, nobody has to call him a butler so you'll be sure he isn't Amos or Andy or Molly Goldberg; he invented his own caricature. Other actors seem equally one-dimensional, unable to do more than skate on the surface of thankless parts.

But Muni and Bette Davis play originals, though Muni's eyes occasionally flash too wide in the Valentino manner. Miss Davis, young, quite beautiful, filled with sex energy, spits out her lines in that cigarette-biting, smoke-exhaling way which has become the symbol of high camp. "You must have an adding machine where your heart is," she tells Johnny Ramirez. These are stars, imprinting their flaming vitality on the screen.

Only a few things date *Bordertown*, studied in a projection room in 1973: the women's clothes (hats and skirt length), the automobiles, the width of men's trousers, and the fact that some of it seems to have been shot on a back lot or a company street, rarely done these days, except with supercheap television films.

Andre Sennwald in the New York *Times* wrote:

> *Bordertown* brings Paul Muni back to the Broadway screen after a discouraging absence, permitting him to scrape the nerves in the kind of taut and snarling role at which he is so consummately satisfying. . . . Mr. Muni brings to the photoplay his great talent for conviction and theatrical honesty, making it seem an impressive account of angry gutter ambitions.

"Kauf" in *Variety* wrote: "Paul Muni in his best screen performance and Bette Davis equallying if not bettering her characterization in *Of Human Bondage*. An interesting yarn, fine direction, and box-office."

It was indeed a box-office bonanza for Warner Brothers. Their ad quotes called for big type:

A GREAT THRILL AWAITS YOU
AS WARNER BROTHERS BRING
THESE TWO SENSATIONAL PERSONALITIES
TOGETHER IN *BORDERTOWN*

= =

THE BEAUTIFUL HELL-CAT OF
OF HUMAN BONDAGE FLINGS A
CHALLENGE TO THE DYNAMIC
STAR OF *I AM A FUGITIVE!*
HEAVEN HELP HER WHEN SHE FINDS
OUT WHAT A MAN SHE'S TALKING TO!

= =

BROTHER, YOU'LL WISH YOU
WERE BACK IN THE CHAIN-GANG
BEFORE I GET THROUGH WITH YOU!

Muni's face snarls from these ads, alongside a sultry Bette Davis in an Empress Eugénie hat.

Muni actually had seven days off to make the transition from Johnny Ramirez to Joe Radek. *Bordertown* finished ahead of schedule on October 10, 1934. Muni's mining film, with a new title, began shooting on October 18.

Interoffice memos should be preserved, like great poetry or the demotic hieroglyphics on the Rosetta Stone. This one deserves to be cast in amber and immortalized in a museum:

TO ALL DEPARTMENTS
The new and final title for the picture now known as BLACK HELL will be BLACK FURY.
Delete "Hell", add "Fury".

JACK L. WARNER

The title change did not affect the quality of the picture. It is a stirring film, sensitively directed, magnificently performed. Hal Wallis, who had taken over as production head of the studio when Darryl Zanuck left to head up Twentieth Century Pictures, pledged daring, courageous films, beginning with this one.

Other studio departments were more cautious:

TO PUBLICITY FROM PRODUCTION-FACILITIES:
In all publicity on the Muni picture, it would be advisable *not*

200

to mention the name of Judge Musmanno. Musmanno has been a liberal lawyer and judge for years and is a sworn enemy of the big coal companies. We will undoubtedly have to send a camera crew to the mines to get long shots, process plates, etc. And if it is known that Musmanno has any connection with our story, the coal companies will absolutely refuse to let us photograph on their property and otherwise refuse to cooperate with us. *After* we've got all the shots we need in Pennsylvania, *after* the picture is completed, we can mention Musmanno's connection with the story as much as we please. In fact, his endorsement will have a definite box-office value. Meanwhile, lay off until it's shot then open up as strong as we please.

If this caution seems lily-livered, the results on the screen justified it. The opening shots of the film are strikingly authentic, a sweeping panorama of an actual mine belching coal dust, a cinematic painting in black and white. Where did the shots come from? Cinematographer Byron Haskins smiled cryptically and simply said that he and a second-unit crew had been on "a little trip back East." And although permissions had been obtained, no mine operator was ready to stand up and admit his coal town had been given a screentest.

Michael Curtiz, the amiable "house director" at Warner's, with a Hungarian accent as thick as goulash, would seem to be an unlikely director for this stark, uncompromising social drama. (His notable pictures later included *Yankee Doodle Dandy, Casablanca, Mildred Pierce* and *Life with Father*.) But he was a magician with a camera, had an instinct for what would play and control of his actors. He was dominating, enormous on a set. Back in the office he listened to Wallis: Curtiz was both father and son on the same picture.

Muni found his director a delight, alternately "light as whipped cream and deep as a mine shaft." Curtiz's malapropisms dwarfed the legendary language of Sam Goldwyn. On *Black Fury*, when a propman came on the set for the third time with a wrong prop, Curtiz shouted, "The next time I send some big damn fool to get something, I go myself."

The studio dug an actual mine into the bowels of Mount Warner on the Warner Ranch, with tunnels and shafts, elevators, drills, lights, shoring, and real coal. No standing sets on back lots were redressed to make do or save a buck. Authentic interiors and a mine company street were built at the studio in Burbank and the old Warner lot on Sunset Boulevard. Muni and the rest of the cast commuted.

Muni spent most of his week off in the studio makeup depart-

201

ment draining away any vestige of the sleek Johnny Ramirez, converting himself into Joe Radek. High up on the wall of the makeup department were rows of dead-white plaster masks, each of a major Warner's star: Bette Davis, Edward G. Robinson, James Cagney, Pat O'Brien, Joan Blondell, and, of course, Muni. The Westmore brothers, in charge of the department, experimented with makeups on the masks. Newcomers would point to Muni's plaster face, asking who it was—unrecognizable because he was rarely seen out of heavy makeup. Women would admire the bone structure of Muni's mask and the sensuous mouth.

Perc Westmore presented Muni with an approximation of a Slavic face topped with a rough-cut mop of blond peasant hair. Muni approved but felt a wig, no matter how expert, would seem false, so they went to work on his own hair. Muni himself had brewed up walnut stain for the jet-black hair of Ramirez. Westmore found that walnut stain doesn't unstain easily. They bleached and bleached, including his eyebrows and the stubble on his chin. Then Westmore literally turned a cereal bowl over and gave Muni a typical 15-cent Pennsylvania coal-town haircut.

When he stared into the mirror, Muni said, "*That* I guarantee you is a Polack, born and reborn." Then he laughed. "Nobody can say I'm not willing to dye for dear old Warner Brothers!"

The Pole was much closer to the Muni character and experience than the Mexican; there is great believability in the happy, irresponsible, wise-stupid, playful, innocent Radek with a warm purr of an accent. This character was part of Muni's own heritage, the Slavic background of his unknown grandparents and his own long experience with peasant roles in the Yiddish theater.

"Joe Radek he likes everybody, and everybody likes Joe Radek," Muni says, and the laughter bubbles up from inside him. He uses a hulking walk. "Bohunk" really describes him: the kidder, the josher, the village clown. Here is another movie-movie, a story which could never be told as effectively on a stage, for the camera pokes into eyes and into souls. Radek is engaged to Anna Novak, sensitively played by Karen Morley. At Slovak Hall, he dances with her, exuberantly, joyfully, singing (damned well) a Polish folk song: "Woman is for man—just like rain is for the dusty ground."

But betrayal is in the air, on several levels. He learns, just as he is counting out the money to buy a farm for his bride, that Anna has run off with another man. His quality of disbelief is fantastic to behold. A little girl, the only one who knows how to read, spells out Anna's farewell letter. Radek's shocked numbness turns into fury and anger, then wildness. There is total vulnerability in Radek, joy of life to be shattered, a blank slate to be written on—and the camera writes. When he is made a dupe of strikebreakers and becomes a pariah in the community, he drinks himself into attempted insensibility. It is *Moshke Chasser* again: a gentle drunk, a nonoffensive drunk, an understandable, motivated drunk, a helpless man, drinking to forget, trying to blot out the iniquities which surround him.

Black Fury is memorable because Muni as Radek, without ever saying it in words, comments on betrayal, on the bloodletting of the human soul, on pain, on personal agony, on social injustice. We are all subject to wounds, he says, we all have scars in our palms and in our feet, we are all crucified by social inequities, we are all brothers and sisters in this wounding.

In 1973 at the Mark Taper Forum, director Wally Chappell asked one of his *Story Theater* actors what he wanted to be. The very young man quietly replied, "I want to be Paul Muni."

What can a novitiate learn, watching Muni on the screen, listening to people with vivid memories of his stage performances? (The young actor missed them, not having been born yet, which was foolish of him.) A Muni emulator can remember a key word: "vulnerability." Divinity, in Ben Hecht's story of a Hollywood Passion, does not photograph. But conviction does. Thought does.

In a reverse way, watching *Bordertown,* you can also learn not to *over*act. Muni himself was often horrified when he caught glimpses of himself "being a *ham-faddo*" on the screen. Get quiet! Less! Relax! When he let his emotions come out through his eyes, with merely a quiver of his back or a glance of pain, he was brilliant. The camera is a microscope and is capable of digging deep into the human mind. Perfectionism plagued Muni. "Be better!" had been his unspoken commandment to himself ever since his teens. It is a torturous state for any actor, but a healthy one.

Muni discovered Louis Untermeyer's poem "Caliban in the Coal Mines" while he was shooting *Black Fury,* and he read it aloud every morning. And although he never actively prayed, he kept in his wallet a ragged copy of Untermeyer's "Prayer," and would often glance at the line "God, keep me still unsatisfied." But his favorite lines of the poem were:

> From sleek contentment keep me free,
> And fill me with a buoyant doubt.

During the third week of shooting of *Black Fury,* on November 2, 1934, Muni's mother died. Just after lunch, she had complained of pains and dizziness. Manuel called an ambulance, and she was rushed to Van Nuys Hospital. Two hours later she was dead. The doctors diagnosed it as diabetes and ultimately heart failure. Bella had been called off the set and hurried to the hospital. Sallie was already dead by the time she got there. Bella drove back to the studio to pick up Muni. On their way home to Van Nuys, Bella quietly told Muni the news. He stared blankly in front of him and said nothing.

Ruth Jacoves, then Ruth Finkel, recalls the funeral. Muni stood dry-eyed, staring down at the open casket, as Ruth came up to him.

"Muni," she said, "she was a very good-looking woman."

"Yes," Muni nodded. "Beautiful. And for the first time in my life I know she won't open her mouth and say something that will cut me."

"Just because you were born to a woman doesn't mean you had to love her," Ruth said.

Muni nodded. "Or that I had to *judge* her. Good-bye, Mama."

The release of *Black Fury* caused a flurry of censorship. The state boards in Maryland and Illinois banned it outright. There were long debates before it was shown, reluctantly, in Pennsylvania. The New York board demanded the cutting of the scene of the brutal killing of Mike Shemanski, John Qualen's vivid parallel to the real-life John Barkowski. Warner Brothers hedged its bet with this program note: *"Black Fury* is not a propaganda picture; it offers no solution to labor problems, but presents human beings in a human story."

Critics hailed the film as "a thunderbolt of film courage" and called Muni's performance his greatest to date. Sennwald wrote in the New York *Times:* "Mr. Muni is altogether superb. By all odds, *Black Fury* is the most notable American experiment in social drama since *Our Daily Bread.*"

Variety's Abel Green, in the language he invented, called the picture: "Canny Burbanking. . . . Plus, of course, the superlative histrionism which Muni usually endows any flicker."

Volleys of complaints were fired from both the far right and the far left. Fiercely topical, filmed at the height of CIO's bitter fights with mineowners, the picture split the opposing sides into hypersensitive partisans, each wanting its own position glorified. But the real villains of *Black Fury* are the strikebreakers, the thinly disguised Pinkerton Men, called Industrial Detective Service in the film.

Judge Musmanno began a personal fight against the banning of the film and any tampering with its truthfulness. He filed an injunction against the elimination of the killing scene in New York.

"It will not hurt the citizens of the Empire State," he wrote in his brief, "to witness the conflict, the war by which both sides grind each other into coal dust. This is fact, not fiction. Cuts will make the picture namby-pamby, a bloodless corpse."

For the New York showing of the film at the Strand, part of the scene remained; only the actual sadistic clubbing of Shemanski was deleted. And a triumphant Musmanno attended the Pittsburgh opening, where not a frame of the final print had been touched.

Hollywood saw *Black Fury* and quickly swept it under the carpet. Academy members gave this brilliant film no awards and no nominations in any category. It was as if Hollywood were saying, "Fine! Be socially conscious—but not that much!"

Muni was exhausted after the two films. He lost twenty-two pounds. He wanted only to retreat to his sunny ranch, pick the mammoth walnuts, and take long walks with the Munis' newly acquired pet, a frisky Airedale affectionately named Simon, after the long-running lawyer in *Counsellor-at-Law*.

He listened to Toscanini records. He read his dictionaries. He played the violin. He had promised himself he would return to Broadway every year; but it was already too late in the season, and he hadn't read a play which fired him up and could lift him from his exhaustion. Besides, he felt it would be unfair to producer, backers, and fellow actors to go into a play in December or January and have to leave it in May.

Warner's promised to spread his next two pictures over a more realistic shooting schedule, with time to breathe between the two. Jake Wilk bought several properties in New York, including a story by W. R. Burnett, the author of *Little Caesar*, and Hal Wallis assigned Abem Finkel and Carl Ericson to develop it. But what else?

Jack Warner, with his eye to the box office, noted that along with musicals and gangster pictures, their biographical films had done all right. How about Muni stepping into the distinguished shoes recently vacated by Mr. George Arliss? Arliss had made three historical films for Warner's: *Disraeli, Hamilton,* and *Voltaire*. But he had packed his biographical bag and moved with Zanuck to become Twentieth Century Pictures' sixteenth- and seventeenth-century's Richelieu and eighteenth- and nineteenth-century's Rothschild. Did Muni have any suggestions?

Muni did not hesitate.

Paul and Bella Muni with their dog, Toto, on their California walnut ranch.

"Beethoven!" he said.

Jack Warner's answer did not thunder back from Burbank like the opening chords of Beethoven's Fifth Symphony.

But Muni, quickly bored with walnuts, went to work. He read every book available on the great composer. He moved his makeup kit into the guest cottage and began experimenting. Suddenly he felt excited as a kid in Cleveland on roller skates. The Toscanini records played at full volume in the cottage which he began to call "my chicken coop."

One day, deep in study, he was wandering at the edges of their property. A neighbor, Mrs. Mischa Auer, leaned across the fence and said pleasantly, "Good morning, Mr. Muni." Totally impervious, Muni moved on, not answering. Later in the day a worried Mrs. Auer saw Bella.

"I hope I haven't offended Mr. Muni in any way," she told Bella. "I said good morning to your husband, and he just walked right by without answering."

"Oh, don't worry about that," Bella pooh-poohed. "He probably didn't even hear you. You see, today he's Beethoven, so naturally he's deaf as a doorknob!"

The release of *Bordertown* and *Black Fury* hard on each other's heels early in 1935 convinced Warner Brothers that Muni was

206

their major star. Jack Warner called Muni in for a personal meeting. The Beethoven film biography was a fine idea, sure, but it was a project that should be developed slowly, gradually, carefully. Meanwhile, there was this screenplay in the hopper, *Dr. Socrates,* and it was a surefire winner. Muni, who had read the original short story, begged off. It was another gangster film, he protested, and hadn't the studio promised to go on to bigger and better things, more uplifting subject matter?

"It's a switch," Warner told him. "Maybe there's a gangster or two in it, but we get Barton MacLane and that whole bunch to do them. You play the antigangster—a small-town doctor. And, Paul, let me talk to you like a father to a son. This will be your greatest role! It was made for you!" (TEST: Anybody who called Muni "Paul" was about as intimate with him as an ice cube.)

Muni said he'd like to read the latest screenplay and would let Mr. Warner know. Finkel and Ericson had been taken off the script and Robert Lord and Mary McCall, Jr., were now writing it. (Eventually Miss McCall received solo credit.) In short, it was an assembly-line screenplay, and Muni looked at the probability of doing it with an eye of a dead fish.

"I don't want to play in *Caesar,*" he explained, "but I don't want to play in *Little Caesar* either. That was yesterday. Where the hell is tomorrow?"

"Which reminds me," Warner said casually, "Eddie Robinson is dying to do the part. I guarantee the actor who plays it will get an Academy Award."

Studio executives undoubtedly told Robinson the same thing about Muni's passionate desire to play *Dr. Socrates.* Often the two were pitted against each other, a manufactured rivalry invented as studio policy. Robinson was bright enough to turn down *Dr. Socrates.* Muni eventually got trapped into playing it.

Radio drama was in the ascendency, and Muni was invited to star in the two most popular Hollywood-originated programs during 1935: *Lux Radio Theatre* and *Hollywood Hotel.* Cecil B. De-Mille was nominal director of *Lux,* but the backstage craftsmen of this Monday night favorite were the skillful adapter, George Wells, and Frank Woodruff, as calm and confident a director as ever hit radio.

Woodruff had difficulty selling Muni as a *Lux* guest star. "He's a makeup freak," the J. Walter Thompson advertising agency executives told him. "He'll never come across on the air. Get somebody with a radio voice like Don Ameche."

Box-office figures on Muni movies changed their minds, and they reluctantly agreed on a property of Muni's choice, an hour-

(Warner Brothers photo)

(CBS photo from Helen Lovett Collection)

Warner's star Dick Powell comes to visit Paul Muni on the sound stage of *Black Fury*. "From us coal diggers to you Gold Diggers," Muni joked.

Cecil B. DeMille greets Paul Muni in his first appearance on *Lux Radio Theatre*.

long version of *Counsellor-at-Law*. It was Muni's first radio appearance, and although he was delighted to be playing his old friend George Simon again, he was terrified of a live broadcast before a live studio audience. (CBS and NBC in those days would rather murder their mothers than allow anything as network-shattering as a transcribed broadcast, and nobody had been clever enough yet to invent tape.) But once Muni sailed onstage, the terror disappeared. The reaction from the live audience felt like the old tennis game.

The response was overwhelming: from radio columnists, the Crosley Rating Service, and particularly the fan mail. "That is the sexiest voice I have ever heard in radio," one housewife wrote. "It's a goose-bump voice," another female listener commented. The organ tones in Muni's low register were rarely heard on the air; later Orson Welles magnetized the nation using a similar range of his Mighty Wurlitzer voice. The Hollywood columnist Jimmy Fidler managed to get Muni's unlisted phone number and asked him how the hell he accomplished this instant radio stardom.

"It's a special makeup I use on my tonsils," Muni kidded in a dead-serious confidential whisper. "Max Factor hasn't brought it out yet. It's a hundred percent chicken fat!"

Hollywood Hotel, sponsored by Campbell's Soups, billed Muni's appearance a few months later as his radio debut, totally ignoring his appearance on *Lux*. Muni and Jean Muir played scenes from *The Valiant*. In her interview spot on the program, Louella Parsons described the work, in her famous la-de-da voice, as *"The Valiants,* Mr. Mooney's very first picture in our wonderful city of Hollllllywooood. And here they are again, appearing through the courtesy of that sweet Jack Warner, Paul Mooooooney, and Jean Mweer." She managed to pronounce "Warner" correctly.

A listener somewhere in the Midwest, dreaming of the glamorous film capital, believed the program was actually coming from a luxurious and exclusive hotel. The actual Hollywood Hotel at the corner of Highland and Hollywood Boulevard, now gone, was a fairly tacky establishment; the Friday night broadcasts came from a radio playhouse. A press release indicates other portions of the program that night included: "the gay young singer Dick Powell, Frances Langford, Ann Jamison, Igor Gorin, Raymond Paige and his orchestra."

Muni resented the velvet-gloved blackmail of the *Hollywood Hotel* series. Louella Parsons agreed to deliver dramatic gueststars every week—without compensation—presumably for favorable mention in her Hearst-syndicated gossip column. Muni found this an insufferable practice but made this one token appearance to silence Warner's publicity department. Bella had stayed home to listen "on the air." When Muni arrived back at the walnut ranch, Bella was full of questions: what was Louella Parsons really like?

"Brilliant. An intellectual," Muni said. "That woman can pronounce *absolutely anything*—except words."

Jack Warner advised Hal Wallis to "get some writers cooking" on biographical ideas for Muni. "Anything but Beethoven. Nobody wants to see a movie about a blind composer!"*

Sheridan Gibney, back on the lot to work with Marc Connelly on *Green Pastures,* came up with a notion called *The Gentleman from Kimberley,* about the South African diamond mines. This seemed a commercial idea, and Gibney was advised to develop it. Another young writer on the lot, Pierre Collings, put together six pages of a rough idea concerning Louis Pasteur. Wallis looked at it, thought it was a possibility, and showed it to Warner, who practically kicked Wallis out of his office.

"We don't want a period piece, and we don't want to hide Paul behind a beard," Warner said. "That face is a star now. Stick

*Producer Henry Blanke swears this is a literal quote.

all those whiskers on him and nobody'll know who he is. If Muni wants to be a doctor, we've got a perfectly good one ready for him. *Dr. Socrates,* not Dr. Pasteur. Who wants to see a picture about bugs?"

The discouraged Collings mentioned his failure to his fellow workers at the writers' table in the Green Room, the studio's commissary. Edward Chodorov asked for a copy and spent a few days adding some material to it, based partly on reading a chapter about Pasteur in Paul de Kruif's *Microbe Hunters.* Abem Finkel, also at that luncheon table, told his brother-in-law about it. The possibility of playing the famous scientist excited Muni.

Chodorov tried to see Jack Warner personally but found "he was tied up in an important tennis match." Muni came on the lot and backed Jack Warner up against the tennis net on his private studio court.

"We'll hold off on Beethoven for a while," Muni bargained. "You're right—it's a long-term project which should be developed over a year or two. But I want to do Pasteur. I want to play it so much I'll even do *Dr. Socrates* first while the other screenplay is being written."

Hal Wallis assigned Collings and Gibney to develop a Pasteur script, with this cheering news to any creative writer: "I don't think we'll ever do it. Jack Warner is dead set against it. But to please Muni and quiet him down, go ahead and write a screenplay, and we'll see when you get through. Frankly, I think it's hopeless."

Muni found the script of *Dr. Socrates* an inoffensive little melodrama. He liked some of the perky dialogue and he rationalized it this way:

"I'll play the other side of the coin—everything the character in *Scarface* wasn't: gentle, unselfish, shy, bookish. Tony Carmonte never stuck his nose in a book in his life. The mild man in *Dr. Socrates* rarely gets his nose out of one."

The film contains a touch of precognition. In a bookstore, while a bank is being robbed across the street, Muni is reading a copy of *The Life of Louis Pasteur.* It was a trailer sneaked in for the film Muni really wanted to make.

From Muni's point of view *Dr. Socrates* was better forgotten, and he rarely listed it in his credits in the years that followed. However, it did introduce him to its director, William Dieterle, and together they created three classics: *Pasteur, Zola,* and *Juarez.*

"In *Dr. Socrates,*" Muni told me, "Dieterle and I were out in the bullpen, warming up."

Dieterle, a disciple of Max Reinhardt's, had co-directed the film of *Midsummer Night's Dream* with Reinhardt. Dieterle was only two years older than Muni, but somehow he seemed like a father figure. He was six feet three, with dark hair and dark eyes, a square jaw and broad shoulders. He always wore well-tailored clothes, elegant but casual, and invariably white gloves, which he rarely, if ever, took off. He had been a matinee idol in Berlin when his future wife, the ubiquitous Charlotte Hagenbruch, discovered him helpless on a sickbed one day in the early twenties. The stars in the heavens, she predicted, would make him well and guide him on to worldwide fame. Dieterle was born on July 15, 1893. On July 15, 1921, when all their rising signs were in their right houses, the nondescript, chubby, round-faced, unpretty Charlotte, was married in Berlin to the handsome actor, director-to-be.

Muni was a bit startled by his director's reliance on signs and portents. Dieterle, in the manner of a Prussian martinet (and how often he seemed to Muni like Philip Weisenfreund), ordered the shooting of *Dr. Socrates* to begin precisely at 9:02 A.M., exactly on the morning of June 6, 1935, and not a second later. They would end precisely at 5:20 P.M. on July 15, a lucky day for both Dieterle and Muni, according to Charlotte, the family seer. Not only were the stars with them, all the forces of numerology agreed, but it was a thirty-four day shooting schedule, and thirty-four was also a magic number for both of them.

At home, Muni told Bella about this. "I think it's nuttier than this whole walnut ranch," he said. "Still, I feel he's a great director. If only he had something and somebody to direct."

Muni, looking remarkably like Ronald Colman in a neatly clipped mustache, went to work, happy to know that writers were also busy close by on the Pasteur project, tentatively titled *Enemy of Man*. His old friend Tony Gaudio was behind the camera, and Muni had exacted a promise from Gaudio to stand by for the Pasteur picture as well.

Touches of humor punctuate *Dr. Socrates*. When the mild-mannered doctor is asked what he thinks of a patent medicine, he replies, "It's a bargain for seventy-nine cents. Most patent medicines are straight alcohol. Mix it with ginger ale and you have a great cocktail."

Muni plays an uncompromising man, long on principle. His integrity shines through, even in this B-picture-level melodrama. If it were not for the presence of Muni and some fairly good photography, it would be just another forgettable, grind-them-out-for-the-block-booking film. (A few years later, in 1939, Warner Brothers reused the plot, called it *King of the Underworld*, starring Humphrey Bogart. Bogie was the Barton MacLane gangster; Muni's part was switched to a woman doctor, and Kay Francis played it.)

The film critics were not to be fooled. Most of them considered it a waste of Muni's talent. Sennwald in the New York *Times* wrote:

> Interrupting his preoccupation with the big things of the cinema, Paul Muni undertakes a bit of minor league melodrama. *Dr. Socrates* is pleasantly unimportant and vice versa. . . . The Warner Brothers know how to hold up a bank and wreck a careening automobile. . . . Mr. Muni shows himself to be an able critic of the drama by resisting any temptation to give the work a false importance in his performance. It is time, though, that the Warners locked up their armory.

The perceptive Leo Mishkin in the *Morning Telegraph* chided Muni: "He should come back to Broadway for awhile, preferably with another *Counsellor-at-Law*. It would do him a world of good."

During the shooting of the picture, Charlotte Dieterle arrived every day at lunchtime to wash her husband's feet as if she were a Geisha girl, always addressing him as "Mr. Dieterle." And she was there the entire day of July 15, helping celebrate his birthday, their anniversary, and the completion of the filming, as the heavens had decreed: exactly on the magic thirty-fourth day and precisely at 5:20 P.M.

The stars may have been propitious. The picture was preposterous.

18

AT Los Angeles County Hospital Sheridan Gibney was conferring with biologists and pathologists who gave him valuable material about anthrax (the sheep disease), hydrophobia, and childbed fever—all vital parts of the Pasteur story. Pierre Collings, ill most of the time, worked with Gibney only about one day a week.

Muni, meanwhile, was reading all he could on Pasteur. He was a master of marginalia. Bella left us all of Muni's books, and we have donated the pertinent ones to the Library and Museum

(MGM photos)

Muni in *The Good Earth*.

Luise Rainer as O-Lan and Muni as Wang.

(MGM photo)

(Ted Thomas Collection)

of the Performing Arts in New York's Lincoln Center, where scholars may study Muni's painstaking analyses of historical characters in the research he did. He vigorously underlined passages in both red and blue—red for facts, blue for emotional values. His scribbling in book margins, some in English, some in Yiddish, say, "Watch this!" or "Try to catch some of this quality!" or "Imp!" (his recurring shorthand for "important").

The first draft screenplay was completed early in July, 1935. Eight or nine neatly mimeographed copies were sent from the stenographic department to the writer's office, apparently, Gibney remembers, "to sit and rot there." But by accident, Muni dropped in at the end of his day's shooting on *Dr. Socrates,* saw a script, and took a copy home with him for the weekend.

Henry Blanke had been loosely assigned as supervising producer of the project and had airmailed a *Pasteur* script to Hal Wallis, on vacation in Banff with his wife then, Louise Fazenda. Whoever left the copy on Jack Warner's desk put it there and ran.

Early Monday morning Muni was waiting in Gibney's office when the screenwriter arrived.

"I love it," Muni told Gibney, at which point Blanke walked in.

"I like it, too," Blanke said. "I think it can be an important picture. But before we all get too excited, have a look at this."

He handed them a three-page single-spaced memo, unsigned, from the front office. Gibney read it aloud. It directed Blanke to take Gibney and Collings off the screenplay immediately and to put a writer named Laird Doyle onto it. It suggested a storyline in which Pasteur is a chemistry major at the university, in love with the daughter of the dean of the medical school. The dean will not allow his daughter to marry Pasteur unless he switches his major from chemistry to medicine. Pasteur refuses, and the girl must give him up. Thus he loses the love of his life. He wins her back eventually when he is acclaimed and famous.

"At the age of eighty," Gibney commented.

The memo went on to order no experimentation on dogs whatsoever, because of the SPCA; the mention of no Russian names of scientists or Mr. Hearst might object and the studio would lose Marion Davies; and no use of childbed fever in the plot because it might frighten women and they'd stop having children. The final page of these orders-from-on-high insisted there be no sheep jumping over stiles because the audience would start counting them and go to sleep. The author of this memorable memo has never stepped forward to demand credit.

214

Muni grabbed a copy of the screenplay, took out a fountain pen and wrote, in large letters across the cover:

I APPROVE THIS SCRIPT EXACTLY AS WRITTEN!!
PAUL MUNI

An hour later Gibney was in Jack Warner's office, "getting hell," the screenwriter recalls.

"How dare you commit such an act of insubordination?" Warner shouted. "An actor should only see a script through regular channels, given to him by a producer, not a writer. Don't you know that?"

Gibney just nodded and listened.

"I told that son of a bitch Chodorov the same thing I'm going to tell you. This picture will never be made. Why, I even asked a waitress in the Green Room, and she never even heard of Louis Pasteur. So forget about it!"

Silently, Gibney handed Warner the script with Muni's hastily scrawled blessing.

Trapped by Muni's contract giving him script approval, the studio started the picture "with most of the executives in the front offices holding their noses." They gave Blanke, as producer, a pitifully small budget, $330,000—the lowest figure possible at the time for an A picture. Even Dieterle hated the script; Charlotte was convinced that the studio was trying to ruin her husband's career by assigning him to it. In short, Dieterle handled the screenplay with kid gloves, white.

No new sets, only redressed ones, were to be used. The biggest set needed was the Academy of Science indoor amphitheater; they repainted a nightclub used in an extravagant Busby Berkeley musical. The whole thing was treated as if the film were eventually to be junked.

Despite the limitations, the spirit was upon Muni, and his dedication and belief shine through. The lighting and photography, compensating for the makeshift production, were masterful. One London critic wrote later: "Tony Gaudio is an artist who has achieved shots worthy of being hung in the world's great galleries."

Clay Campbell, a makeup man often considered a genius at his craft, was assigned to Muni. Pictures of Pasteur were plastered around the walls and mirrors of the makeup department, and the beard went on hair by hair. Muni was never satisfied. Finally they shaped a beard that seemed identical to the photographs. Muni insisted they test the makeup with still shots before they settled on it completely. "The camera," he said, "will see things that we're missing." But then he squinted into the mirror and shouted at his image. "My God, that's not Pasteur! I look exactly like Ulysses S. Grant!"

The discouraged Clay Campbell raced to the research department and brought back a photograph of General Grant. He placed it beside Muni's mirror; sure enough, they were dead ringers. "But, look," Campbell said, ripping down a picture of Pasteur. "Pasteur and Grant look enough alike to be twins!"

Modifications were made, during which Campbell lost five pounds. When Charlotte Dieterle heard about the similarity of the American general and the French scientist, she rushed to announce that Grant and Pasteur had been born the same year, 1822, and though one was born in April and the other in December, they were both born on the twenty-seventh day of the month. To Charlotte, this was an important portent.

Shooting began on August 15, 1935, and the picture finished exactly on schedule, on September 27 (oh, lucky day!), with a minimum of retakes. "It was practically the way a current television show is shot," Gibney recalls. The title was changed several times, from *Enemy of Man* to *The Fighter* to *Death Fighter* and finally to *The Story of Louis Pasteur*. If the stars weren't all exactly at their zenith, Charlotte Dieterle noted, at least there were the right number of letters in the final title.

It's a beautiful picture. Muni plays it in a kind of rabbinical style: the scholar, the courageous unflinching scientist, always with wit. Audiences sense in every foot of the film that there is a mind at work, ears listening, eyes watching: thought and intelligence are captured on celluloid.

Dick Moore, today a New York advertising executive and editor of the *AFTRA* magazine, recalls his experience working with Muni in *Pasteur* and later in *Zola*. He was Dickie Moore then, six years old.

"Muni never treated me as a kid actor, always as an equal, never with condescension. The feeling I got was great authority, enormous stature, I don't mean height, but wherever he moved, he *filled the vacuum!* That's the feeling I had later on, in the audience watching him in *Inherit the Wind*. And I felt the same way when I saw him in person."

A classic screen-mother story is told about Moore *mère*. Dickie flashed his huge brown eyes at his mother one day during the filming of *Pasteur* and moaned, "Ma, why can't I go out and play like the rest of the kids? Why do I have to be an actor?"

"But, Dickie," she said reasonably to her tiny six-year-old, "it's what you've wanted *all of your life!*"

The distinguished actress Josephine Hutchinson (today Mrs.

(Ted Thomas Collection)

Muni receiving the gold statuette Oscar for his performance in *The Story of Louis Pasteur*.

(WB photo by Bert Longworth) **Left: Pasteur among his test tubes.**

Staats Cotsworth), who played Pasteur's wife, remembers how impressed she was with Muni's perfectionism and the depth of his preparation.

"One of the mistakes young actors make today is to think they can go onstage or on camera and do whatever comes into their minds. And it probably isn't as good as if they'd had a line or musical score in their heads beforehand." Muni, she recalls, seems to have prepared an entire symphony.

How much did Dieterle direct? Not too much with Muni. He would say simply, "You know what to do—go ahead and do it!" Dieterle was less kind to others in the cast. Miss Hutchinson remembers his shouting at Anita Louise, "Anita, for Christ's sake, don't be so *Hollywood!*"

Gibney ran up a sizable bill at the County Hospital for all the slides (anthrax, hydrophobia), which were painstakingly accurate as seen through the microscope and the eye of the camera. "Send us a bill," Gibney said. "Oh, I'm not allowed to take money," the biologist-pathologist said. "But I could use a shipment of monkeys." So Blanke arranged to have forty monkeys shipped from Africa. For the first time in film history, the official tender was monkeys instead of money.

217

Two final memos must be included in the record book:

> In the official billing, Paul Muni's character role is described as "Dr. Louis Pasteur."
> Please eliminate the "Dr." part of it since he is not a doctor.
> Kind regards.

Another bolt of inspiration was passed down from on high, addressed to all concerned from an unnamed executive:

> Just had brilliant idea how to make the film completely acceptable and commercial. Have voice-over or film crawl at finale saying: "And to this day, housewives all over the world are grateful to this man, because he invented pasteurized milk."

Hal Wallis, Jack Warner, and Henry Blanke had enough sense to ignore that suggestion. To Warner Brothers came glory and sizable box-office receipts, even without the enlightening epilogue. Not long afterward Jack Warner was invited to Paris, made a Chevalier of the *Légion d'honneur,* and soundly kissed on both cheeks for producing, "to the glory of France, of science, of Men of Good Will throughout the world, and to the enduring art of the cinema," a picture he never wanted to make.

Muni didn't attend the sneak preview of *Pasteur* in Santa Barbara, but Henry Blanke, with tears in his eyes, phoned Muni to report that at the final fade-out the audience stood up and cheered and applauded for five minutes; this had never happened before at a preview.

The next day a studio electrician told Muni that he had taken his nine-year-old son along to the preview. The boy was silent all the way back to Los Angeles. Just as they arrived home, he turned to his father and said, "Daddy, will you buy me a microscope?"

"That," said Muni, "is a better ovation than any cheers and applause."

After the success of *Pasteur,* the studio didn't want to let Muni out from behind a beard ever again. They rushed to prepare other properties, including even Beethoven. (Did he wear a beard? Never mind, we'll put one on him.) After all, critics throughout the world echoed the London correspondent who wrote: "Warner Brothers deserve every congratulation for having the intestinal fortitude to make what must be considered strictly a prestige picture. But it will live through the years."

I asked Sheridan Gibney, as the writer of two and a half of

Muni's films, how he evaluated Muni as an actor. Observing Muni on the set, later on the screen, performing *your words,* what did he do that made him so effective and memorable?

"I think he is one of the really great actors of this century," Gibney said. "The reason? He made the words his own. I believed them when he spoke them. I think this was his great gift."

Muni received hundreds of letters, some from statesmen and famous authors, and Muni was awed. He would write multiple drafts, attempting to answer them with intelligent simplicity; he would curse himself for not writing easily, and he'd rip up his replies and start again. International celebrities, visiting California, would invariably ask to tour a motion-picture set. This terrified Muni. "What in hell can I say to an Einstein or a Milliken or a Shaw? My God, they're not interested in what *I* have to say."

When H. G. Wells visited Hollywood in December, 1935, the Academy of Motion Picture Arts and Sciences gave the celebrated author a banquet. Wells had asked to meet only two stars: Charlie Chaplin and Paul Muni. The novelist-historian was speechless after the final course of the dinner: a showing of *Pasteur* in the Academy projection room on the balcony of the Hollywood-Roosevelt Hotel. The place was jammed with Hollywood nobility: Cecil B. DeMille, Norma Shearer, Jack Warner, Hal Wallis, William Dieterle, Walt Disney, and Mr. and Mrs. Chaplin (Paulette Goddard at the time). But when the lights came up, Wells wanted to speak only to Muni. "Wells talked to me as if I were really Louis Pasteur, and expected me to say, 'Oh, send my regards to Dr. Lister.' This fluent and prolific author looked at me, tongue-tied; I guess he was waiting for me to speak pearls of wisdom. And all *I* wanted to do was listen to *him.*"

"I have no small talk," Muni often said. Despite his omnivorous reading and study, he felt his lack of formal education would reveal him as "a blithering idiot." And so he shied away from parties, avoided most social functions. "I hide in public," Muni once told me.

One letter Muni answered from a noncelebrity changed that young man's life. Max Foster, a fourteen-year-old in Garnett, Kansas, had seen Muni in *Bordertown*. "To me," Foster says, "he was the epitome of all actors." The boy was suddenly stricken with malarial fever and not expected to live. His mother wrote Muni, saying how much a letter from him would mean to the boy's recovery. Muni answered in his own hand, writing about Foster's career, but meaning his health and indeed, his life:

Jan, 2, 1936

My dear Max: —

Your several letters have been received and I have been extremely busy and so have been unable to write you... I want you to know that I have enjoyed receiving them. If it's a career you seek in the movies or in the theatre by all means stick to your guns, [but] stick: in other words [fight]! where there is no conquest there is no victory — — grit and perseverance. You must have talent, or you wouldn't write the way you do. So don't be discouraged, and you will ultimately attain your goal. My sincerest wishes that in some future time you will climb to the pinnacle of success

A happy New Year to you.

Paul Muni

P.S. I have mailed you a photograph, and hope you will like it

Is it ironic that a man of such infinite talent misspelled the word "talent"?

The doctors in Kansas say that Muni's letter made the young Foster battle for his life; from the day it came he continued to improve. Later he and his family moved to Hollywood, and the Munis "adopted" him. Today Foster is an executive of the Los Angeles Philharmonic.

Bella and Muni often said, "You think we have no children? We have four. A daughter and three sons. Bethel Leslie. Jerry and Bobby. And Max Foster."

"We know about Lawrence and Lee," friends tried to figure, "and you inherited Bethel when she acted in *Inherit the Wind*. But who's Max Foster? Did you adopt him legally?"

"No, no," Bella answered.

"Then where's he from?"

"Oh," Bella said, "we found him in the mail."

Mimi Levee, the wife of Muni's agent, remembers the day Muni took her to lunch at the Players Restaurant on the Sunset Strip and asked her wistfully, "Tell me. How did you manage a family in this town?"

Beyond his growing sons, M. C. Levee had established a family atmosphere representing actors, directors, and songwriting teams.

Instead of a sterile office building, his agency was headquartered in a rambling house at the corner of Crescent Heights Boulevard and Fountain Avenue. He conducted business on a sunny patio over lunch he prepared himself with flair and style. Levee, a gourmet cook, took delight in serving his clients quiche Lorraine, fish soup, and marinated steaks while studio contracts were being marinated simultaneously.

When the Munis were invited to lunch at 1 P.M., they invariably arrived ten minutes early but walked around the block so they could ring the front doorbell precisely on the hour. Levee cooked up another concept to make his agency something beyond "flesh peddling." He combined business management and public relations all under the same roof. Ivy Wilson (a warm and witty woman of eighty-six when I talked to her in 1973) recalls that her job as head of publicity for Levee consisted mainly in keeping clients' names out of the newspapers for occasional indiscretions, a task she never had to perform for Muni. She also remembers Bella with special affection. The busy Mrs. Wilson had been driving a battered 1929 Model-A Ford. Bella organized all the Levee clients, who mutually bought her a snub-nosed Willys as a present.

All of 1936 and a month into 1937 was *Good Earth* time for Muni. An eleven-month shooting schedule was luxury compared to the five weeks spent on making *Pasteur,* the quickie which became a classic.

For Irving Thalberg *The Good Earth* was the climax of a career which was to end too soon. Thalberg never put his name on any of the films he made; he was the "anonymous genius," F. Scott Fitzgerald's *Last Tycoon.* In the last year of his life he was involved in making independent films, still under the umbrella of MGM. He planned three "monuments": *Romeo and Juliet, Marie Antoinette* (both starring his wife, Norma Shearer), and *The Good Earth,* which he had been planning and preparing since the book came out in 1931.

Louis B. Mayer had said he didn't want a film even about American farmers; who the hell was interested in a film about Chinese farmers, for God's sake? Thalberg pointed out that this was a picture about the land, about a marriage, and about human dignity.

In 1934 he had sent a crew to China headed up by director George Hill (not George Roy Hill, who was still in elementary school). From Shanghai, they shipped back 2,000,000 feet of film; even without actors, it would have been a movie 370 hours long or the equivalent of 185 average feature-length films. (Muni loved statistics—if you quoted any to him, you'd win every argument.)

Alexis Touloubov, the art director of the Chinese expedition, bought up entire farms, including authentic gear, equipment, and artifacts which were to make the picture meticulously accurate. Eighteen tons of properties and furniture were shipped back to MGM. Not long after he returned from China, George Hill, a great strapping man, committed suicide. Thalberg assigned Victor Fleming as director; when Fleming became ill, Sidney Franklin took over. Multiple scripts were written: one day Thalberg put them all in one pile, and they towered above his head. Karl Freund created sepia tapestries as cinematographer. Rarely is sound given a significant part in the entire mood of a picture; Douglas Shearer turned sound effects for *The Good Earth* into a symphony of dramatic, emotional meaning.

Thalberg personally assembled the cast for the picture. He phoned Muni and asked him to read Pearl Buck's Pulitzer Prizewinning novel. (It was her major work and later the main reason she was awarded the Nobel Prize.) Muni and Bella came to lunch at the Thalberg-Shearer oceanfront home at 707 Pacific Coast Highway late in September, 1935, a few days after Muni's birthday.

"I love the book, Mr. Thalberg," Muni said. "And I would be honored to work with you. But there are three reasons I can't possibly do *Good Earth*. First, I'm under contract to Warner Brothers."

"I think I can make a deal to borrow you," Thalberg assured him.

"In the second place, I'm about as Chinese as Herbert Hoover. I won't look Chinese, no matter how much makeup I use, and I won't sound it."

"You'll *be* it," Thalberg said. "Which is what I want."

"But the third and main reason," Muni said, "is that I'm too old for the part. Wang Lung starts out as a kid—twenty years old—on his wedding day. A couple of days ago, Mr. Thalberg, I was forty years old. How do you tell a camera—and an audience—that an old character actor is a kid? Hell, I never even played a twenty-year-old when I was twenty years old!"

"I've got an instinct about it," Thalberg said. "I'm convinced you can do it. You can *act* it!"

Thalberg told Muni and Bella about Clark Gable's initial refusal to play the role of Fletcher Christian in the original *Mutiny on the Bounty* film. "I'm a coal miner from Cadiz, Ohio," Gable had protested to Thalberg. "What the hell would I be doing on Her Majesty's Ship *Bounty,* for Christ's sake? Besides, I have terrible legs, I'll look God-awful in knee breeches. You're miscasting me. You're going to ruin me. And your picture."

"I told him the same thing I'm going to tell you," Thalberg said. " 'It's a marvelous part. If it doesn't come off as I say, I'll never again ask you to play anything you don't want to play.' Well, Clark did it, and the rest is history. And I'll make the same deal with you, Mr. Muni. And I hope we can make many, many pictures together in the future."

Muni was sold. The problem then was to convince Warner Brothers, which didn't want Muni to go over to the enemy. Thalberg negotiated an involved deal, in which he borrowed Muni, as well as Leslie Howard (for *Romeo and Juliet*), and had to lend Warner Brothers Clark Gable, who found himself trapped in Burbank in a forgettable film with Marion Davies called *Cain and Mabel*.

"They traded us like baseball players," Muni told me many years later. "Warner Brothers got Gable; Thalberg got Leslie Howard, me, and an outfielder."

In November, 1935, Muni traveled to San Francisco with his old friend Max Siegel, who was then working for Thalberg on Marx Brothers pictures and had the assignment to cast the rest of *Good Earth*. Muni met and talked with as many Chinese as possible, observing every nuance of walk and shrug and rhythm. "For my purposes, the trouble with most of the Chinese in San Francisco," Muni said, "was that they were too Americanized." Muni sought out more Oriental Asians in San Francisco's Chinatown, sat with them, ate with them, philosophized with them.

Later Muni spent many hours with Major General Ting-hsui Tu, who was lent by the Nanking government as technical adviser on the picture. (After World War II, Muni learned, Tu was executed for "improper conduct" by the new Chinese regime.) Muni read books on Chinese art, history, customs, and enrolled in an extension course at UCLA in Chinese music. His favorite piece of research was a saying of Confucius, who designated the ranks of society in this order of worth: (1) scholar, (2) farmer, (3) artisan, (4) merchant.

When shooting began early in February, 1936, four years had gone into the preparation of the film. MGM announced it as "the longest production effort in the history of the screen." To the workers in the makeup department, it seemed as if Muni had spent the entire four years at their mirrored tables in infinite experimentation.

The makeup which eventually satisfied Muni (and the camera) was subtle and simple: no slanted eyes, no involved facial reconstruction. He simply shaved off half his eyebrows and built up the area just above his eyelids into a convincing Mongolian or epicanthic fold. He also shaved part of his head. He lost weight.

Beyond that his amazing transformation consisted entirely of attitude and belief. To that point in film history most Orientals had been stereotypes: the stock laundryman, the villainous opium dealer, or the oh-so-clever Charlie Chans, most of them speaking singsong pidgin English. The inscrutable East had been cinematically screwed. In the performances of Muni and Luise Rainer, however, there is dignity, simplicity, understanding, humor, believability, most of all humanity. In 1973, perhaps justifiably, pressure groups are insisting that only Orientals play Orientals. But if that had happened in the case of *Good Earth,* we would have missed two of the most memorable performances in the history of the screen.

Pulitzer Prize playwright Marc Connelly wrote the final screen treatment, laying out the structure of the story. The late Tess Slessinger then wrote a screenplay. Frank Davis, one of Thalberg's production associates, was assigned to work with her on technical details. (Six weeks later he married her.) Talbot Jennings, a favorite of Thalberg's, wrote still another draft, and Claudine West, who worked closely with Sidney Franklin on many projects, added bits here and there. The final credit reads: "Screenplay by Tess Slessinger, Talbot Jennings and Claudine West, with additional dialogue by Marc Connelly." Davis recalls that his wife often said that Connelly wrote some of the most telling lines of the film, including the moving ending, and should have had major credit.

Muni, who had been terrified to play youngness, is most effective in the early scenes. It is an interesting switch. Most performers think character acting, when you are young, usually means pretending to be older or hiding under mountains of makeup. Muni, age forty, is totally convincing as an open-faced twenty-year-old. He does it all with a young spirit bubbling inside himself, with naïveté, with innocence, with youthful tenderness, wonder, incredulity, and a joyful, giggling charm. He learned how to master body language: the waddling walk, the quick-dipping bow, the rice bowl close to his lips as he shovels in a hasty meal, the wiping of his hands on his backside.

This simple saga, designed in Thalberg's words, "to catch the soul of China," was miraculously dramatized by the unfailing rule of "taking infinite pains." This was true of Muni and of Metro's scenic magicians. For eleven months Chatsworth became China. Five hundred acres were purchased in the San Fernando Valley, the rolling fields terraced after the Chinese fashion; a walled city was constructed, with streets and shops, farmers' huts erected, the ground plowed and seeded with authentic Chinese farm products, an artificial river constructed, then pumped dry for the famine scenes.

Bella saved some notes Muni took during the shooting:

> I don't believe it. I forget the camera and think I am really
> on a farm on the other side of the world. The hundreds of
> Chinese extras. The water buffalos, my new friends, actually
> brought from China, and such actors! I seem to hear the mourn-
> ful call of doves and smell burning joss-sticks in the air. Buddha
> seems to brood. It's all old and oriental—and just think, WE
> ARE TEN MILES FROM THE CORNER OF HOLLYWOOD
> AND VINE!

(Today that Chatsworth location is a shopping center jammed
with supermarkets: alas, not even a Chinese restaurant com-
memorates its Oriental glory.)

A play of *The Good Earth*, dramatized by Owen Davis and his
son Donald Davis, had been produced by the Theatre Guild in
New York in October, 1932. The cast is of historic interest: Claude
Rains played Wang, Alla Nazimova was O-Lan, Sydney Greenstreet
was the uncle (played in the film by Walter Connolly), Henry
Travers was the father, and several bits were played by Vincent
Sherman (later a film director-producer). Thalberg was unconcerned that the play only ran fifty-six performances and purchased the dramatic rights as well. He sensed the cinematic values
of this saga. The end result on the screen is a rare combination
of intimacy and spectacle. It is a personal story, but with the
grandeur of a Greek tragedy: man against the forces of nature,
man against the gods.

The celebrated operetta composer Sigmund Romberg, searching for plots for new musical plays, asked us, "Where are the
plums? Every good story and every respectable plum pie has to
have at least one good *plum!*" This is doubly true in a motion
picture; conscientious producers search for one spectacular sequence where the camera can catch a great cinematic climax,
where the production money can be spent and seen vividly on the
screen. *Good Earth* has not just one plum but four: a storm, a
famine, a revolution, and (the most cinematic) a plague of locusts.

Sam Marx, Metro's story editor at the time, and Frank Davis,
Thalberg's assistant, explained to me how this powerful and stirring effect was achieved on the screen. They began with newsreel
footage from Africa of an actual storm of locusts, sweeping,
panoramic shots, conveying the feeling of millions of hungry black
locusts against an empty sky. But Sidney Franklin, a painstaking
and immaculate director, wasn't happy with stock footage. A huge
white screen was constructed at Culver City. Tiny pieces of burned
cork were shot out of pressure guns; wind machines blew them
against the white screen. These and the African locusts were inter-

mixed and double-exposed against the live actors in Chatsworth. Franklin was still unsatisfied and asked his tricksters at MGM to keep working on more convincing special effects. Then word came, as if God were watching and decided to be part of the action, that a plague of grasshoppers was expected in Utah. A camera crew was flown there instantly. They brought back not only shots of millions of grasshoppers against a Utah sky, but several barrels of live grasshoppers to scatter over the Chatsworth actors, more than anxious to fight them off. The final result was a blending of all these elements for a stunning, almost overwhelming climax.

On September 14, 1936, six months through the filming of *The Good Earth*, Irving Thalberg died at the age of thirty-seven. His death shocked the industry. Muni rarely wept, but tears filled his eyes at the tragic funeral. When *The Good Earth* opened the following January, it contained the only credit Thalberg ever received on the screen:

To the memory of
IRVING GRANT THALBERG
We dedicate this picture
His last great achievement

Groucho Marx, master of early-day bitter humor, remarked, "Why is it that all the really great men die young and all the *shmucks* live to be a hundred?"

Albert Lewin, one of Thalberg's associates, completed the film as nominal producer. Later a director (*The Picture of Dorian Gray, Moon and Sixpence*), Lewin once made a statement which Sam and Bella Spewack used in their satiric play about Hollywood, *Boy Meets Girl*: "They hate me here at the studio because I have a college education."

The Good Earth finally cost $2,816,000, a fortune in those days, but made more than $500,000 profit, unlike *Romeo and Juliet*, which lost Metro $1,000,000.

Good Earth opened in New York in February, 1937. The critics raved, and long lines formed at the Astor box office. Ironically, Frank S. Nugent, the *Times* critic, wrote: "Paul Muni, flawless in the early sequences, seemed to me to step out of his Chinese character in the post-famine episodes, talking, walking, reacting more as Muni than as Wang Lung."

A month later the Academy Awards banquet at the Biltmore Hotel brought honors to both stars of *The Good Earth* for pictures released the previous year. Miss Rainer won as Anna Held over Norma Shearer's Juliet. (Her famous telephone scene in *The Great*

226

Ziegfeld did as much for AT&T as Don Ameche.) Muni, with a pointed Van Dyke beard, shy, smiling from inside, accepted his Oscar for *Pasteur* from Victor McLaglen, who had won for 1935's *The Informer*. Muni said, "I will try to continue to work to make myself worthy of the Academy's high and meaningful honor." "Me too," McLaglen added.

In 1971 Bella gave me Muni's heavy gold Oscar. After her death, I clutched it all the way across country, carefully wrapped in swaddling clothes, to deliver it at her instructions to the Theatre Collection of the Library and Museum of the Performing Arts in Lincoln Center. (There, Bella hoped, "it could be an inspiration for aspiring young actors.")

Tony Gaudio received an Oscar that night, too, but for *Anthony Adverse*, not *Pasteur*. Sheridan Gibney went up to accept, for himself and the ill and absent Pierre Collings, four Oscars—one each for the original story of *Pasteur*, one each for the screenplay. Tragically, Collings committed suicide two months later. (Note to Sheilah Graham: Gibney did not, as reported in your book *The Garden of Allah*, "hock" either of his Oscars. I lifted and admired them in Gibney's home in Sepulveda, California, on a steaming September day in 1973.)

What shocked the assembled movie nobility that night in 1937 at the Biltmore was George Jessel's announcement, following the ritual ripping of the envelope, that *The Great Ziegfeld* had won over *The Story of Louis Pasteur* as best picture. "Hollywood," one newspaperman commented, "is interested only in lavishness. There seems to be just one formula for screen success: tits and tights!"

But Bella was ecstatic at Muni's personal triumph. She tried to control her emotions but found herself simultaneously smiling and crying. After all, her husband had won in an impressive field of competitors: Gary Cooper, Walter Huston, William Powell, and Spencer Tracy. A *Daily Variety* lady reporter describes how Bella looked that night: "Mrs. Paul Muni, with hair parted Wally Simpson style, wore a green figured gown made with a peplum, a diamond brooch, high neck line, laced green sandals, a mink coat." But the look on her face was more like the Queen of England than Mrs. Simpson.

Manuel drove them back to the walnut ranch in a sleek black limousine, rented for the occasion. At every signal light (there were no freeways in those days) Manuel slid the separating window back and applauded.

Muni was silent, weighing the golden Oscar in his hand, staring at it, as if trying to evaluate its true meaning. Finally he spoke: "Bella, does this mean that finally I've *really* passed my *proba?*"

(*Warner Brothers photos*)

Three ages of Zola.

19

Muni found it difficult to pass a vacant lot without buying it, any lot, any piece of land. Several times, early in the morning, driving down Ventura Boulevard to Burbank or heading northwest to Chatsworth, he would instruct Manuel to stop the car when he saw a wooden "For Sale" sign. He would dig up the sign and leave a note: "It's sold. Phone me after 7:00 P.M." And he would scribble down his home phone number.

"Bargain! Haggle! It's part of the game," Bella advised when she learned about this. "Pretend you don't really want it and you'll get it for less."

"But I do want it," Muni said.

Part of Muni's land hunger came from playing Wang Lung, who believed passionately that good earth beneath a man's feet was more permanent and precious than life itself. Once Muni explained his longtime "theory of land" to his cousin-in-law, writer Sidney Ellis (Annie Thomashefsky Edelstein's son).

"When I was a kid, I couldn't stand to beg. I don't mean with a tin cup or even a tingle-tangle tamborine. It would wither me up when I saw my father or mother asking somebody else for a favor: a bed to sleep in, a slice of potato. Usually, when you stayed for a few nights with strangers or friends, or even relatives, the main family would eat first, and our family would be fed *afterwards*, the crumbs, the leftovers. And there was always the feeling in the air, 'It's nice to see you, but good-bye already!'

This happened not only in Europe, but more than once in Cleveland and Chicago. Ben Franklin once said, 'Fish and house-guests begin to smell after the third day.' I never wanted to be a smelly fish!

"So I decided, thirty, thirty-five years ago even, that the one thing I wanted to have, that I *had* to have, was a place nobody could ever tell me to leave. When you own the land, nobody can ever say, 'Get moving, you bum!' And when I buy, I want to pay cash—no mortgages, because then a bank can tell you to leave. I want to own it. And then nobody can ever throw me out."

Muni never did this for profit, and often, when he sold property, all he asked was what he had paid for it. Bella's investments were a different kettle of blue chips. In the mid-thirties she bought General Motors at 10, Chrysler at 7, and great hunks of IBM, General Electric, Eastman Kodak, all at bargain prices, and never cashed them in. "They're old friends who happen to live in my safe-deposit box," Bella used to say. "Why should I kick them out?" Muni, on the other hand, never had any luck in the stock market. On the set he listened to tips, bought speculative nonsense, and lost his shirt. Finally, he turned all the stock purchases over to Bella. She continued to buy IBM although I doubt if she ever really understood what a computer was. Did it matter?

Muni won two other awards for *Pasteur*: the Minneapolis *Journal* Medal, awarded by the Motion Picture Critics of America, and the Volpi Cup, presented in Italy. Muni did not go to Venice to receive the Italian award and hesitated at first about even accepting by mail. He had no liking for Mussolini or any brand of Fascism. But the studio assured him this was an award from his performing peers in Italy and not officially from the Italian government.

Just before the Academy nominations, Muni appeared on *Lux Radio Theatre* in *Pasteur*. The advertising agency did not have to be convinced this time of his fame or the quality of his radio voice. Cecil B. DeMille was all smiles: Muni was the toast of Hollywood, the hottest actor around.

The library at the Motion Picture Academy still has a copy of a memo written by program director Frank Woodruff to executives at Lever Brothers and J. Walter Thompson: "This program tops any show we've done. It was human. Muni gave a magnificent performance with a supporting cast worthy of playing this show. Barbara Luddy's Madame Pasteur deserves special mention."

Muni was beginning to love radio and asked his agent to arrange more appearances. "It's theater of the imagination," he said. "Close your eyes—hey, you don't even have to look—and the whole play, the whole world starts spinning inside your head. And every *klutz* with a ballsy voice is suddenly a good-lookin' gent. One breath of wind and you're on a mountaintop. A few waves and you're in the middle of an ocean. That sound-effects fella—he paints scenery. And *fast!*"

During the final interview of that *Lux* appearance, Muni announced his next two projects publicly for the first time:

MUNI: Well, Mr. DeMille, I have two pictures to make: ESCADRILLE at RKO co-starring Miriam Hopkins and then THE TRUTH IS ON THE MARCH for Warner Brothers. The latter is based on Zola's unforgettable document: "I ACCUSE!"

Muni wanted to say "J'Accuse!" but an agency executive (not Woodruff) thought it would sound like "Jack Cooze" and Muni lost his fight for bilingual literary accuracy.

Escadrille had its name changed to *The Woman I Love* (cashing in on King Edward's famous phrase about Wally Simpson) and was Muni's second loan-out from Warner's. He agreed to do it, primarily as a favor to its producer, Albert Lewis, an old friend who had helped discover him for Broadway and later brought him to Hollywood. But Miriam Hopkins turned out to be anything but a woman he loved, and the picture was a near disaster.

Muni welcomed the role of Lieutenant Claude Maury as a change of pace. He dreaded being typed and thought the dashing World War I aviator would be red meat and romantic contrast sandwiched between his two historical chunks of bread; it turned out to be a very thin slice of ham.

The property, based on a best-selling French novel, *Équipage*, had been made into a French film, directed by Anatole Litvak. RKO decided to remake it and hired the original director. It was Litvak's first Hollywood film. Albert Lewis, reminiscing in his Brentwood apartment in 1973, told me what happened:

"To play the important part of the husband, the studio wanted Charles Boyer, who had a commitment with RKO for one more picture. I held out for Muni, and because of our friendship, I was able to make a convenient deal for him on a loan-out from Warner's, after he saw the French film. Miriam Hopkins, with whom I had an unfortunate experience at Paramount when she defected from a Gable picture, was suggested by the studio to play the wife. She was now under contract to RKO, and over

(Photo by Alex Kahle from the Max Foster Collection)

Amelia Earhart visits Muni on the location of *The Woman I Love.*

my objections, she was set. The studio had reason to regret this decision when Miss Hopkins again proved herself a disturbing element during the shooting. Muni refused to tolerate her behavior on the set. I threatened to remove her. The director offered to resign in protest. It was a miracle that the picture was finished at all. Miss Hopkins was not given another picture to do at RKO, but she gained a husband. She 'won' Mr. Litvak!"*

During the shooting of the picture the famous aviatrix Amelia Earhart visited the set. A fan of Muni's, she was happy to pose for a photograph with him. Muni remarked later, "It was the only time during the making of the film that I really felt like an aviator—by association."

The reviews of *The Woman I Love* were unkind: what the hell was the great Muni doing in this unfortunate tangle of celluloid? But *Good Earth* and *Pasteur* were playing simultaneously, and the public generously forgot Muni as the dashing aviator, who died for love and at the box office.

Muni was also comforted by the fact that Warner Brothers was preparing a monumental work, one he could approach with total belief and dedication. Two writers with little experience in the screen medium, Geza Herczeg, a Hungarian, and Heinz Herald, a German who had been a dramaturge for Max Reinhardt, wrote a ten-page synopsis about Zola and the Dreyfus case entitled *The Truth Is on the March.* They took it to their friend, director Ernst Lubitsch at Paramount. Lubitsch read the short synopsis, said

*Miss Hopkins did marry Anatole Litvak in 1937; he was her third husband. The marriage had a short run—less than two years.

it was a wonderful idea, but advised them to take it to Henry Blanke, his former associate, then an assistant producer at Warner Brothers. Blanke, Wallis, and Warner, Lubitsch insisted, had the only actor who could play Zola: MUNI.

Blanke remembers how he sold the idea to Jack Warner.

"He was on his way to Europe. I drove him to the railroad station and acted out the whole idea, very dramatically, even the ripping off of Dreyfus' epaulets and the breaking of his sword. Warner said, 'Go ahead, get to work on it. Only change that goddamn title.' "

Almost a year was spent preparing the film, with detailed research, numerous screenplays, and the construction of fifty authentic settings. It was Muni's thirteenth picture (Charlotte Dieterle declared it his lucky number), and it made him, according to *Time* magazine, the First Actor of the U.S. Screen.

For four weeks, Muni and all the Westmores experimented on makeup, taking still shots every time they thought they were close. Four different ages in *The Life of Emile Zola* were required, so the picture was shot backward. Muni grew his own beard and grayed and augmented it for Zola's final years. In the course of the making of the film, he grew younger, clipping and darkening the beard until the last scenes shot were the opening of the film, the young Zola in his early twenties. Each day before shooting, Muni spent three and a half hours in the makeup department. It was an exhausting but gratifying labor. The still photos of the young and old Zola side by side give some indication what a master sculptor Muni was, not with clay, but with hair and greasepaint; most of it was accomplished with the indefinable art of a consummate *actor*.

Muni read everything available about Zola, every word of the Dreyfus trial transcripts, and many of Zola's works in translation, particularly his earliest success, *Nana*. Muni discovered through research some famous Zola gestures and idiosyncrasies: the stoop-shouldered walk, an eccentric laugh, the way Zola tucked his dinner napkin under his collar, how he held out his hands in front of him and thoughtfully tapped his stomach. Muni tried to make all these his own.

One day he stormed into the studio research department. "I want to know more," he said.

"But, Mr. Muni, we've given you everything we could find on Zola."

"I think I know about Zola now," Muni answered, impatiently. "Almost. Almost. Now I want to know something about his ancestors."

232

Bette Davis asked to play the tiny role of Nana, the streetwalker. "At that stage in my career," she says, "it would have proved a sensational stunt. Besides, I realized it was going to be a great picture, and I wanted to be part of it." Jack Warner said she was too big a star and wouldn't let her play it. Erin O'Brien-Moore was sent out from New York to be Nana.

William Dieterle was assigned as director. The final screenplay was written by the original two writers, with the addition of Norman Reilly Raine. The supporting cast was brilliantly chosen: Gale Sondergaard, Joseph Schildkraut, Morris Carnovsky, Donald Crisp, and Louis Calhern. For the first time in his entire career, Muni was happy about a character, a theme, a story, and the total significance and pertinence of the work. Zola was a man who crusaded passionately against injustice, particularly in the case *célèbre* where Dreyfus had been the victim of vicious anti-Semitism. Muni climbed into the skin of the great author and was equally eloquent in crying out against inhumanities plaguing the world; with Hitler threatening all Europe, Muni's passion fused past and present.

Shortly before William Dieterle died, he spoke about Muni: "We had the same theory about picture making—that films should do more than just entertain, that there's always been a vast audience hungry for pictures with meaning.

"There was no harder worker in Hollywood than Paul Muni. Once he started a picture, that was his life. He wasn't satisfied merely resembling Pasteur or Zola physically. He wasn't content until he could think as they thought and feel as they felt.

"He was a thorough man, a thoughtful, sensitive man. That's why he was easy to direct. You didn't have to tell him what to do. He *knew*. In *Zola* we made the *J'Accuse* scene and the address to the court over and over—not because I was dissatisfied, but because he was. The stage was hot. He wore a heavily padded suit and an uncomfortable makeup. It was a long scene—six and a half minutes without a cut. Yet not once did he complain. He worked until he was exhausted. The grips and the electricians and the camera crew applauded when he finished this moving scene without a flaw. But he came back the next day to do it all over again.

"He was a totally unselfish man. I never saw him try to steal a scene. And when the picture was completed, he gave credit to everyone but himself. After the preview of *Zola*, I went home to find a long telegram from him thanking me for making it. From the wire, you would have thought he had nothing to do with the film, and that the preview audience liked it for the photography, the writing, the direction and the performances of every player but Paul Muni."

The preview at Warner Brothers Hollywood Theatre on August 9, 1937 was a memorable evening for Muni. He rarely attended public performances of his films, but with *Zola* he agreed to come, out of mingled curiosity and pride. He and Bella hurried into the theater, and during the running of the film, he slumped in his seat. When applause broke after key scenes, Muni whispered to Bella, "Maybe it's not too bad!" Muni's tablecloth speech was greeted with cheers. Morris Carnovsky, as Anatole France, delivered the final line of his eulogy to Zola, "He was a moment of the conscience of man," and the audience rose to its feet. Regina Crewe of the New York *American* attended that preview and reported what happened immediately after the showing:

> I witnessed an unforgettable scene. As Paul Muni left the theatre, the audience jammed the stairs, lobbies, aisles and sidewalks to render homage to him in an ovation such as I have never witnessed. It was almost—if not quite—as thrilling as the portrayal he had just given upon the screen. The great crowd didn't mob Muni in its enthusiasm. Rather, it parted so that he might pass through, bowing acknowledgment. For there was respect amounting to awe mingled with the ecstatic enthusiasm inspiring the demonstration.

Warner Brothers, with equal respect amounting to awe, began billing him as *MR*. PAUL MUNI, usually in large script letters. It was meant as an honor to their most distinguished player, but in later years, in retrospect, Muni thought it was a mistake.

Frank S. Nugent in the New York *Times* called *Zola* "The finest historical film ever made and the greatest screen biography. . . . Paul Muni's portrayal of Zola is, without doubt, the best thing he has done."

On August 16, 1937, *MR*. PAUL MUNI made the cover of *Time*.

One hot day Muni impetuously told Bella that he felt they should have a "shack by the ocean, where it's cool and we can breathe some sea air." He jumped into his car and drove toward the beach, searching for a retreat.

When he came home to the walnut ranch, he told Bella he had bought "a little place in Palos Verdes." The next morning he drove her out to see their "shack by the sea." It was a huge Spanish-style mansion, impaled on a hillside, thirty-five miles from Hollywood.

Bella loved it as much as she could love anything in California. Their view of the expanse of the Pacific Ocean was magnificent: the wide crescent of the Santa Monica Bay curving away for nearly forty miles. When she saw the Olympic-size swimming pool, she said, "Ah Munya, you have finally gone Hollywood!" "Gone?" said Muni. "Of course I've gone. This is about as far away as you can go and still work in this town."

They moved in even before they began to decorate it. Bella wanted to do it all herself, so there were empty rooms for many months. They loved having breakfast on the patio bathed in sunlight, with the ocean as a backdrop. Muni bought a telescope and watched ships passing at sea.

Their Airedale, Simon, loved it too, bounding around the terraces and the wide outdoor staircases; Muni took him for long walks through the winding paths of the Palos Verdes Estates. Muni would say casually, "I'm going for a walk," and Simon would already be at the entranceway, barking and pawing at the door.

"We'll have to start talking in Yiddish," Bella suggested. "That dog understands every word we say!"

They tried. Even "I'm going for a walk" in Yiddish made Simon bound for the door.

"We're damn fools," Muni said. "That's George Simon. And lemme tell you, that Airedale is a Yid!"

Then the fog moved in. Their view disappeared as if the Pacific had been erased. The fireplaces were lit, the outdoor breakfasts canceled, the telescope abandoned. "If I walk out onto the patio in this fog and look at my watch," Muni complained, "I can't even see what time it is! Dig up our passports, Bella, we're taking a trip. A long one."

They booked passage on the Grace liner *Santa Paula*, through the Panama Canal, to New York. They'd had such a glorious experience coming the other way, just five years before, and they had met some enduring friends, particularly Ben and Goldie Goetz. And this time there was no script to study—they could leave the Dictaphone at home! M. C. Levee, Muni's agent, was in the process of negotiating a new, more elastic contract with Warner Brothers which gave Muni more leisure between pictures. Why not go around the world?

Jake Wilk had purchased two properties, a play by Franz Werfel and a novel, *The Phantom Crown*, by Bertita Harding. Both were on the same significant area of human liberty, the story of Maximilian and Juarez, the liberator of Mexico. Warner, Wallis, and Blanke all decided not to rush, to take an entire year in preparing it. Muni was free to travel. He called it "the first vacation of my life."

But this trip through the Canal was a nightmare. Tourists poked cameras in their faces, brandished open fountain pens and autograph albums at Muni, asked ridiculous questions about the sex habits of Hollywood stars, and—worst of all—just stood and stared at them.

"I feel like a monkey in a zoo," Muni said.

"If you don't want to be recognized"—Bella shrugged—"then don't be a movie star."

"I don't want to be a star. If you have to label me anything, I'm an *actor*—I guess. A journeyman actor. I think 'star' is what you call actors who can't act!"

They inspected the locks in Panama, took an auto trip into the jungle, sipped free samples at Havana's rum distilleries. But Muni was restless, and they arrived in New York fatigued and unhappy.

Muni and Bella saw some plays, including their friend Ben Hecht's *To Quito and Back*, Clifford Odets' *Golden Boy* (with an array of old friends on stage: Luther Adler, Morris Carnovsky, and the grown-up office boy from *Counsellor*, Jules Garfield), and the Orson Welles-John Houseman modern-dress *Julius Caesar* (Muni considered Welles "the hope of the American theater"). During the performance of *Caesar*, Bella remembers Muni silently mouthing along with the speech "Cowards die many times before their deaths;/The valiant never taste of death but once."

"See, Bella," he said, "you wait long enough, you finally get to say the lines."

But Muni was uneasy on the audience side of the curtain. He found relaxing extremely hard work. He longed for another play, "one, please God, with guts."

They canceled further theater-attending plans and booked passage on another ship, headed for the Mediterranean. Although he had never been there before, Muni felt he was coming home when their ship, the SS *Patria*, arrived at Palestine's newly liberated port of Haifa. His arrival on a sunny February morning in 1938 created as much excitement as the opening of Tel Aviv's window to the sea.

Bella and Muni were sped by car toward Tel Aviv with a police escort; a British officer had been killed on that road two days before.

The *Palestine Illustrated News* wrote:

> There can be no doubt about it: Tel Aviv is excited. Muni, the world-famous film star, is here. His wonderful personality, his easy and familiar manner of conversation, the lack of all

affectation and the absence of visible manifestation of that thing known as artistic temperament made a deep impression; and there was a deeper realization of those qualities that make Muni the great artist he is.

The *Palestine Review* rhapsodized in print:

> Tel Aviv always finds something to be jubilant about. It is a sign of her perennial youth. And this time it is Paul Muni and the permit to land passengers at her port. Mainly Paul Muni. Marlene Dietrich could not expect such a welcome nor Greta Garbo such an unheralded reception. Last Tuesday everybody seemed to be rushing towards his hotel. "Have you seen Paul Muni?" "What! You haven't seen Paul Muni?" or "When did you see Paul Muni?" He is a brilliant actor, he is one of us, let us go and mob him.

At his hotel every effort was made to give him the delights of French cooking. When an elaborate gourmet feast was set before them, Muni looked at it ruefully. "Please," he said, "take it away and bring me some good Jewish food."

But Muni was astonished to learn that there wasn't a kosher dill pickle or a hot-corn-beef-sandwich-on-rye available anywhere in the Holy Land. But he did get his fill of sour-cream salad.

Somehow the adulation seemed less harrowing to Muni in Palestine. He enjoyed the sunshine, the taxi drivers who recited Shakespeare, the fervor in the air of pioneers dreaming and working toward the day when Israel would attain statehood. On his final night in Tel Aviv Muni agreed to a short public performance for charity. The film of *Zola* had not yet reached Palestine; Muni gave a preview to the packed auditorium at the Concert Hall in the Fair Grounds. On a bare stage, without makeup, jutting his chin out, Muni chilled his audience with Zola's fiery and impassioned plea for justice and the rights of men. To the audience, many of whose families were still trapped in Hitler's Third Reich, it was an evening of deep emotion and significance. In response to the wild applause, Muni dredged out of his subconscious a half-remembered speech from his Yiddish theater days and switched from Zola to an old *melamed*. He recited Sholom Aleichem's *If I Were a Rothschild* in Yiddish. (Almost a generation later lyricist Sheldon Harnick turned this into "If I Were a Rich Man" in *Fiddler on the Roof*.) The unrehearsed Muni didn't miss a syllable.*

---

*Harnick recalls a great line from this version: "If I were a Rothschild, I'd be *richer* than Rothschild!"

The mayor of Tel Aviv, Israel Rokach, could hardly speak his thanks; the audience was pounding its feet on the plank floors, shouting bravo in Yiddish, Hebrew, English, and Russian. Mayor Rokach thanked Muni for his performance on behalf of charity, then declared warmly that Muni had endeared himself to the people of Tel Aviv. "Keep your promise," he said, "and come back next spring. Next month. Next week. Don't leave!"

The following morning the Munis sailed from Haifa on the SS *Polonia*. While they were on the warm seas, touching the isles of Greece, the New York Film Critics were giving Muni, in absentia, their award as best actor of the year for *Zola*. The master of ceremonies at the Rainbow Room, Robert Benchley, also announced *Zola* was chosen best picture.

A few weeks later the Academy Award ceremonies, postponed for a week owing to California floods, was further dampened by a wave of absenteeism at the Biltmore Bowl. The press departments at Warner Brothers and MGM pleaded with Muni to return to be there in person. Both *The Good Earth* and *The Life of Emile Zola* were nominated as best picture, and Muni was nominated as best actor for *Zola*. (If their release dates had been spread out to different years, Muni would undoubtedly have also been nominated for *Good Earth*, but Academy rules prohibited a double nomination in one calendar year.)

"Why be there?" Muni argued. "It'll be less embarrassing for everybody if I'm in Palestine or Greece. I don't want to go sit there with egg on my face, looking as if I'm expecting something that will never happen. Nobody wins two years in a row!"

Luise Rainer did. Obviously thinking the same thing, she was at home in Beverly Hills. She had to be yanked out of her bedroom slippers by a frantic phone call from an Academy official who knew the results. (Press releases had been prepared just ahead of time.) She climbed into an evening gown, her husband, Clifford Odets, squirmed into a tuxedo, and they arrived at the Biltmore in time for Miss Rainer to get her second Oscar in a row, this time for *The Good Earth*. It had never happened before and began a rumor that such "tempting of the gods with overpraise was a jinx and a curse." Perhaps. "Or more likely," Sam Marx comments, "the gods of the studios find Academy winners suddenly overpicky and overpriced."

Spencer Tracy, who won as best actor for *Captains Courageous*, heard it all over KNX radio from a bed at Good Samaritan Hospital, where he was recovering from surgery. Mrs. Tracy accepted for her husband, who won over Muni and three other seemingly unbeatable candidates: Fredric March in *A Star Is Born*, Charles

Boyer in *Conquest*, and Robert Montgomery in *Night Must Fall*. (Is it any wonder we sigh over the halcyon days of great movies and great stars?)

Joseph Schildkraut, the unforgettable Dreyfus of *Zola*, wasn't even listening to the radio. He had gone to bed. His agent discouraged him from attending the ceremonies, convinced that the best supporting actor award would go to Ralph Bellamy for *The Awful Truth* or H. B. Warner for *Lost Horizon*. Pepe Schildkraut only agreed to get out of bed and race downtown when that urgent unknown voice on the telephone assured him, absolutely, that he had won. Typical aftermath: Schildkraut never was cast in another role at Warner Brothers.

Dieterle had been nominated, but lost out to Leo McCarey. Karl Freund won an Oscar for his incredible photography for *The Good Earth*, and the trio of Zola screenwriters won for the best screenplay.

With fantastic opposition, including *The Good Earth*, *The Life of Emile Zola* won for best picture. Jack Warner, justifiably and deservedly jubilant, accepted, then handed the gold statuette to Hal Wallis.

Muni rejected one award. When a tugboat full of reporters and photographers met their ship coming into New York Harbor, one young man had a package tucked under his arm. He whispered hoarsely to Muni, "I have an award here, and you and my company can get a lot of publicity with all these photographers here."

"Forget it," Muni said bluntly, returning to his stateroom. Later Muni found out that it was an overeager publicity man, promptly fired, who was trying to give him a bronze statuette presented by the Manischewitz Foundation. "Now, if he had slipped me a box of egg matzohs," Muni said, "I would have grabbed it."

Jake Wilk met the boat. Muni begged off further press conferences, accepting only one invitation: a Passover Seder at the Wilk home in Scarsdale. On the drive out, Wilk told Muni of still another honor. In a worldwide poll, Ivrim, an honor society of Jewish students, had selected the 120 greatest living Jews for a Jewish Hall of Fame. Wilk began reading the list:

"Scientist Albert Einstein, Actor Paul Muni, Supreme Court Justices Brandeis and Cardoza, Musicians Mischa Elman and Jascha Heifetz, Authors Emil Ludwig, Arnold and Stephen Zweig, Sculptor Jacob Epstein, Composers Maurice Ravel and Oscar Strauss, Director Max Reinhardt, Scientist Sigmund Freud, Radio Engineer David Sarnoff, French Statesman Leon Blum, and many, many others. Just think, Muni, you're the only actor on the whole list!"

"Please, Jake," Muni warned, poking him with an elbow, "don't say that too loud. Jehovah, who is Jewish—or used to be—might be listening, and He'll get jealous. Look—He isn't even on the list!"

"But He's not another actor," Bella said.

"Don't be too sure," Muni added.

Author Max Wilk, Jake's son, who was seventeen then, remembers that Seder:

"Muni regaled the table with jokes, Yiddish mostly, and had everyone in stitches. That was a side of Muni that should be noted; he was a supreme raconteur and enjoyed telling jokes. It gave him a chance to act out all his characters from the Yiddish theater: old Jewish women with limps, peddlers, doctors, bums, waiters. When Muni told you a story, he *became* those people."

The joke about the kid who was terrified of kreplach (the Jewish improvement on ravioli) was Muni's favorite. He embroidered it elaborately, turning it into an exercise in the absurd, acting all the parts. He began by contorting his face as a frightened little boy, screaming as in a terrible nightmare at the sight of a helpless little kreplach. In the next scene, a kindly old doctor advised the bent-over mother (Muni leaped back and forth playing both roles) to use logic, reason, calm persuasion: knowledge would triumph! At the climax of this epic yarn of psychological verities Muni pragmatically cooked kreplach, rolling the dough, chopping the meat, sprinkling on the flour.

"See? Good eggs. Nothing to be frightened of there."

"No, Mama."

"Flour. Beautiful white flour. Nothing to scare you?"

"No, Mama."

"And meat. You love meat, *boychick*."

"Yes, Mama, I love meat very much."

"See? See? We put the meat in the middle, and we fold the dough like this, and like this, and we get some beautiful, delicious. . . ."

"Achhh!" the boy screamed in ridiculous and irrational terror. *"KREPLACH!!!"*

Muni once told me that he only liked to hear or tell jokes which contained some universal truths. This one old story contained more truth than he probably realized. Totality frightened Muni rather than the separate one-by-one, day-by-day events of his life.

Perhaps the trouble was that when he put them all together, they spelled kreplach.

The Santa Fe Chief brought Bella and Muni back to California after their five-month trip abroad. Jack Warner, Hal Wallis, and Henry Blanke were all on the station platform in Pasadena to greet them.

"The three wise men," Muni commented as he came down the train steps.

Warner was full of news as a limousine sped them toward Palos Verdes. *Zola* had been big, important, erasing from the public mind any frivolities of the past: Warner Brothers was no longer the studio which made merely gangster pictures or razzmatazz musicals. They had pledged to "combine good citizenship with good picture-making." If *Zola* had won awards, critical praise and box-office success, well, "you ain't seen nothin' yet!"

For *The Phantom Crown* (and they just might consider changing the title to simply *Juarez* in honor of their greatest star) they had set aside a budget of $1,750,000, the most money the studio had ever spent on a single picture. Even better news: not a camera would turn for seven months; Muni would have ample time to prepare. Screenwriters were at work; at Burbank the studio research department had gathered more material about the man Juarez than you could find in all Mexico. To supplement that, a trip was planned for Muni (along with Wallis, Blanke, and director Dieterle) to go to Mexico in person. They had been personally invited by the Mexican President, Lázaro Cárdenas himself. They'd leave any time Muni was ready.

"Let me go to the toilet first," Muni said.

But Muni was pleased. The character of the liberal leader and liberator Benito Pablo Juarez was totally different from anything he had ever played. He began hypnotizing himself into the skin and soul of this stolid Zapotecan Indian, whose face was like a granite monument and whose convictions and spirit were Lincolnesque.

Dr. Herman Lissauer of the studio research department showed Muni a staggering array of material: 372 books, documents, letters and albums of rare and authentic photographs. There was too much material, enough for a dozen motion pictures. Or at least two.

Wolfgang Reinhardt (son of Max) and John Huston (son of Walter, and in his predirecting days) were hard at work, along with author Aeneas MacKenzie, attempting to make this sprawling document of human liberty into a single viable screenplay. Meanwhile, Muni seemed not merely to read the voluminous research, but to absorb it into his viscera. His makeup experiments were lengthy and elaborate. This was to be the first picture to use the new Eastman Plus-X negative. Tony Gaudio promised startling innovations: fifty percent less light would be required, richer blacks would be possible in the shadows, a textured three-dimensional effect would be achieved, and the actors could work in greater comfort.

Wallis, Dieterle, Blanke, and Muni spent six weeks in Mexico, following the footsteps of Juarez as if visiting the stations of the cross. They all were dedicated to historical accuracy and pleased that the Mexican government, which had previously been hostile to any attempts to dramatize the story of Juarez, was now receptive and cooperative.

Muni met and interviewed two elderly survivors of the Juarista army of liberation, Colonel Gabriel Morena and General Ignacio Velásquez. Muni quizzed them endlessly, not merely about the battles they remembered, but about the man Juarez, probing for the tiniest detail of habits and gestures. Did he ever smile? How? Did he ever laugh out loud? Joyfully? Did he ever weep? Describe his voice: soft? throaty? dynamic? What did it feel like when Juarez walked into a room?

Wallis recalls the afternoon they paused in their search and research for a welcome glass of tequila at a sidewalk café in Mexico City. "It's one of the few times I ever saw Muni relax, unwind, laugh, joke, and play the rather difficult but charming role of Paul Muni."

M. C. Levee had negotiated a new contract for Muni which was the envy of Hollywood. Muni told his agent, "Fine. Good work. But I don't give a damn about anything but the stories, the scripts. If they're good, it's all that matters. If they're lousy, I'll be lousy, no matter where you put my name or how many 'misters' they use in the billing."

In fact, Muni went personally to Jack Warner and requested a waiver of the provisions of paragraph 9 of his contract, in which he was to get sole star billing above the title. He asked that Bette Davis, who played the mad Empress Carlotta, get equal billing with him. Brian Aherne, who was magnificent and touching as Maximilian and won an Academy nomination for it, complains in his book *A Proper Job* that he was informed on his first day's work on *The Phantom Crown* that the title had been changed to *Juarez* because Muni had a clause in his new contract requiring every picture he made to be named after the character he played: Pasteur, Zola, Juarez. There was no such clause. Aherne's more careful research might have pointed to Muni's next film: *We Are Not Alone*.

Charlotte Dieterle was delighted with the title; it contained six letters, a lucky omen. So much so, she claimed, that this magic number must be saved for the title alone and not wasted during the shooting of the picture with six-letter words like "Camera!" or "Action!" Dieterle, brilliant in every department except this, agreed. Every shot began with his shouting an eight-letter direction: "Here . . . we . . . GO!"

The numerology-astrology-demented Charlotte also decreed that the picture could not begin on the scheduled date of November 15. Dieterle obligingly and dutifully shot one insert of a poster being ripped from a wall on October 29, 1938, a more propitious day for the stars (in heaven, not in Burbank).

For Muni, the film was a passionate statement for democracy and the dignity of all men at a time when the world was in flames. "When a monarch misrules," Juarez says, "he changes the people. But when a president misrules, the people change him."

Much like his portrayal of Lepack years before in *The Thieves*, Muni chose to underplay the role of Juarez totally. He gives the impression of a giant, stolid and unmoving. It is almost impossible to believe this is the same man who played Zola and Pasteur, for Muni cut away all extraneous gestures or the flamboyant use of props. Later Muni felt he had been too faithful to the original, not allowing himself an artist's prerogative of adding coloration to the historical character. He blamed only himself for the fact that *Juarez* was far less popular than his previous biographical films.

Men still alive who had known Juarez personally were astonished at the physical resemblance. The makeup included not merely the high Indian cheekbones and the straight black hair, but his entire body padded and looming large, with massive shoulders and a bearlike bulk.

Muni asked Dieterle to shoot his first sequence the way Muni had done Du Arun in *Wolves* on the Yiddish stage so many years before. The character of Juarez plays his introductory scene with his back to the camera. Only the hulking shoulders and the brown leathery hands are seen.

Watching in a darkened projection room in 1973, I find it a beautiful and meaningful motion picture, with Muni giving his most restrained and in many ways one of his best performances. True, it is two movies, and the opposing parties never meet; perhaps fiction would have abetted fact through an invented *scène-à-faire*.

It is ironic that the Mexican Community Council has pressured Los Angeles television stations not to show *Juarez* in these enlightened seventies, giving as their reason: Mexicans should play Mexicans.

Discussing the film with producer Henry Blanke at his home in Brentwood in 1973, I mentioned that I had read that somebody was planning a Broadway musical on the subject. He shook his head sadly. "It should be an opera," I said. "It has the size and scope and power and bravura of grand opera."

The New York critics praised the film with reservations. The Los Angeles Mexican community may not remember that its greatest ovation was received in Mexico City. Warner's had been hesitant about a splash opening there; Mexicans had turned thumbs down on any *Yanqui* attempt to film south-of-the border history, booing *Viva Villa* off the screen and even banning for many years Eisenstein's *Thunder over Mexico*. Warners carefully arranged a private screening for El Presidente. Cárdenas loved it and requested that its premiere be held at Mexico's National Theater in the Palace of Fine Arts, the first time a film was ever shown in this great hall devoted only to symphonic concerts and classic works of drama.

Without even seeing the film, the newspaper *La Prensa* screamed in print that this was an outrage: the film glorified and glamorized Maximilian, Juarez was played like a wooden Indian, and the ending of the picture was an affront to their national honor. The latter refers to the final fade-out of the picture, where the

Muni as the Mexican liberator in *Juarez*.

(Helen Lovett Collection)

244

saddened Juarez pays his last respects to the murdered Maximilian, lying in his coffin, and says, "Forgive me."

Riots were expected on that June night in 1939 when *Juarez* opened at the Palace of Fine Arts, searchlights fanning the sky along the Prado. The first full-faced view of Muni drew gasps, then applause, a tribute to his amazing resemblance to their national hero. There was scattered hissing at the arrival of the Hapsburgs, but just as many passionate shushes. Moment after moment, speech after speech elicited applause and cheers.

The ending was the test. Soldiers, hidden in the side aisles, rose to an alert, expecting the worst. On the screen, Muni as Juarez walked into the cathedral, moved solemnly toward the casket, and stared down at it. There was a barely audible click from the projection booth. Muni's mouth moved silently. The line was cut; *La Prensa* was deprived mechanically of its attack weapon. The fade-out was met with an ovation.

Muni was unable to return to Mexico City for that opening, though he had been invited. He was already at work on his next picture.

But people who attended claimed the entire audience fully understood the line, unspoken and unheard: compassion and greatness, respect for another human being—even his enemy —were all eloquently there in the Muni-Juarez face and in his soul.

20

MUNI was king of biographical films, despite the fact that *Juarez* was not the box-office success of *Pasteur* and *Zola*. Every studio story editor in Hollywood received stacks of treatments from screenwriters eager to dramatize their favorite historical characters, the recurring suggestion for each: "Borrow Muni, he'd be perfect for the part." Some of the biographical ploys were sound; others were absurd.

One eager promoter managed to penetrate Muni's security cover and got to him in person. Muni only agreed to see him because a relative of a relative assured him that the young producer had an idea "which would revolutionize the film industry." Muni listened attentively.

"Here's the concept, Mr. Muni," the producer said, fairly froth-

Muni at home with his two dogs at Palos Verdes.

ing at the lips with his notion. "It's the basis of not just one, but a whole series of films for you. It's a switch. Instead of going right in the front door of a historical character, we do the side door approach. The real historical character is never seen. You always play the brother!"

Breathless, the young man waited for a reaction. Muni was stone-faced.

"Don't you see? THE BROTHER OF NAPOLEON! THE BROTHER OF ABE LINCOLN! THE BROTHER OF SUSAN B. ANTHONY!"

"Yes, yes," Muni said, his voice rising in a crescendo. "I know just the brothers I want to play—Morris Mussolini! Irving Hitler! Now—out, out! And use the side door!"

Muni had a "kitchen cabinet" to help him search for proper material. Bella was the head reader, but Ruth and Abem Finkel read and discussed scripts with Muni. Later Ted Thomas replaced Abem as Muni's chief literary adviser. Biographical film dramas of Albert Einstein, Simón Bolívar, Haym Salomon, Alfred Steinmetz, Victor Hugo were suggested. Muni primarily wanted to play Beethoven and then let epic biographical material alone for a while. As for Haym Salomon, somebody at the studio mentioned it would be dangerous to show a Jew involved with a revolution, even the American Revolution. Besides, who would believe a banker lending money at such a low interest rate and dying bankrupt?

Ted Thomas tried to steer Muni toward the classics, onstage and onscreen. "Why wait for a new play to come along? Sure, do a great contemporary work when you find one," Ted suggested, "but meanwhile, play Cyrano! And you'd be brilliant in Molière! And why not Shakespeare?"

The Bard frightened Muni. "I'd have to study a lifetime to master even the rhythm of the language," he said. But *Lear* intrigued him. He recorded some scenes, but erased them immediately, not even letting Bella hear them. *Richard III* also seemed a possibility. Stage producers were constantly suggesting Shylock. "In a world sick with the Hitler disease," Muni worried, "if one person felt presenting *The Merchant of Venice* was anti-Semitic, then it would be a mistake to do. Hamlet? I was never that young. Besides, how could I top Thomashefsky as the *Yeshiva Bocher*?"

Sam H. Harris tried tempting Muni back to Broadway in William Beyers' dramatization of the Nijinsky biography. Muni thought the role was fascinating and totally different from anything he had ever done. He felt he could even master the moments in the play requiring a dancer's poses and attitudes. But finally he turned it down in a letter to Max Siegel, who was back working for Harris. "Though I admire the vitality of the story," Muni wrote, "I find certain pathological elements repulsive to me." Later Ted Thomas and his brother, Dr. Milton Thomashefsky, wrote an entirely new play on Nijinsky, *Man of Genius*. Muni toyed for more than two years with the possibility of playing it. (During that period, the playwrights collected $40,000 in option money, but the work was abandoned when Nijinsky's wife, Romola, threatened suit for invasion of privacy.)

Muni was not militantly antihomosexual; it was simply a subject he refused to discuss. If somebody gossiped to him that a fellow actor or a director loved not just his fellowmen but his fellow*man*, Muni quickly said, "Don't tell me about it. I don't want to know. As far as I'm concerned, such things don't exist."

Muni appeared on *Screen Guild Theatre* on March 5, 1939, in a daring radio drama by Norman Reilly Raine, *Bridge of Mercy*, based on a previous script by True Boardman, *Quality of Mercy*. The subject matter was mercy killing; Muni, seeing his wife in severe pain during a terminal illness, puts her to sleep. In the final scene, he goes to his death in the electric chair, punished by society for his "misdeed." In many ways it was a milestone for radio, allowing a dramatization of controversial subject matter on the air. The *Screen Guild* broadcasts, sponsored by Gulf Oil Company, were a joint effort of the Motion Picture Relief Fund, the Screen Actors Guild, and the Screen Writers Guild. Unlike *Hollywood Hotel*, stars were not pressured to appear on it; the fees normally paid them went to their own worthy charity, the Motion Picture Country Home.

George Cukor was announced as director of the broadcast, but it was entirely window dressing; Cukor merely lent his name. Extremely minor historical note: the master of ceremonies for that *Screen Guild* show was George Murphy, later United States Senator from California.

Thomas H. A. Lewis, the program's director, and Austin Peterson, the story editor, remember Muni's meticulous detail, going over every line during their script conferences. Lewis recalls Muni repeating, "I'm not a popular actor like Clark Gable, remember that." The program originated from the El Capitan Theatre on Hollywood Boulevard opposite Grauman's Chinese (later from Earl Carroll's Theatre Restaurant). Elegance was the keynote. The courtly and highly theatrical Huntley Gordon, representing the Motion Picture Relief Fund, handed orchids to all the ladies of the cast and a carnation to each of the gentlemen. Josephine Hutchinson, who played the wife in the broadcast, remembers a dismayed Muni, holding his boutonniere at arm's length and saying quite seriously, "What's this for? I can't go to the electric chair wearing a carnation!"

Muni continued to find radio fascinating. He was scheduled to appear with Orson Welles, whose *Mercury Theatre* broadcasts were then sponsored by Campbell's Soups. The property chosen was Kressman Taylor's startling anti-Nazi novella *Address Unknown*. Diana Bourbon, then head of the Hollywood office of Ward Wheelock advertising agency, remembers that neither CBS nor the agency had any objections but the sponsor felt it was too controversial. "To hell with them," Welles said, and continued to rehearse the entire week. The day before the scheduled broadcast the advertising manager of the company came to the studio, listened to a rehearsal, and ordered it canceled. Muni was paid off, and an earlier Welles broadcast, without Muni, was repeated. The indignant Muni ordered his agent not even to cash the check. "Shred it up," he said, "and make it into soup!"

On May 8, 1939, Muni performed his third *Lux Radio Theatre* broadcast, *The Life of Emile Zola*, with Josephine Hutchinson especially requested by him as Madame Zola. DeMille was away on vacation, and Leslie Howard was the guest host. Howard, who had just completed starring in and co-directing the screen version of Shaw's *Pygmalion*, was in Hollywood for the filming of *Gone with the Wind*. Muni admired Howard, particularly his voice and British poise.

"I think it's wonderful that you managed to keep the title *Pygmalion*," Muni told him. "Most studios would have changed it into *Lonely Love* or *The Passionate Professor*."

Howard had to admit there were difficulties. "Some people," he said, "fully expect *Pygmalion* to be an animal picture. Do you know that I've heard it called PIGMY *LION!*"

Jake Wilk sent Muni a James Hilton novel he had just purchased. Muni read it and liked the gentle British doctor, but felt the studio should wait for Leslie Howard and cast him in it. "I'm just too Jewish for the part," Muni said, wanting to be convinced. M. C. Levee, who also handled Howard, whispered to Muni a little-known fact: the polished and poised English star had been born Leslie Howard Stainer and was also Jewish! "Then maybe Weisenfreund can do it," Muni said and agreed to play Dr. David Newcome in *We Are Not Alone*. It turned out to be his favorite screen role. And Bella's.

Henry Blanke recalls that when Muni saw the first screenplay, he was disappointed. "It's chicken-shit," he said. Blanke assigned it to Milton Krims (coincidentally a member of the Thomashefky family and another of Bella's talented cousins), who had been a contract writer at the studio for many years, completely independent of the Munis. Blanke teamed Krims with James Hilton. When the final script reached Muni, he sighed blissfully. "Ah! Now—chicken *salad!*"

Before the shooting was scheduled to begin, Bella and Muni decided they needed another vacation. They sailed for Hawaii on the liner *Matsonia* "just long enough to step ashore in Honolulu and climb back aboard." Muni could not avoid reporters when the ship docked in the Islands. He was floored when one asked if the trip was a honeymoon.

"Yes, I guess you'd say it is," Muni answered. "Even though we've been married slightly more than eighteen years."

"To the *same woman!*" the reporter gasped. Muni remembered it as the most astonished reading he'd ever heard.

Edmund Goulding, a gracious and charming Englishman beyond his legendary capacity as a ladies' man, was the director of *We Are Not Alone*. The cast pleased Muni very much: Flora Robson as his wife, Una O'Connor as the cook; the rest of the company were equally distinguished performers. Dolly Haas (now Mrs. Al Hirschfeld) was tested for the role of Leni, the lost and lovely Austrian girl, but it was finally played by Jane Bryan, whose beautiful face and unaffected performance illuminated the screen. At the completion of the film, she retired and married a millionaire. "I could never again," she explains, "find such a wonderful part."

Muni was also enchanted by his role: Hilton's gentle humanitarian, the "little doctor" who had wit and total honesty. But two days before shooting began, he almost quit. Bella felt that they should see Hilton's most recent motion-picture success, *Goodbye, Mr. Chips*. Muni loved it, but after the screening he was in despair. "How can I ever match Robert Donat's truthful performance? It would be arrogant of me to play an Englishman in a Hilton story." Bella had to force him not to call the studio and resign.

MUNI WITHOUT WHISKERS! read a sign tacked up in the makeup department. Muni wore his own mustache and just the slightest bit of greasepaint. "It was a pleasure to play a nonepic," Muni remarked, "and not have to spend half my life putting on and talking off beards."

Onscreen, Muni looked very much like James Hilton. Flora Robson was remarkably like a tall, stern, humorless Bella. The little country doctor plays the violin and makes his rounds on a bicycle. Nobody dubbed for Muni on the fiddle; in fact, he had to play less well than he could; the little doctor was not supposed to be a virtuoso. But it took him several weeks to master the bicycle. "I can roller-skate," Muni told Goulding. "But I guess I'll have to learn this two-wheel trick; you can't get anybody to dub me on the bicycle!"

We Are Not Alone, set in a tiny British village in 1914, is a simple and moving story. Goulding's direction, the totally convincing sets, the gentle performances, make it authentic Hilton and valid storytelling. Bets were lost by experts certain it was shot in England and not in Burbank.

Raymond Severn, Muni, and Jane Bryan in *We Are Not Alone*.

(WB photo by Bert Six)

Two love stories are eloquent in their understatement. Muni expresses total fatherly affection for his son, Gerald, unaffectedly played by seven-year-old Raymond Severn. His unspoken love for the quiet Austrian girl, Leni Krafft, seems natural as sunrise. The doctor and the girl are innocently accused of the murder of his wife. In the courtroom at their murder trial, the counsel for the Crown ruthlessly cross-examines him: "Do you or do you not love Leni Krafft?" Puzzled, vaguely, the doctor answers: "Do I . . . love . . . Leni?" "That was my question," the counsel thunders. The silence is beautiful as the camera slowly pans around the courtroom in the deathly quiet of an uninterrupted shot. No one dares breathe until the doctor answers. The camera comes to rest on the doctor, moves to a close shot of him as he shakes his head and is completely bewildered. Then gradually, his face lights into an incredulous smile. "Why . . . I hadn't thought of it . . . but"—(then with matter-of-factness and complete conviction, though it will hang him)—"of course I love her."

It is a classic moment, one of the most moving sequences ever seen on film.

In almost every scene, the character reveals his warmth and dedication. "Strange how words can be true and yet have no truth in them," the doctor says. And later: "I don't know why anybody hates people. Things. Ideas. Qualities. Yes. But never people." How Muni-ish are the lines "I hear an apple a day keeps the doctor away. If I eat enough, I may get away from myself altogether—and I think I'd like that."

The outbreak of World War I is part of the film. By grim coincidence, World War II began while the picture was being made. Everybody on the set was deeply affected; many of the lines and situations had poignant double meaning, particularly to Flora Robson and the other English actors. They rushed to radios between takes for news of the bombings and constantly read newspaper reports of endangered villages back home so similar to the one in the film. The title line refers to the companionship of death, the final agony shared, unjustly and uselessly, by World War I soldiers in the trenches. Muni's conviction in his reading of "We are not alone" now included the millions already dead or still-to-die in the 1939–45 European holocaust.

Blanke remembers that on previous pictures Edmund Goulding always roped off an area around the camera, primarily to sit and rewrite the screenplay during the shooting, with a beautiful secretary at his side. The ropes came down for *We Are Not Alone*. Hilton was on the set a great deal, and Muni would not tolerate the changing of so much as a comma.

About working with Muni, Jane Bryan says, "He was such a *private* person—and I was (and am) very shy. Almost all of our communication was in shared heartbeats while filming."

We Are Not Alone did only modest business. Ironically, the gentle message of the picture, an appeal against prejudice toward the Germanic girl, may have militated against its commercial success. Audiences of 1939–40 were in no mood for a heroine on the enemy side, despite Jane Bryan's tender and heartbreaking performance.

The New York *Times* critic Frank S. Nugent (later a screenwriter, hired away from his brickbatting position by Darryl Zanuck) called Muni's performance "flawless" and the film one of the best of the year. Hobe Morrison in *Variety* caught exactly what Muni was trying to do:

> Although the leading part isn't as spectacular as other recent Muni roles, it offers more depth and naturalness and the star gives a penetrating, spontaneous and ingratiating performance. . . . He not only achieves the necessary light touch in the part, but he has dropped the mannerisms with which he adorned such character parts as Zola, Juarez and others. It is a stirring performance, direct and subtle.

Impulsively, abruptly, Muni sold the Palos Verdes house almost as fast as he had bought it. He considered an hour's ride to the studio every day and another hour back a waste of time. With the biography of Beethoven next on his schedule, he needed those two hours in the makeup department. They rented a small house just ten minutes from the studio. Simon, the Airedale, hated it; his rambling spirit needed more grass than a tiny backyard.

Author Louis Golding was formally introduced to Simon one day and wrote: "He's a strange creature who combines the qualities of a bear and a lamb, and in that respect is not wholly unlike his master." Like Muni, Simon hated restriction, and he ran away. Muni was indignant. "If that's what he thinks about us, let him stay away. I won't let him in the house if he *ever* comes back." But Bella, an Airedale lover, roamed the streets looking for him. Four days later a muddy but innocent-looking Simon bounded through the door and back into Muni's arms. Muni hugged the wanderer and cried with relief.

Muni had not performed in a Broadway play for seven years. He longed to go back and swore he would the moment he could find a play which inspired him. Bella missed New York very much.

"I have made the transformation," she said, not convincing anybody, "from city sparrow to meadowlark." But the sparrow in her constantly wanted to fly home to Manhattan. Muni joked with Bella about it. "Don't worry," he'd say. "We'll find a play and you can go back and grub crumbs in Times Square."

Their main luggage on the move into town consisted of tall piles of playscripts. Muni sat on a sun porch converted into a study, a stack of plays at his side. Bella would prop herself up in bed with an equal pile of multicolored manuscripts on the bedside table. They traded scripts silently. Muni walked unenthusiastically into Bella's room, tossed a script on her bed. Bella looked up, with a *Nu?* on her face.

"It's a maybe," Muni said. "But I'm looking for an *absolutely*. I'm looking for a *wow!*"

One day Fred Hoar, the accountant from the M. C. Levee office, delivered Muni's weekly check from the studio and a package of fan mail. "Except for the ten-thousand-dollar dole from Warner Brothers," Bella said, riffling through the mail, "there doesn't seem to be anything important." At the bottom of the stack was a telegram. She ripped it open and read it aloud to Muni.

HAVE NEW PLAY. WOULD YOU BE INTERESTED IN READING IT? AM IN MALIBU VISITING KURT WEILL. GL 4-2909.
                                        MAXWELL ANDERSON

Bella waved the telegram in the air like a flag. Muni, without a word, went to the phone and called Anderson. The next afternoon Mrs. Anderson delivered a manuscript neatly bound in the familiar Brandt and Brandt red binding. Muni told her he'd read it within the next few days. Muni looked at the title, *Key Largo,* and headed for the sun porch. Bella had to bludgeon him into dinner first, but he raced through it, then headed for his easy chair. Bella remained in the living room, trying to read a book, but paying no attention to it.

After a few minutes, Muni poked his head out, "We just might be going to New York." He smiled. "Get your feathers dusted." Then he disappeared again. Bella smoked cigarettes, chain fashion, pacing the living room, waiting for the verdict of that one-man jury. After an hour and a quarter, Muni came slowly back into the room.

"It's a beautiful play," he said. "Full of ideas. Full of poetry. I've read the prologue and the first act. The only trouble is—I'm all wrong for it."

"Okay," Bella said, knowing exactly how to handle him. "In that case, I'll go back to New York by myself for a couple of weeks. Back to civilization!"

"Wait!" Muni said. "There might still be a chance. Lemme read the last act."

At eleven o'clock, Muni stood in the doorway, a dazed glow on his face. "That Max Anderson sure as hell can write," he said, almost with reverence. "You wanna read it, Bella?"

"Not tonight or I'll never sleep. I'll get up early and read it in the morning."

Bella was awake at dawn. When she finished reading the play, she walked into Muni's room with a breakfast tray, the red-bound script under her arm. Muni piled his pillows under his head, took one sip of coffee, then stared at his wife, waiting for the unspoken signal he knew so well. Bella's face did not shrug.

"If you don't do this," she said, tossing the script on his bed, "I just might divorce you."

An hour later Muni was on the phone to Anderson.

"I love your play," he said. "But which part do you want me to play? McCloud or the old blind father? I'll do either one."

"McCloud of course," Anderson said.

"In that case," Muni warned, "you'd better come over and have a look at me. McCloud's a young man, and I'm no spring chicken!"

The Andersons spent the next afternoon and evening with the Munis from four until past midnight. Muni wanted to read the whole play aloud, not as an audition but to get the feel of it. Anderson was delighted. Muni was nervous but grew in confidence and fervor as he read of a disillusioned idealist who rediscovers his faith as he battles the gangsters of the world, finding at last a reason to live and a reason to die.

When Muni finished reading *Key Largo* aloud, Anderson told Muni he was perfect as McCloud, whose battlefield was his own soul. Muni quickly dismissed the compliments, only wanting assurance that "I won't ruin your play. I don't respect forty-year-old actors who still think they can play college freshmen."

Anderson stared at Muni and smiled. "I originally conceived King McCloud to be about thirty-five. Now that I've had a good look at you without makeup, I think we should make him twenty-eight!"

As one of the founding members of the Playwrights Company, Anderson was his own producer and had the power to sign a contract. Bella raced for a piece of stationery and a fountain pen. The contract, half a page long, was signed that night in North Hollywood.

"Hey! Hey!" Bella shouted, almost cheering. "We're going to New York!"

Warner Brothers promised to keep working on the Beethoven project. Muni and Bella traveled across country again. "We are pioneers, heading in the other direction," Bella said. And to a young actor who asked for her advice, she added, "Go East, young man, go East!"

After reading and considering more than 200 plays, Muni felt that at last he had "one with guts." But he was concerned about being out of practice for the stage. "Coming back, after so many years, I feel like Rip Van Winkle," he worried. "I hope I'll know what to do with my feet."

He was delighted with director Guthrie McClintic, set designer Jo Mielziner, and with the Playwrights Company, which included, in addition to Maxwell Anderson, Robert Sherwood, S. N. Behrman, and Muni's old friend Elmer Rice. The cast was equally distinguished: José Ferrer, Uta Hagen, Karl Malden, and for old time's sake one of the *Four Walls* gangsters, Averell Harris. A tiny walk-on role was played by Ethel Jackson, the original American star of *The Merry Widow*.

John Fearnley (later an eminent theater director) was assistant stage manager and played one of the tourists. He recalls the early rehearsals onstage at the Ethel Barrymore Theatre in New York. McClintic and the cast sat around a table for six days, discussing every ramification of the play before the blocking began. Fearnley remembers only one instance where a scene's meaning was unclear to Muni. McClintic came to rehearsal the following day with a paraphrase of the scene neatly typed on several pages, not to replace Anderson's poetry, but to illuminate it from another perspective. Muni read the pages, and his troubled face suddenly lit up with a smile. "Aha!" he exclaimed. "You have penetrated my thick skull by showing me the backside of the coin. Now I understand the front side. Thank you, Mr. Director."

Key Largo opened at the English Theatre in Indianapolis on October 30, 1939. Muni insisted that he not be billed as MISTER. Elmer Rice and S. N. Behrman were there in the capacity audience which welcomed Muni home to the theater. Muni caught a cold in Indianapolis but never missed a performance. But he maintained an offstage silence during their stops at the Hartman Theatre in Columbus, the Hanna Theatre in Cleveland, and the Erlanger Theatre in Buffalo. Muni wanted to go visit Woodland Avenue and have another look at Case-Woodland School while in Cleveland, but he concentrated totally on the play. Their last stop pre-Broadway was the Colonial Theatre in Boston.

Elliot Norton reported in the Boston *Post:* "Paul Muni, who doesn't look anything like Al Capone and very little like Louis Pasteur, arrived here last night for his first stage appearance in seven years. Like the gangsters he so vividly portrayed before he got to impersonating more dignified celebrities, he wasn't talking." Norton went on to note the invasion of Boston by the famous, which included Ethel Merman, Bert Lahr, and Betty Grable, all in Boston for *Du Barry Was a Lady.* For that event, composer Cole Porter had imported every social register, show-biz and café society headliner known to man. But Norton called Muni's modest arrival in Beantown the high point of the week.

Boston in November was cold. The reviews were warm. Offstage Muni hugged a radio, listening to the horrors of the Nazi blitzkrieg and the outrageous slicing up of Poland.

There were lighter moments. The Munis loved the Hotel Ritz and the food at Locke-Ober's Restaurant. Muni remarked that the fella who declared Boston clam chowder unkosher must have been anti-Semitic.

Max Wilk remembers that Boston winter:

"I had worked at Warner's the previous summer as a messenger boy in the publicity department. Muni was making *We Are Not Alone,* and I was lonely—being eighteen. He'd take me in a corner and *shmoose* with me. And when he opened in Boston in *Key Largo,* I was there with a friend of mine from Yale, and the two of us went backstage at the Colonial. We were going to a formal dance at Harvard, and we were both wearing full dress (my first, and may I add, my last), and when the doorman ushered me into Muni's dressing room in that outfit, Muni was absolutely flabbergasted. He stood up and then solemnly said, 'Maxie! My God, you look like a . . . a . . . penguin!' Which broke us all up.

"Oh, hell, I don't know what he was like to other people—probably a pain in the ass to some, and a meticulous perfectionist—and who cares? To us he was a friend."

The cast and backstage crew didn't consider Muni a pain in the ass, but they felt he was aloof. Alan Anderson, the playwright's twenty-one-year-old son, was stage manager. "To watch Muni play a scene," he recalls, "took a whole lot out of you. He was not just an actor; he literally became whatever character he played. Backstage he was nervous; I suppose all really great actors are. But that nervousness, that intense eagerness to play the scene just right, was never transmitted into a finished product. The final scene, the other actors told me, 'tore them apart with its intense validity.' "

(Photo by Richard Tucker)

Paul Muni, Uta Hagen, and Harold Johnsrud in *Key Largo*.

The opening of *Key Largo* at the Ethel Barrymore Theatre on November 27, 1939, was a triumph for Muni but yes-no for the play. Brooks Atkinson in the New York *Times* wrote:

> *Key Largo* is a mixture of Mr. Anderson at his best and worst. Mr. Muni is one of the most believable actors on stage or screen and, if memory serves, he is a finer grained artist now than when he went west.

In a Sunday follow-up, Atkinson added:

> Mr. Muni's simple, direct style of playing and the magnetic force of his personality give the play a solid footing. Although he gave some memorable performances on the stage before he left Broadway, he never gave as fine a one as this. In a more obliging part he would have the town by both ears instead of one.

Muni again had double exposure in New York when *We Are Not Alone* opened at Radio City Music Hall two weeks later. Bella was drunk on playgoing, joyful about being back in a city "alive with theater." John Fearnley remembers Bella coming backstage at the Barrymore Theatre on a gray, sleeting matinee day in December.

"Isn't it lovely today?" Bella enthused.

"It's terrible out, Mrs. Muni," Fearnley said. "Just dreadful."

"Oh, no"—Bella smiled in her Mona Lisa way—"it's beautiful. And it's so good to be away from those everlasting blue skies in California!"

During the run of *Key Largo,* Claire Edelstein, Annie Thomashefsky's daughter (later Claire Friedland), served as part-time secretary to the Munis ·while she was attending Hunter College at night. "I would come to their suite at the Ambassador Hotel every weekday morning about eleven," Claire recalls. "When Bella opened the door, she would either put her finger to her lips to *shoosh* me because Muni was in the middle of a temper tantrum, or it was 'Hello, darling, how are you?'—and that's the way I knew the mood of the day. Some mornings Bella would whisper to me at the door: 'Today's Muni's day for *weltschmerz.* Over his Cream of Wheat he's aggravating over what to aggravate about!' "

Key Largo played 105 performances in New York, then went on an extended tour to Philadelphia, Chicago, San Francisco, ending at the old Biltmore Theatre in Los Angeles in June. Uta Hagen and José Ferrer had been married more than a year but behaved like newlyweds backstage, trying at every available moment to precipitate an act of God so they wouldn't have to go on the road tour. Mrs. Ferrer was sufficiently pregnant by January, with God's help and her husband's, to bow gracefully out of the cast. Helen Beverly, then Mrs. Lee J. Cobb, replaced her. Two other additions to the road company were Tom Ewell and Joseh Pevney, later a stage and film director.

Muni felt very deeply about the shattering news from Europe: the invasion of Denmark and Norway, the conquest of the Netherlands and Belgium, the fall of France. Tortured, restless, Muni only seemed happy when he was onstage and could declare fervently his opposition to the Fascists of the world.

In spring of 1940 Muni was awarded the Delia Austrian Medal of the Drama League of New York for "the most distinguished stage performance of the year." Still touring with *Key Largo,* Muni was unable to be in New York to accept the medal in person, but he was proud to receive it by mail. (The Tony awards had not yet been established, and this was one of the theater's meaningful honors; Maxwell Anderson accepted for Muni.)

At the close of the play Muni reported back to Burbank, where he had seven more pictures to make for Warner Brothers under the terms of his existing contract. Muni had brought great prestige to the studio, but art was battling box office. *Juarez* and *We Are Not Alone* were not financial bonanzas. In early July, 1940, at a conference with all the studio executives present, everyone was long-faced and solemn. This was no time for Beethoven, they declared. Audiences wanted escape, frivolity. They had a perfect role for Muni to do next—a fugitive hiding from the law in the California mountains.

Muni read the screenplay and turned it down. "I don't want to play another gangster," he declared.

"For God's sake, Paul, you should listen to me," Jack Warner said petulantly. "After all, I gave you *Pasteur!*"

Muni studied the multiple scripts on hand on the life of Beethoven. He was equally displeased with them. They had been ripped apart, stitched together, falsified with ersatz commercialism; the stature of the great composer had not been caught on paper. "I have choice of properties," Muni said, "but nothing to choose."

In a dramatic gesture, Muni literally tore up his contract. He refused to take a penny in settlement. All he wanted was his liberty. The day after Muni walked out, William Dieterle also asked for his release and was granted it.

Humphrey Bogart took the part Muni had turned down; *High Sierra* elevated Bogart from secondary roles to stardom. The picture was a critical and box-office hit.

Muni was free. And he hated it.

Out of the studio "harness" Muni made only seven more motion pictures in his lifetime and a token cameo appearance in an eighth. No actor alive could match the stature and importance of the classic roles he had created for Warner Brothers and for Thalberg at MGM. As the years passed, he came to realize that there were two sides to the burden of "being under the yoke" of a contract, advantages as well as disadvantages. Despite his protests to be independent, Muni missed the protective paternalism of a studio.

Papa, even in the form of the often difficult and sometimes obtuse brothers Warner, was gone from his life. Creatively, Muni was an orphan at the age of forty-five.

(Photo by VanDamm)

Jessica Tandy and Muni in *Yesterday's Magic*.

21

MUNI sulked and suffered. He swore he would never work again or at least take a long vacation: a year, five years. But two hours with nothing to do drove him crazy.

"Relax, Munya," Bella said.

"I'll relax tomorrow," he said, pacing, fidgeting. "Did any scripts come in the mail? Call Mike Levee and tell him to find us some radio broadcasts. I want to work. I can't sit on my ass and grow walnuts."

Bella seemed to be the only one left in the world he could trust. He had cut himself off from his literary advisers. When Abem Finkel left his wife, Ruth, and started living with another woman, Muni righteously refused to see him anymore and took Ruth's side in the matrimonial split. Ted Thomas broke away from Muni the day they had such a fierce shouting argument in an open convertible that a police officer stopped them to find out what was wrong. "That day, discussing Muni's future," Thomas remembers, "he spoke the saddest words I've ever heard from an artist. 'I'm a commodity, Teddy,' Muni said. 'I'm a product that has to yield a profit!' " Thomas got out of the car, walked away, and didn't see Muni again for many years. "Why?" Thomas explained. "My god degenerated into a mortal."

It is difficult to fathom this complex, self-tortured, and contradictory man. A storefront psychoanalyst might easily say that Muni's workomania was based on his fear of rejection. Wasn't the great public an adoring parent? Did he protest too much that he distrusted applause; was audience approval really a kind of all-embracing mother love?

Muni impulsively accepted the first offer that came along. Ironically it was from Twentieth Century-Fox, the reorganized version of the studio where he had begun and nearly finished his screen career eleven years before. Two weeks after he tore up his Warner Brothers contract, Muni signed to star in *Hudson's Bay*.

"I've never done an adventure story before," Muni rationalized. "And it's a good lusty part, different from anything I've ever played."

Muni hid elaborately behind a thick beard and an even thicker accent as Pierre Radisson, a French-Canadian trapper in this semihistorical icebox of a saga on the birth of the Hudson's Bay Company. A week into the shooting, Muni realized he had trapped himself. Director Irving Pichel would not allow Bella on the set, and Muni was lost in the snow.

Muni did enjoy working with a huge protean actor, the young Laird Cregar (Muni called him Sam, Cregar's real first name), but fifty days of wind machines blowing sleet in his face felt as if he had been sent to Siberia. Muni hired Marcel de la Brosse, a stage actor who had played a French waiter in Cregar's stage production of *Oscar Wilde,* to help him with his dialogue; Brosse became Muni's stand-in so he could be on the sets constantly to listen and correct Muni's garbled-syntax dialect. Muni kept the Dicta-phone running in his dressing trailer. When Brosse heard one cylinder replayed, he was startled: "It was so amazing, that I was scared. I knew it was Monsieur Muni, but I thought I was listening to my own voice!"

The character of Radisson had lines like "Canada—she my wife—no woman—joost Canada." Muni plus a flight of angels could not make this patois sound immortal. He mugged outrageously, perhaps as compensation, and nobody on the sound stage was courageous enough to tell the celebrated actor, "Less!"

Bosley Crowther, in his first review of a Muni film, wrote: "The combination of an epic tale and Academy Award winner Paul Muni was too much for the boys at Fox. Their *Hudson's Bay* is as static and ponderous as a bale of furs."

Why did Muni, usually astute in his choice of stories and roles, choose this? One can only speculate. Unlike many actors, he was never in love with himself. But he didn't like being "a temperamental son of a bitch"; he wanted to masquerade as this jolly, carefree French trapper, a far cry from the moody, tortured Muni. There was an element of resentment, too. Though he himself had torn up the Warner Brothers contract, why had they let

261

him go so willingly? Why didn't they fight to keep him there? This hasty acceptance of a new part, particularly from a studio which had fired him, would prove that somebody else really wanted him.

In January, 1941, when *Hudson's Bay* was released, Muni reacted to the reactions by putting the walnut ranch up for sale. He declared he was turning his back on the picture business forever. Hollywood didn't want him, and he didn't want Hollywood. What a paradox that on the day the ranch was sold, Muni was named, in a poll taken by the show-business periodical *Billboard*, as "one of the five greatest performers within the memory of living man." (The other four were John Barrymore, Charles Chaplin, Helen Hayes, and Enrico Caruso.)

Bella had strangely mixed feelings. Hardly a day passed when she didn't sigh, "Let's go back to New York." But now for the last time she walked around the ranch, touching the branches of the almond trees she had planted, feeling vaguely like O-Lan of *The Good Earth* whose peach stone had grown into a blossoming miracle. And how odd that the Concord grapes she had wanted "right by the window, where you can reach out and pick them," were finally bearing fruit.

They made arrangements for Simon, their "senior citizen Airedale" to be shipped back East just as soon as they had a proper place for him. A coach dog, called Toto because he was spotted like a clown, had been added to the household. Regretfully, they gave him to neighbors.

Once Muni made a decision, he was locked into it. He did not waver or look back. If he had any emotions about leaving the walnut ranch he loved, he refused to admit them. He wished he had a play to go back to, but it was too late in the season. Perhaps next fall. He phoned Lucy Finkel, Bella's sister, who was now operating a talent and literary agency out of the Wellington Hotel in New York, to find a play for him.

He also phoned attorney Jonas Silverstone to get real estate brokers to work. They were moving East permanently, away from the sunshine and open spaces. But wasn't it possible to combine the best of both worlds? Living in New York didn't necessarily mean being squeezed into an apartment or a hotel, you didn't have to turn into a cliff dweller; there were country places. Long Island. Bucks County. Connecticut.

Two days after Bella and Muni arrived back in New York, a broker drove them out to Long Island. As impetuously as he had sold the walnut ranch, Muni bought ten acres of land and an old Tudor mansion in Brookville. He considered it a steal for

$25,000. They were surrounded by the Brookville Country Club, sea air wafted from the Sound, trees and grass abounded, even a gate cottage was available if guests came to call. And Shubert Alley was only an hour away.

In the entire year of 1941 Muni appeared in no play in a legitimate theater and on no motion-picture sound stage. He was forty-five years old, soon to be forty-six. He had never spent a whole year offstage, out of action, lying fallow, since it all began for him in 1908, when he was twelve.

Muni made frequent trips into New York, haunting bookshops and stationery stores. He bought more paper clips than he could use in a lifetime. He brought home fountain pens by the boxful, dictionaries of every variety, and the latest style wire recorders to replace his Dictaphones.

"You'll bury yourself in office supplies," Bella remarked.

Muni sat in his newly furnished study in Brookville, turned on the newfangled recording machine, and had nothing to record.

He leaped at the chance to do two radio broadcasts originating in New York, half-hour biographical dramas on the *Cavalcade of America* series sponsored by DuPont. The scripts seemed a bit stuffy and documentary, but they were parts Muni enjoyed. He played Edwin Booth in March and Simón Bolívar in October. Otherwise, the only dramatic event in 1941 for Muni, and for everybody, was the bombing of Pearl Harbor on December 7 and America's entry into World War II.

Two offers arrived almost simultaneously for Muni to return to the New York stage in *King Lear,* one from the Theatre Guild and one from Billy Rose. Theresa Helburn of the Guild wrote:

> I believe you would give such a magnificent performance that it would be a landmark in the theatre. The right new vehicle is often difficult to find and *King Lear* has so much beauty and is so seldom seen in the theatre because of the difficulty of casting it rightly that I cannot resist urging you to consider it. We feel it has some of the greatest poetry Shakespeare has ever written. We feel, too, that the public, torn by world conditions, will turn more gratefully than ever to the kind of release and uplift that Shakespeare gives them. Do think this over and if you are interested, let us discuss production ideas.
>
> Your persistent and profound admirer,
> THERESA HELBURN

Billy Rose's offer was more terse via Western Union. Muni sat down and tried to answer both of them.

"If I were twelve years old," Muni wrote, "I'd be brash enough to attempt Lear in a second. Now that I am older, I am perhaps wiser and simultaneously more careful." Then he was stuck. He looked up and saw Bella, who was watching him struggling with the letter. He showed her what he'd written. Their dialogue went something like this:

BELLA: "Careful!" That's a fancy word that means scared.

MUNI: I've never played Shakespeare. Not even in Yiddish.

BELLA: You never played Zola—until you played him.

MUNI: All right, I admit it. I'm afraid of Shakespeare.

BELLA: If everybody was so afraid of him, nobody'd know who Shakespeare was.

MUNI: So? That's his problem.

BELLA: You've got to work, Munya.

MUNI: Who says? Are we hungry?

BELLA: Yes. I am. Hungry to see you on a stage again.

MUNI: What if I flop?

BELLA: You've flopped before. So what? Don't you have the right? The world won't come to an end. Who remembers *Hi, Nellie!*?

MUNI: Was *Hi, Nellie!* so bad?

BELLA (pleading): Take the part, Munya. I can't stand having you around the house all day.

MUNI (thoughtfully): What if I make a *Hudson's Bay* out of *King Lear*?

BELLA: So he'll get wet. Stick your neck out!

MUNI: No!

BELLA: You think doing nothing is *safe?* An actor has to act. You're playing Lear right now—a foolish-wise old man, hiding in Brookville surrounded by ungrateful paper clips!

He never sent the letter. He phoned a polite no, via Lucy, to be conveyed to both the Guild and Billy Rose. Muni desperately wanted to work, particularly on the stage, but Shakespeare was a *terra incognita.* He wished he could have spent a lifetime, like his peers in England, growing up with Shakespeare, so that it was as much a part of him as his bloodstream or the lining of his brain.

Prophetically, Herman Shumlin made Muni an offer in 1941, fourteen years before he was to direct and produce Muni's most successful Broadway play. Shumlin wrote:

I understand that you admired *Watch on the Rhine,* and I am wondering if you would be interested in taking out a company for a tour. While I realize that this is an unusual proposal to make to you, it seems to me that the importance of the play at this time and the major importance of the part as an acting part justifies my writing to you.

Muni replied, in his own hunt-and-peck typing:

Dear Herman Shumlin,

I really thank you for considering me for *Watch on the Rhine* when you send it on tour. The truth however is that I have never followed anybody in a second company and can not be reconciled to doing so now. It's really my loss. It's a great play and in my opinion Paul Lukas' performance can not be equaled. He is so extraordinarily right for it that I doubt if anybody could match him. It would be a shame to deny the audiences on the road the pleasure of seeing him in it.

Kindest regards,
Paul Muni

Many years later, Muni told me, "It was a mistake. I should have played it. Lillian Hellman writes brilliantly. The play said something important about human dignity, and it was a blast against the Nazis. But I meant what I wrote Shumlin about Paul Lukas. Nobody could have been better."

Early in 1942 Muni appeared as a guest on the *Kate Smith Variety Hour* in a ten-minute dramatic playlet, *Task Force.* It was written by my partner, Robert E. Lee, just before we met and began our collaboration. It was a moving radio drama, not unlike the film *Commandos Strike at Dawn,* which Muni played later but which had not been written at the time. Ted Collins, Kate Smith's producer, had agreed to pay Bob Lee $10 for the script but reneged on the payment because Bob worked for Young and Rubicam, the advertising agency handling the show. Finally, Collins relented, and Bob did receive payment: a hand-me-down tuxedo from the generous producer. Bob says his real payment was the chance to work with Muni.

"I want to do a stage play," the restless Muni told Bella. "But it's got to do one of two things: make some kind of contribution to social consciousness or make people happy. Better if it does both."

Lucy found Muni a play, the last of the Theatre Guild's '41–'42 season, and Muni grabbed it. Emlyn Williams' *Yesterday's Magic* had played 700 performances in London as *The Light of Heart,* first with Godfrey Tearle, then the playwright himself in the lead. Williams had a notable play, *The Corn Is Green,* running successfully on Broadway, and Muni had admired his taut and suspenseful *Night Must Fall.* In New York *Yesterday's Magic* turned into

265

yesterday's cold tea for both star and playwright: it neither entertained nor added a whit to social or theater history.

For Muni, psychologically the play felt like a masochistic confessional. Though Muni was never an alcoholic, this saga of the dead end of an actor's career, drowning in liquor and self-pity, attempting a triumphant comeback in *King Lear,* was bleeding in public, wearing sackcloth and ashes for all the world to see.

The auspices were promising, including a thoughtful and understanding director, Reginald Denham, authentically British and a playwright as well *(Ladies in Retirement).* The cast was the best the Guild could assemble: Jessica Tandy, Alfred Drake, Brenda Forbes, James Monks.

"What a crazy character!" Denham said about Muni when we talked in the spring of 1973. "I met him first in 1942 at Lawrence Langner's house down in the Village about a month before rehearsals started. The meeting was arranged for me to get acquainted with Muni and for him to see if he wanted to bother with me. I didn't find him the easiest man to talk to. When I came in, Muni was having a violent argument with Langner, who had just made a disparaging remark about some actress, implying that she was a lesbian.

"Muni suddenly turned on Langner with great scorn. 'I loathe gossip. I loathe anything to do with this chitchat of Broadway. How do you know what those two people were doing? Have you been in bed with them?' I thought we were never going to talk about the play. But finally Langner turned to me and said, 'Well, Reggie, what do you think of Mr. Muni as the lead in the play?' I said, 'Does it matter what I think if he's already been engaged?' They laughed and assured me that he'd been hired, so I agreed it was a fine idea. Muni appreciated my frankness. He asked me if I'd ever seen Godfrey Tearle play the part in London. I hadn't and said so. Muni immediately began unselling himself for the role. 'I feel I'm not fitted for the part. Tearle's a tremendously successful, good-looking actor and here I am, a squat character, undersized—how can I possibly play this great old actor?'

"I answered, 'Well, Mr. Muni, it's all a question of inside, you know. Look at Kean, do you think he could play the part? He was a squat little man, but with the inner fire that delivered, and I think you have that.' Muni agreed to do the play if I promised to come down to his place in Long Island every weekend and help him with his English accent. I felt the accent wasn't important, but he insisted he needed it. Granville Barker once said, 'There are two kinds of actors: those who *express* their personalities and those who *suppress* it.' Muni was a suppressive actor."

Just before rehearsals began, Bella's sister, Lucy, suddenly took sick. The doctors diagnosed it as leukemia. Lucy grew weaker and weaker in a painful eleven-month illness. Bella hardly left her side, first in Lucy's room at the Hotel Wellington, then through the many harrowing months at Mount Sinai Hospital.

Muni attempted to turn himself into Maddoc Thomas, the character of the play, an actor who has sunk so low in his career that he is forced to play Santa Claus at Selfridge's Department Store. Muni was drunk, not with liquor, but with autohypnosis, forcing himself to forget Lucy's illness, Bella's absence, and his own restless, compulsive need-to-be-needed.

Muni's insecurity because of the lack of his "seeing-eye wife" (Bella concocted that phrase) was compounded by the presence at rehearsals of Molly O'Shann Williams, the playwright's wife, constantly seated in the front row. Emlyn Williams, on war duty in London, was unable to come to America.

"Molly scared the bejesus out of Muni," Denham recalls. "She was there on orders from Emlyn not to change a bloody line. We tried a few word substitutions, an American equivalent of an English phrase so that the audience here could understand it better, but she'd say, 'No, Emlyn wants it to be exactly as it was in London.' She wasn't aggressive, she was simply adamant. She was the Rock of Ages."

Jessica Tandy (then Mrs. Jack Hawkins) had been evacuated from London and played, brilliantly, the crippled daughter in the play. To make more money to send "Bundles to Britain," she doubled as a radio actress in New York, playing the Princess in *Mandrake the Magician.* Louis Jourdan was originally the young-man-next-door; but Mrs. Williams asked him to "drop his French accent," and he walked out after two rehearsals. His substitution, Alfred Drake, had his first critical success in a nonmusical part. (An earlier play he had been rehearsing that season, *The Admiral Takes a Wife,* dealt with—of all things—frivolous social life in Pearl Harbor and was abruptly canceled on December 7.)

Yesterday's Magic tried out at the Shubert in New Haven, the National in Washington, and the Forrest in Philadelphia. Out-of-town critics praised Jessica Tandy and Alfred Drake but dismissed Muni as "miscast as a ham actor." (Was that a compliment? Muni was never sure.) News from Lucy's hospital bedside was dire: the doctors had given up hope. Muni felt he was at the low point in his life.

Broadway seemed spooky. On this first season after Pearl Harbor, the entire Times Square area was browned out. Very few serious plays were successful. The mood of theatergoing was summed up by Howard Lindsay, who told us about what happened almost every night at *Life with Father,* which had almost hit 1,000 performances at the Empire Theatre. "After the final curtain," Lindsay said, "the audience just stayed in their seats, hanging on for a few more minutes to that cozy, uncomplicated past they'd just seen onstage, not wanting to go out onto cold Broadway of 1942 and read all the terrible headlines of the moment."

The opening-night audience at the Guild Theatre on April 14, 1942, greeted *Yesterday's Magic* with militant indifference. The play lasted fifty-five performances.

Atkinson shrugged.

A few weeks later, a transatlantic radio broadcast was arranged, part of an English-American amity program. Emlyn Williams had wanted very much to come to New York to play Morgan Evans, the young Welsh miner in *The Corn Is Green,* opposite Ethel Barrymore's Miss Moffat (he had played it with Sybil Thorndyke in London), but the war prevented it. So they performed a brief scene on this international wireless hookup, with Miss Barrymore in a studio on Madison Avenue and Williams at Broadcasting House in London, both wearing earphones and fighting great washes of static which sounded as if the Atlantic waves were part of the broadcast. The interference cleared miraculously for a conversation immediately following between the British playwright-actor and his wife, Molly. She was in America, it was announced, because he couldn't be. Their stilted but crystal-clear conversation went something like this:

MOLLY: Hello, Emlyn. Are you there?
EMLYN: Yes, Molly. How are you?
MOLLY: I'm fine. How are things in London?
EMLYN: It's black here, Molly.
MOLLY: How are the boys?
EMLYN: Safe in the country, away from the bombing. How's the play?
MOLLY: Which play, Emlyn?
EMLYN: Oh—both.
MOLLY: Well, *The Corn Is Green*—with Miss Barrymore, you've just heard her on the wireless over your earphones, she's brilliant, smashing.
EMLYN: How's *Yesterday's Magic,* that terrible title they gave it in America?
MOLLY: Well, it's—(LONG PAUSE)—it's all right, Emlyn. It's playing.

The entire public heard this, Muni was convinced; nobody missed it. Slumped in his dressing room, Muni listened on his superheterodyne with the curved top and the cloth front (long before the days of transistors). This international broadcast declared publicly—not just to America but to the world—that his play was "all right," and he wasn't really in a class with the Barrymores! And his brave playwright was "over there" watching out for German bombers. Muni, "over here," felt as if somebody had kicked him not in the guts but in the groin.

Muni rushed into another film, one which would let him say something about the war effort. It was his way of fighting the forces of evil, in uniform, a gun in his hand. Producer Lester Cowan had purchased a *Cosmopolitan* magazine short story by C. S. Forester about a Norwegian patriot and underground resister. Irwin Shaw was hired to write the screenplay. Muni went into *Commandos Strike at Dawn* with passion and conviction amounting to near ferocity.

From mid-July until early September, 1942, the company shot the film in Victoria, British Columbia, a rugged coast that resembled Norway, but still 1,400 miles away from Hollywood and a continent's distance from New York, where Bella remained at Lucy's bedside.

The excellent cast included Anna Lee, Lillian Gish (her first picture in eleven years), Sir Cedric Hardwicke, Robert Coote, Rosemary DeCamp, Ray Collins, and Lloyd Bridges as a young soldier in one of his first film roles. Borrowed Canadian troops of four famous regiments (the Canadian Scottish, the Royal Rifles, the Sault Ste. Marie and Sudbury, and the Rocky Mountain Rangers) were all part of the film: authentic commandos staging a raid onto the rocky shore of Vancouver Island. Sometimes they were available; sometimes they were mysteriously absent. When they reappeared on location, they volunteered no information,

Muni dancing with Anna Lee in *Commandos Strike at Dawn*.

and everybody in the cast was instructed not to ask questions. John Farrow was simultaneously the director and a lieutenant commander of the Royal Canadian Navy. He never went to bed at night knowing whether or not he would have his soldiers for the next day's shooting. Muni was unusually patient.

In the film, Muni plays Eric Torensen, a shaggy, peace-loving villager. Unable to stand the Nazi savagery, he tells his neighbors, "Nobody is going to get victory as a gift. We will have to change over from the murdered to the murdering, we must learn to be gangsters, thugs, useful with the knife, dynamite, club and poison."

The picture ends, though Torensen is killed, on a note of hope: "For we wrestle not against flesh and blood but against principalities. Against powers, against the rulers of the darkness of this world, against spiritual wickedness in high places."

The lovely Anna Lee (now the wife of novelist Robert Nathan) reminisced warmly about the film, in which she played a young English girl in love with Torensen. John Farrow called her in and said, "Anna, we have a certain problem. Paul Muni doesn't like any kind of physical contact." Miss Lee thought this might be because Bella was always on the set, but on *Commandos* this wasn't true.

"It was very difficult, when we were playing a love scene, even across a restaurant table, not to touch him, to pat his arm," she remembers. "I literally held my hands behind my back or in my pockets."

But she admired his concentration, his dedication, and his passion about his work. Muni, in turn, had great admiration for the discipline and training of British actors. She had long repertory experience, and Muni could feel it. "Most American actors never get that kind of opportunity," he commented.

Maureen O'Sullivan, married to Farrow, was pregnant with Mia at the time. Farrow laughed when Miss Lee confessed her double-edged problem: Muni the misogynist, Farrow the fabled ladies' man—both on the same set!

Muni tried to explain, mostly to himself, his reluctance to film love scenes. "I am not a woman hater," he said. "I think they are far and away the most beautiful fifty percent of the universe. Love scenes can be very moving. But for myself, the invasion of privacy, the camera climbing into bed with me, is not something I want on film. I've never gotten over feeling awkward when called upon to do a lot of kissing. It's just that I'm—well—not sure of myself when trying to play a great lover. Casanova I'm not!"

Muni was wounded during the filming; he received a six-inch gash in his left arm while climbing through barbed-wire entanglements. When the strenuous shooting in Vancouver was completed in September, 1942, he returned briefly to Hollywood. Anna Lee recalls a startling switch during a postfilming publicity session. She and Muni were summoned to Columbia Pictures Studio at Gower and Sunset for stills, which were shot on a sound stage roof. Muni was in a helmet, wielding a revolver. Suddenly he tossed aside his battle gear and said, "These are love scenes, for God's sake. I'm supposed to be crazy about this girl. With a gun in my hand, it'll look as if I'm trying to kill her."

Then Muni seized Anna Lee and bent her backward as if he were Rudolph Valentino and she were Vilma Banky—and kissed her passionately on the mouth. His eyes were sparkling like a little boy's, and he suggested pose after pose, romping about while the startled cameraman clicked away.

"It may have been the real Muni coming out of his shell," Miss Lee says. "I'm certain he knew of John Farrow's warning to me that he never be touched. After about twenty minutes of somewhat torrid embraces, during which Muni was obviously enjoying his 'Valentino' act—*and* my poorly hidden shock at his sudden metamorphosis—he remarked with the mischievous gleam in his eye, 'The trouble with you Englishwomen is—you're so reserved!' He really was a dear man!"

Alas, none of those rooftop still photographs seems to have been saved in the publicity files.

Commandos Strike at Dawn did fairly good business and is still shown constantly on television, though badly gouged to make way for advertising. Muni would be appalled at the multiple commercials; *Late Show* watchers in the seventies seem to see more Fords than fjords go by.

Muni gave an understated and sincere performance which was admired by the critics. Bosley Crowther wrote in the New York *Times:* "It is clearly apparent that Mr. Muni had his heart and soul in the picture, and that its most affecting moments are largely due to him."

Before Muni returned to New York, he bought more California land, ten acres along the rolling hillsides and deserted dunes of Trancas beach, twenty miles north of Santa Monica. With most of the coastline blacked out (there had been a scare with a Japanese submarine spotted just off Santa Barbara), Muni was practically handed the land. "Someday," he said, "I'm going to build a tiny shack here, a wart of a house, where I can be a twenty-four-hour bum!" He paid cash for the land: $1,000. In 1973 not an inch

271

of it is available; if it were, the ten acres would cost almost $1,000,000.

Muni phoned Bella for reports of Lucy. Bella wept incoherently; it had been impossible for her to read any new plays; she hardly ate or slept. Muni returned to New York. But for what? Can a man retire at the age of forty-seven? To Muni that seemed immoral. Tortured when he was working, festering with impatience when he was not, Muni was constantly at war with himself.

Then his old friend John Golden phoned. "For years, dear Muni," he said, "I've wanted to have you back under my management. But I've never found the right play, the suitable play. So what would you think about a revival?"

"A revival never works," Muni said. "It's like drinking your own bath water. What do you want to revive, John, *Four Walls*?"

"No. Eleven years ago a lot of ten-year-olds who are twenty-one now never had the chance to see you do *Counsellor-at-Law*. Elmer Rice agrees it's exactly the right time to bring it back."

Muni was silent, thinking. Golden continued to sell.

"I've just brought back *Claudia* at half-price tickets and it's jamming the theater. *Counsellor-at-Law* will do twice as well."

"Sure"—Muni shrugged—"if you cut prices. But *Counsellor* is a big production: thirty people in the cast, six scene changes. You'll lose your shirt."

"I don't think we'll have to cut prices. The play is still fresh and vital, and I've got an instinct about this, Muni. I want to do this for the only sound reason I know for putting on any play, new or old."

"What's that?"

"Because it's damned good entertainment."

Muni paused. Bella was too busy to ask. He took a deep breath. "When do we start rehearsals?"

They began three weeks later with Elmer Rice again directing. To Muni it was a homecoming: to a director he respected, a producer he liked, and a role which was like putting on a comfortable pair of old shoes. And the Royale Theatre shared a stage-door alley with the Plymouth next door, which had been *Counsellor's* first Broadway home.

Many of the cast also came back, including Jennie Moscowitz as his mother, and even a part for weeping Clara Langsner, his wife in *We Americans*, his mother in *Four Walls*. Muni was equally pleased with new cast additions: Olive Deering as his adoring secretary, Joseph Pevney as Harry Becker, and Joan Wetmore as his wife. And he thought Ann Thomas was the very flower of Flatbush as the comic telephone operator. "Where did you get that authentic Brooklyn accent?" Muni asked her. "By listening," she answered. "Brooklynites aren't as confused about their *R*'s as most people think. They don't say 'goil' for girl. They say, 'She's a very modrin gurrl'—like that. But they definitely say 'modrin' for modern!"

"In the modrin theater," Muni told her, "you are my kind of gurrrl!"

Bella stayed at the hospital, constantly at her sister's side. She held Lucy's hand, looked into her once-beautiful face, now thin and pain-withered, and read poetry to her. Lucy's favorite verse was about a butterfly; Bella was reading it aloud when Lucy died on a November night in 1942.

Rehearsal was canceled the day of the funeral. Lucy was buried alongside her mother in Washington Cemetery. Their father, Morris Finkel, who might have been by Emma's side, lay beyond the gates of the cemetery in unholy ground designated for suicides.

Bella spent the rest of her life trying to recover from the shock of Lucy's death. She never fully succeeded. She began collecting butterflies: butterfly pins, butterfly paintings. And every time she saw a real butterfly fluttering across a field or a lawn she said, "Ah! Lucy has come to visit!"

The *Counsellor-at-Law* revival opened on November 24, 1942. Very little was changed from the original production except topical references: Babe Ruth became Joe DiMaggio; a sailing at the French Line pier was switched to a flight at LaGuardia Airport. The critics felt Muni had grown in stature as an actor in the eleven-year interval. His playing had more subtlety, more finesse, more restraint. Lewis Nichols covered the opening for the New York *Times* and wrote:

> A new generation of theatre-goers have seen either the play without the actor or the actor without the play; now they are together where quite properly they belong. . . . The evening, of course, is Mr. Muni's. With a soft voice and a loud roar, with quietness, gentleness and fierceness in turn, he dominates the role. . . . He is seven or eight Paul Munis, smooth and accurately setting forth as many phases as there are types crossing the threshold of the office. He *is* the *Counsellor-at-Law*, no exception being granted.

John Golden's prediction was right. Audiences thronged to the Royale. The revival run lasted the entire season and then went on a lengthy tour the following spring and summer. Golden billed it as "a performance I have never seen equaled in the theater since Richard Mansfield. Muni is our foremost actor in a great portrayal of an East-Side-Exquisite!"

Muni received a personal fan letter from Mayor Fiorello

LaGuardia. But his greatest thrill of the run was the backstage visit, just before Christmas, of First Lady Eleanor Roosevelt. Olive Deering and other actors huddled in the corridor to watch and listen. Mrs. Roosevelt, who had attended the matinee performance, stood in the doorway of Muni's dressing room. Muni, on his feet, looked at her with respect and near adoration. In that unmistakable, not-to-be-imitated voice, Mrs. Roosevelt said, "In Great Britain, they give their finest actors knighthoods. In Japan, deserving artists are designated as national treasures. Here we have nothing to give you but our applause and our affection and our gratitude. But if I had the power, Mr. Muni, you would be declared an American knight and one of our national treasures!"

Muni, speechless, could only mutter, "Thank you, Mrs. Roosevelt." After she left, he stared for a long time at the space she had occupied in the doorway, still taking measure of the great lady.

"*That*," Muni whispered, "is a *MENSCH!*"

"You mean," the stage manager asked, "that you think she wears the pants in the White House?"

"No!" Muni said indignantly. "That's not what it means! A *mensch* is a . . . a . . . a *MENSCH!* A courageous human being. An individual with dignity! And that lady, *boychick,* is a *MENSCH!*"

22

MUNI never wanted to know beforehand when celebrities were in the audience, particularly his acting peers. If he was aware that Charlie Chaplin or Laurence Olivier or John Gielgud was seated out front and he was onstage it was torture for him. So he issued an order to stage managers, cast, and company managers:

"Please don't tell me! Afterwards, fine. Lemme explain this with a story. There was this fella who had been through the great Johnstown Food—and he bragged about it every chance he got. Well, finally he died. And when he reached heaven, he asked St. Peter, 'Hey, is it all right if I tell people up here about what I did in the Johnstown Flood?' St. Peter looked at him and nodded his head and said, 'Help yourself. But just remember—NOAH will be in the audience!' "

Muni as Joseph Elsner in *A Song to Remember*.

Each night a taxicab was waiting for Muni on Forty-fifth Street. He would bundle up almost beyond recognition, avoiding autograph seekers, and catch a midnight train at Pennsylvania Station to Long Island. On the forty-five-minute ride, Muni would read the next day's New York *Times* and *PM*, a now-defunct intellectual tabloid he found fascinating. He carried a new playscript under his arm almost every night, brought it home to Bella like an offering; he wanted her to read it first. But the plays they studied seemed upstaged by the war, dramatically anemic alongside the headlines.

Occasionally Muni offered his services as a bus boy at the Stage Door Canteen, the American Theater Wing's down-one-flight, just-west-of-Broadway haven for servicemen. Alfred Lunt was usually there washing dishes, Brock Pemberton was emptying ashtrays. Lunt and Muni would joke with each other about how rarely they were recognized by the young soldiers, sailors, and marines. "Now, if Johnny Weissmuller washed dishes," Lunt commented, "there'd be a riot in the kitchen!"

Sol Lesser produced a film, *Stage Door Canteen*, directed by Frank Borzage. The cast included theater and motion-picture greats, alphabetically from Judith Anderson to Dame May Whitty. In a brief cameo, shot backstage at the Royale, Muni played not a real-life bus boy but a real-life actor named Paul Muni, wishing a fledgling actress good luck on her first theater audition. Shot against the pipes and radiators of an empty stage, his scene with young Cheryl Walker lasts a grand total of fifty-nine seconds. A highlight of the picture was the newcomer Lon McCallister in a few speeches from *Romeo and Juliet* with Katharine Cornell playing the balcony scene as she hands out oranges in a chow line.

In the spring of 1943, before *Counsellor-at-Law* left for its road tour, Muni appeared as the narrator of a stirring pageant at Madison Square Garden, *We Will Never Die*. Billy Rose and Ben Hecht formed a team to present this appeal for a state of Israel, still unborn except in the minds of dreamers, and to protest horrifying Nazi crimes of genocide against millions of Jews in Europe.

Moss Hart directed the pageant, with music composed by Kurt Weill and the fiery words of Ben Hecht. At the two Sunday performances 40,000 people jammed into the old Madison Square Garden, with 20,000 more outside listening over loudspeakers. In addition to Muni, the cast included Edward G. Robinson, Frank Sinatra, Ralph Bellamy, George Jessel, John Garfield, Stella and Luther Adler. At the climax of the pageant, fifty Orthodox rabbis recited Kaddish, the prayer for the dead, in unison. This moving and effective pageant was a prelude to *A Flag Is Born*, staged on Broadway three years later.

Counsellor toured the major cities of the East Coast during the unusually sultry spring of 1943. Max Siegel went along as company manager because Muni was on a percentage and needed somebody to tally the take. Siegel became ill in Boston, so Bella phoned Ted Thomas. Thomas flew to Boston for a reconciliation and to become company manager pro tem. Ted re-created for me Muni's personal Boston Tea Party:

"HOT, HOT, HOT! Boston humidity too! Wednesday matinee. SRO. No problem figuring statement when all the tickets are sold. Just add standing room hard stuff to capacity. Go backstage during middle of Act One with statement to show Munya figures and get his signature. He comes offstage fuming, furious, livid. What's the matter? He leads me to the wings and invites me to look out: the entire audience from orchestra to gallery is fanning themselves with programs. 'Bastards! Bitches! How can I act with that swish-swish going on?' I explain about the heat (no air conditioning then). I can't open any exit doors because of some construction work nearby. Doesn't satisfy him. 'It's hotter onstage than it is out there. I'll stop 'em—I'll stop them fanning programs if—' His cue comes, and he walks back onstage. I go out front to the box office, get his share, and take it to the bank. When I return, Muni's acting 'all out.' Talent, projection, empathy, and involvement are going to make the audience forget the heat and short-circuit the fanning programs. But in the middle of Act Two, the audience wins. Muni picks up a sheaf of papers from George Simon's desk, walks to the apron rim, sits down with his feet dangling into the orchestra pit, fashions the papers into an impro- vised wind maker, and fans himself in tempo with the audience programs. The curtain has to come down, Muni's pulled offstage. And the most pagan of all theatrical sins took place: the audience got its money back. Everybody apologized to everybody after it got a little cooler. And it never happened again."

A week after the tour ended, Muni became restless at Brookville and sold the Long Island house. "All I want is what I paid for it," Muni told the broker, who quickly wrote him a check for $25,000. Later Muni learned that the quick-grabbing broker sold the gatehouse alone for that amount.

Bella reluctantly accompanied him back to California. Muni's agent, M. C. Levee, and his wife, Mimi, rented them a large house in the Hancock Park area of Los Angeles, at the corner of June and Oakwood. Along with the house, they inherited a cook and a housekeeper, Isabel and Jess Colbert, who had been with the Levees for twenty years. The Colberts pampered the Munis. "Heaven," Bella said, "does not consist of angels playing harps. It's breakfast in bed and somebody to run the bath water."

Muni began to build his Wart on a bluff overlooking the deserted beach at Trancas. Bessie Thomashefsky moved to California about that time and held court in the living rooms of Hollywood friends.

"How come you left New York?" Muni asked La Thomashefsky. "I thought you loved it madly, that you swore you'd never leave it. What made you change your mind, Aunt Bessie?"

Muni, joking offstage with Luther Adler, during rehearsals of *We Will Never Die* **at Madison Square Garden. Adler writes: "Muni had moments of great warmth and charm —when he was young and indestructible."**

(Luther Adler Collection)

"Two very good reasons, Munya," she said. "In the first place, *absolutely everybody* has left New York. And in the second place, it's getting too damned crowded!"

Muni's more logical reason for returning to Hollywood was a call from Sidney Buchman, then Columbia Pictures' front-running producer-screenwriter. Muni admired him ever since his playwriting days and *This One Man*. Buchman, a handsome, gracious, and talented man, was one of the few people able to handle the head of the studio, the monolithic and often Neolithic Harry Cohn. Buchman knew of Muni's interest in a film biography of Beethoven. Well, they weren't going to film that, but something very close, a motion picture which would wed classical music to biographical storytelling: The Life of Chopin.

"I'm too old," Muni said. "The most exciting parts of Chopin's life are the romantic scenes with Madame George Sand."

"That's not what we want you to play," Buchman said. "There's a better part: Chopin's teacher, Joseph Elsner. The main influence in Chopin's life. You're perfect for it."

Buchman promised a screenplay as soon as possible. Muni went to work on his usual research. All he could find was that Elsner, besides being Chopin's mentor, had composed *Stabat Mater*. Muni compensated by reading everything available on Chopin and the history of the liberation of Poland.

The picture went through many modulations of title. It began as *The Song That Lived Forever*, lived briefly through several offkey mimeographings as *A Love of Madame Sand*, and ended up as *A Song to Remember*. Buchman adapted it from a story by Ernst Marischka, but it had long been contemplated at the studio. Frank Capra had talked about making it, had even worked on a screenplay himself. It took Buchman twelve years to get the project reactivated. Harry Cohn consistently soft-pedaled the idea, in concert with Jack Warner's deafening of the Beethoven saga across the hill in Burbank.

Charles Vidor, assigned as director of the picture, had constant feuds with Cohn. "When I die," he said, "I wish to be cremated and have my ashes thrown in Harry Cohn's face!"

Muni read the script, signed the contract for a great deal of money, and found himself in the untenable position of being a major star in a supporting role. It might have helped if Bella had been there to restrain his overripe performance. But Vidor, hearing rumors of her Svengali-like effect on her husband, banned Bella from the set.

Cornel Wilde attempted, as an actor and at the keyboard, to play Chopin. The unbilled and unseen hero of the sound track was José Iturbi, unable to take credit because he was under contract to MGM. As George Sand, Merle Oberon was dashingly handsome in male attire, even brandishing an unsmoked cigar. The Los Angeles *Times* critic, Philip K. Scheuer, on the set for the first day's shooting, remembers Miss Oberon's entrance when her fellow players saw her in tight trousers. Muni gave two short appreciative whistles.

"See what happens to pants," Muni observed admiringly, "when a woman wears them!"

Nina Foch was just beginning in films (she had only done one minor picture, *The Bride of the Vampire*) and remembers how Muni helped her in this, her first important film, though she was still an obscure Columbia contract player. Muni had met Nina's father, the famous Dutch symphonic conductor Dirk Foch, on one of his frequent transatlantic crossings. Muni called the nervous and distraught young actress into his trailer on the first day of shooting.

"How's your father?" Muni asked.

"He's fine, Mr. Muni," Nina answered, shaking and frightened, having hardly slept the previous night.

"Well, I want to talk to you. Since you've just started in this business, I have an important question to ask you: Do you want to be an actress or do you want to be a whore?"

"I-I-I want to be an actress, Mr. Muni."

"Well then, you have to work. You have to become good!"

And he went on to advise her to take regular leaves of absence from her seven-year studio contract to go work on the stage, to study, to grow. Remembering Muni's words, Miss Foch broke away courageously from the constricting life of a contract player and went back to Broadway. One of her best roles and a great advance in her dramatic career was, ironically, in the Chicago company of *The Respectful Prostitute*.

Miss Foch also recalls the difficult death scene in *A Song to Remember*. Muni was pleased to have his old friend Tony Gaudio as cinematographer, but the early elaborate Technicolor film required blaring hot lights. In the middle of a climactic shot, one of the set arcs sputtered and died. Muni was at the emotional peak of a scene, when the director called, "Cut!" In great fury, Muni shouted, "I can't turn this on and off like a faucet!"

"All the people on the set shook in their boots," Nina remembers. "But as the years passed, I discovered that's a very funny line. I'm indebted to Muni for it—because whenever it gets sticky on a set, I scream out loud in mock drama, 'I can't turn this on and off like a faucet!' and the whole set breaks up. Of course, strangers watching think I mean it, but the crew just laughs like hell."

The faucet poured too freely in Muni's overmeticulous, over-fussy performance in *A Song to Remember*. Harry Cohn was so unimpressed with the entire project that he didn't want to pay Muni any more salary when the filming ran four weeks over schedule. Instead, he offered him a percentage of the picture's gross. Muni grudgingly accepted and eventually made five times as much as he would have if he'd continued at his regular salary figure.

When the film was completed, Harry Cohn held up its release for a long time, still feeling classical music wasn't box office. When it was finally shown, Chopin music made the *Hit Parade*, millions of records were sold, and the composer became known in the hinterlands. All this helped to make the film financially successful, though it was historically and artistically suspect.

Not too many years later, Sidney Buchman was summarily dismissed from Columbia by Harry Cohn when the writer honorably refused to name names before the witch-hunting House Un-American Activities Committee; it was a colossal waste of one of Hollywood's most shining talents.

The film was kidded outrageously in many areas. At one point, the sick Chopin spits up blood onto the white piano keyboard. *The Harvard Lampoon* mercilessly called the picture KETCHUP ON THE KEYS.

Despite its financial bonanza, for Muni *A Song to Remember* was a film to forget.

Muni appeared on numerous wartime radio programs. Several times he recited Edna St. Vincent Millay's "Lidice," a tribute to the murdered village in Czechoslovakia. In the summer of 1944 he was driven to the Air Force base in Santa Ana, California, to appear on *Soldiers with Wings*, an entertainment program designed primarily for Air Force recruitment. The entire staff of the program was in uniform, including Major Eddie Dunstedter and his enlisted-man orchestra, director Ted Steele, and producer Freddie Brisson (later married to Rosalind Russell). Tom Adair (currently a celebrated lyricist-producer) was one of the enlisted-men scriptwriters and remembers Muni's trepidation about appearing in a comedy sketch. Just before they went on the air, Muni said, "My God, I'm as nervous as a bride!" But Muni was a more seasoned comedy performer than he believed, and the huge live audience of servicemen roared its approval. His leading lady in the sketch was swimming-star Esther Williams, whose husband, Ben Gage, was one of the cadets on the base. A few weeks later Muni ran into Fanny Brice (who had once called Muni "the greatest actor of our century").

"You've worked on the Metro lot with Esther Williams," Muni said. "Tell me, Fanny, do you think she has talent?"

"Talent?" the famous Funny Girl brooded. "Wet yes, dry no."

Muni visited innumerable military hospitals, including four in Texas. "Not being the popular type of entertainer," he noted, "I limit myself to personal conversations with the men. I'm not a stand-up comic like Bob Hope or a stand-up sex symbol like Carole Landis."

Muni felt his greatest contribution to the war effort would be to make a picture or find a play which would illustrate the universality of the human spirit, the dignity and decency of men everywhere; this, he believed fervently, could be his greatest weapon in fighting savagery. So when Sidney Buchman offered him *Counter-Attack*, Muni agreed to do it immediately after he completed *A Song to Remember*.

The screenplay by John Howard Lawson was based on a stage play by Janet and Philip Stevenson, which had been moderately successful in New York the previous year. It, in turn, was based on a contemporary wartime Soviet play, *Pobyeda* by Ilya Vershinin and Mikhail Ruderman. The film went through several title changes: *Counter-Attack* to *One Against Seven* (a far more apt description of the plot), then back to *Counter-Attack* again. Muni plays Alexei Kulkov, an uneducated Soviet paratrooper, holding seven Nazi prisoners at bay in a subterranean room beneath a German-held town. The confinement makes the action theatrical but not highly cinematic. Muni's performance is taut, likable, unmannered, and filled with Slavic clowning, which came naturally to him from *Black Fury* and his many antic roles in the Yiddish theater. Zoltan Korda directed and welcomed Bella to the set. When Muni's intensity grew too large for the camera, she stared him into restraint.

Muni asked for Tony Gaudio as cameraman, but he was unavailable for the assignment. "Tony knows how to climb inside my face," Muni said. But unlike matinee idols and most ladies of the screen, Muni never worried which side of his face was more photogenic. He had a slightly offbeat right ear, but that didn't faze him at all. "If they're going to judge my acting by whether my ears match, you don't want an actor, you want a soup tureen!"

But he was delighted that James Wong Howe, one of the best cinematographers in Hollywood, was assigned to *Counter-Attack*. Muni loved the story about Jimmy's opening a Chinese restaurant and used to kid him about it. The Chamber of Commerce sent out a dim-witted still photographer to shoot the façade of Howe's new establishment. The cameraman set up his tripod in the middle of Ventura Boulevard where he had to dodge traffic. Finally,

Howe walked out and said politely, "Excuse me. You're liable to get killed out here. So may I make a suggestion? If you use a longer-focus lens, you can get just as good a shot of my restaurant from the opposite curb." The photographer turned to Howe indignantly. "Listen, China boy—I'll take care of the pictures, you take care of the noodles!"

Muni's most difficult ·scene in *Counter-Attack* was his fight to stay awake and guard his prisoners after many days and nights without sleep. The trick was to act totally exhausted without putting an audience to sleep. Muni, with Korda's help, accomplished it with brilliant punctuations of tension and humor.

The general pretending to be a German enlisted man was played by an actual former Nazi officer, Harro Meller, who had never acted before. One night Meller was arrested for strutting along Hollywood Boulevard wearing storm-trooper boots. The casting may have been authentic, but Muni preferred working with more experienced actors; besides, the thought of the man's past made him shudder.

Marguerite Chapman, playing a Russian partisan, was the only woman in the cast. She and Muni weren't even introduced until the first camera setup began. ("Hell," she says, "later I did an entire picture with Marilyn Monroe, *Seven Year Itch*, and never met her!") Regarding Muni, she recalls: "I wasn't frightened. After all, I told myself he was a human being. A genius, sure. I had great awe of him, but I didn't let it get to me."

Muni and Marguerite Chapman in *Counter-Attack*.

(Marvin Paige Collection)

They broke the claustrophobic tension of the set with joking. "Bella was there to help him," Miss Chapman recalls, "but the other actors didn't resent it. I wish I'd had somebody like that on the set. As for Muni, I learned during *Counter-Attack* that very bright people can be very simple people, not as complex as we think they are. He was warm and hardworking and an inspiration to the rest of us."

She also remembers Harry Cohn always calling her Margaret.

"My name is Marguerite," she told him. "You spend all that money putting me under contract and spelling the letters of my name out on marquees. So at least pronounce it right, Uncle Harry."

"From now on," Cohn assured her, "I will always call you Marguerite, Margaret!"

Somebody asked Muni just how many actors there were in the Screen Actors Guild. He thought for a minute and then answered with mock gravity, "I'd say about one in every hundred."

The cast of this film proved, however, that good actors weren't a rarity in Hollywood's performing factories. Muni admired the work of Ludwig Donath, who was a vicious, snarling Hun in *Counter-Attack*, a switch for Donath, who had just played the lovable, waltzing Papa Jolson. A few blocks away at Armed Forces Radio Service, we enlisted Donath whenever we needed the strident voice of Adolf Hitler for a documentary. This wise, gentle, and peace-loving man was able to simulate a perfect voice double for the scourge of the century.

Bosley Crowther in the New York *Times* praised the philosophic maturity of the film and Muni's honest performance. But the timing of a picture's release is vital. During the first week in May, Truman, Churchill, and Stalin announced the end of the war in Europe and proclaimed May 8 as VE Day. Eight days later *Counter-Attack* opened at Loew's Criterion in New York. Suddenly it was a very stale piece of strudel.

Muni performed in a radio broadcast in the fall of 1945 for writer-director Arch Oboler, who has never forgotten his experience working with Muni. In my book *Off Mike*, I described Oboler as "a broadcasting great; one of radio's bad boys and good angels" and suggested that his name is really a verb which could be conjugated: *I obol; you obol; he, she, it oboles*.

In 1944 Oboler produced a weekly program, *Everything for the Boys*, starring Ronald Colman, sponsored by Auto-Lite every Tuesday night on NBC. (While still in uniform, I made some contributions to the overseas sections of the series.) For one of the Auto-Lite broadcasts, Oboler wrote a script, *This Living Book,* a parallel of the Old Testament with the life of a young American. The advertising agency and sponsor promptly turned it down as "too arty." Moral to writers: never throw anything away. The following year Oboler produced a sustaining series of twenty-six half hours on the Mutual Broadcasting System, *Arch Oboler's Plays.* For the final program, he dug out *This Living Book.* On a whim, he sent it to Muni. "Of course I'll do it," Muni replied. Muni's total salary: $21.

Muni was narrator of the program which included rich passages from the Bible; Muni read them like an Old Testament prophet. Gordon Jenkins wrote a stirring background score.

"I stood in the control room," Oboler recalls, "and I wept. That was not merely an actor out there in the studio; it was as if Moses were standing at the microphone. He was magnificent—ninety feet tall!"

Irony: after the broadcast on October 11, 1945, the advertising agency called Oboler and indignantly complained, "Why in hell didn't you give us that script for the Auto-Lite series?"

The end of hostilities in Europe inspired Muni to search for a dynamic way of dramatizing peace. He felt that Alfred Nobel was a biographical figure worth investigating: the drama of a man who made all his money inventing destructive dynamite, yet left his fortune to award prizes in the constructive arts of literature, science, and peacemaking. Could this dual nature be brought to life on the screen? And could he play it effectively? Muni began what was to become a four-year monomania about Nobel, a desire to illustrate the conflicting war and peace within every individual man.

Muni retreated to his newly built Wart in Trancas with a stack of books on Nobel. "I am a hermit by the sea," Muni said. The ocean was an inspiration to him. He lived on scrambled eggs and sour-cream salad and drove into town to be with Bella just once a week. Bella shrugged philosophically. "Regularly Muni has to run away. It's part of his nature, and I understand it. Argue with him about it and he runs faster and further."

During his retreat, Muni wrote notes to himself, trying to appraise his past and chart his future:

> Why would anybody ever want to become an actor? Tell your-self the truth. Is there some insufficiency in a person which

makes him want to be somebody else? Is he a driven, impulsive showoff? (*I* don't feel like one. Bragging makes my flesh crawl!) Yet! I am unhappy if I am not working. But why is it that when I *am* working, I want to RUN, GET OUT, CAST IT OFF! Perhaps some day I should play Freud. Then maybe I'll become Freudian enough to understand this crazy Munya. I know people think I'm *mishuga*. Why shouldn't they think that? *I* think I'm *mishuga*!

Do actors go through this kind of slave market of their bodies and minds and personalities for the money? For the fame? Hell, most actors spend so much money to show the world how successful they are they never have any left. How few are savvy enough to save or invest or have a wife who invests? The rest get caught in the marry-her-quick, divorce-her-quicker treadmill. Going from one wife to another is like having a different audience every night in the theater: somebody new to adore you. Actors, baseball players, ballerinas, and butterflies last a season and then are gone. One white hot moment or two and it's over. Maybe that's what makes it so fascinating and desirable and dangerous. You climb Mount Everest and how long do you stay up there? Nobody builds a house or opens a delicatessen on that highest peak. You stand there for a split second, plant your flag, and then, in order to breathe, you've got to come down again.

Muni found one book he thought could be the basis of a screenplay about Nobel: Herta E. Pauli's *Alfred Nobel: Dynamite King, Architect of Peace*. He personally purchased an option for the film rights. M. C. Levee, Muni's agent, took the book and a rough outline of the idea to every studio in town. They all turned the project down: the idea wasn't commercial, peace isn't interesting; and besides, they said, "Muni is no longer a box-office attraction."

"To hell with them," Muni told Levee. "I'll produce it myself!"

23

MUNI was unhappy when producers and studios besieged him with offers, but far more unhappy when they didn't. He wanted to work at his trade but felt that if a single frame of exposed film was not up to his full acting potential, then all the good work he had done previously would be forgotten, obliterated.

"If you want to be a great actor, you don't go in the movies,"

Muni as Tevya in *A Flag Is Born*.

Luther Adler once told him. "The industry doesn't encourage acting."

"And does the great American theater encourage it?" Muni protested. "Where in God's name do we find it, Luther—that shrine to art? That place an actor can act without feeling like an idiot or a piece of lox slapped at an audience by a producing fish peddler? Show me where a working craftsman can practice his profession and I'll race you there!"

Muni recalled one plan early in the forties when Cornelia Otis Skinner, Blanche Yurka, and others wrote and phoned him: would Muni become part of an American national theater company? He answered promptly: ABSOLUTELY. COUNT ME IN. He believed it was shameful that the American stage had no continuum, no plan, no enduring shape. Even the Yiddish theater, in its heyday, made more sense; a production didn't burn its scenery on the Jersey flats the day after it closed. In a hoped-for national theater actors could play multiple roles, neither trapped in a long run nor humiliated by a short one. Once they had learned to work together, they would not suddenly be set adrift after a closing to hunt desperately for a new family, a new working home. The dream: a permanent American ensemble of dedicated performers, a theater not built on Broadway's hit-or-miss quicksand.

"For a theater like that," Muni declared enthusiastically, "I'll do anything. Bits! Even a crossover in a beard!"

A committee of actors went to Washington to confront President Roosevelt. Cornelia Otis Skinner pleaded: "Mr. President, every country in Europe the size of Rhode Island has a national theater. Why not the United States?"

Roosevelt indicated his enthusiasm for the idea but pleaded that "I'm a little busy right now." He arranged for the committee to see the Vice President. The Honorable John Nance Garner listened attentively and told the group of petitioners, "I'm the wrong man to talk to. I've never seen a stage play in my entire life."

We can almost forgive Mr. Garner, since he coined a highly theatrical phrase to describe the "high office" he held: "The Vice Presidency," he said, "isn't worth a pitcher of warm spit!"

Roosevelt's ultimate Vice President was a piano player named Harry Truman. After Roosevelt's death, the committee tried to see the new President. He was too busy finishing the war in the Pacific. The committee gave up.

* * *

Early in 1946 Producer Charles R. Rogers sent Muni a screen-play of *Me and Satan*. The rights had been purchased for $60,000 from Harry Segall, the author of *Here Comes Mr. Jordan*. Muni turned it down. He wanted to concentrate on finding a workable screen approach to the Nobel material. "Besides," he told his agent, "fantasy hardly ever works. If, as George S. Kaufman said, satire is what closes Saturday night, fantasy is what closed *last* night."

Rogers was persistent. He hired screenwriter Roland Kibbee to collaborate with Harry Segall on an entirely new script. This version, called *Me and Mr. Satan*, had a lot more substance, and Muni was tempted. But again he said no. A third screenplay was prepared, this one titled *Angel on My Shoulder*. Muni and Bella read it. The Nobel project was shoved aside. Muni said yes.

(Gilbert Miller once advised us, "If there's an actor or actress you really want, remember—casting is a courting game. They want to be wanted. 'No' from an actor doesn't always mean 'ab-solutely no.' On one play I had twenty turndowns from the star I wanted. But finally she agreed on my twenty-first offer. It was Helen Hayes, and it became her most famous role, *Victoria Regina*. The number of no's you get doesn't matter; you only need one yes!")

Eddie Kagle in *Angel on My Shoulder* was Muni's twenty-first motion picture role. In the kingdom of Hollywood, where Bette Davis and Edward G. Robinson each made more than ninety films, this seemed like a princely few. In a way, Muni was going back to his start in pictures (discounting the early misses at Fox); the character of Kagle was not unlike the tough, lower-class hood of *Scarface*. And although he had sworn never to play another gangster, he considered this a chance to comment on that character, to caricature it slightly, to kid it. He was beginning all over again, and within the framework of one film, he could illustrate and illuminate the progress of a man from beast to a rational, sensitive human being. Perhaps the picture contained more fact than fantasy.

Claude Rains, who had been a heavenly Mr. Jordan, is a hellish Nick in this film, Mephistopheles in the flesh. He makes a deal in hell with Kagle, a murdered gangster, to fuse his spirit with a lookalike back on earth, a judge whose humanity is causing a shortage of customers in the nether regions. Muni becomes the judge, in love with a beautiful young lady played by Anne Baxter. The major set of the film was a huge papier-mâché hell. The picture was made at General Service Studio; the cast called it General Service Inferno.

Muni had respect for Rains as an actor and found Anne Baxter one of the best young actresses around. He was fascinated to learn that she was architect Frank Lloyd Wright's granddaughter. (Muni was always lured to the minds of the world, the senior creators, the good gray intellectuals.)

"I was very much impressed with the idea of working with the great Muni," Miss Baxter recalls. "I'd seen all of his pictures, and he did things as a performer that I envied. I would love to do on film what he has done; but very few actresses ever get that opportunity. Oh, Bette Davis shaved her head once and became Queen Elizabeth, but somehow the multiple characterizations, the intricate makeups, the long preparation for a role aren't often permitted the female of the species."

Muni allowed himself a romantic scene or two in *Angel on My Shoulder* for the first time. "He seemed to be a very lonely man," Miss Baxter remembers, "a boy-child really. And Bella was Mama. Bella discreetly left the set during the slightly torrid scene. I found Muni a fascinating, attractive man. But he was essentially *sous-cloche*—a spirit enclosed under glass, under a glass bell jar."

"Under a Bella jar," I added.

Archie Mayo was the director. "He was primarily a canner," Miss Baxter notes. "Do the take, do the cover shot, reverse angle, close-up, and get it in the can, like sardines!"

Mayo leaped to gags and funny business; Muni disapproved. "It was like a Big Boy hamburger directing a fine gourmet Wiener schnitzel," Miss Baxter says.

Somehow the picture seemed jinxed. Muni caught the flu. Then Anne Baxter was out sick. An assistant director died in the course of the shooting. The bad luck climaxed on the final day of shooting. Anne Baxter remembers that her mother picked up a newspaper in San Francisco and read *MURDER ON SOUND STAGE*, then saw a huge picture of Anne beneath it. The Los Angeles *Times* reported it this way:

FILM WORKER KILLED:
MUNI HIS HOST

Hollywood, April 4—

A real-life slaying today climaxed a party celebrating conclusion of a gangster movie.

Police found Edward W. Gray, 31, studio electrician, dying beneath a film set backdrop.

Detective Sgt. Stanley W. Johnson said Gray, who succumbed in a hospital, was murdered. Attendants said his skull was fractured, his jaw broken and his palate pierced.

As is often the case on conclusion of filming a picture, the cast and crew of "Angel on My Shoulder" joined in a party at the General Service Studio. Paul Muni, gangster star of the movie, was host.

Muni's last scene was laid in Hell, with Claude Rains playing the Devil. A bar had been set up on the sound stage and more than a score of tables had been arranged in front of the huge "Stairway into Hell" set.

The electrician was found beneath a 60-foot seascape backdrop.

Muni and Miss Baxter were both called to a coroner's inquest. The tabloids continued to print black headlines; any scandal in the movie colony was joyful compost for the gossip garden.

Muni was dismayed. All publicity rankled him. But to be at the center of a scandal was a sickening experience. No one suggested that he was actually implicated in the man's death. But it *was* Muni's party. And he found himself compelled to perform, in real life, a role which he would never have considered in a play or film—not even the murderer or the attorney for the defense! (Perhaps every courtroom needed a resident playwright.)

Muni had never even met Gray. The body wasn't found until three hours after everybody left the set. During the inquest, it was learned that Gray was an uninvited guest, not even a member of the crew of *Angel on My Shoulder*. Evidently he had drunk too much at the party and had climbed up onto the catwalk above the set to sleep it off (a favorite retreat of hiding studio workers). The nine-man jury found his death the result of an accidental fall.

Anne Baxter recalls the inquest: "I automatically felt guilty just being on a witness stand." Muni began his testimony with the statement that he could be of very little help, having left the party early, which he didn't frankly consider had been a "joyful celebration."

"Without seeming facetious," he told the jury, "if that was a 'joyful party,' I wonder what a dull one would be. All the people were exhausted. It was supposed to be a little shindig to show goodwill, but we were all dog-tired."

"Did you see any drinking?" asked Deputy District Attorney S. Ernest Roll.

"Oh, yes," Muni replied. "Miss Baxter had a glass of milk, Joan Blair had Coke, I had one scotch and soda, and Mrs. Muni had a sherry. Others went to the bar. I don't know what they were drinking." Part of the testimony of the caterer's bartender indicated that three cases of bourbon, a case of scotch, and four cases of beer were consumed.

290

The attorney for Donna Gray, the electrician's widow, was Sam Yorty, later mayor of Los Angeles.

The practice of celebrating the finish of a film was officially stopped at most studios. Muni, who rarely attended parties and practically never played host, swore he would never go near a party again—his own or anybody else's

Angel on My Shoulder did not lose money for United Artists, but it did not make any either. The critics dismissed it as adequate hokum and praised Claude Rains' performance over Muni's. The picture was quickly forgotten. Muni, in despair, was certain he had been tossed onto the junk heap of his profession.

The Munis bought a rambling house at 525 Louise Avenue in Encino "designed for retirement." On May 8, 1946, Bella and Muni celebrated their twenty-fifth wedding anniversary by staying home. They had a full bottle of Concord grape wine. They stared at each other and silently drank a toast to their quarter century together.

"I don't know how you stand me," Muni told Bella. "I'm impossible to live with."

"More impossible to live without," Bella said quietly.

Why did they never have children? Many friends and many relatives have varying speculations.

"I've got a baby," Bella said. "One of the biggest and most famous babies in the world. Munya."

"Bella never wanted children," Muni once told his brother Joseph.

"Muni never wanted children," Bella told Ruth Jacoves. But did Bella worry about her own possible inadequacies as a mother? Did she feel children would be competition for the star who claimed he never wanted the spotlight, who had a monomania for privacy and a passion for undisturbed work? Or did Bella worry about children of her own going through what *she* had experienced as a child? Or was she superstitious that there was a curse on her family?

In the summer of 1946 Muni accepted the leading role in a pageant-*cum*-message, *A Flag Is Born*, written by Ben Hecht, scheduled to open at the Alvin Theatre in New York early in September. The official producer was listed as the American League for a Free Palestine, and Jules J. Leventhal was named in the program as "in charge of production." But Ben Hecht ran the show, pouring his passion, his conviction, and his anger into this frankly propagandistic stage work. The motto of the sponsoring organization was "It is 1776 in Palestine." Hecht assembled the best theater brains he could find: Kurt Weill wrote the background score; Luther Adler was hired to direct. Nobody was to get a salary beyond the required Equity minimum, so they went for the top cast they could find. They considered Edward G. Robinson and Elizabeth Bergner, among others.

"Let's go for the bucks," Luther Adler told Hecht. "The biggest draw. How about Muni to play Tevya? And for the wife, Zelda, the best we can find. Let's get Celia Adler, my oldest sister." Ben wondered who could play the impassioned boy. "I've got a great kid for you," Adler suggested. "He's damn good. No 'name,' but can he act! Kid called Brando."

Robert Downing, currently a drama critic in Denver but then one of New York's leading production stage managers, remembers how rumors swept Broadway. Everybody was asking Muni, "Why would you want that crazy kid Brando in your cast? He's trouble. He keeps white mice and lets them run across the stage. He's a nut. Why in God's name do you want him in the company?"

Muni had a simple answer: "He's the best we have."

The company rehearsed in the bare studio just above Al & Dick's Restaurant on West Fifty-fourth Street. At first Brando mumbled his role, and it began to concern Muni. Adler went to Hecht and told him of Muni's worry. To smooth things out, perhaps they should get rid of Brando and hire some standard good actor.

"Good actors bore me," Hecht said. "I'm curious to know what this guy Brando is going to do. He intrigues me."

As a ploy during rehearsal, Adler took Brando aside and asked him to cut loose in his scenes with Muni, *really* let go, overact.

"He was fantastic," Adler recalls. "Marlon uncorked, and Muni suddenly thought he had a tiger by the tail. Brando was incredible: flash, violence, electricity. My sister Celia has owl eyes, but when she opens them in astonishment, they're like saucers. When Brando started to perform, Celia's eyes became soup bowls. Muni turned scarlet; his lips began to tremble; then he got a kind of foolish grin of approval on his face."

Bella often spoke of Muni's admiration for this twenty-two-year-old actor. Years later, Brando returned the compliment. "I admire and respect very few actors," he said. "Spencer Tracy is the kind of actor I like to watch . . . Tracy, Paul Muni, Cary Grant. They know what they're doing. You can learn from them."

Observing Brando during rehearsals of *A Flag Is Born*, Muni commented, "How the hell can an actor like that come from Omaha, Nebraska?" Brando told Muni he had studied with Stella Adler and with Katherine Dunham. "That," Muni said, "accounts for the fact that you move like a panther." Asked about his experience, Brando modestly refrained from mentioning that he had played three Broadway roles, including the kid in *I Remember Mama*, the lead in *Truckline Cafe*, and Marchbanks in *Candida*.

"My first role," Brando told Muni, "was a giraffe in *Bobino* across the street at the Adelphi Theatre in 1944."

"Ahhh," Muni murmured. "That's a difficult character part. It's a makeup I've never tried!"

In *A Flag Is Born* Muni took the symbolic generalization of a wandering, dispossessed Jew and gave it a heartbeat, a poignancy, an inspirational individuality. The rehearsals, for Muni, seemed like forty years in a wilderness of soul-searching. "Why should this play be different from any other play for Munya?" Adler speculated. "He went through his usual torture. He set hurdles for himself to jump, higher and higher with the passing years. But always he cleared them beautifully—with ease and grace and talent."

For this tribute to Jewish survival, Muni demanded painters, artists from Palestine, if possible, to draw the face, the portrait of this universal Jew. "I want to know what this fellow *looks* like. Hebrew painters can draw him—and I'll copy the makeup exactly."

Adler laughs, recalling Muni's self-flagellation.

"A Palestinian painter he wanted yet—to tell this great Master of Makeup how to be a Jew. My God, in his acting career, he'd played every kind of Jew that ever existed!"

But Adler was bright enough not to agree instantaneously with Muni. "If you yessed him, he'd get suspicious. He thought you were conning him. So to Muni you always gave a Yiddish yes-no."

On his own, without the demanded paintings, Muni experimented with beards, finally narrowing down the field to one vaguely resembling his beard from *We Americans*. Muni's climactic "tablecloth speech" of the play was an address to the assembled diplomats of the world, but he had an actor's block about it. During their final week of rehearsals onstage at the Alvin Theatre, Muni brought a chair down to the footlights and spent half an hour telling his director why he couldn't possibly learn it. "Peroration on peroration on peroration," Adler describes it, all about retention, memory, concentration, and Muni's total inability to master the speech in time to open.

"Muni," Luther said slowly, "I know you're speaking the truth. That's not a speech, it's a whole play, and if you want to blame

Ben Hecht, all right—but I know where you come from and where *I* come from, so I'll say one word to you: *souffleur*. You want prompters? You can have as many as you like. You're at a lectern. We'll have a script there with letters the size of your hand; nobody's gonna walk out if you turn a page. But in addition: there'll be a prompter inside the lectern. Also one stage right. One stage left. One in your beard. And one in your *tochus!*"

Opening night, Muni was letter-perfect. The prompters, not quite as ubiquitous as Adler had promised, closed their books. Muni received a standing ovation. Brooks Atkinson, less than fond of the Hecht playscript, gave the star a rave:

> Mr. Muni is giving one of the great performances of his career. He is a man of mind and understanding. Without sentimentality, without heroics, he is speaking . . . with an actor's eloquence. Mr. Muni's greatest gifts are now on view at the Alvin and they give this playgoer a feeling of profound gratitude.

In the final scene, Brando as the young Jew fashions a battle flag from the dead Tevya's prayer shawl, then joins the underground fighters; it was a moving and memorable moment. From the play's profits, $275,000 went to the cause of a newborn Israel. The converted ocean liner which became the flagship of the Israeli Navy was named the SS *Ben Hecht*.

Muni particularly treasured one of the huge stack of opening night telegrams:

> PAUL MUNI
> ALVIN THEATRE WEST 52 ST
> DEAR MUNI WHEN I AM OLD I WILL REMEMBER YOU
> AND TONIGHT AS ONE OF THE THINGS THAT MADE
> THE WORLD SEEM A LITTLE WONDERFUL
>> BEN HECHT

Later, when asked to describe Muni, Hecht commented, "He's the only actor I know who has a lyric mind!"

Muni remained with the play at the Alvin for the season. Luther Adler replaced him as Tevya; then Jacob Ben-Ami played it for the lengthy road tour. It was an emotional and financial success.

When Elia Kazan asked Luther Adler to recommend a young actor for the film version of *Gentleman's Agreement*, Adler suggested Marlon Brando. John Garfield had a previous commitment or tax problems or both, and Kazan offered Brando the part. "No," Brando responded, "I want to stay with the play. I want to keep doing what I'm doing. These people are persecuted, and they need help!" Ben Hecht wired Brando:

DEAR MARLON. THE JEWS HAVE BEEN PERSECUTED FOR 3000 YEARS. THEY LIKE IT. TAKE THE JOB.

BEN HECHT

Garfield finally cleared both conflicts and played the part. Brando was not to explode onto the screen until *A Streetcar Named Desire* five years later.

In Hollywood's appalling Red hunt, Muni was not directly attacked or named, but he was alarmed to see so many writers, directors, and actors he admired riding in the tumbrils down Sunset Boulevard. If anyone wishes to chart the death throes of the major motion-picture studios, the cancer began in 1947, when they succumbed to the virus of reaction. Witch-hunting and suppression of free thought were personified by the House Un-American Activities Committee and the dawn of the Age of McCarthyism. In many ways the studios began their own downfall; they were scrapping themselves.

Bella and Muni stayed in Encino for just three weeks. "You could feel the forces of repression like a plague of locusts," Bella recalled. "Nobody had to build the set of a ghost town to film a Western. Everybody seemed to have gunned himself down. We turned around and came back to New York, taking the first attractive offer that came along."

It was for a summer tour of *Counsellor-at-Law*. Muni had never played summer stock, and he welcomed the opportunity, particularly because it involved an imaginative young director, Marc Daniels. (He was to become a close friend of the Munis' for the rest of their lives.) It was a festive cast, including Annie Thomashefsky as Mama Simon, Vivian Vance, Fredd Wayne, Sidney Lumet, Pat Harrington, Sr., Adele Longmire, and Joseph Weisenfreund's step-daughter, Deloris Hudson. Muni had a good time. The tour included only two stops: Marblehead, Massachusetts, and Princeton, New Jersey. The playhouses were not the bucolic *Babes in Arms*-type barns, but the high school in Marblehead and the traditional McCarter Theatre in Princeton. Both places were so packed that standees perched on the windowsills. A return engagement was scheduled in Marblehead to meet the demand for tickets. Muni insisted that the cast split all the receipts, with the lowest-paid player getting the highest percentage of the cut. Vivian Vance, later Lucy's sidekick on the celebrated TV series, *I Love Lucy*, is rumored to have had an adoring crush on Muni, onstage and off.

Muni once explained to me his theory of backstage romances. A new company, assembling for the first time, was a natural crucible of emotional attraction: a lot of handsome people thrown together into a tight working situation would inevitably prove to be a hotbed of bedding down. In a summer company the atmosphere was even more conducive, not unlike a summer cruise: men in white ducks always seemed to be heading toward pretty girls in white shoes. Muni's theory originated with an old stage doorman who recommended the "Five Day Test."

"The first day of a rehearsal, everybody in a company falls in love with somebody else," the old doorman observed. "Boys fall in love with girls; girls fall in love with boys; boys fall in love with boys. The oldest character man in the company always falls for the prettiest ingenue. If you're lucky, sometimes it works the other way around, and the young ones fall for the old ones. This happens to anybody who still has his eyesight and a few glands left. But take my advice, kid. Always wait five days. At the end of that time, if you still want it *then* do something about it. But you usually don't."

Muni found that to be true in almost every instance. After five days, most initial crushes disintegrate into indifference.

Whether Vivian Vance's summer adoration of Muni was for five days or forever she intends to recount in a book of her own she is writing. I can't wait.

The sellout success of *Counsellor-at-Law* was proof of Muni's box-office draw. Bella was baffled by the blindness of the motion-picture studios. Down the street so-called blockbuster movies were playing to empty houses. But at the Marblehead High School auditorium people were lining up around the block to get a glimpse of Muni in a play fifteen years old.

On the final night of the summer-stock adventure the cast gave Muni a silver platter, with all their signatures inscribed on it. (Opening and closing night gifts are part of the generous backstage tradition of the theater. Bella gave that plate to Marc Daniels after Muni's death; she gave me the silver cigarette box the Playwrights Company had presented Muni after *Key Largo:* it is a collector's item, containing the engraved signatures of Maxwell Anderson, Robert Sherwood, S. N. Behrman, Elmer Rice, company manager Victor Samrock, and attorney John Wharton—it sits proudly on the shelf of my theater library in Malibu.)

In the fall of 1947 Warner Brothers produced a movie of *Key Largo*. Muni was not even considered. He was too old for McCloud (called Frank in the film instead of King McCloud), so Humphrey Bogart played it. He was too young for the old father, D'Alcala (renamed James Temple), so Lionel Barrymore played it. He was too distinguished from the aura of Pasteur and Zola to play another gangster (now called Rocco instead of Murillo), so Edward G. Robinson played it. These were easy rationalizations. The truth of the matter is that Warner Brothers and every other major studio considered Muni "box-office poison." As far as the film business was concerned, Muni was sent out to pasture like an aging useless horse for six interminable years.

24

MUNI was determined to realize the film project based on the life of Alfred Nobel, even if he had to produce it, direct it, act in it, edit it, and go around the country with film cans under his arm and show it in high schools and barns. He had another inspiration. Why not a co-star? And why not the immortal Swede herself—Greta Garbo? Certainly there must have been a "mystery woman" in Nobel's life. It would be poetic justice doing a film with the "I-want-to-be-alone" star, since he himself had once been called the "Male Garbo." Problem: all research indicated that Nobel, a bachelor all his days, had an explosive antipathy to the female sex. There was a hint of a romance in the Herta Pauli book, but was it enough? On the banquet table of literature and history, was it kosher to serve up a totally fictitious woman behind the scenes? No. Penetrating research would surely uncover that missing heroine! When he found her, then he would approach Garbo.

In August, 1947, a new contract was drawn up extending Muni's option on the Pauli book until May 14, 1948. The original agreement was dated May 14, 1945: Muni had been struggling to lick the Nobel story for almost three years. Back in California, he found a kindred spirit in the literary colony which had sprung up in Santa Monica Canyon: a German writer named Alfred

Neumann (not to be confused with the film composer-conductor). Neumann wrote three treatments and two screenplays of Nobel in German, with Muni haltingly translating page by page.

"If there was a difficult way to do something," one of Muni's friends remarked, "he'd find it. I think Muni had his wisdom teeth extracted through his rear end."

Muni was an unwilling producer. He wanted to get out from under the responsibility of creating anything but the character he would ultimately portray on the screen. But where could he find a producer of size? He kidded with Neumann about being his own *macher*. "I find myself," he complained, "fitting that old definition of a producer: a man who knows what he wants but can't spell it!"

Muni and Neumann believed they had a valid premise:

> This is the story of "the loneliest millionaire in the world", a strange and complex being who planned for peace while he grew rich from death and destruction. The very contradiction of his deeds has given rise to all manner of speculation as to the motives that inspired him.
>
> In this film, no conscious attempt will be made to aggrandize or distort the character of Nobel. He will be presented in the light of what is known of the man today against the background of the world in which he lived—a background of war and peace so analagous to our present world situation that its outcome is only now being mirrored in tomorrow's newspaper.

Muni felt he needed an experienced screenwriter, so he took the stack of material to Ben Hecht, who studied it, wallowed in it, and turned it down. "I don't think there's a picture in it," he told Muni. "It's a story that can't be licked. Sorry, old friend, but I won't touch it."

Stubbornly, Muni packed up the material, and he and Bella returned to New York again in January, 1948. Muni arranged to get all the Nobel research and their embryonic screen treatments to playwright Robert E. Sherwood.

"It's dramatic without being a drama," Sherwood reported. "It's very difficult to bring to life a man who was so lonely, frustrated, distrustful, and unhappy. Where do you begin with a character so self-effacing, so colorless? Alas, Mr. Muni, the creator of dynamite was no dynamic personality."

Muni was persistent. The contradictions of Nobel's life: the creator-destroyer, the self-tortured genius, the wanderer—all resembled the unsolved and unexplained battleground of Muni himself.

In desperation, Muni phoned Joseph Rothman, an experienced

filmmaker, then involved with industrial motion pictures in New York and a veteran of the business since the age of twelve. He was also Ruth Rothman Finkel's brother, which made him "almost a member of the family." Muni asked him to dinner, proposed that they work as partners on the project, explaining his multiple approaches in the past, frankly admitting his failures, and indicating he had only four months left on his option of the Herta Pauli book.

"Muni and Bella were overboard with the idea of doing something to promote world peace," Rothman recalls, "and felt this would be it."

Rothman read through the mass of material and reported back. "Muni, I hate to disappoint you, but I think this is the most ponderous hunk of crap I've ever read."

Such candor didn't make Muni angry. He only really trusted people who disagreed with him. Humbly, Muni asked Rothman's advice and counsel. Rothman convinced him that to bring to life the kind of film Muni envisioned would require not arm's-length library research, but actually going to Stockholm and to Paris, to dig into authentic on-the-spot color and perhaps penetrate the mystery of Nobel's personal life.

Detailed incorporation papers were drawn up for a Paul Muni Production Company with Muni and Rothman as partners. Muni, careful almost to the point of cowardice, never signed the papers. Meanwhile, Rothman began discussions with executives of MGM and Columbia International to determine their interest in the distribution of a film on Nobel starring Muni. Both companies had large sums of frozen funds in almost every country in Europe which could be used for financing the production abroad. Both studios were interested, depending on the final script and cast.

MGM and Columbia executives were, however, a bit hesitant about Muni's ability to carry the film at the box office and discussed a possible co-star. When Rothman mentioned Muni's suggestion of Garbo, the studios assured him that he had a deal if that casting

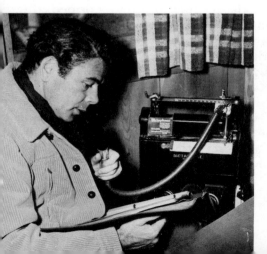

Muni dictating in his four-year search for the story behind Alfred Nobel.

were consummated. For obvious reasons, Rothman didn't tell that to Muni.

For almost the entire months of February and March, 1948, they met daily at Rothman's apartment to discuss and analyze the multiple scripts, treatments, notes, and individual scenes Muni had amassed in the course of three years. A secretary stood by to take copious notes on the salvage operation. During their pre-Swedish exploration Muni was searching for the big scenes, the moments, the "plums." They hit upon one approach which fascinated them. Following Nobel's death, his living relatives had contested his famous will; Muni and Rothman thought they might do the entire picture as a court-trial, with each witness telling a different version of Nobel.

Muni also met with Naboth Hedin, head of the American-Swedish News Exchange in New York, who arranged for full cooperation by the Nobel Foundation. Passage was booked on the Swedish liner *Gripsholm* on March 27, 1948. But something troubled Muni. Every time he'd ask Hedin about details of Nobel's private life the Swedish representative would grow silent. "I don't know," he'd say. "Perhaps nobody knows."

Ten days before they were scheduled to sail, Rothman received a call in the middle of the night from California. Abem Finkel, Bella's brother, had been found dead, a possible suicide. Rothman had the unhappy task of conveying the tragic news to Bella; he was convinced she would be flying back to California immediately and it would be the end of their trip to Sweden.

Rothman found it almost impossible to get the words out. The phone conversation to Bella at two in the morning seemed like some grotesque echo chamber across the few blocks of Manhattan to their hotel. He could sense the fumbled reach for the telephone, the darkness in the room, the fatalistic numbness of Bella's silence.

Abem had been having a difficult time. After his estrangement from Bella and Muni and his divorce from Ruth, he had fathered a son (also named Abem), but the writing jobs had stopped, the studio doors had closed. But at last he had a contract in his pocket for another screenplay assignment. Like the father he had hardly known, he was a great wine drinker, and he celebrated the event by having a bottle of expensive wine at every one of his favorite Hollywood restaurants. Chelios, the *maître d'* at the Hollywood Brown Derby, remembered serving him and later told Ruth that Abem, though alone, had never seemed happier. But later that night Abem drove down the coast to Tijuana. He bought pills there he could get without a prescription. He had his picture taken by a street photographer alongside a striped burro. Ted

Thomas, who was summoned to the border to claim the body, found the photograph; it showed an antic Abem, pointing to the donkey and to himself as if to say, "Just look at the two jackasses!"

Abem had evidently stumbled back to the American side of the border. In a lonely men's room, he swallowed all the pills. The border police found him sprawled on the floor dead.

As compassionately as possible, Rothman told Bella. She did not react. Rothman realized the gravity of the moment: Bella was the last of the family—Morris, Emma, Lucy, Abem, Bella—a theater dynasty, all so handsome, so talented, such promise, such hope. Now there was only Bella.

After a long pause, speaking in a voice which seemed half like an old, old lady and half like a lost little girl, Bella said simply, "Don't tell Muni."

"Can I help make arrangements for you to get back to California?" Rothman asked. "You'll want to go to the funeral."

"No," Bella said quietly. "It would upset Muni if I was away from him now. We're going on the trip to Sweden. Nothing must spoil it. This is the most important picture in Muni's career."

They sailed, as scheduled, on the *Gripsholm*. Muni didn't find out about Abem until many months later.

With the tunnel vision of her mind focused completely on Muni's career, Bella did not weep for her brother. Almost a year later, her normal philosophic calm was broken by delayed tears. She would wake up in the middle of the night sobbing helplessly. Her doctor suggested a psychoanalyst. She dismissed the idea: it was an expensive self-indulgence, a theatrical performance by a *ham-faddo* for an audience of one. But finally she put on the face of a Beverly Hills countess and decided to try it—once. Half-way through the first session, the psychoanalyst looked at the outwardly unperturbed Bella as if she were the standard, rich, bored Hollywood wife. "I think, Mrs. Muni," he said, "that you seem to be a perfectly adjusted and rational human being. Perhaps you have had no tragedy in your life." Bella stared at him with disbelief and then she "let him have it." She told him about her mother and father, about Lucy and Abem. It was her first and last visit. "The psychoanalyst," Bella told us wryly, "took immediately to his couch!"

On the ten-day crossing to Göteborg, Muni and Rothman worked every day to chart fresh approaches to the Nobel script, seeking to lighten what both felt, but did not say out loud, was basically unentertaining material. They hoped to find more magic ingredients on Nobel's home ground in Sweden.

"This trip was intended to be a combination of business *and* pleasure," Rothman states. "But getting Muni to relax and enjoy himself was next to impossible, particularly when he was so immersed in a project. His passion for work was compounded by a look in his eyes: this is my last big chance!"

Muni showed his usual reticence toward reporters and photographers when the boat docked at Göteborg, but he seemed inwardly pleased at the massive press turnout. Most of the newspapermen accompanied the Muni party on the three-and-a-half-hour train trip from Göteborg to Stockholm. Some of them spoke a lilting broken English; others conveyed their questions through a translator. Muni and Rothman, in turn, asked the reporters questions about Nobel. There were awkward pauses, an unspoken air of innuendo and skepticism. When Rothman asked about romance in Nobel's life, one reporter smirked, a girl giggled.

Muni learned very little about Nobel from the reporters. Though Nobel prizes had brought international fame to the Swedes, nobody in Sweden seemed to have much admiration or feeling for the man himself. Perhaps, Muni rationalized, this was because the scientist-philanthropist had lived and worked in Sweden only a few years of his early life. Most of his time had been spent in Russia, Germany, France, and Italy. And possibly many of his fellow countrymen resented his forsaking Sweden to become an International. The air of mystery was a dramatic plus, Muni argued. But Muni began to have qualms when one reporter asked, "Why don't you do a picture about Sir Basil Zaharoff, Mr. Muni? He, at least, was a self-admitted Merchant of Death!"

They were ceremoniously bowed in at the Grand Hotel in Stockholm and provided with the services of a young man from the Swedish Cultural Society who acted as escort and interpreter. And they were cordially welcomed to the Nobel Foundation headquarters by its executive director, Ragnar Sohlman.

Muni was impressed with the magnificent structure and the air of solemn dignity. Sohlman, a charming octogenarian, led Muni to Nobel's own desk, opened a drawer, and handed him a pair of eyeglasses which had been worn by Nobel. Muni took them carefully and put them on. As they touched the bridge of his nose, Muni transformed himself into Nobel as an old man, not unlike one of his characters from the great days of the Yiddish theater. Everybody laughed. But Muni remembered in later years that it was the first and last time he ever actually played Nobel.

They visited one of Nobel's only living relatives, a half-deaf niece in her eighties, who served them tea and repeated one phrase in Swedish again and again. The translation—"He was my uncle, he was my uncle"—was their total enlightenment from this tedious teatime visit.

Sohlman escorted the Munis and Rothman to the site of the

original Nobel laboratory-factory, now an empty lot. The lab had been blown up eighty years before. Sohlman did not mention it, but Muni and Rothman found out: Nobel had accidentally set off a blast which killed his younger brother; as a result of the explosion, Nobel had been driven out of Stockholm. Certainly this was dramatic; but could a viable screenplay be fashioned from a latter-day Cain?

Muni began to wonder if the biography he had optioned was more fiction than history. Still, the prospect of making a film in Sweden had alluring facets. Production salaries and other costs were roughly a third of what a film would cost to make in Hollywood or New York. The film critics and film directors of Sweden provided an interesting but unproductive evening with Muni as guest of honor. The ritual and protocol of a Swedish formal dinner seemed incredible; it started at seven and ended at midnight. The eight-course dinner climaxed at midnight with an additional "snack," a huge raw chopped steak, difficult for the normal American stomach to handle. Ingmar Bergman, then comparatively unknown on the international scene, was present—but seemed cool and distant. Why did he never offer Muni a film? And why hadn't the Swedish film industry itself ever contemplated a Nobel project, before Muni's visit, or since?

When they left Sweden on April 20, 1948, they had gathered nothing but undocumented rumors and no facts beyond what they could have discovered at the New York Public Library. They traveled via Malmö and Copenhagen and then to Paris by train. To cross postwar Germany required a military visa, and it was a profoundly depressing journey for Muni. He never left his compartment. Though the tracks had all been replaced, most stations and buildings along the route were twisted metal and rubble.

The lights had not yet been turned back on in Paris (July 14, 1948, was the first night Paris again became the City of Light; I was there.) And though food rationing was still in effect, the Hotel George V was bubbling with Gallic festivity. Stella Adler was also a guest, and she made Muni laugh. Whenever they met, they would suddenly, as if by conditioned reflex, put on an entire show, even in a hotel lobby, not for anybody else, but for themselves: playing a variety of Yiddish theater types—*shmendricks* and old grandmothers combing their mustaches and hard-of-hearing "old farts" trying to dance a waltz.

Muni was persuaded, against his will, to hold a press conference for French film critics and reporters. It was a mistake. One newspaperman declared loudly that "no respectable Frenchman ever attends American movies; the puerile quality of anything filmed in America is beneath French intelligence and taste." When they emerged from the conference, Muni and Bella found that not merely one, but *two* of the major film theaters on the Champs-Élysées were showing Walt Disney's *Bambi*, with lines of waiting customers around each block.

Rothman and Muni hoped to find in Paris some further trace of a woman in Nobel's life. Herta Pauli's book recounted a love affair between the Dynamite King and Bertha von Suttner. But Paris, where the "romance" was supposed to have taken place, proved a literary dead end. Nobel, they found, had hired Bertha as a secretary for one short week; then she fled to marry another man. Everybody they encountered seemed to be hiding something, to be covering up; even scholars with documented historical data were hesitant to talk, shy to disclose any further facts of Nobel's private life.

Muni had a growing suspicion, never proved, that Alfred Nobel was homosexual. He had never married, and facts uncovered in Paris indicated Nobel was constantly hiring handsome young assistants and had built houses for them. In the more permissive cinema world of the 1970's this might have been acceptable subject matter. In 1948 it was impossible. For Muni, this suspicion cast a shadow over a project born and developed with cherished idealism, but now dead from unproved rumor. How could he ever play the man?

Further travels to Italy and the South of France seemed like a protracted bout of running away. Joseph Rothman saved multiple books and manuscripts and endless memos of their fruitless adventure, including his unsigned contract. Muni tore up or burned every shred of material he had accumulated. Four years of work went up in flames and blew away in the coastal sea breeze off the alien coast of Italy.

Back in New York in the fall of 1948, Muni, who had threatened to go into permanent retirement, performed his first live television drama on *Philco Playhouse*. NBC bragged that there was a potential audience of a million. It seemed staggering then to reach that many viewers in one Sunday night hour. Muni chose a carefully cut version of *Counsellor-at-Law*. Fred Coe was producer-director, with Neva Patterson playing the devoted secretary. *Life* magazine, saluting the "maturity of television," wrote: "The Philco productions are elaborate and expensive, costing an average of $17,000 each to produce!" Twenty-five years later a comparable program would cost at least twenty-five times as much.

Muni was fascinated but fearful of the immediacy of live television, a wedding of film techniques and theater, with hidden cameras poking through picture frames and actresses making quick changes behind the sets. The new medium was further described by *Life*: "Despite TV's frequent crudity—and huge expense compared with its trembling sister, radio—it has an 'it's-happening-right-there-while-I'm-watching' quality—that makes the whole world of entertainment, journalism and politics want to get into the act." Live drama on television has, unfortunately, disappeared. News events starring performers on the political stage still shatter us with the adrenalin impact of first nights. But actors who only act are no longer so lucky.

Bella and Muni decided to stay in New York. He wanted to perform in more television dramas and went on a search for appropriate material. Neva Patterson remembers Muni's racking headaches during the *Philco* experience and his extreme nervousness, which somehow miraculously disappeared the moment the camera's little red light flashed on. "Never worry," Bella the worrier told the even more worried Fred Coe. "Munya's a firehorse. Sound the bell and he'll be there!"

Muni's headaches were undoubtedly caused by a recurring ambivalence in his feeling about his work. He was torn between two desires: on one hand, a drive for perfection, which he sometimes vaguely approached through the mechanics of retakes in the film medium; on the other hand, his stage-bred instinct of "Now! They're watching me now. It's all happening for the first time!" More than anything, the firehorse wanted to race to fires.

Marc Daniels came to Muni with a suggestion for a live TV version of Sidney Howard's *They Knew What They Wanted*. Muni read it and agreed. "If they want me, I'll do it," he said. Daniels went to the producing executives of *Ford Theatre*. Sure, they said, it's a famous play, and sure, it would be great to have Paul Muni as its star—but it's essentially a story about a mail-order bride who has a baby with a man who's not her husband. Daniels protested that the play had deeper philosophic depths, but the golden age of television drama included golden fences of presumed morality; *Ford Theatre* turned it down.

Muni's old friend John Golden phoned. "I am a one-man committee dedicated to bringing the great Muni back to Broadway. Is there any play you've wanted to do but just haven't gotten around to? Name the play and name the date, and we'll start rehearsals."

"I've always steered clear of Shakespeare," Muni answered. "But maybe about five years from now, if I study every day and I get some help, I just might be able to play Shylock in *Merchant of Venice*. And I'll be just the right age. Actually it should take a whole lifetime and I'm not sure how much of one I have left.

But give me five years to bone up on the part, and we can set the date right now; five years from tonight."

"You may be the right age by then, Muni," Golden noted, "but I'll be well past eighty. I may not be able to see you or hear you. How about something we could start next week?"

"What about reviving *They Knew What They Wanted*?" Muni suggested.

"It's a deal," Golden said. "We don't even have to shake hands. Take my telephone word for it. Start learning the part!"

They Knew What They Wanted had been presented first in New York by the Theatre Guild in 1924, twenty-five years before, and a glow of perfection lingered in the critics' memories about the Pulitzer Prize production, which starred Richard Bennett, Pauline Lord, and Glenn Anders. (At the other end of the time spectrum, Frank Loesser transformed the play in 1956 into his remarkable "Project Three"—his third Broadway musical and his code name for it during its preparation; it became the near-operatic *The Most Happy Fella*.)

Muni tried to get Golden to hire Marc Daniels as the director, but Daniels was tied up in television commitments. Muni was pleased with the cast: Carol Stone, Edward Andrews, Henry Jones, and Charles Kennedy from the original Theatre Guild cast. But Muni lacked proper respect for the director, Robert Perry, who had effectively directed Miss Stone in *Dark of the Moon*.

My fellow Ohio Stater Eileen Heckart (later to win an Academy Award) was Carol Stone's understudy. She remembers the director who brooded in the front row of the Music Box Theatre during rehearsals, making vague suggestions which Muni never seemed to "hear."

"I was seated in the back of the theater, in Row S with Bella," Heckie recalls. "Bella leaned over and whispered softly to me, 'I wish Muni wouldn't wear those carpet slippers.' At which Muni, on stage, roared, 'What did you say, Bella?' "

In January and early February, 1949, the company played in Wilmington, Philadelphia, and then Boston. The reviews were good, though the critics felt the drama seemed dated and that Muni was "too Italian." Muni himself was unhappy. What did the play say for the world of 1949? What did it contribute to the thinking of the moment? His restlessness was compounded by the fact that a masterpiece was trying out simultaneously in Philadelphia: Arthur Miller's *Death of a Salesman*.

Max Wilk remembers traveling to Philadelphia in January of 1949 with his father. "We saw the Miller play at the Locust Theatre in the afternoon and were absolutely shattered. (Try seeing that play sitting next to your father sometime.) Then we had dinner

306

at Frankie Bradley's and went over to the Forrest to see Muni. Afterwards we visited with him and told him how great the Miller play was. When we left, I vividly recall Jake saying, 'Instead of that period piece Muni is in, he should be playing the lead in the Miller play.' How's that for my father's theatrical astuteness?"

Anyone who thinks a star automatically hogs billing, credit, and the exclusive attention of the press should read a wire (now part of the Muni Collection in Lincoln Center). In Muni's own painstaking printing, the copy of the February 2, 1949, telegram from Boston reads:

MR. JOHN GOLDEN
246 W. 44TH STR.
NEW YORK N.Y.
WOULD APPRECIATE IT IF YOU WOULD GIVE CAROL STONE MORE
IMPORTANT BILLING. SHE VERY RICHLY DESERVES IT. BEST WISHES
FOR YOUR GOOD HEALTH.

MUNI & BELLA

They Knew What They Wanted, with more prominent billing for Miss Stone, opened at the Music Box in New York on February 16, 1949. It was a pallid evening in the theater. Six nights before, *Death of a Salesman* had opened right next door at the Morosco. Arthur Miller's play rocked the town, while the Sidney Howard play seemed like a musty museum piece in contrast, mostly because *Salesman* was a new, free-theater form. Muni wished he could switch stages.

The critics declared the revival a mistake. Atkinson in the *Times* labeled it an unhappy choice for Muni and felt the production was unable to blot out the memory of the original. Other critics castigated Muni for his overelaborate performance. In *Lies Like Truth*, Harold Clurman blames the sixty-one-performance near fiasco on the fact that Muni had virtually directed himself. Clurman's valid point was that every actor, no matter how skillful and painstaking, needs the dispassionate eye of a director he trusts.

Broadway was disappointed. Muni, who claimed not to have read a single review, knew what was wrong: his audience was not responding, not "playing tennis" with him.

The revival died quietly the first week in April, 1949. On Easter Sunday, Muni starred in an hour-long Passover radio play, *This Year Israel*, on a coast-to-coast CBS network for United Jewish Appeal. It was a curiously muted performance, as if he were saying to his audience, "I'm no longer a major star. Why the hell are you listening to me?"

H. M. Tennant planned a midsummer opening of *Death of a*

Salesman in London, in association with the Arts Council of Great Britain. When Elia Kazan and Arthur Miller offered Muni the role of Willy Loman in London, he grabbed it. Muni studied the play, felt it was "one of the best, if not the best play I've ever read," but did not go see Lee J. Cobb perform in New York, feeling he should create the part from the ground up. And he pledged to himself he would listen to his director.

Bella and Muni sailed on the *Queen Mary* for London late in June. Muni worked with Kazan on the role the entire trip across. Rehearsals began at the St. James Theatre on July 2. Binkie Beaumont, head of the Tennant office, was the reigning producer of London (he had eight other shows playing simultaneously in the West End). Beaumont rented the old Nell Gwynn house in Chelsea for Bella and Muni, but Muni was rarely there; he holed up in his dressing room at the theater, with his Dictaphone his constant companion. It was a difficult, exhausting role. Muni refused an invitation to go to the U.S. ambassador's Fourth of July party on the embassy lawn. "I'm not Paul Muni," he said. "I'm Willy Loman, and I don't think Willy would have been invited." Bella was never fond of the Nell Gwynn house. "It smells of cabbage," she complained.

Jo Mielziner came to London to duplicate exactly his famous set for the play. Early in rehearsals the cast moved to their own theater and were able to rehearse right in the set, that necessary luxury so often denied American actors. The Phoenix in Charing Cross Road seemed an appropriate theater to Muni. "Perhaps," he told Bella, "I, too, am rising from the ashes."

Half the cast was brought from America, under a special dispensation from British Actors' Equity, since the play itself was so American. Kevin McCarthy and Frank Maxwell played the two sons, Katherine Alexander was Linda, Bessie Love (an American already resident in London) was the woman in Boston. Ralph Theadore as Charley was later replaced, owing to illness, by that giant of an actor Finlay Currie.

Though it was mid-July, Muni was always cold. He came to rehearsals bundled in multiple mufflers. He was eager to "do justice to the play"; to Muni, Willy Loman seemed to be the part he had been looking for all his life. Muni's films had been successful in England, but he had never appeared on the London stage in English; the half-remembered adventure with Maurice Schwartz, the Yiddish Art Theatre, the moved bench—all seemed a lifetime ago. Had it really happened to somebody else?

The epic role of Willy Loman was played in New York by Lee Cobb with size, with bluster and braggadocio. Muni approached the role from the opposite direction. He was more the "little man"

Arthur Miller originally conceived. The showoff side of Loman was conspicuously missing in Muni's performance, but the interior man emerged with shattering poignancy.

Rehearsals were strenuous, often painful. Kazan attempted to re-create all the effective moments of the New York production. Often he worked through Bella in trying to reach Muni. Katherine Alexander proved to be another problem; she had never played a character role, never before been anything on a stage but Katherine Alexander. "She was faced," Eric Johns of *Stage* noted, "with the problem of blotting out her own personality and emerging as Linda Loman." It was difficult for Kazan to convince her even to use a gray wig. Before he sailed for America, Kazan had to put her on her honor to draw in every wrinkle of the final agreed-on makeup. Muni, always so eager to submerge Muni, could never fathom the thinking of such a performer.

Frank Maxwell, who played Happy with five different stars as Willy Loman, still shakes his head in wonder at the emotion Muni brought to the role. One line, in Muni's interpretation, seemed to synthesize the entire play:

WILLY: You know, Charley, you're the only friend I've got.

"Nobody's ever read that the way Muni did," Maxwell recalls. "Willy suddenly realizes that the guy next door whom he's really loathed all his life is the only person in the world who's his friend. Well, as Muni did it, it was an incredible moment in the theater. I had to make an entrance right after that line, happy, joyful, full of good spirits. So I forced myself not to watch the stage, or I'd break into tears. No matter how many times I heard it, I always bawled."

Twenty-six days of rehearsals seemed too short a period for Muni to crawl inside a part almost as long as Hamlet. No out-of-town tryout, no warmup in the provinces had been scheduled. Muni pleaded for more time. (He always pleaded for more time; if producers listened to him, he would have kept plays forever in rehearsal!) Previews were unheard of in London and unlawful by British Equity rules. Several audience-invited dress rehearsals were planned, and Muni found them helpful, sensing a communion with an audience.

But for Muni, the opening night, July 28, 1949, was a nightmare. He fluffed several times and was convinced he had destroyed the entire play. Nervously, he fell back on an overdetailed performance. Even then, the audience gave the play and Muni's performance fifteen curtain calls. Muni gracefully waved away the audience clamor for a curtain speech.

(Photo by Angus McBean)

The London production of *Death of a Salesman*. Left to right: Kevin McCarthy, Sam Main, Paul Muni, Frank Maxwell.

Gadge Kazan and Arthur Miller convinced the party-shunning Muni to come to the opening-night celebration at Binkie Beaumont's elegant Georgian house. Bella was amazed when Muni agreed to go. He entered the party, still playing Loman, hunched over, with a heavy scarf around his neck. Beaumont set Muni on a thronelike chair in the far corner of the room. That evening all the elite, the royalty of the British theater, lined up to pay court to Muni. Laurence Olivier was there with Vivien Leigh (then starring in the West End in *A Streetcar Named Desire*). John Gielgud congratulated Muni, as did Ralph Richardson, John Clements, and Noel Coward. All of them declared how wonderful Muni was. "Oh, no, no!" he protested. "Terrible. I was terrible!"

That night Noel Coward told Muni a secret about one of Beatrice Lillie's classic comedy bits, in which she plays an elegant grande dame who lifts her skirts and roller-skates offstage; she had been inspired by the legend of Muni as a roller-skating old man in the Yiddish theater. "No legend," Muni noted. "It really happened. Oh. Advise Lady Peel always to carry a skate key!"

The London reviews for *Death of a Salesman* were excellent. Kazan and Miller sailed the next day for America, admittedly disappointed in Muni's opening-night performance. If they had waited a week, they would have seen Muni grow in strength in the role as he simplified, cutting away all extraneous *shtick*, becoming eloquent as this universal father.

Kevin McCarthy, in an interview with Michael Gerlach, states

310

that at first he found Muni's acting too rich, too filled with detail. But after the traumatic opening night, Muni began to polish and perfect. "Then," McCarthy says, "I was spellbound, filled with admiration for Muni's discipline as, night after night, he tightened and refined his performance. Finally it came out clean and strong!"

"To Paul Muni," Arthur Miller said later, "acting was not just a career, but an obsession. Despite enormous success on Broadway and in Hollywood, he threw himself into each role with a sense of dedication that can only be explained one way: he was pursued by a fear of failure."

Bob Lee recalls a conversation in Santa Barbara many years afterward about the London production of *Death of a Salesman*:

BELLA: Arthur Miller said Muni's feet never quite touched the floor.
MUNI: I never quite touched the audience either!

It wasn't true—just another of Muni's exercises in incessant self-deprecation.

When his six-month London contract was complete, Muni withdrew from the cast. They could have played longer, but Muni was ill and required elaborate oral surgery. Beaumont contemplated approaching Fredric March and Florence Eldridge, but abandoned the idea and closed the play in January, 1950. March eventually did the motion picture, with Kevin McCarthy playing Biff as a result of the London production.

"This is the last play I'll ever do," Muni declared. "I'll never appear in front of the public again."

London was cold and wet; Muni insisted that Bella travel to the States aboard the *Île de France* with the other returning Americans. "Why should you stay here and have toothaches with me?" Muni said. Frank Maxwell recalls Bella's lonely crossing. He and Hiram Sherman (returning from his London run in *Brigadoon*) tried to cheer her up. Her only other comfort was a full pound jar of caviar dead center of her table in the dining salon at every meal, including breakfast.

After the completion of his oral surgery in London, Muni spent a month alone in Switzerland, trying to rest. He found it impossible. "It's a beautiful place," he wrote Bella. "But not for an actor. If I were a mountain or a cuckoo clock or a chocolate bar, I guess I'd like it here. But a performer, even if he's retired, has to see a stage sometimes—even from the audience side. Here you get seven matinees a week of the Matterhorn. I can't stand it. I'm coming home."

(Photo by Manuelli)

Muni with Vittorio Manunta in _Stranger on the Prowl_.

25

MUNI was certain that the _Queen Mary_ took longer crossing the Atlantic than Columbus did. When he reached New York, he decided to fly to California, where Bella had gone to reopen their house in Encino. Muni stopped being afraid of flying the day he learned that the "fortune-teller" who predicted he would die in a plane crash had fallen off a ladder to her death in her own kitchen.

A few days after Muni's return to California a surprise for Bella arrived at the pier in San Pedro: an elegant new automobile Muni had purchased in London. The Bentley was an expensive contrast with their usual Dodges and Buicks. Bella christened it "the Duchess."

A long famine began for Muni as an actor in 1950. Bella thought it was a sacrilege, a waste. "He's only a kid of fifty-five," she said. "My God, in the Yiddish theater, stars still played _juveniles_ at fifty-five!" But where were the parts? Where were the offers? Where were the plays and the films? Had all the writers been silenced? Were all the daring producers hiding their heads in the sand at Malibu?

"I'm not completely retired," Muni said, contradicting the flat finality of his London declaration. "I'm _semi_retired. That means:

312

still breathing. And we'll hope for a miracle. The perfect play. I don't have to appear in it. Maybe I'll produce it. Maybe I'll direct it. Maybe I'll do both. If it runs, fine; if it doesn't run, fine. All I care about is that I myself can like it and get excited about it."

Muni barricaded himself in a study filled with dictionaries, tape recorders, record players, piles of office supplies waiting to be used. He edited and snipped together voices of famous men he admired: Roosevelt, Churchill, Robert Oppenheimer. Muni had a radio in every room of the house, and he would walk around, turning them on and forgetting to turn them off, so that a different station would be blaring cacophonously from each room. Bella would follow him around the house turning them off. Muni wrote notes to himself and left them around the floor where he could be reminded of what they said by stepping on them. Usually they contained nothing more urgent than "Watch Edward R. Murrow on Channel 2 at 7 P.M."

A black-and-white television set was enthroned at the end of the Encino living room. Muni liked Murrow but would talk back to other commentators and newscasters and occasionally to a Senator. "You're crazy as a bedbug," he'd shout. Bella thought Muni sounded so convincing that she expected the guy on the TV screen to turn suddenly and say, "Shut up already, Munya!"

Were any good motion pictures still being made? Five or six a year, Muni was told.

"That many?" He laughed. "Out of three hundred? Listen, if a man set out deliberately to make lousy pictures and put something terrible, something bad in every one—even with a plan like that, he couldn't help making five or six good ones out of three hundred—by mistake!"

But Muni admired some of the pictures coming out of postwar Italy, particularly Vittorio de Sica's *The Bicycle Thief*. In spring of 1952, when an offer arrived for Muni to star in a "picture of the streets" to be shot in Italy, he agreed to do it. Nobody had offered him a part in a film for six years, and he was bone-tired from resting.

Producers Bernard Vorhaus and John Weber put together a combined Italian-American company to make two versions of a film, originally called *Encounter*, one for American, one for Italian release. The title was changed to *Embarkation at Midnight* and was released in Italy as such: *Imbarco a Mezzanotte*.

The picture, which eventually had a sparse and unfulfilled showing in America as *Stranger on the Prowl*, was written by Ben Barzman and directed by Joseph Losey on the streets of Leghorn and Pisa and at the nearby Tirrenia studios. Muni and Bella were not unhappy they had made the long ocean trip. "We are refugees in reverse," Bella commented. Muni admired Losey as a director and felt the screenplay, though basically merely a manhunt, had overtones of *I Am a Fugitive* and an unspoken plea against injustice.

Muni plays a vagrant, a derelict, hungry and unshaved, prowling the bombed-out dock fronts of Leghorn, attempting to peddle his revolver to raise money for illegal passage on a departing ship. He steals some food and accidentally suffocates a woman in a dairy shop. Escaping from the police, he is joined by a skinny Italian boy who has stolen a bottle of milk. The relationship between the two fugitives has warmth and dimension; the authentic Italian background gives it some of the flavor Muni admired in *The Bicycle Thief*. Joking with the cast, Muni began calling the picture "The Milk-Bottle Thief."

Vittorio Manunta as the waif Giacomo shows a genuine adoration for Muni as the nameless character, "The Man," who in turn grows from hostility and suspicion of the fatherless boy to bewildered affection. As in *We Are Not Alone,* there is the silent look (as much Muni himself as the characters he was playing?) which says, "This is the lost child I myself was. This is the son I never had."

Joan Lorring (happily now returning to acting) has an effective if abbreviated role as a housemaid who hides the two fugitives. The film, unfortunately, ends in melodrama: a rooftop chase and plunge to death reminiscent of the Bill Sykes finish of *Oliver Twist.*

The tragedy of the picture came in its censorship, not by moralistic bluenoses, but by political assassins. Roy Brewer, the rabid Red hunter and boss of the International Alliance of Theatrical Stage Employees, ordered all the projectionists in his union to refuse to show the picture. He denounced the producers, director, and screenwriter of *Stranger on the Prowl* as subversives. Although a United Artists release had been promised, co-producer Vorhaus invested his own family inheritance to complete the film and lost it all. Muni was indignant and horrified.

In the book *Losey on Losey,* Director Joseph Losey says, "It was the first European picture made by Americans to be a casualty of the blacklist. It never appeared in its original form, all of the people who were in any way implicated in the witch-hunt had their names taken off the credits, and the picture disappeared." The credits emerged as: "Produced by Noel Calef [read Vorhaus-Weber], Directed by Andrea Forzano [i.e., Joseph Losey], Screenplay by Andrea Forzano [read Ben Barzman]."

When the picture was finally shown in November, 1953, more

314

than a year after it was shot, the New York *Times* pleaded for more Muni: "His absence is to be deplored. *Stranger on the Prowl* proves, if nothing else, that the screen could use his services more often."

The film shows up with startling regularity in the more enlightened seventies in the dark spaces of the night on minor TV channels, sliced into ribbons, still with the same disguised credits. But there are moments when the screen seems twice incandescent; the man, the actor, cannot be buried or forgotten.

Muni and Bella returned to their hideout in Encino. "Munya is Heebie and I am Jeebie," Bella reported. "And this house is full of the Heebie-Jeebies. Can Múnya retire? He says every day, 'Absolutely!' Me, I've got only one comment: *Ossir*. Can the sun stop shining?"

When the sun blazed too hot and the temperature topped 100° in the San Fernando Valley, Muni switched hiding places and drove the Duchess down to his seaside Wart in Trancas.

He made one brief television appearance in June, 1953, in an off-season, underpublicized hour-long drama on *Ford Theatre* on NBC: *The People vs. Johnson.* Muni returned to his favorite acting role, an attorney, this time defending a truck driver played by Rex Reason. It was not a notable hour and was quickly forgotten.

Early in the fall of 1953, the enterprising Michael Ellis and James Russo, conducting a stock theater in Syracuse, New York, phoned Bella and inquired about Muni's availability for a pre-Broadway tryout of an R. C. Sherriff play, *Home at Seven.* They had presented an amazing lineup of stars for previous productions in this out-of-the-mainstream theater company. "How did you get all those actors?" a rival producer inquired. "A very simple formula," Ellis answered. "We *asked* them."

Bella advised the producers to mail the script to Encino special delivery. Muni and Bella read the play as soon as it arrived. *Home at Seven* was a mild mystery-suspense drama, but the role of the confused English bank clerk appealed to Muni. (It had been played in London three years before by Ralph Richardson.) When Muni agreed to do it, the Syracuse papers trumpeted the opening as the first tryout for a Broadway play in twenty-four years—since the lusher days of old when Syracuse was a major way-stop. This event, plus the great star attraction of Muni, was certain to do sellout business.

Muni flew to New York; Bella followed by train. Michael Ellis remembers meeting Muni at La Guardia Airport, then driving him into town to the Meurice Hotel, a favorite of many British actors, where a reservation had been made for Muni. He signed the register, then the desk clerk said haughtily, "May we have a bank reference please, Mr. Muni?" Ellis was embarrassed, but Muni waved him aside, carefully wrote down the names of eight banks, then turned on his heels, walked out, and went to live at the Warwick Hotel.

Herbert Ratner directed two weeks of rehearsals in New York. The supporting cast was good. Muni was particularly enchanted with a new young actress, the beautiful, bubbling Betsy Palmer, who was later to play in the film *The Last Angry Man* with him.

When the play opened in Syracuse, nobody came. The Astor Theatre, with the exception of a few stragglers, was empty. Muni was baffled; he had not seen this happen since the days in London when the Kid Twist gang threw rocks at his father's Whitechapel theater stoop. Bella was equally concerned; certainly Muni had not lost that much of his draw. The producers, who had run a successful series of plays at a bargain price of $3 top, investigated. At first there was silence wherever they inquired. Then they uncovered the fact that Syracuse residents had received threatening phone calls, ordering theatergoers to stay away from the Astor, and the mails had been flooded with unsigned letters accusing the producers of hiring actors who were Communists or who belonged to Communist-front organizations. Muni, who never joined anything beyond required unions, was not accused by name, but many of the other peformers who had appeared at the Astor that summer and fall were smeared with one devastating (and completely inaccurate and unjustified) stroke.

Lawrence Johnson, organizer of the Veterans Action Committee of Syracuse Supermarkets, and John Dungey of the Syracuse chapter of the American Legion were the head witch-hunters. Their vicious publication, *Spotlight,* was causing as much trouble as *Red Channels*. Both were apostles of antisubversion, especially anything or anybody daring to make an appearance in their sacred Syracuse. Senator Joseph McCarthy was their messiah and savior.

The play closed. The theater closed. "How do you fight these maniacs?" Muni protested. "You sit here and try to figure out what to do—and all you end up with is a *shrieking silence.*"

(Muni was not vindictive enough to gain comfort from any man's death; it was cold solace when he learned that Lawrence Johnson died, alone and discredited, in the Town and Country Motel in New York during the John Henry Faulk trial in 1962.)

Paul Muni, actor, made no public appearances whatsoever during the entire calendar year of 1954.

(From the Collection of Jerome Lawrence)

Painting of *Inherit the Wind* by Staats Cotsworth.

26

THE "Texas Tornado"—as friends affectionately and accurately called Margo Jones—ran a remarkable theater-in-the-round on the Fair Grounds in the city of Dallas, Texas. She had an incredibly optimistic policy: she presented only new plays.

We met her after every major producer on Broadway had turned down our play, *Inherit the Wind*. Harold Freedman, the Buddha of Brandt and Brandt and the dean of play agents, had given up. Next, we had taken the play to a famous Hollywood agent, thinking there might be a film in it. The agent personally returned the play to me at my beach house, held the script at arm's length as if it smelled bad, pointed toward the fireplace, and said, "Toss it in there, light a match to it, and *burn it!*"

We didn't burn it, but we put the play away in our files and tried to forget it. Then one day, while Bob Lee and I were typing on my patio, working on a new play, a distinguished-looking gentleman with prematurely white hair and a charming thick Southern accent wandered along the beach, stopped, squinted at us, and asked, "You writers?" We nodded. "You playwrights by any chance?" We nodded again. "My name's Tad Adoue," he said. "I'm Margo Jones' general manager—and she's lookin' for new plays. You got anything?"

I raced into the house, dug out a play (not *Inherit the Wind*), and gave it to him. The next day he sauntered by again, returning the script. "I don't like this play much," he drawled. "You got anything else?"

"No!" I said. "Now get lost."

"What about *Inherit the Wind*?" Bob suggested.

I shrugged, went to the files, and gave Tad Adoue a copy, convinced it would be the last we'd ever hear of it. Without telling us, Tad read the play that afternoon and immediately airmailed it to Margo in Dallas. "I double-dog dare you to produce this," Tad scrawled on an accompanying note. Two days later Margo was on the phone to Harold Freedman in New York inquiring about the rights.

"You don't want to do this play, Margo," Freedman told her, doing the hard sell in his commanding telephone whisper. "They'd crucify you down there in the Bible Belt."

"Exactly why I want to do it," Margo said. (That lady had more guts than any human being I've ever known.)

A few days later we flew East and met the dynamically enthusiastic Miss Jones at Rosamond Gilder's Gramercy Park apartment. "I love this play," she said. "I want to do it right away. Can you come to Dallas to work on it with me?"

We began rehearsals with her resident company in Dallas in December, 1954. *Inherit the Wind* exploded into life the night of January 10, 1955. The theater rocked. We all went back to Margo's apartment at the Stoneleigh and waited for the reviews. Margo made everybody in the room read John Rosenfield's and Virgil Miers' incredibly enthusiastic notices out loud over and over again. And then she kicked off her shoes and danced and sang in the center of the floor with tears running down her cheeks.

Every divinity student at Southern Methodist University was assigned to see the play. We still call Tad Adoue God-Pappy. We began the Margo Jones Award to honor Margo's memory and salute annually anybody who can match her daring in the borning of new plays and playwrights. From that beginning in Dallas, the play has never stopped. It has been translated and produced in twenty-eight languages. The agent who wanted to burn it has never forgotten the fact. But best of all, we met Paul Muni, found in him a new father and friend, and were able to bring him a part to climax his stage career.

After the Dallas opening, Bob Lee flew East, playscripts in hand. I remained in Dallas to take notes at subsequent performances. Margo asked us to offer the play for Broadway production first to her friends Howard Lindsay and Russel Crouse, then producing works other than their own. Lindsay told Bob Lee, "Look, it's a fascinating play, but if we produce it, we won't finish writing

318

our *own* play." At that point, Crouse strolled into the room. Lindsay said, "Buck, can you imagine what Mr. Lee has just done?" Crouse sighed and answered with resignation and professional certitude, "Mr. Lee has *written a play!*"

Harold Freedman took a copy to Herman Shumlin. As director-producer, Shumlin had presented some of the most vigorous plays of ideas of the century. He had admired the play previously; now, inspired by the critical and audience reception in Dallas, he agreed to produce it. But he wanted to wait until September to begin. "No," we said, "we want to do it now." "By the time we cast the play properly, and get out of town, then into Broadway," Shumlin warned, "it'll be April, the end of the season, and then we'll be going into the summer and it'll be hot." "It's hot right now," we insisted. "Let's do it *now!*"

We all went on a casting prowl. Bob and I felt the juiciest role was the William Jennings Bryan-like Brady, and the fall of this giant would be most appealing to a star name. (A brilliant supporting gadfly of an actor could play the Darrow-like Henry Drummond of our play.) Herman Shumlin flew to Paris to see if he could lure the mammoth Orson Welles. Bob Lee flew to California in an attempt to tempt Lee J. Cobb back to Broadway. Both actors turned down the role of Brady, though they allowed they might just consider Drummond, a far more attractive part. We allowed both would be wrong for it. But we agreed that we should shift our ground and try to find a star to play Drummond.

When we all reassembled at Shumlin's office in New York, somebody mentioned Paul Muni. His name hadn't even been included in the long list of every possibility and impossibility in the casting directory. "He's retired" was the flat verdict. "He's declared publicly he'll never do another play. It's a total waste of time."

We wasted our time making endless additional lists. Somebody even mentioned Milton Berle. The number of stars and near stars who turned down the part could only be equaled by the number of stellar producers who had ignored the play.

Shumlin decided to try to find Muni; hell, the worst he could do was say no. We managed to uncover the private phone numbers in Encino and Trancas. Neither number answered. Celebrity Service was unable to establish a current location. Actors' Equity and Screen Actors Guild only had old addresses. Friends in the Yiddish theater hadn't heard from Muni for years. Shumlin traced down a rumor that the Munis were in Europe. He tried half a dozen agents and twenty European hotels. No luck. Terese Hayden, working as assistant director and casting consultant, discovered Muni's New York contact: attorney Jonas Silverstone.

319

Coincidentally, Silverstone was Margo Jones' lawyer, as well as Bella's cousin. "Sure," Silverstone told Terry Hayden. "I know exactly where Bella and Munya are. They're about three blocks away from you at the Dorset Hotel."

Shumlin immediately phoned the Munis at their hotel. Bella took the call. She said that it was very nice of Shumlin to inquire but explained that they were in New York on vacation, to *see* plays, not to read any. Besides, Muni had definitely decided to retire. There had been too many heartbreaking experiences, too many disappointments, and she doubted there was a play anywhere strong enough to convince Muni to return to Broadway after a six-year absence.

"I've got that play in my hand," Shumlin said in that fierce tone which has given him the label "Broadway's Angry Man."

Bella sighed. "Drop it by the hotel," she said. "We'll glance at it."

Shumlin didn't trust messengers. He took it over himself.

Muni and Bella were just on their way out to dinner and then were going to the Belasco Theatre to see Menasha Skulnik and Berta Gersten in Clifford Odets' *The Flowering Peach*. Shumlin quickly told Muni about the pertinency of *Inherit the Wind* in this period of repression of freedom of thought. He urged Muni to read it as soon as possible. Muni took the play, weighed it in his hand, and smiled.

"I used to know a producer," he said, "who could take a script like this and just by the touch of it would know whether he wanted to do it."

"How does this one feel to you?" Shumlin joked. "Will it run?"

"With proper casting," said Muni, "it should run two and a half hours!"

They laughed, and both the Munis promised to read it during the week they were in town. Then Muni and Bella went out into the crisp January night. Shumlin crossed his fingers.

That was a Thursday. They didn't take a week. Friday afternoon Muni agreed to do the play. Early Saturday morning, with no secretary on duty in Shumlin's office, Bob Lee and I typed Muni's contract.

To celebrate and to introduce us to our star for the first time, Shumlin arranged for all of us to meet for cocktails late that afternoon in the bar at the Dorset. Muni shook our hands. "That's a damned good play," he said. "My pores tell me."

Bella smiled at us appraisingly. Shumlin wanted to order champagne, but Muni protested that all he wanted was ginger ale. But Bella ordered a sherry and toasted the play. *"Lechayim,"* she said, then quickly felt that she had to explain. "That means 'to life.' We've been in California where there isn't much."

You don't have to translate," Shumlin said. "You see, one of this playwriting team is Jewish and one isn't. Guess which."

Muni squinted at both of us, then nodded his head wisely, and pointed a finger at Robert E. Lee.

"That," Muni declared positively, "is the Yid!"

Bob is a Methodist-turned-Congregationalist who had never tasted hot pastrami, a kosher dill pickle, or a blintz until I forced them down his untutored throat at the age of twenty-three. (Now he is an incurable blintz addict.)

On March 7, 1955, we began rehearsals on the stage of the National Theatre on West Forty-first Street. Muni had returned to California for a month to study the playscript and to experiment with various makeups in concert with the Westmore brothers and then with William Tuttle.

Ten days before rehearsals began, Muni was back in New York, already in his dressing room, working, studying, trying on and taking off a variety of faces.

Peter Larkin was engaged to design the two-level set, in which the entire town could be as much on trial as the defendant. Agents, who can be creative contributors instead of destructive play burners, helped with the casting: Jane Broder came up with the happy inspiration that Ed Begley play Brady. (Ed was an old friend of ours from radio days.) He became a perfect foil and worthy antagonist for Muni in the battle of giants. For the Mencken-like Hornbeck, Bill Liebling brought over a young actor who had the acerbic intelligence and cocky impertinence ideal for the role—Tony Randall. (The play made him a star.)

Shumlin had a special affection for the National Theatre. He had directed several other plays there: *Grand Hotel, The Little Foxes,* and *The Corn Is Green.* (It is now the Billy Rose Theatre.) Shumlin had the star dressing room cleaned up for Muni's painstaking prerehearsal experimentations. No other play was in the theater at the time, so the stage was available for rehearsal.

Shumlin remembers his initial apprehension about Muni's overemphasis on makeup:

"Muni felt that he didn't resemble Darrow enough. So he concentrated on trying to duplicate the expanse of Darrow's forehead, which was quite high. Muni had a very thick head of hair, and Darrow was balding. I pointed out to him that I didn't think it made any difference; what was important was *behind the forehead*!

"But I knew enough about Muni, mostly what I'd been told about him, to realize that he was one of those actors who functioned both from an outward realization of appearance, makeup and clothes, as well as an *interior* examination of the character and his own feelings. I've always felt that it was a natural point of view for an actor to have: what he wears does something to him right away—when he puts on a costume, it helps him become the character automatically.

"Muni phoned and asked me to come over to his dressing room. I went to the theater with a certain trepidation and anxiety. Well, the door was open and I stared at his reflection in the dressing-room mirror. He had created, it seemed to me, a whole new head. It wasn't just a wig or a piece, it seemed like a solid head-enclosing mask that went straight down to his ears and made his head much higher with a lot of exposed skull. Also he had separately applied a great deal of false nose.

"I was unprepared for it. It all seemed artificial; I didn't know how it could be used on a stage. But I was careful what I said to him, knowing of the importance of working in his own way toward a character, an image. I said I thought it was interesting, but wasn't there just a bit too much? Maybe the forehead was too high, maybe the nose needed reduction. 'Let me work on it,' he said.

"Three days later he called back. The makeup was less exaggerated, and I complimented him on the change. Always in the back of my mind was the thought that we wanted just Muni, not a lot of makeup. I suggested still a little less. He never bridled, never argued, just asked for more time to work on it. On the third visit, the makeup was almost gone. By the time we got to dress rehearsal, the only thing he did was whiten his hair."

In the course of rehearsals, all of us, including the other members of the cast, were amazed how the externals, so important to Muni at first, had been discarded. The character of Drummond crept into his face, his mind, his posture, his walk, replacing the makeup with a higher performance truth. Muni shoved out his belly, without padding, so that occasionally he almost looked pregnant. (That was difficult to do, projecting a belly without affecting his vocal strength.) It was a startling physical transformation.

Shumlin describes his directorial approach to Muni:

"I said to myself that I was working with an actor of such tremendous ability and imagination and knowledge that *I am going to learn a lot!* I wanted to let him *go free* with the life force of the actor to live onstage, because I knew that whatever I felt the part should be, *he* would know better! I wanted to see his great talent work out intuitively and instinctively.

(Photo by Staats Cotsworth)

Paul Muni and Ed Begley in *Inherit the Wind*.

"Of course, he did a great deal of private work at home, every day and during the night with tape recorders, even putting a speaker under his pillow because he was always worried if he could remember his lines. Nevertheless, as soon as he got up in his part and started to act, when he had to take over the stage, you knew that what was happening was a concentration of all of his years and all of his thought. I remember talking to him about the Stanislavsky Method, and he said: 'Oh, I read that book, but we always knew about that in the Yiddish theater! And nobody read a book!' "

Staats Cotsworth, who was Reverend Brown of the play (his wife then, the late Muriel Kirkland, was Mrs. Brady), recalls the beginning rehearsals:

"I remember mostly the apprehension of the cast at the s-l-o-w preparation Muni went through. Very slow. At first we could hardly hear him. He had his nose in the book, and he mumbled and muttered and went back over things, and we suddenly thought: 'Oh, my goodness, it's going to take forever.' And then suddenly, in the second week, there was a sudden blooming of excitement as the words began to form themselves into thoughts, into ideas, and Muni put himself into it and everybody was *spellbound!*"

Muni has often been accused of being a humorless man. Bob and I found that offstage he had a delicious wit and onstage his comedy timing could match Jack Benny's or any other major comic's. (We had learned something working with Benny and used the technique with Muni: we gave him his own *protection.*

323

Following a major laugh, we usually managed to give Muni the next line, sometimes within his own speeches, as in the "Cain's wife" sequence. Students of comedy should go to Jack Benny scripts in the archives; they will find that most expected laughs are carefully and deliberately followed by:

BENNY: Hmmmmmm

or

BENNY: Welllll

thus allowing the star to control the timing of the entire show and to make certain nobody else in the cast "steps on a laugh." Muni was able to do this brilliantly throughout *Inherit the Wind,* often with a line, often instinctively with a shocked look or a disparaging gesture.)

We'll never forget the day during rehearsals when Muni came in with a folded copy of the tabloid New York *Daily Mirror* and a mischievous look on his face as if he'd swallowed a box of birds. A key moment in the play (perhaps *Inherit*'s tablecloth speech) is Drummond's memory of a rocking horse he had cherished as a child and his disillusionment when he discovered that the bright golden paint of the shiny exterior concealed nothing but rotten wood. (In later years we used this speech as a lesson to young playwrights: *Look behind the paint, and if it's a lie, show it up for what it really is!* This can be a key to the subject matter of infinite plays: look behind the paint of your government, your parents, your religion, your university, mostly yourself.) Originally we had called the rocking horse of Drummond's memory Golden Girl, invented completely from our imaginations.

When the entire cast was assembled and Muni had an audience, he carefully unfolded the newspaper. It read: GOLDEN GIRL ARRESTED. In the tabloid account, Golden Girl was the name of New York's most celebrated, $100-a-night call girl. Rocking with helpless laughter, the tears running down his cheeks, Muni read the speech from the play, including the lines: "I woke up in the morning and there was Golden Girl at the foot of my bed. . . . I climbed into the saddle and started to rock and it *broke!*"

Muni laughed for twenty minutes. We changed the name of Golden Girl to Golden Dancer.

The out-of-town opening night at the Forrest Theatre in Philadelphia on March 31, 1955, was apprehension time for Muni, meeting an audience for the first time. He asked stage manager David Clive to stand close to the proscenium portal at stage right with promptbook in hand. Though he had mastered the lines, Muni wanted a *souffleur* on hand as extra insurance.

"If I need help," Muni told Clive, "I'll put my finger in my collar as if I'm hot—and you throw me the line."

During Act One, Muni used the mannerism when he didn't actually have to be prompted. Clive, following instructions, whispered the speech. Muni was furious and blasted the young stage manager at the end of the act, ordering production stage manager Burry Fredrik to take over as prompter.

But suddenly in Act Two, Muni went blank. He stared at his opponent in the witness chair, put his finger in his collar, but no cue came. Never stepping out of character, Muni marched to the proscenium, got his line from Miss Fredrik, turned, and said, "As I was saying," and sailed through the rest of the performance. Muni made his temporary lapse seem like part of the blocking. Despite an ovation at the final curtain, he was convinced that he had ruined the entire play and wouldn't allow anybody backstage into his dressing room after the opening.

On subsequent nights, my partner and I went back to compliment Muni, to chat with him. "You were great tonight," we said.

"Get out!" he screamed. "It was terrible, terrible. Don't tell me how great I was—I'm awful. Tomorrow night don't even come backstage."

The next night, per instructions, we stayed away. When Herman Shumlin came into his dressing room, Muni looked around, worried. "What's the matter?" he asked. "I was so bad tonight the boys didn't even come back?"

The first chapter of this book recounts the tumultuous opening night at the National Theatre in New York on April 1, 1955. *Inherit the Wind* became one of the longest-running serious plays in the history of the American theater. Muni played every night as if it were an opening. "Why not?" he said. "To the people out there, paying too much money for tickets, it's all happening for the first time!"

Muni won every award it was possible for an actor to receive in the theater: the Antoinette Perry Award (the Tony), the Donaldson Award (signed for the critics by Walter Kerr, for the actors by Katharine Cornell), the Variety Critics Poll as Best Actor of the Year, the Outer Circle Award, the Newspaper Guild Page One Award, the Lamb's Club Award, and the Albert Einstein Commemorative Award for Achievement in the Arts. (He was pleased that the other recipient was Edward R. Murrow, and he declared, "It's a joy to receive this in memory of Albert Einstein, my fellow fiddle player.")

Bella returned to California just long enough to sell the house in Encino, though Muni insisted on keeping the Wart at Trancas beach. They rented an apartment on East End Avenue. "Thank you," Bella told us, "for bringing us back to New York. I frankly don't give a damn if I never see another orange as long as I live."

The New York *Times* headlined:

MUNI'S SECOND FLING WITH FAME
From great renown on stage and screen in the Thirties, he went into semi-retirement in the Forties. Today, once more, his star shines bright on Broadway.

"Vindication!" Bella said triumphantly.

Herman Shumlin remembers Muni's grace in the face of personal disaster. At the end of August, when Muni could see nothing but a vague shadow out of his left eye, Bella asked Shumlin to accompany Muni to the eye specialist's office for a final verdict. Would the eye have to be removed?

They waited in an inner examining room. Muni was philosophically calm and even, to Shumlin's amazement, began to joke. The doctor came in quickly, took a file, and said, "Hello. I'll be just a few minutes. How are you?" Then he disappeared.

Muni grinned and shrugged. "How am I? That's a question! Would I be here if I was all right? You know, it would be interesting sometime, when somebody asked, 'How are you?' if you really *told* them—the whole works. Like maybe you were standing in a railway station and a guy rushed by just as the train was ready to leave, and he asked you that question, and you grabbed his shoulders and held onto him, and you told him everything: what was wrong with your family and your head, the whole kit and kaboodle. And he missed his train, and maybe he missed his whole life."

Muni began to laugh, and Shumlin sat there and thought: "My God, you're wonderful!"

The panorama of the courtroom during the trial in *Inherit the Wind*.

(Photo by Staats Cotsworth)

Muni was deeply touched when almost fifty people, mostly total strangers, offered him their eyes. "All my life I've been suspicious of the human race," he told me. "I guess I was wrong."

The play reopened triumphantly with Melvyn Douglas, sans mustache, on September 19. Over the years there have been many rumors backstage in Broadway playhouses and buzzing through the dressing-room trailers alongside Hollywood sound stages that Muni was even more difficult than the "difficult customer" label he gave himself. The company of sixty-five in *Inherit the Wind* didn't think so. They loved Douglas, but they adored Muni. On September 22, on Muni's sixtieth birthday, the entire company sent Muni a Torah, each inscribing a handwritten or hand-lettered greeting—some with artwork—on the parchment scroll. They wrote that they missed his turning upstage at the curtain calls each night, smiling and saying warmly, unheard by the audience, *"Danke schoen, meine liebchen!"* Muni treasured the scroll, which was eight feet long by the time all the members of the cast included their messages. (Bella left it to me.) Here is Ed Begley's entry:

Muni, I have re-written this several times. But what I went to say has just got to be said simply. So here goes. I love you. And no matter what success I may have in the future nothing can top the thrill of working with you. I look forward to that day when we work together again.

Sincerely and affectionately,
Ed Begley

For the Christmas which came to us early that year (see Chapter One of this book) Muni tested himself for his return to the play by driving all the way across the country alone, with no help, in the Duchess.

Melvyn Douglas took a second company on the road for a year-long tour. At the Huntington Hartford Theatre in Hollywood the following summer, Muni—on vacation from the Broadway company—came onstage to thank Douglas for what he had done

(Columbia Pictures Photo)

Muni as Dr. Sam Abelman in *The Last Angry Man*.

so brilliantly "to keep the play warm during my personal crisis in New York."

I asked Herman Shumlin his appraisal of Muni as an artist: "We had a company of over sixty in *Inherit the Wind*. Some of the extras have since become famous: Simon Oakland, Michael Constantine, Bradford Dillman, George Furth (who wrote *Company*). But hardly anybody left the cast during that long, long run. I used to look at them in the courtroom scenes and see how absorbed they were, mesmerized—and several times I would say to these people: 'Don't you get tired, just sitting there watching every night?' Invariably, I'd get the same answer: '*Muni absolutely fascinates me every performance!* I'm held by him, he never leaves the character—and I always find something new in it!' These people who sat through that play night after night for more than 800 times were *enthralled* by him! Muni is in a class by himself. Both on the stage and on the screen there was a kind of personal revelation that came out of him in every performance he ever gave."

The echo still sounds down the years from Second Avenue: "That is an *actor!*"

27

FOR his entire professional career Muni fought a constant battle against being typed, being "pigeonholed" by an audience. He never wanted a paying customer to say, "I know exactly what to expect of him!" He was continually, restlessly searching for change. He didn't want to be stuck in a rut. Having been typed as a bearded child, he sought barefacedly to surprise audiences, to give them what they didn't anticipate, even what they didn't want: this was the reason for his successes and perhaps equally the reason for his failures. His test for a role: did the man have substance? When you touched him, was he *flesh*? Was the character larger, deeper, broader, more brilliant, more dazzling, more totally fascinating, more intelligent than the man he downgraded and despised—the *nothing* Muni? (You might say that Muni had the arrogance of almost masochistic humility.)

In late February, 1956, after he had been comfortably back in the role of Henry Drummond in *Inherit* for three months, Muni agreed to do a half-hour filmed television show in New

York for CBS' *G.E. Theatre*. "A fella named Mort Abrams, a TV producer, wrote me a nice letter," Muni explained. "He phoned. He came to visit. He has good taste. He sent me a script, and I thought I could do it. After all, it was based on a short story by Sinclair Lewis; how wrong can you get?"

But it was shot in two and a half days, and it was an agonizing experience. Nevertheless, the telecast on March 4, 1956, turned out better than he expected. In *A Letter from the Queen,* dramatized for television by O. J. Powers, Muni played a ninety-year-old United States Senator from a past so distant most people thought he was dead. Senator Lafayette Ryder was described by Lewis as "a lively old relic with the mind of a Machiavelli and the force of Genghis Khan." His prize possession was a letter from Queen Victoria. Muni had never played a Senator. In pungent scenes with Christopher Plummer and Polly Bergen, Muni was brilliant; this television episode should be revived and treasured as a collector's item. In it Muni delivered some memorable lines:

> Teddy Roosevelt once told me never to trust a Roosevelt. They'll double-cross a politician for a constituent anytime.

Referring to his own bygone era:

> Foreign policy wasn't reached with one eye cocked on the cover of a news-magazine.

Muni in *A Letter from the Queen* on *G.E. Theatre*.

And prophetically years ahead of the confused '70's:

> This country was built by men. If it survives it must be maintained by men!

Even in this almost-forgotten television half hour, Muni grappled with ideas, with lines he could play with conviction and wit.

In November, 1956, Bob and Janet Lee's daughter was born. They named her Lucy, a longtime family name. Bella, pleased to have another Lucy in her life, became the official godmother. After he left *Inherit the Wind*, Muni came to visit. Jonathan Lee, age five, took a commemorative snapshot of the great actor saying "Coochie-coochie-coo" to the year-and-a-half-old Lucy. With camera poised, Jonathan said with professional aplomb; "Mr. Muni, would you mind cheating your face a bit more toward the camera?"

Watching Muni that day, I thought of something Los Angeles *Times* critic Cecil Smith once told me: "There's an old show business saying: *he's too good an actor to be a star.* Paul Muni was one of the few actors of our century who proved that was erroneous, who gave the lie to that statement. The man who played in *Scarface* and the man who played *Zola* and the man in *Inherit the Wind* were all different people. Only a great actor could do all those roles. Aside from Olivier, I think he was probably the most impressive actor of our times."

Muni said "Coochie-coochie-coo" again to Lucy without the slightest resemblance to Pasteur or Juarez. Then I thought of a comment by Michael Levee, the producer-son of Muni's onetime agent, M. C. Levee: "How many actors ever get to play more than two great roles in their lifetimes? Muni played at least ten! What a rarity!"

He was also brilliant saying "Coochie-coochie-coo" to Lucy Lee, with a five-year-old director calling the shots.

In 1958 Muni played in a memorable television program and in a disastrous stage musical. It marked his fiftieth year as a performer.

Playhouse 90 offered him the role of the aging war-horse of a lawyer in *Last Clear Chance* by A. E. Hotchner. It was Muni's twenty-second legal role—but far different from his Drummond of *Inherit*. In this live ninety-minute telecast from Television City

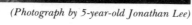

(Photograph by 5-year-old Jonathan Lee)

Lucy Lee with Muni.

(Photo by Bob Clouse)

Muni in *Last Clear Chance* **on** *Play house 90.*

in Hollywood, Muni played an attorney who defends his own son against possible disbarment for concealing evidence. His opponent (Department of Old Times) was Luther Adler. George Roy Hill directed. United Press critic William Ewald wrote the most accurate description of what the TV audience saw on the night of March 6, 1958:

> The play wasn't the thing last night. The thing was Muni. Muni turned in a dill pickle of a performance—a performance with salt and bite that dripped with brine.
>
> He unbagged more tricks in his 90 minutes than I have ever seen over a comparable period on TV. And make no mistake about it, they were tricks.
>
> He smacked his lips; tugged his vest, nose and ear lobe; drove his right fist into his left palm; ran a forefinger along a wrinkle in his forehead; brought his hands together in a soft clap; scratched the heel of his hand, his knuckles and his head; and dove his hands in and out of every pocket in his costume.
>
> But Muni's intelligence and authority turned this calisthenic grab-bag into something more than just a series of actor's tricks.
>
> Watching Muni was a little like watching Willie Mays hit a triple (losing his bat, sliding into third when he needn't, slapping the dust off his spotless trousers). Grandstanding, yes. Excessive, yes. But somehow all very right and more to the point, exciting to watch.

One thing the audience never realized: Muni was "pecking corn" in the tradition of a Yiddish theater actor waiting for his next line from the prompter. Director George Roy Hill went beyond cue cards or the electric Teleprompter. Production pressures turned him into television's first *souffleur*. During rehearsals, Hill found Muni was unable to commit his lengthy role to memory; his diminished vision made a Teleprompter useless. So Hill came up with the idea of having the aging lawyer wear a hearing aid; not only would this serve as a line of communication from the control room, but it seemed an appropriate character touch as well. Speech by speech through the live hour and a half broadcast, the director (not trusting anybody else with the delicate timing) read Muni's next line to him (unheard by the audience) through the earpiece, in each instance just before it was delivered to the camera and the audience. As he listened, Muni used "cover-up business." To a watcher it never seemed like a prompting device; here was a lawyer who *thought* before he spoke, a rarity not just with most lawyers but with most human beings.

Muni topped Willie Mays. He hit not merely a triple but a homerun. His dill pickle performance won him an Emmy nomination as one of the best television actors of the year.

"Before I die," Bella said, "I want to see Muni singing and dancing onstage again in white tie and tails. That's how I remember him best. He was the most handsome then, back in the *singen* and *tanzen* days of the Yiddish theater. And that's the way I want the world to see him. They'll fall in love the way I did—with a great entertainer named Munya."

Edwin Lester, the potentate of the Los Angeles Civic Light Opera Association, had often heard the rumor that the mighty Muni might be tempted into a musical, particularly if Bella could get her long-cherished wish to see him cavorting in white tie and tails. Lester thought he found the perfect opportunity in the role of Kringelein in a musical version of Vicki Baum's *Grand Hotel,* to be called *At the Grand.* But the best laid schemes of men and musicals gang aft agley.

Vicki Baum's best seller, originally called *Menschem im Hotel* (*People in a Hotel*), began a chain reaction of books, films, and plays in which one setting (a train, a plane, a ship, a dinner party, a desert island) was used to tell multiple stories. To make this kind of omnibus-plot work, you need *all* stars or *no* stars. The film of *Grand Hotel* had two Barrymores (John and Lionel), Greta Garbo, Joan Crawford, Wallace Beery. *At the Grand* had Paul Muni.

Muni was lured to it by Luther Davis' literate book, by a lilting score by Robert Wright and George Forrest, but mostly by Bella's persistent vision. The setting was shifted from post-World-War I Berlin to contemporary Rome ("Hollywood-by-the-Tiber"), and Kringelein (the role played by Lionel Barrymore in the film version) was changed from an accountant into a scullery worker in the kitchen of the hotel who has always dreamed of "getting upstairs." When he finds he has only a short time to live, he moves out of the kitchen and uses his life's savings for a final fling as a guest. In the big second act number, "I Waltz Alone," Kringelein (says the script) sings and dances in white tie and tails. Perhaps it was added deliberately to snag Muni. Muni was snagged.

Thirty-two years before, Muni had sung and danced (and had enjoyed himself doing it!) in *Maytime* and *Student Prince* in the Yiddish theater. But he had never been a song-and-dance man on the English-speaking stage or screen. This was certainly a change of pace, a challenge, a "way to end the way I began." Again Muni's life was coming full circle.

"I loved the music," Muni told critic Cecil Smith, "and I liked the Davis script. And my part—the little man, Kringelein— delighted me. But I had to know that I could do it.

"They rented a hall, and I sang the songs and danced for the composers and writer, director Albert Marre, and producer Edwin Lester. They said yes, it's right; you can do it. Still I had to get the approval of one other tough critic. I recorded my songs on tape and listened to them. And I asked myself, 'Munya, can you do it?' And I said 'Munya, I think you can do it!' You know what that proves? You should never listen to a critic."

Bella and Muni moved into the penthouse apartment of the Chateau Marmonte on the Sunset Strip in West Hollywood. (So many New York actors use it as a West Coast headquarters that we have often labeled it "Sardi's with beds.") Muni went through his usual elaborate preparation phase, including daily and nightly sessions with multiple tape recorders. But then he began to have irrational apprehensions about the show.

"What if they vulgarize it?" he moaned to Bella. "What if they turn it all into a girlie-girlie show, a sex opera, burlesque? I'd be disgraced!"

Bella and Muni attended the chorus auditions and the early dance rehearsals so that Muni could be worked into the musical numbers. As if putting on horse blinders, Muni (through Bella) made a strange request: the dancers should not be allowed to wear those tight, revealing leotards. Why not tutus or something less provocative?

Once full rehearsals began, Muni had an almost paranoiac delusion that director Albert Marre and his wife, Joan Diener, were his enemies. Miss Diener was playing the Garbo role, which had been switched for *At the Grand* from a ballet dancer to a Callas-like opera singer. Miss Diener, a lady of ample talent, is often auto-upstaged by her equally ample breastworks, which make Jane Russell look like Freddie Bartholomew. Muni, usually a lover of personal liberty, perhaps failed to consider that physical attributes constitute part of a girl's constitutional rights; to him the front of Miss Diener was simply an affront.

In many ways, Muni was a Jewish puritan. Using the weapons of his pretended enemies, he would curse anybody who cursed onstage. He demanded changes in costume designs, eliminating obvious cleavage in what he felt were too-scanty outfits for the girls of the chorus. In his scenes with Joan Diener, he never looked at her.

"She's a very intelligent girl," Bella insisted. "She was a psychology major at Sarah Lawrence College."

"Me, I'm an uneducated slob," Muni said. "And I see nothing above her neckline."

It would take more than a psychology major to analyze the panic which reigns backstage at any musical-in-the-making which is not an instantaneous hit. Muni was unprepared for the infighting, the backbiting, the chaos. He covered up his own insecurity with a kind of moralistic fervor, which antagonized the rest of the cast.

"The show was a tremendous failure," Luther Davis says with remembered sadness. "And of course with any disaster, there's an awful lot of blame to be divided. But Muni got the show on; it was his reputation that got it produced. He did everything he'd contracted to do even though some of it cost him a great deal of courage and energy. Beforehand, neither Bella nor Muni understood how much work, how complicated a contemporary musical is."

With his salary based on a percentage of the box-office gross, Muni was making $10,000 a week, but he signed a contract covering only the Los Angeles and San Francisco engagements, a total of ten weeks. Beyond that, *At the Grand* was scheduled to go into the Forty-sixth Street Theatre in New York. Producer Roger Stevens agreed to pick up the option. Stevens' general manager Victor Samrock told me they had a million-dollar advance in New York with sellout houses to the end of the year, the many theater parties based mainly on the alluring idea of *Muni in a musical!*

"Onstage at the beginning of rehearsals Muni was adorable,"

Luther Davis recalls. "He was full of enthusiasm. Though he talked his songs, he was a brilliant talker and made every phrase count. We were all terribly excited. Whenever he became Kringelein, even in a dance step, he was wonderful."

Offstage, Muni turned into a terror—mostly to himself. The creative staff of the show did everything to please Muni. He wanted to be "the little man" onstage, so they cast as many tall people as possible for striking contrast. Muni wanted a death scene; they had never planned for Kringelein to die onstage, not in a musical, but they wrote the scene to make their star happy.

Muni began to get the feeling of a lavish show around him, out of his control. In addition there was the unanticipated sexuality he had feared. Somebody argued that it was a necessary part of a musical: every man in the audience should want to lay every girl in the chorus, every woman in the house should have a burning desire to bed down with every man in the cast, with suitable variations of that rule of thumb depending on sexual predilections.

"Maybe," Muni brooded, "but not for me. I can't stand up there in front of two thousand people every night feeling like a pimp!"

He began fighting everything he had previously liked. He was unable to sleep at night and would prowl around the Chateau Marmonte penthouse, growling into tape recorders. The following day he would criticize the material even more.

One morning he called the director, the composers, and the book writer to a 10 A.M. meeting at his apartment. He sat them all down and faced them as if it were a classroom, though he seemed to Luther Davis more like a lion tamer. Muni said he wanted to play them a tape of suggestions on how to improve the show, made the previous night when he couldn't sleep at all. The tape spun. There were long passages of silence. It was an agonizing experience for Marre, Wright and Forrest, and Davis. They sat there until 1:30 listening mostly to pauses. Finally, Muni's voice on the tape declared a middle-of-the-night maxim about empathy for a leading character, a way of making an audience feel and react.

"I know what you mean," Davis noted, trying to be helpful. "It's one of the great pieces of information George Pierce Baker passed on to us at the Yale Drama School."

Muni stood up and stalked out of the room. Bella, who had been sitting silently in a corner, followed him out. All of them were startled and looked at each other innocently: what had happened? Bella walked slowly back into the room and said in a funereal voice, "I think you'd all better go now." They simultaneously spilled out their concern: was Muni ill? What's the matter?

(Photo by Rothschild)

Muni as Kringelein in *At the Grand*, getting the glamor treatment from hotel attendants.

Had they offended Muni in any way? Why had he suddenly left the room in a huff?

Bella looked steadily at Davis. "He doesn't like to be reminded that you all went to college and he didn't," she said. "And he thinks you're trying to put him down."

Years later Davis still shakes his head in disbelief. "It never occurred to me that you could 'put down' this great theatrical genius by mentioning that you had miserably matriculated at Yale!"

At the Grand opened at the Los Angeles Philharmonic Auditorium (on Sundays it was a Baptist Church) on July 7, 1958. Like so many overelaborate musicals before, the show was nearly destroyed by the tyranny of scenery. The multiple turntables didn't work at the final dress rehearsal and barely worked on opening night. In addition, there was an unexplained bomb threat in the theater; it was a valid motivation to postpone until they could slap the sets into smoother working order—but Lester decided to open on schedule. Nothing bombed except the show.

Muni himself received a warm reception from the audience and the critics. "Broadway will soon see its newest and most unlikely musical star," the AP reported. The audience cheered his number, "A Table with a View," in which the warm and wistful Kringelein, on a ladder, expressed his desire for retirement, not to be stuck

337

in some dreary old people's home—but to sit at a special table upstairs in the café of the Grand Hotel Roma and watch all the world go by. In Act Two, dancing with young Neile Adams, and then all by himself in "I Waltz Alone," Muni—in white tie and tails!—was triumphant. The show itself received "mixed notices." (George S. Kaufman once defined that as "good and rotten.") Onstage Muni sparkled; it seemed to an audience as if a mug of beer had turned into a magnum of champagne. Offstage he wanted to kill himself.

His sleeplessness became chronic. All night he would pace back and forth in the Chateau Marmonte penthouse, but refused to go out onto the terrace. At the curve of Sunset Boulevard, a huge, sixty-foot high figure, a garish plaster girl in hot pants (advertising a Las Vegas hotel-gambling joint) revolved constantly, floodlighted just outside Muni's window. Irrationally, Muni would shout at it, "It's the whore Hollywood! The whore show business! The mother-whore of this whole damn world!"

Herman Shumlin was summoned from New York. (He had guided the straight play of *Grand Hotel* to a 459-performance run in 1930 and had directed Muni's most resounding New York success.) They suggested the possibility of Shumlin's taking over the show. "Muni did a lovely job," Shumlin recollects. "He loved singing and enjoyed the little dance steps. But the show was a mess." Shumlin turned it down.

In August the musical moved to San Francisco for a five-week run at the Curran Theatre and did sellout business. Plans were made for the New York opening. Edwin Lester proposed a further month of tryouts and polishing in Philadelphia. Muni, exhausted and unhappy, asked for his release. Without Muni, nobody in New York wanted the show.

The last performance in San Francisco on September 9, 1958, was a night of horror for Muni. Hit or flop, members of the company desperately wanted the show to continue, however briefly. They blamed Muni for throwing them out of work. Backstage on closing night they hustled him cruelly, elbowing him in the dark between scenes; one chorus girl even slapped a bare breast in his face. The whirling turntables felt as if the earth beneath him were moving; Muni came offstage like a lost and beaten King Lear.

At the final curtain call, Joan Diener, wearing her own full-length mink, turned upstage toward Muni, and grandly opened her coat, like a latter-day *Fraülein Else*. Underneath she was stark naked—except for a single long-stem rose between her legs.

* * *

In February, 1958, Columbia Pictures producer Fred Kohlmar sent Muni a copy of Gerald Green's novel *The Last Angry Man*. This fictionalized account of Green's own father, Dr. Samuel Greenberg, a Schweitzer of the Brooklyn slums, had been a Book-of-the-Month Club selection in 1956. (Coincidentally, we tried to get the dramatic rights for a Broadway stage play of the work, also for Muni, but Harry Cohn, who had purchased the book in galleys, refused to release it. It might have been a more complete acting adventure for Muni if he had done it first on the stage.) Muni didn't pay much attention to the book when it arrived; he was committed to *Playhouse 90* and then, for the rest of the year, to *At the Grand*. Shooting for *The Last Angry Man* was scheduled for early fall.

"Why even read it?" Muni shrugged. "If I like it and can't do it, it'll break my heart."

Daniel Mann was assigned to direct the picture (he had done many notable works: *Come Back, Little Sheba* and *Rose Tattoo* on both stage and screen) but was unhappy about the long list of casting possibilities. Nobody but Muni seemed right or even a remote possibility for the fiercely individualistic Dr. Sam Abelman of the film. When Mann heard that Muni might be withdrawing from *At the Grand*, he phoned to San Francisco, then sent Muni another copy of the novel and Gerald Green's screenplay.

The character of Dr. Sam, a living symbol of integrity, appealed to Muni. This actor, who "never went along with the herd," was amazingly similar to this nonconforming doctor who hated "the new age," the age of the "galoot," the fast buck, the something-for-nothing crowd. (A "galoot" in Dr. Abelman's dictionary is any petty creature who takes but never gives.)

"Sure, I'm tired and sick," Muni told Bella. "My bones only want to lie down. But what this film says is important—about what medicine should be and what doctors should be. To play an honest doctor would be something—particularly a Jewish doctor helping poor people. So it'll kill me. Abelman dies at the end of the picture. Make sure they schedule that scene last. He'll die, and I'll die. It'll be a dramatic finish for both of us!"

"You bet," Bella commented wryly. "Where should we phone you for retakes? Heaven? Or do you intend to go to hell with the rest of us?"

After *At the Grand* closed, Muni and Bella traveled directly from San Francisco to New York, where location shots were to be filmed in Brownsville, Sheepshead Bay, and Prospect Heights. At his first meeting with Danny Mann, Muni was pleased with his director's combined stage and film background. In addition, Mann told Muni about his own father, a "last angry man of law," who had been Sholom Aleichem's attorney. Mann recounted his teen-age experiences working for his father, serving a summons on Maurice Schwartz whenever he performed Sholom Aleichem plays without permission. Muni told Mann some of his early encounters with Schwartz, when it was not only *Hard to Be a Jew* but hard to be an actor.

Muni met the rest of the cast of *The Last Angry Man* for the first reading around a long table at a Columbia Pictures office in Manhattan. The cast was formidable: Luther Adler, Nancy Pollock, David Wayne, Betsy Palmer, Claudia McNeil, and three unknowns at the time: Billy Dee Williams, Cicely Tyson, and God-frey Cambridge. Muni was shy, hesitant, wary, worried.

Then and later Luther Adler tried to calm Muni.

"Look," Adler would advise, "just take it easy, baby!"

"Don't call me baby!" Muni shouted back, then quickly apologized, explaining his apprehension about his heart condition and his one sightless eye.

"Munya," Adler said soothingly, "what is there in this whole world that you really want to look at entirely? *Half* is enough to see!"

Muni liked that and relaxed. There weren't many relaxing moments in the months that followed. A six-week shooting schedule stretched into seventeen weeks. With the exception of the ill-fated Italian film, Muni had not worked in front of a motion-picture camera for twelve years. Though he was scrupu-lously on time for every scene and every setup, many delays were caused by a recurring cue from Muni: "Can I say something?" Everything would stop while Muni discussed a point in the script at length. But when anybody said yes, he would scream, "Don't agree with me! I'm not a writer. I'm a poor son of a bitch of an actor who's asking a question. Don't accept my question as an answer!"

In an attempt to speed up the delays, Fred Kohlmar, the pro-ducer, assigned a studio contract writer to sit on the set and "service" Muni. Whenever a line of dialogue was challenged, the writer would propose possible alternates. When Muni ad-libbed a suggestion, the writer would almost snap to attention. "Yes, yes!" he'd say. "That's it!"

Muni would stare at the writer with the eye of a dead fish. He simmered with dissatisfaction, suspicious that he was "being handled, coddled."

"Any writer who thinks I'm a good writer has got to be a lousy writer," Muni murmured in disgust.

At one point Muni stopped everything on the set and shouted, "Too many words!" Then he unbound his script, carefully laid all the pages on the floor, and pointed down. "Look! It's the size of an Army blanket!" Then, in the character of Dr. Abelman, he tiptoed over the pages.

"What are you doing, Muni?" the director inquired.

"I'm going over my lines!" Muni shouted back.

Early on, while they were still in Brooklyn, the hypochondriac-playing-a-doctor was afflicted merely with shyness and a passion for privacy. And Bella was there to help. But with a curious self-contradiction, Muni had a sense of a living audience in the neighborhood people and the shopkeepers who were adoring fans. Howard Thompson of the New York *Times*, covering the location shooting on Brooklyn's Strauss Street, reported one happy bellow from a housewife at an open apartment window:

> "Hey, Goit, look—it's Paul Muni!"
> Another window opened.
> "Well, I'll be damned—it is. Bless his heart!"

Back in Hollywood the blessings were not so abundant. Muni respected his director but insisted they work even on Saturdays and Sundays. Every weekend Mann would go over Muni's miles and miles of notes on his many tape machines set up in the Wart shack at Trancas beach.

Two weeks after they were back in Columbia Studios on Gower Street, Bella had a mild heart attack and was ordered to stay in bed. Without Bella on the set, Muni felt lost. He would grow faint, seem to suffer sympathetic heart attacks himself.

"I can't do this today," Muni would say in the middle of a rehearsal and retreat to his dressing room, complaining he was having trouble with his eye, his heart, his memory. But if Danny Mann began working with Luther Adler or David Wayne, Muni would pop out of his dressing room and declare, "Okay, I'll go. I can do it now."

Muni's geysers of temperament were compensations for an unwilling awareness of his own growing inadequacies and his diminishing powers.

"He was no longer the giant who really controls a film," Mann recalls. "At one point, when he couldn't remember some lines, we put a page of script on a chair where the camera wouldn't see it. But it was a tragic moment. 'What am I doing?' Muni moaned. 'After all these years in the theater, after all these years in film, I can't remember words and have to look at a piece of paper!' He was confronted with the reality that at that moment of his life he wasn't what he wanted to be."

Luther Adler remembers stopping his director in a studio alleyway. "Danny, I know Muni a lifetime and I want to do something to help you and to help him. Muni has a lot of virtues, but he's got one fault; every now and then he gets the 'cutes' and there's almost no stopping him, but you've got to."

Mann doubled up with laughter. "Twenty minutes ago, Luther," he said, "Muni stopped me on this very spot and whispered, 'Listen, I don't have to tell you what a wonderful actor Luther Adler is and all that, but every now and then that boy goes overboard!' "

Mann describes vividly the scene in the picture when Muni-Abelman gets a heart attack:

"He was climbing the long flight of stairs in the Brooklyn police station, which we had built on a sound stage. I was riding the camera boom, following him up. Three-quarters of the way, where we had planned it, he had his attack. He leaned over the banister; when he came up again; his face was completely sunken in. He looked like a different man. I went over and congratulated him and asked him how he had achieved that remarkable transformation. I thought it was marvelous. Smiling mischievously, he opened his hand and showed me his false teeth. He had a kind of childlike glee about it."

Muni loved James Wong Howe, the brilliant cinematographer. "Jimmy, how can you stand photographing this ugly face?" Muni asked in his usual lifelong pattern of spitting on himself. "Aren't you afraid it'll break your camera?"

"Your face isn't even on the film," Howe told him. "This camera is designed to shoot your insides: your soul, your integrity."

For a man with heart trouble to play a character who dies of a heart attack may be carrying Stanislavsky too far. For the final deathbed scene, Muni insisted on having a doctor, a heart specialist, on the set so the second-to-second death-throes would be realistic and authentic. The director had a young first-aid man from the studio standing by, and that satisfied Muni. But the "specialist" had nothing to do; Muni seemed to know instinctively how to die.

"It was almost as if Muni's whole life had been geared to this moment of death," Mann remembers. "He relished it. He was excited about playing this scene—and all of his creative juices were flowing."

It is a superb moment on film. Luther Adler, playing a fellow doctor, jumps on the bed, attempting artificial respiration, begging

342

him to live, hating him for dying, pounding on him to live, *live*, go fishing!

When the scene was over, Muni got up, winked at the crew.

"Don't call the funeral parlor yet," he said. "I think I'm still breathing."

Despite the delays and the difficulties, the other actors loved and respected Muni. Though the extended schedule cost Nancy Pollock the role (which she had created on Broadway) in the film version of *Middle of the Night*, she speaks of her experience working with Muni without regret: "He was a superb performer. When I watched him, everyone else faded into the background."

Why? What did he have? What techniques, what tricks?

"You use a word," Danny Mann comments, "which in my younger days would have been condemned: 'tricks.' Muni had the technique of creating inspiration. He was able to synthesize, weave into the fabric of his performance things he knew would be effective. How did he do it? Trial and error, work, doing it again and again, a lot of private preparation and *thought*. A lot of research. Dr. Abelman in anybody else's hands couldn't have been complete; Muni brought to it *personal concentration*. There was a *force*. Whatever he did was more arresting than what anybody else did—by virtue of his *presence*, his size. He could sit in a chair and you would look at *him*: the man gathered in all of your attention because he was *so involved in what he was doing!*"

Hollis Alpert in *Saturday Review* headlined his notice:

TO A GREAT HUMAN BEING

> Mr. Muni seems to have created Dr. Abelman like a sculptor working with living materials. . . . The gestures are not the mannerisms of an actor, but of a real person who, astonishingly, isn't Paul Muni at all. This is character creation, the real thing, and what, it seems to me, acting is all about. . . . Paul Muni carves another niche for himself in screen history.

The Last Angry Man was chosen for the Royal Command Performance film in Great Britain. Muni received his fifth Academy Award nomination. Bella, strong enough to travel, insisted on returning to New York, and Muni went with her. He asked James Wong Howe to accept the Oscar for him "in the unlikely chance that I might win." It was *Ben Hur*'s year. Charlton Heston's bravura charioteer, Judah Ben Hur, won over the gentle Thoreau-quoting Dr. Abelman of Brooklyn.

It was the last angry actor's last film.

Muni as a nonagenarian in *Saints and Sinners*. (This is a frame of the film, cut out because of the fly on Muni's nose; he couldn't see it because of his bad eye.) Muni inscribed this to Marc Daniels: "CUDENA DUN IT WIDOUT YOU."

(Marc Daniels Collection)

28

IF it weren't for Muni's own joylessness, he would have been a joy. Despite his shouted protests that he never wanted to act again, nonacting was nonliving. He was tortured by his own uselessness. He dramatized the emptiness of "total retirement."

The East End Avenue apartment in New York was an armed camp. Bella, swallowing pills for her heart condition, was frantic.

"For Muni," she said, "a misplaced paper clip is a national tragedy. Getting up in the morning is a federal case!"

Was the public's attitude toward Muni a classic example of America's actor sickness? We all crave heroes—presidents with charisma, sexy senators and governors, teachers we can love, preachers we can turn into fathers. But mostly we want gods and goddesses on our stages, screens, and TV sets: idealizations of ourselves. If the face isn't a male collar ad or a female blonde Venus, then we want intellectual giants: mammoth IQ's, instant answers, prefabricated philosophies, packaged religion, magic, fairy tales, Santa Claus, Superman. We idolize them; then we forget them.

Muni was convinced he was never handsome, never intelligent, never talented, never able to open his mouth and say the word "the."

"I'm no good," he muttered. "I never was worth anything. I'm nothing."

Then he would retreat into a near-catatonic silence, which alarmed Bella. She pleaded with him to get help. He spoke only long enough to shout her into tears.

Not everybody forgot Muni. Herman Shumlin brought him an early edition of Edward Lewis Wallant's novel *The Pawnbroker*. Shumlin felt that it would be a great motion-picture property for Muni, that if Muni agreed to do it, he could get the financing and they could shoot the picture right there in New York. Muni read it, but his discussions with Shumlin were vague, irrelevant, elliptical, and finally Muni just muttered, "I don't think so." (Five years later the film, starring Rod Steiger, was made by other hands.)

Bella took Shumlin aside and wept. "I can't stand it any longer. He hates me. He really hates me. It takes me two days to recover from some of the things he says to me!"

Muni hated only himself. When he was separated from Bella for more than a week, a few times on opposite coasts, he would be on the phone demanding that she fly to California or setting the date for his return to New York.

Bella pleaded with him to confer with a psychiatrist. (She distrusted them but felt it was a last resort.) Muni made several appointments and broke them. Finally, he did listen and sat silently in a psychiatrist's office. The doctor told him he needed twenty-four-hour care and recommended an exclusive mental home ("rest home" was the euphemism) in Connecticut. "Why do I need a rest home?" Muni pleaded. "*Rest* is what I'm sick of!"

When he no longer had the energy to resist, he finally nodded his head and committed himself to the mental home. But when he arrived in Connecticut, he was uncooperative. "I may be *mishuga*," he said, "but nuts I'm not!" He couldn't stand it. After a week he returned to New York and the silence of the East End apartment.

Bella felt that the apartment itself might be to blame; though it was expansive and expensive, to Muni (who loved land) it still seemed "cliff-dwelling claustrophobia." So Bella began searching for another country place, close enough to New York so that she could come in to see the theater she loved, far enough away so "Muni could breathe."

Jonas Silverstone, their attorney cousin, tries to fit in one of the missing pieces of the jigsaw puzzle of Muni's life in his description of that incident:

"A friend of theirs whose name I choose not to remember 'had just the place' up in Connecticut, and Bella agreed to buy it without even seeing it. We closed the deal in my office. After it was over,

Bella and I drove up to see the property. It was a prefabricated kind of house, which was nothing. Muni went there two or three times and just refused to go ever again. It had lovely land, but the building was just not to his liking. Though there were twenty or thirty acres, it was completely hidden and cut off from the world with a high hedge. It had privacy, which to my mind was imprisonment.

"I had a long talk with Bella on the way up and back—just the two of us in the car heading for a town way above Danbury. I laid bare what had been resting in my gut for years about Muni and Bella and their relationship and what all this did to Muni. Bella cried, and I think she hated me for the rest of that drive; but obviously I must have been truthful or our relationship would not have continued.

"I told Bella that I thought she had failed Muni very substantially by constantly 'hiding' him, by claiming always to provide him with privacy: she had doomed him to be closeted and cloistered. Muni loved people! It's hard to believe, but basically he was a very gregarious man, who loved being in the company of other men and women. I told Bella that *she didn't mother him, she smothered him.* That was the exact expression I used."

Why did Muni let this happen? Was he a docile man who hated to fight? A thousand people who shared sound stages with him would argue that point. Perhaps it was the duality of Muni: so much of his energy went into Muni the actor that only a few shorts volts were left for Muni the human being. Was Jonas Silverstone right? Did Bella, in her passion to protect Muni's career, have a stifling effect on Muni the man?

Ted Thomas, a lifelong Muni watcher, comments, "Take away Bella and I doubt if Munya would have survived the sinking of the Yiddish theater. Let's face it: there were other actors around at the time who were also great, but who got lost in the shuffle—maybe because they didn't have a Bella around to confuse, irritate, help, trip, and inspire an actor into a star. *Viva Bella!* I wouldn't have lived in her girdle for all the money in MGM!"

Then Thomas quotes Cesare Lombroso, the Italian-Jewish turn-of-the-century psychiatrist, who must have had somebody like Muni in mind when he wrote: "A genius is a man whose brain is devoted ninety-nine per cent to one function, leaving one per cent to cope with all the other functions of life."

* * *

The Munis never lived in Connecticut. Two weeks later the property was again in escrow and Muni was headed back to California and his Wart on Trancas beach. There he found comfort and a measure of peace staring out at the unpacific Pacific.

Muni's fiddle lay in its case on a closet shelf, unplayed. He never touched it again.

In the summer of 1959 my partner and I, in concert with Herman Shumlin who was set to direct and produce, offered Muni *Only in America,* a play we had written about Harry Golden, the Yankee conscience of Charlotte, North Carolina. Muni read it five times. Bella urged him to do it. "It would be a family reunion," she said.

Muni phoned us. Bob Lee and I drove out to Trancas. Muni handed us the script sadly, shaking his head. "I'd like to do this, but I can't. It wouldn't be fair to you, or to the play, or to an audience."

Then he looked away from us, and his voice was strange and distant.

"It's natural to grow old—that happens to everybody. But it's indecent to be sick. An actor needs energy, memory, concentration. For me, *boychicks,* it's all gone."

(The play ran less than a month in New York but played for a full year when Herschel Bernardi starred in it on the West Coast. We can only speculate what the play would have been like on Broadway with Muni as this "Yiddish Will Rogers.")

The couple who couldn't live with each other but couldn't live without each other had their last home together in a hillside villa overlooking the ocean in Montecito, a suburb of Santa Barbara. Reluctantly, Muni finally sold his Wart and the profitable acres around it, parcel by parcel.

Their first telephone call of welcome was from the rabbi of the tiny Santa Barbara congregation. "We have a very small temple here," he told Bella, "only about twenty families, but we'd be honored if you and Mr. Muni would become members."

The nonjoining Bella was polite. "Thank you for calling, Rabbi," she said, "but I'll be frank with you: we're mostly Jewish in our stomachs. So you can help us out with that. For God's sake, where's the nearest kosher delicatessen?"

The rabbi had to admit there wasn't one he knew of within a hundred miles of this WASP enclave. So my partner and I began sending monthly "Care Packages" to the Munis of Montecito: bagels, lox, corn beef and pastrami, Jewish rye breads, and salamis three feet long—all shipped in dry ice from Linny's in Beverly Hills or Cantor's on Fairfax Avenue. There was an inadvertent omission in one package.

"What kind of writers are they?" Muni complained when the package was dumped onto their dining-room table. "They forgot the kosher dill pickles!"

We drove up to see them as often as possible. Muni was warm and affectionate, but each visit he seemed more withdrawn. He told us how thrilled he was when Ed Begley dropped in one day, to present his new young wife and embrace his friend-opponent of *Inherit the Wind*. Beyond that the visitors were few: Ruth Jacoves (formerly Ruth Rothman Finkel) came when she could, as did Marc and Emily Daniels. It was Daniels who convinced Muni to make one last television appearance on the *Saints and Sinners* program late in 1962.

"You're Jesus," Muni told Daniels. "And I'm Lazarus, raised from the dead! A couple of Jewish boys."

The Ernest Kinoy script was about a man of nearly one hundred and his wife, almost as old (played by Lili Darvas), who were about to celebrate their diamond wedding anniversary when they decide to get a divorce. Muni and Bella came in from Montecito and stayed at the Beverly Wilshire Hotel for the week-long shooting. When he rehearsed privately with Daniels, Muni was letter-perfect. When he got onto the set, the lines disappeared from his memory. Muni felt humiliated before cast and crew members. Painfully he got through the ordeal.

Early one morning, halfway through the shooting, Bella and Muni were coming down in the hotel elevator when suddenly Muni said, "Why are we doing this?"

"I don't know." Bella yawned.

"*I* know!" he said brightly. "We need the money!"

(In their wills, the Munis left almost $2,000,000 to the City of Hope for cancer research and to Brandeis University for student scholarships.)

They were back in Montecito when the filmed *Saints and Sinners* program was broadcast just before Christmas of 1962. I watched it with admiration. Despite the difficulties of the shooting, Muni was unable to camouflage his personal wit and wisdom. His speech about how old people should be treated was one of the best table-cloth speeches of Muni's career. When I phoned them just after the broadcast, Bella answered. (Muni wouldn't come to the phone. "He's allergic to compliments," Bella said.) Jokingly, I asked Bella if, like the wife in the TV play, in all her years with Muni she'd ever contemplated divorce.

"Oh, no," she said with mock solemnity. "Murder, yes. Divorce —never!"

She began to laugh. Later somebody told me it was an old joke; but we both roared, and it was good to hear a joyful Bella again.

For almost five years, Muni's health declined. Bella hired two nurses, Mrs. Agnes Wolford and Mrs. Helen Lovett, who were devoted to the Munis. The nurses found they had not just one but two patients. Bella's frequent attacks were as painful to Muni as his own.

Muni read deeper and deeper into philosophy, studied his dictionaries, watched television alternately with delight and scorn, stared out at the Pacific Ocean, and waited to die.

On his seventieth birthday, he strode erectly around the house. Ruth Jacoves, who was there, remembers his saying, "Look at me. I'm seventy. But I'm not stooped over. I don't have a high, thin, trembling voice. My hands don't shake like jelly. But when I was a kid, that's the way I played seventy-year-olds. Frankly, I was a more convincing seventy-year-old when I was twelve!"

A few weeks later my partner and I drove up to Montecito, a belated birthday gift in hand: the new unabridged edition of the *Random House Dictionary of the English Language*. Muni made a ritual out of opening the heavy package and then weighed it with delight.

"A dictionary?" Bella shrugged. "Muni needs a dictionary as much as Mr. Webster does!"

"Turn to page 941," Bob suggested.

Muni flipped the pages elaborately, wetting his finger like an ancient Talmudic scholar.

"Let me see, let me see," Muni mumbled. "Here on page 941 we have MUMBO JUMBO—'a meaningless incantation or ritual'—exactly what celebrating a birthday is! Or my adopted sons bringing a present yet for their *alter-cocker* papa. Not in the dictionary, but also mumbo-jumbo!"

"Look in the second column," Bob said.

Muni pulled his eyeglasses onto the bridge of his nose and looked down the column. Suddenly he stopped, visibly moved. Silently he pointed to an entry and showed the dictionary to Bella.

It read:

mung′ bean′ (muñg) 1. the green or yellow, edible seed of an Asian bean. *Phaseolus aureus.* 2. the plant itself. [*mung* < Tamil *mūngu* << Skt *mudga*]

mun·go (muñg′gō), n., pl. -gos, a low-grade wool from felted rags or waste. Also, mungo, moungo. Cf. shoddy (def. 1). [?]

Mun·hall (mun′hôl′), n. a city in W Pennsylvania, near Pittsburgh. 17,312 (1960).

Mu·ni (myōō′nē), n. 1. Paul (*Muni Weisenfreund*), born 1895, U.S. actor, born in Austria. 2. a boy's given name.

Mu·nich (myōō′nik), n. 1. German, München. a city in and the capital of Bavaria, in SW West Germany. 1,157,300 (1963). 2. any dishonorable appeasement. Cf. Munich Pact.

"I'm in a dictionary, for God's sake," he shouted. "At last somebody has defined me!"

Twice Muni was confined to the Cottage Hospital in Santa Barbara with pneumonia. His heart condition grew more serious. In the summer of 1967, an ambulance took Muni to the Good Samaritan Hospital in Los Angeles, where a pacemaker was put into his failing heart. After the operation, he wanted to go home. "I prefer being near the sea," he said, "and near my dictionaries."

Back in Montecito, confined to his bed, he kidded with his nurses. "An enema? Why not? But let's trade. You give me one, I'll give you one." But the pain in his chest was too intense for him to laugh.

Bella hung some family pictures on the wall opposite his bed. When he opened his eyes and saw them, Muni pointed toward his mother's photograph and said weakly; "Take her away." Bella removed it. Only Philip Weisenfreund's picture, taken in Chicago when Muni was thirteen, remained on the wall.

The sunset over the Pacific was brilliant on the evening of August 25, 1967. Bella sat at Muni's bedside holding his hand as the shadows deepened in the room. He was barely breathing. He moaned but seemed to try to stop himself, as if wishing to spare Bella.

She leaned in closer.

"Are you in pain?"

"Sure. What else is new?" And he laughed a little.

Bella tried to smile but moved away from the bed so Muni wouldn't see her crying. Distantly she heard him, a whisper, deep in his throat, as if directing himself:

"Munya, be a *mensch!*"

She rushed for the nurses. When they lit the lamp in the darkened room, the light fell across the photograph of Philip. Muni opened his eyes and spoke to the picture.

"Papa," he said, "I'm hungry."

And that was all.

I shivered when I saw a bulletin board at the cemetery gate, with movable letters almost like a movie marquee. It read:

TODAY—PAUL MUNI

Many retired Yiddish actors filled the chapel on the cemetery grounds, but almost nobody from the film colony came to the brief service. At the graveside, Jonas Silverstone and I murmured the Kaddish. In the chapel, at Bella's request, Bob Lee spoke:

"Paul Muni has asked that there be no eulogy for him. He doesn't need a eulogy.

"What Muni has done on the stage is theater history. His films will certainly be run as long as there is a projector on this planet to show them.

"He said to Bella a few weeks ago that he only hoped a friend would stand up and say: 'He wasn't such a bad guy.'

"This vast understatement is typical of the man.

"The paradox of Muni is that his genius was illusion, but he had contempt for anything which was sham. In a business of pretending, he hated pretense or pretentiousness.

"So there was a constant restlessness within him, a creative restlessness.

"When he was working, nothing mattered but *getting it right!*

"I don't think Muni ever really heard the applause; and if he did, he didn't believe it.

"We all have our own stories about Muni: his tenacity, his wit, his shy generosity, his dignity.

"We mourn the departure of our friend Muni, we pray for comfort and strength for his Bella.

"We rejoice that we have had the privilege of knowing him, and being inspired by him.

"Someone defined God as the voice within us which keeps saying: 'It isn't good enough!' If that's true, then Muni has lived very close to God. *He wasn't such a bad guy.*"

Muni with Bette Davis in *Bordertown*.

29

MUNI, who never wanted a eulogy, received a lot of them in the multiple tapes I recorded as I was researching this book. If *Actor* is a proper designation for Muni, *Actress* would be the appropriate description of Bette Davis. She rarely, if ever, agrees to a taped interview. In this instance she made an exception, to tell me her impression of Muni. She had shared two motion pictures (*Bordertown* and *Juarez*) with him and, like Muni, was a studio rebel, with the same mixed feelings he had about the advantages and disadvantages of a star contract.

Hollywood, October 9, 1973

BD: Is this a biography or an autobiography?
JL: A biography.
BD: The only way to do it. I disapprove of autobiographies. There was such a vogue for them once. Now where do we begin?
JL: When you first met Muni.
BD: When I did *Bordertown*. That was after *Scarface*. It was his beginning, and he played himself. He did in *Bordertown*,

too—and I think you'll agree he was a terribly attractive man—as himself. What happened to him with the disguises I don't know. I remember going to Mexico City shortly after we made *Juarez* and seeing statues of Juarez, and I said, "My God, it's Paul Muni!" Jack Warner made a brilliant remark to producer Heinz Blanke: "Why did we have to hire Muni? You can't find him!"

JL: Blanke sends his best to you. A wonderful man.

BD: One of the greats. He and Hal Wallis really made films for Warners that were *firsts*. They did *Pasteur* and *Zola* with Muni. They were beautiful, but you couldn't find Muni behind the makeups. Many critics say about me, "She's always the same." This is not true, but unless there's *some label* of the personality for the public to recognize, you'll never be a big star. They've *got* to find you each time—someone they know. John Barrymore played many great parts, Sarah Bernhardt played many great parts, but there was always a Barrymore underneath, a Bernhardt underneath. You cannot disguise your personality completely. I've worn millions of makeups, but always there was the personality. Why did Muni start hiding so? Because he wrecked his career with it.

JL: He was a "self-wrecker"—partly because of his childhood.

BD: What was his birth sign?

JL: He was a Virgo.

BD: My mother was a Virgo.

JL: Are they self-destructors?

BD: Well, they're not the strongest people in the world.

JL: He was strong when he was in another role, but not when he was himself.

BD: And yet he had every indication as a young man that he had a terrific personality. And intelligence. He was a genius with scripts—analyzing a script, knowing what was wrong with it. At the end of *Bordertown*, Mr. Muni said to me, "Don't ever have a director, you don't need one." I said, "Mr. Muni, the day will never come when I don't need a director! And want one!" Muni himself never trusted any director—except Bella, whom I really adored and who had one hell of a life. But what happened to Muni was that, in effect, he became his own director, his editor, everything. The way I feel: you *cannot do it alone.* I can be a hundred times better with a good director. Muni was brilliant. *Utt*erly. Articulate. A real intellectual—but he was his own worst enemy. Why did he "hide" behind the characters so much?

JL: He wanted to do a great variety of parts, never repeating himself . . . and he didn't like himself very much.

BD: You know, I have a theory. It's taken me sixty-five years to realize this—I don't think *any* of us who loved playing characters liked ourselves. Do you agree?

JL: Absolutely.

BD: It's taken me years to figure it out. I used to say, "Why do I love playing other people?" I didn't *like* myself very much. Muni didn't like himself at all. Once you have a certain amount of success, you have to have more regard for yourself, but this didn't seem to help him. It made his problem worse and worse and worse. You know what I've often wondered? If Bella hadn't gone along with him as much as she did, she might have helped him.

JL: She tried. But by helping him too much she probably hurt him. That's part of it. She overhelped him. He should have relied on himself and his own instincts more.

BD: And she became his complete mother.

JL: Mother-companion-director-agent.

BD: Did he have a great mother?

JL: Oh, no. He had a terrible mother. He had a horror of a mother.

BD: So Bella became his mother, and he started to rely on her: the mother he never had. That's understandable.

JL: Right. A little bit "twopenny Freud," but it does help explain him. Now, tell me about William Dieterle.

BD: I first made a picture with Dieterle called *Fog over Frisco*, his first film at Warner's. Then Muni found him, and Dieterle gave up his identity to Mr. Muni, and that was Dieterle's funeral. He ended up doing all of Muni's films and looking toward Bella for approval after every scene—like everyone else. Dieterle could have been one of the most important directors in Hollywood.

JL: Tell me. Do you think that Warner Brothers hurt Muni calling him "*Mr.* PAUL MUNI"? Did they ever bill you as "*Miss* BETTE DAVIS"? I think the only two people they did that to were Muni and George Arliss.

BD: Which was right for Arliss. But in that day for Muni it was, in my opinion, detrimental. If they want to call me, "MISS BETTE DAVIS" at sixty-five that's a totally different matter.

JL: You said in your book, and I think rightly, that Muni did things for the dignity of the actor. He fought the studio just as you did.

354

The poster for *Bordertown*.

(Courtesy Warner Brothers)

BD: Oh, boy, *did* he!!!

JL: Do you think it was laudable of him?

BD: Yes! We all had to! I don't think any of us, including Muni, would have had important careers. Cagney, Bogart, Muni, and me. It takes a lot of guts to fight a studio, for they are really in charge.

JL: And they sued you in England and you lost the case, didn't you?

BD: You know what my fight was: directors and scripts. I knew that if I didn't stop getting poor directors and bad scripts, then it was over. Actually I *won,* because when I came home, they never treated me badly again.

JL: Who was the most sympathetic spirit in the front office?

BD: Hal Wallis. Muni would never have had *Zola,* all those parts, unless Hal had been in charge. I think, under Wallis, Warner Brothers for ten years was a studio that will never be equaled (well, we know it won't be equaled now!). Hal was the one who bought all those great properties for me.

JL: Muni performed most of his best roles at Warner's. Do you think it was a mistake that he turned his back on the studio system?

355

BD: The studio contract system made stars! Nobody can be made a star again in the same way. We had ninety men in the publicity department. By the time one of your films came out, the whole world knew about it! They waited a year to bring *Dark Victory* out, timing its release properly, preparing the ground. Now I look at a New York paper and I say, "Who's that? What's this?" With all of the contract problems, those were *better* problems than the young actors have today. *You don't learn through the parts which are easy for you!* Nobody's playing anything anymore that's tough for them. It's all typecasting, and I know there was type-casting then, but not as much.

JL: That was part of Muni's motivation. He was fighting to be different every time.

BD: Well, I wanted to be different, too. But I never used that much makeup. For instance, he could have accomplished his purpose without that rubber face as Juarez. They could have fixed his nose a bit, given him some Mexican eyes, but we would have recognized Muni. What do you call your book?

JL: *ACTOR.*

BD: That is the *perfect* title for Mr. Muni. He was a consummate actor. He had no other life! I can have another life when I'm not acting. Muni didn't *exist* except as an actor. That was really another tragedy. He never had any release. Acting is a marvelous profession: you can go off for six months and recharge your battery and forget you're an actor and come back renewed and refreshed. Muni *never* forgot he was an actor.

JL: He didn't know how to relax. He never learned. If a young actor today were trying to analyze, trying to learn something from Muni, what would you, who worked with him, who observed him, say he had?

BD: Dedication. Sweat. Muni never stopped working. Because he loved it! Muni didn't love just the lights and the fame, he loved the *doing* of it. What is gone from today is *the love of doing it!!!* And it's going to take you fifteen years to be a Paul Muni, of just doing it and learning by your mistakes.

JL: He never had a frame of film on him until he was thirty-three.

BD: Muni had an incredible thing which is very important. He could play two things at one time. Every actor has to learn to do that. You don't just play one thing *head on into the camera!* There's something else going on in the back of your

356

head that makes you *say* this; that's the thing you have to project.

JL: In other words, *thought* has to be photographed.

BD: Thought is the only thing. The camera catches thought. If there's ever a moment when an actor stops thinking, the audience stops being interested.

JL: What was your feeling about working with Muni for the first time?

BD: Remember—I was a very young actress then, with half the experience of Muni. So number one, I was enormously thrilled to work with him. I had seen him many times and respected him. When we finished *Bordertown*, I respected him even more. And *learned* from him! *Really* learned from him. And he was beautiful to me—you know, that's part of being a star. Today actors don't know what a star is! A star is not just a big name that supposedly can act—*a star is in charge* of the whole project. Muni was a *star* in charge of a set. I found this a great experience. Because this was the first real honest-to-God *star* I had ever worked with. A star takes center stage. I had a scene in *Bordertown* where I wake up in the middle of the night. I put cold cream on my face and curlers in my hair. I had a fight with the studio—Wallis came on the set and said, "You can't look like that on the screen!" I said, "That's how this woman would look in bed!" Muni stood up for me. He also stood up for me in the mad scene in the courtroom. I think of him many, many times in my life. You want one phrase to sum up Muni for your book? *He was an actor's actor!*

WHEN I built a house overlooking the Pacific Ocean, Bella gave me two flowering trees to plant at either side of the entrance. These coral trees blaze with color; the branches twist toward the sky, reaching for the light. They seem to lean toward the ocean, as if wanting to catch the spray. Because Muni had loved the ocean, too, the trees were to be a memorial to him. So I named them, placing tiny signs at the foot of each trunk: THE MUNI TREE. THE BELLA TREE.

Bella Muni with playwright Jerome Lawrence.

(Photo by Rusty Morris)

They were bush-high when they were planted. Now they are giants. The trees require affection and light. They love music, as the Munis did. And each year the trees grow taller.

The school kids from the mesa above me use a path we have cut alongside the trees as a shortcut to school. The other day, a nine-year-old girl with long blond hair like Lewis Carroll's Alice, stopped for a moment and pointed to one of the tiny signs.

"What's a Bella Tree?" she asked me.

"Bella is a woman's name. It means 'beautiful.' She was the wife of a very great actor."

The girl's thirteen-year-old brother, with an intense, listening face, came up behind her.

"What's a Muni Tree?" he asked.

"That was the actor's name: Paul Muni. Sometime look in your *TV Guide* and watch some of his movies."

A few days later I saw the boy standing alone, silently staring at the Muni Tree. He turned suddenly when he saw me heading for the garage.

"I stayed up and watched that *Zola* movie on TV last night," he said. "Hey! How do you get to be an actor like that?"

"You work hard," I told him. I wish the boy had also watched Rudolf Nureyev on the *Dick Cavett Show* several nights before.

358

"Do you ever want to act?" Cavett asked the famous dancer. Nureyev looked incredulous, as if somebody had asked that nine-year-old girl to step onto the stage of the Bolshoi Theater without an instant's training or practice and immediately become a prima ballerina. "It takes a whole lifetime, no?" Nureyev said. "If you're not trained for acting, how can you just go and act, you know? Shouldn't you learn a profession properly—and not just wish, not just have a fantasy, a whim?"

Bella lived four more years. But she was lost without Muni. "Nobody recognizes me," Bella told Bob Lee's wife, Janet. "Nobody knows who I am without Muni. I'm the caboose—but the train's gone."

Roberta Thomas (Ted's wife and Michael Tilson Thomas' mother) remembers Bella's eloquent way of conveying the idea that an issue or a person was dead. Silently Bella brought her open hand down in front of her face—as if a theater curtain was being lowered. And it came down with a finality, not just like a velour curtain, but like a two-ton asbestos drop.

Bella tried living in New York at the Plaza. She tried to write about Muni. Finally she came back to California. She lived with her nurses at the Beverly Wilshire Hotel, then in a rented house on Camden Drive. When she read a new play of ours (she always got the first copy) or watched a Marc Daniels-directed television show, her criticism was intelligent, to the point, and full of wit. We named her "President of the Let's-Not-Kid-Ourselves Club."

After she suffered a stroke, she began to hallucinate. She was convinced that somebody was photographing everything she was thinking and remembering and then projecting all of it on a huge movie screen in the basement of the Camden Drive house. Only Bob's son Jonathan, a nineteen-year-old electronics buff, was able to convince Bella—with quiet scientific logic—that nobody had yet invented movies like that.

In October, 1971, Bella was propped up in bed, her dinner tray in front of her. She was staring at a photograph of Muni when she died.

Bob Lee spoke these words at Bella's funeral:

"A few weeks ago, Bella asked Jerry Lawrence, my writing partner, to say a few words when this time might come.

"Well, Jerry is in New York for the rehearsals of our new play —and he has asked if I would be his stand-in. But I'm not speaking only for Jerry—but for *all* of us—all the hosts of friends Bella and Muni have made in their lifetime.

"Last Thursday afternoon, Janet and I parked by the white picket fence on Camden and dropped in to say hello to Bella. (This has become one of our happy rituals when we are in Beverly Hills.)

"As many of you have done, my wife and I followed Bella's ups and downs over the past months. She really seemed to be improving. Bella knew that we were going to the Soviet Union, and she told us some very funny stories about the visit she and Muni had made to Moscow, sometime in the thirties. I told her we were also going to Kiev—and a distant look came into her brown eyes and she said, 'My father was born in Kiev.' Janet told her that I was studying Russian and she said, 'Say hello.' Well, this was one of the few words I thought I knew. Bella listened; then she said: 'You think anybody in Moscow is going to understand that?'

"And then this remarkable friend—who, only a few weeks before, was suffering from aphasia, a speech impairment because of a stroke—was now 'palatilizing' the complexities of Russian! If I ever learn to say *Zhdrast-vyee-tyeh* so anybody can understand it, I can thank Bella. Of course, we didn't have any way of knowing this (the irony of it), but while she was teaching me to say hello in Russian, we were actually saying good-bye.

"It is impossible to think of Muni without Bella—or of Bella without Muni. This is what made the past few years so difficult for Bella, with Muni gone.

"In a time and in a profession where marriage is growing more and more meaningless, the Munis demonstrated that a committed wedding of spirit and mind and talent and soul can be the greatest reality of life.

"So real, in fact, that when Bella lost Muni, she simply could not regain again the fullness of living.

"But she *tried!* In New York, she tried, but winter and loneliness defeated her. Here in California, her body grew weaker—in spite of the loving attention of Mrs. Wolford and Mrs. Lovett, the same nurses who had attended Muni in Santa Barbara.

"Now, from time to time, Bella had great pain, and she had to have relief from that pain. But she never lost touch with what was going on. The TV set was at the foot of her bed. She watched David Frost with friendship and Agnew with dismay. She never lost her ability to laugh at little things and to get angry at big ones.

"Many of you here have known Bella far longer than I. And you will remember that Bella Finkel was a very important star before she married Muni. She had to decide, really, between her career and his. She chose to be Mrs. Paul Muni. And a great measure of Muni's success was due to her.

360

"Bella's mind was full of rich, clear memories. She was contemplating a book. Jerry and I encouraged her to work on it—but I don't know that she got much beyond a great title: *The Men in My Life*. Bella knew, better than any of us, that Muni was *many* men. He was Tony in *Scarface*, James Allen in *I Am a Fugitive from a Chain Gang*, Louis Pasteur, Zola, Juarez, George Simon in *Counsellor-at-Law*, Henry Drummond in *Inherit the Wind*—he did not play these roles, he was these men!

"And Bella was the wife of them all.

"We will never know—we can only guess—how much *she* gave to the brilliance of *The Men in Her Life*.

"In a sense, an era is now past.

"We must close a book which was lived and acted—but never written."

(Photo by Josh Weiner)

Acknowledgments

My gratitude to many hands, minds, memories:

ROBERT E. LEE for permission to print his tributes to Muni and Bella and for editorial counsel over and beyond the call of duty.

TED THOMAS for constant counsel on this entire project, for multiple contributions, many taping sessions, and for sharing his vast personal knowledge of the Yiddish theater and of his cousins, the Munis.

ROLLAND "RUSTY" MORRIS for infinite precision and pains co-ordinating the research material, for long hours typing the taped interviews and the manuscript, and for aid in selecting and organizing the photographs.

Research assistance in multiple cities: J. B. ANNEGAN and FRANCIS RICHARDS in New York, RUSSELL LEE LAWRENCE in Philadelphia, BRUCE VILANCH in Chicago, WARREN MARVIN in London, RAY TAYLOR in Detroit, ROSEMARY LEWIS and ESTHER FRIEDMAN TAPS in Cleveland, GAVIN KERN and DAVID SAURER in Los Angeles.

The THEATRE COLLECTION of the LIBRARY & MUSEUM OF THE PERFORMING ARTS in Lincoln Center, New York, has the best collection of Muni memorabilia, including annotated scripts and books. PAUL MYERS, THOR WOOD, DOROTHY SWERDLOVE, and ROD BLADEL have been of continuing help during the research and writing of this book.

The librarians at the ACADEMY OF MOTION PICTURE ARTS & SCIENCES in Hollywood have been patient, helpful and creative. My thanks to MILDRED SIMPSON, JUDY POLANSKY, and MARLENE MEDIVIN.

The YIVO INSTITUTE FOR JEWISH RESEARCH in New York supplied much Yiddish theater background material. DINA ABAMOWICZ is the guiding spirit.

The library at the UNIVERSITY OF JUDAISM in Los Angeles was a friendly enclave of major reference materials on Yiddish subjects.

FRANK WELLS, president of WARNER BROTHERS, generously opened his studios and studio files for my research on Muni. RUDY FEHR arranged for the screening of all the relevant Warner Brothers films. SYLVIA RABIN was of incalculable help.

My thanks to the morgues and microfilm services of many newspapers: NEW YORK *Times*, PHILADELPHIA *Inquirer*, CHICAGO *Today*, PHOENIX *Republic*, LOS ANGELES *Times*, CLEVELAND *Plain Dealer*.

The following public libraries were generous with their help: New York City, Cleveland, Pasadena, Santa Monica, Glendale, and Beverly Hills.

MAXINE WOOLEVER, owner-manager of Hollywood Photo Accessories

Company, took personal interest in providing polarized copy negatives and restored prints, which were in many cases, superior to the originals entrusted to her lab. Other photo work by ACTORS ONLY, QUANTITY PHOTOS, and PARAGON LABS.

I must list the following alphabethically. My meetings with each of them were enlightening and enthralling. Without their help, this book would not have been possible:

GEORGE ABBOTT   Taped interview, New York, June 7, 1973.

TOM ADAIR   Interview, Burbank, April 20, 1973.

BRUCE ADLER   Taped interview, New York, October 30, 1973.

LUTHER ADLER   Multiple interviews, letters, wires, photographs. Taped interview, New York, June 11, 1973; interview, Beverly Hills, October 18, 1973.

MARY ASTOR   For permission to print excerpts from her book *A Life on Film*.

ARTHUR BALLET   Interview, San Diego, September 6, 1973,
of the Office of Advanced   and for his careful reading of the manuscript.
Drama Research

SONYA BAYARD   Multiple interviews throughout 1973.
the widow of Elias
Weisenfreund

PETER BELLAMY   For his correspondence about Muni's Cleve-
drama critic, Cleveland   land beginnings.
Plain Dealer

JACOB BEN-AMI   Taped interview, New York, June 14, 1973.

JOHN BERENDT   For supplying me, by long-distance telephone, with copy from the *Dick Cavett Show*.

JACK BERNARDI   Taped interview, Malibu, July 9, 1973.

HENRY BLANKE   Taped interview, Brentwood, September 28, 1973, and multiple telephone calls.

KERMIT BLOOMGARDEN   Taped interview, New York, June 13, 1973.

TRUE BOARDMAN   For the loan of scripts of the *Screen Guild* broadcast and for background material.

DIANA BOURBON   Phone conferences, October, 1973.

PROFESSOR   Conference, September 1, 1973.
DAVID BRADLEY

JANE BRYAN   Correspondence, October–November, 1973.
(Mrs. JUSTIN DART)

ALBERTO CAVALCANTI	Conference, Hollywood, June 21, 1973.
MARGUERITE CHAPMAN	Taped interview, Los Angeles, August 1, 1973.
JAN CLAYTON	For her help in arranging various interviews.
DAVID CLIVE	Telephone conference, November 14, 1973.
STAATS COTSWORTH	Taped interview, Santa Monica, April 11, 1973, and for his generous permission to reproduce his *Inherit the Wind* painting and photographs.
DOUGLAS CRANE	For counsel and help in contacting source material.
CHERYL CRAWFORD	Interview, Beverly Hills, March 16, 1973.
JACK DANIELS	Telephone interview, August 18, 1973.
MARC and EMILY DANIELS	Taped interview, Malibu, April 27, 1973, and the loan of source material.
BETTE DAVIS	Taped interview, Hollywood, October 9, 1973.
FRANK DAVIS	Telephone interview, August 16, 1973.
LUTHER DAVIS	Taped interview, Santa Monica, November 14, 1973.
REGINALD DENHAM	Taped interview, New York, June 8, 1973.
ROBERT DOWNING drama critic, Denver *Post*	For correspondence recalling many theater stories.
MICHAEL DRUXMAN	For running the film of *The World Changes* for me.
MICHAEL ELLIS	Taped interview, Bucks County, Pennsylvania, June 13, 1973.
SIDNEY ELLIS	Taped interview, Malibu, August 10, 1973.
JOHN FEARNLEY	Taped interview, Malibu, January 12, 1973.
ALBERT FENN *Life* photographer and grandson of Morris Finkel	Taped interviews, June 7 and June 14, 1973, with Mrs. Fenn participating the second time, and for arranging for me to meet Jacob Ben-Ami.
NINA FOCH	Taped interview, West Hollywood, May 1, 1973.
MAX FOSTER	Taped interview, Malibu, May 19, 1973, and for permission to use letters and photographs from his collection.

364

MICHAEL FOX	Taped interview, Hollywood, August 8, 1973.
CLAIRE FRIEDLAND	Taped interview, New York, June 10, 1973.
DR. MICHAEL GERLACH	For sharing source material obtained for the preparation of his excellent thesis, *The Acting of Paul Muni* / University of Michigan, 1971.
SHERIDAN GIBNEY	Taped interview, Sepulveda, California, September 25, 1973.
BEN GOETZ	Taped interview, Beverly Hills, August 21, 1973.
HARRY GOLDEN	Correspondence and counsel on the Yiddish theater.
ANNA GOLDFARB	For translating Yiddish source material.
GENEVIEVE GOLDHURST	Memories of Muni's mother.
JOSEPH GROSSMAN	Taped interview, North Hollywood, April 20, 1973.
ROBERT HARRIS	For putting me in touch with Yiddish theater personalities.
HOWARD HAWKS	Taped interview, Palm Springs, California, August 30, 1973.
EILEEN HECKART	Stories re: *They Knew What They Wanted* via correspondence.
FRED HOAR accountant for M. C. Levee	Telephone interview, September 14, 1973.
JOSEPHINE HUTCHINSON	Taped interview, Santa Monica, April 13, 1973, and the loan of background material.
JIM HUTTON	For helping arrange Muni screenings.
CHRISTOPHER ISHERWOOD	Interview about Berthold Viertel, Santa Monica, August 20, 1973.
HENRIETTA JACOBSON	Taped interview, New York, October 30, 1973.
IRVING JACOBSON	Taped interview, New York, October 30, 1973.
RUTH JACOVES	Taped interview, Palm Springs, California, May 2, 1973 and many letters and telephone conversations following.
SAM JAFFE	Interview, Hollywood, May 4, 1973.

PAULINE KAISER formerly PAULINE SIEGEL	Taped interview, New York, June 11, 1973.
WILLIAM KOPPELMANN of Brandt and Brandt	For lending me *Key Largo* material.
HY KRAFT	Taped interview, New York, June 11, 1973, and numerous letters following, as well as permission to quote from his book *On My Way to the Theater.*
MILTON KRIMS	Taped interview, Hollywood, May 1, 1973, and the loan of much source materials.
DAVID LAPP	Phone conversations, Egg Harbour City, New Jersey, summer, 1973.
JACK LARSON	Taped interview, Malibu, May 20, 1973, about behind-the-scenes material at Warner Brothers.
ANNA LEE (Mrs. ROBERT NATHAN)	Taped interview and correspondence, October 20, 1973. My thanks also to her son for further background material on *Commandos Strike at Dawn.*
JANET WALDO LEE	For many stories and impressions of the Munis from her photographic memory.
JONATHAN LEE	(Ditto)
MERVYN LEROY	Taped interview, West Los Angeles, August 22, 1973, and for the loan of source material from his private collection.
MICHAEL LEVEE	Taped interview, October 7, 1973, and for steering me to his mother, his uncle, and to many individuals who worked with his father, M. C. Levee.
MIMI LEVEE (Mrs. M. C. LEVEE)	Phone interview, October 18, 1973.
SIDNEY LEVEE	Taped phone interview, September 13, 1973.
ALBERT LEWIS	Taped interview, Brentwood, January 15, 1973.
THOMAS H. A. LEWIS	For sharing his memories of the *Screen Guild Show.* Ojai, California, October, 1973.
REA LINDENBERG	For unearthing Weisenfreund family material, Philadelphia, summer, 1973.
MARGARET LINDSAY	Taped interview, West Los Angeles, September 12, 1973.

MICHAEL LORING	Malibu, August 8, 1973, for aid in translating Yiddish.
JOAN LORRING	Correspondence, New York, 1973.
LOS ANGELES CIVIC LIGHT OPERA ASSOCIATION particularly Mrs. BETTY RICHARDSON	For help in assembling background material on *At the Grand,* Los Angeles, November, 1973.
HELEN LOVETT	For lending me a great deal of Muni material.
ARTHUR LUBIN	Taped interview, Los Angeles, August 17, 1973, and for the loan of all his collected memorabilia on *This One Man,* including the original unpublished manuscript of the play.
DANIEL MANN	Taped interview, appropriately at Trancas, California, November 10, 1973.
SAM MARX	Taped interview, Malibu, August 13, 1973.
FRANK MAXWELL	Taped interview, Los Angeles, May 30, 1973, and for the loan of London *Death of a Salesman* material.
JAMES .T. McCAFFERTY drama critic, Columbus *Dispatch*	Advice and counsel.
LON McCALLISTER	Taped interview, Malibu, April 30, 1973.
JAYNE MEADOWS	Interviews, Encino, December, 1973.
RICHARD MOORE	Taped interview, New York, June 11, 1973.
MILLIE MURRAY formerly, executive secretary, M. C. Levee Agency	Interview, Los Angeles, September 15, 1973.
PAUL NATHAN	Taped interview, Malibu, August 18, 1973.
ARCH OBOLER	Interview, Los Angeles, November 30, 1973.
GEORGE OPPENHEIMER	Numerous stories about the Yiddish theater.
MARVIN PAIGE	Numerous conferences, July–September, 1973, and for permission to browse through his comprehensive collection of film memorabilia.
BETSY PALMER	Telephone interview, New York, June 13, 1973.

367

HARRY PARRATTO librarian, Philadelphia *Inquirer*	For permission to Xerox material from his paper's morgue.
NEVA PATTERSON	Several phone interviews, summer, 1973, and for the loan of the *Life* magazine spread on *Counsellor-at-Law* television production.
ELLEN SIEGEL PERKISS daughter of MAX SIEGEL	Taped interview, New York, June 8, 1973, and for the loan of letters, snapshots, and the out-of-print acting edition of her father's play *We Americans.*
AUSTIN PETERSON	For information about Muni's radio broadcasts, Los Angeles, October, 1973.
NANCY R. POLLOCK	Taped interview, New York, June 14, 1973, and continued correspondence thereafter.
LUISE RAINER	Taped interview, London, England, September, 1973.
SYLVIA REGAN	Taped interview, New York, June 13, 1973.
The late ELMER RICE	For sharing his memories of Muni.
DAVID and NAOMI ROBISON	Taped interview, Woodstock, New York, October 31, 1973, mostly about their attendance at the Mexico City premiere of *Juarez.*
JOSEPH ROTHMAN	Taped interview, New York, June 9, 1973 and frequent long-distance phone calls, comprehensive letters and the loan of a great deal of material on the entire Nobel adventure.
JUDAH RUBINSTEIN research associate, Jewish Federation, Cleveland	For help in tracking down sources of Yiddish theater in Cleveland.
MURRAY RUMSHINSKY	Taped interview, North Hollywood, April 30, 1973.
BORIS SAGAL	Conversations about the Yiddish theater, 1973.
LESTER SALKOW	Taped interview, La Costa, California September 14, 1973.
DOROTHY SANDS	Correspondence, spring, 1973.
DORE SCHARY	Taped interview and a corned beef sandwich lunch, New York, June 6, 1973.

ERNEST SCHIER drama critic, Philadelphia *Bulletin*	For asking his readers for material about Muni's Philadelphia days, from which we received numerous responses.
PHILIP K. SCHEUER formerly drama critic, Los Angeles *Times*	For his recollections of Muni, 1973.
HERMAN SHUMLIN	Taped interview, New York, June 6, 1973.
JONAS SILVERSTONE	Taped interview, New York, June 5, 1973, and for continuing aid on this project.
KURT SIMON	Phone interview, September, 1973.
SIDNEY SKOLSKY	Phone and in-person recollections, 1973.
CECIL SMITH columnist and critic, Los Angeles *Times*	Taped interview, May 14, 1973, and for his personal memories of Muni and allowing me to Xerox all the material on Muni in the *Times* files.
LEONARD SPIGELGASS	Taped interview, Malibu, January 14, 1973, and for background material on the Yiddish theater, plus subsequent conversations about Edward G. Robinson.
LEE STRASBERG	Taped interview, Los Angeles, April 13, 1973.
MORRIS STRASSBERG	Taped interview, San Juan Capistrano, May 24, 1973, and numerous follow-up telephone conferences.
JACK SWANSON drama critic, Phoenix *Republic*	For allowing me to browse through his newspaper's extensive clipping files.
ROBERT A. THOMAS	For her graciousness in lending material and sharing her memories of the Munis. Interviews, North Hollywood, April 4 and May 30, 1973, and Malibu, July 11, 1973.
WAYNE THOMAS	For running many Muni films.
HARRY THOMASHEFSKY	Taped interview, Los Angeles, April 19, 1973, and for the loan of source material.
MYRTLE TULLY widow of author Jim Tully	Interview, Malibu, July 18, 1973.
ABBOTT VAN NOSTRAND Samuel French, Inc.	For digging up and gifting me with one of the few remaining copies of the out-of-print play *Four Walls*.

HELEN VERBIT — For steering me toward source material on the Yiddish theater.

SALKA VIERTEL — For permission to quote from her book.

JOSEPH WEISENFREUND
brother of Muni — Taped interview, North Hollywood, April 12, 1973, and for the use of family pictures.

EDWARD WESTON
Actors Equity — Conference, Malibu, July 10, 1973, and for helping me track down many actors.

MAX WILK — For generous help via multiple correspondence and for permission to use his boyhood impressions of Muni.

IVY WILSON — Numerous conferences, Hollywood, summer and fall, 1973—and for the chance to browse through her carefully preserved memorabilia of the M. C. Levee era.

Most of all, my gratitude must go to BELLA and PAUL MUNI, for all the books, photographs, letters, and memorabilia which they so generously left as a legacy to Lawrence & Lee . . . and for sharing their lives with us.

Index

An asterisk appearing before an entry
indicates a performance by Paul Muni.

372

374